About Island Press

Since 1984, the nonprofit Island Press has been stimulating, shaping, and communicating the ideas that are essential for solving environmental problems worldwide. With more than 800 titles in print and some 40 new releases each year, we are the nation's leading publisher on environmental issues. We identify innovative thinkers and emerging trends in the environmental field. We work with world-renowned experts and authors to develop cross-disciplinary solutions to environmental challenges.

Island Press designs and implements coordinated book publication campaigns in order to communicate our critical messages in print, in person, and online using the latest technologies, programs, and the media. Our goal: to reach targeted audiences—scientists, policymakers, environmental advocates, the media, and concerned citizens—who can and will take action to protect the plants and animals that enrich our world, the ecosystems we need to survive, the water we drink, and the air we breathe.

Island Press gratefully acknowledges the support of its work by the Agua Fund, Inc., The Margaret A. Cargill Foundation, Betsy and Jesse Fink Foundation, The William and Flora Hewlett Foundation, The Kresge Foundation, The Forrest and Frances Lattner Foundation, The Andrew W. Mellon Foundation, The Curtis and Edith Munson Foundation, The Overbrook Foundation, The David and Lucile Packard Foundation, The Summit Foundation, Trust for Architectural Easements, The Winslow Foundation, and other generous donors.

The opinions expressed in this book are those of the author(s) and do not necessarily reflect the views of our donors.

Principles of
Ecological Landscape Design

Principles of
Ecological Landscape Design

Travis Beck

Washington | Covelo | London

ISLAND PRESS is a trademark of the Center for Resource Economics.

Library of Congress Cataloging-in-Publication Data

Beck, Travis.
  Principles of ecological landscape design / Travis Beck.
       p. cm.
  Includes bibliographical references and index.
    ISBN 978-1-59726-701-4 (cloth : alk. paper) -- ISBN 1-59726-701-5 (cloth : alk. paper) -- ISBN 978-1-59726-702-1 (pbk. : alk. paper) -- ISBN 1-59726-702-3 (pbk. : alk. paper) 1. Ecological landscape design. 2. Ecosystem health. I. Title.
  QH541.15.L35B43 2012
  577--dc23

                                                                          2012022172

Printed using Franklin Gothic Condensed

Typesetting by Lyle Rosbotham
Printed by

⊕ Printed on recycled, acid-free paper

Manufactured in the United States of America
10 9 8 7 6 5 4 3

Keywords: biodiversity, biogeography, biomes, climate change, competition, disturbance, ecology, ecosystem management, edge effect, keystone species, landscape, landscape ecology, microclimate, plant communities, plant populations, soils, succession, Sustainable Sites, water

To those who taught me ecology and biology,
especially *Mr. Tolley, Richard Irwin*, and *Dr. Ralph Boerner.*

Contents

Acknowledgments

This book is the culmination of a long process of thought and discovery, reaching back to graduate school and before. Therefore, more people have offered ideas, assistance, and support than I can name here. Above all, this book stands on the shoulders of the many ecologists whose articles I consulted and of all those who generously shared their work and experiences with me as case studies.

However, there are several individuals and institutions whom I would especially like to thank. Martin Quigley was an essential ally and made numerous contributions. Carol Franklin offered encouragement and advice, as well as a case study and the Foreword. Erica Beade of MBC Graphics went above and beyond the call of duty in her preparation of illustrations for the book. The dedicated staff of the LuEsther T. Mertz Library at the New York Botanical Garden helped my research go smoothly. The main reading room at the New York Public Library's Schwartzman Building provided a congenial atmosphere for many hours of writing. Sarah Paulson hunted down several key images and was endlessly patient and supportive during the final push.

At Island Press, I am grateful to Heather Boyer, who adopted this project immediately, proved patient during its maturation, and pushed me to complete it when the time came, and to Courtney Lix, who has kept tabs on the entire process. Kate Lu obtained numerous permissions to help finalize the art package.

Writing a book proved to be a rewarding and demanding undertaking, and I am grateful to everyone who helped push the project forward.

Foreword

The desire for informed sustainable, ecological, and regenerative design is increasing in every country, accentuated by recognition of the increasing severity of a wide variety of ecological crises (from the dead zones of many oceans to global climate change). A growing dissatisfaction with the ugliness and wastefulness of conventional development is accelerating this interest. Historically, plants for human landscapes were brought together for medicinal, economic, or aesthetic purposes. Now, a new paradigm is finally catching the popular imagination. In this era of threatened environmental Armageddon, ecological design, and in particular ecological planting design, is finally being understood as a critical tool for our ultimate survival. With the loss of almost all our undisturbed natural landscapes, there is also a growing appreciation of the beauty and function of our indigenous landscapes.

Many professionals and nonprofessionals, from a variety of different disciplines and backgrounds, claim an expertise in creating natural plant communities to meet the growing demand for sustainable designs. Engineers, architects, landscape architects, restoration specialists, passionate volunteers, and others often find themselves in charge of the restoration of deteriorating plant communities or actual habitat re-creation. Engineering firms routinely turn out planting designs for floodplains and riparian corridors or planting plans for rain gardens and biotreatment swales, with little knowledge of the relationships of individual plant species to specific environmental conditions such as water tables or contours.

However, there may be light at the end of the tunnel. Cities big and small, throughout the country, are adopting new form-based zoning and performance standards for stormwater management measures and are asking designers for smart growth plans and green infrastructure. As mandates from the Environmental Protection Agency and other government agencies encourage more environmentally respectful designs in our metropolitan areas, and as the public increasingly sees the need for less ugly and wasteful land use practices, attention is being focused on the successful design, installation, and establishment of native plant communities in appropriate environmental conditions that will sustain them. Additionally, nonprofit conservation and land management organizations, educational institutions, and public officials charged with evaluating and overseeing the implementation of mandated programs and practices want to see attractive, successful solutions, measured by clear performance standards.

Until recently, the establishment or repair of native plant communities has been relatively unsophisticated. Ecological restoration and habitat re-creation are very new disciplines. Research into many aspects of plant ecology is either lacking entirely or discussed only in scientific articles, where the language is unfamiliar and the goal is not the translation of research into design actions. Compounding these problems, the older natural sciences often had a tradition of isolation. Even scientists within the same discipline often had difficulty communicating with their peers. (Until recently, soil scientists specialized in either soil structure, soil chemistry, or soil biology. They failed to communicate with each other and to understand soil as an interacting medium, where all these components are interdependent.)

Only a few books have tackled the subject of linking the structure, function, composition, and organization of landscapes directly to ecological processes. Richard T. T. Forman, professor of landscape ecology at the Harvard Graduate School of Design, has been one of the first authors to call our attention to the fact that spatial patterns reflect these processes. He has written a number of books and articles introducing designers to ecological ideas, particularly *Landscape Ecology Principles in Landscape Architecture and Land Use Planning*, with Wenche Dramstad and James Olson (1996), and *Land Mosaics: The Ecology of Landscapes and Regions* (1995).

Principles of Ecological Landscape Design, by landscape architect Travis Beck of the New York Botanical Garden, is an excellent expansion of earlier books on this subject. This wonderful book is the most comprehensive exploration of a planting design approach based on the principles of plant ecology yet to be provided to designers.

Principles of Ecological Landscape Design interweaves very clear descriptions of critical ecological processes to explain the effects of biogeography, foodwebs, nutrient cycles, plant and animal interactions, and many other factors on species composition, function, and spatial organization in natural plant communities. Each principle of plant ecology is paired directly with the implications for planting design, including the ecological processes that have shaped broad landscape configurations such as edges, centers, the fragmentation of a landscape, and the connections between landscapes.

For ecological planting design to be more than greenwashing, this book provides much-needed and long-awaited access to principles, strategies, and specific directions. It allows us to understand, with scientific rigor, the full requirements of establishing thriving plant communities in appropriate habitats, with appropriate plant companions and in requisite numbers and densities. It offers us both an overview of the central issues and a concise, easy-to-use reference. In many ways, this book is recognition of our newfound sophistication and of how far we have come since the era of "progress" of the 1950s to the 1980s and since Ian McHarg wrote *Design with Nature* in 1969. With our increasing need to change the destructive plans and practices of the recent past, and with our growing familiarity with ecological ideas, this book is an indispensable next step, firmly linking the breadth and depth of essential ecological processes directly to design actions. In doing so, Beck has given us a new and better toolbox for ecological planting design.

Carol Franklin, RLA, FASLA
Founding Principal, Andropogon Associates, Ltd.
Philadelphia, PA
May 2012

Introduction

Here, at the beginning of the twenty-first century, we find ourselves in an unprecedented situation. More than seven billion humans dominate the planet in ways we never have before. Our ever-expanding megalopolises creep out into landscapes cut over for timber, mined for fuel, bisected by roads, grazed by livestock, drained and plowed for farming, put back to cover, abandoned and regrown, parceled for houses, or opened for recreation. Even the most pristine wilderness areas are subject to our legislated forbearance. The rain that falls on them is enriched and polluted by our activities elsewhere, and the climate they live under is shifting by our hand.

As human influence over the planet grows, and as the built environment increases in prominence, the landscapes we design and manage will play an increasingly important role. From now on, the ecological function of our planet can come only from a network of preserved, restored, managed, and constructed landscapes. To maintain the function of this network, and the quality of life that it offers, we will have to change the way we think about landscape design.

A landscape, in its first meaning, is a depiction of scenery, and this has been our conventional approach to landscape design. Think of New York City's Central Park, a site to which the origins of landscape architecture in the United States are often traced, and the High Line, one of the most talked-about contemporary landscapes. In these master works, art imitates nature or perhaps an idealized nature already represented in art.

Some assume that Central Park, with its pastoral fields and tangled woodlands, preserves a remnant of the farmlands and wilds that once occupied the center of Manhattan. In fact, in 1857, when the competition for the design of Central Park was announced, the site was a tract of rocky swamps. In their winning entry, Frederick Law Olmsted and Calvert Vaux conjured both English and American scenes. The "Greensward" Plan, as the designers called it, featured broad meadows and contoured lakes, similar to those found in the English countryside or, more accurately, in the English countryside as reimagined by "landscape improver" Capability Brown. The plan also included dramatic rock outcroppings, cascades, and dense woods, like those in New York's Hudson River Valley and Catskill Mountains, or again, more accurately, like those in the landscape paintings of the Hudson Valley School. Olmsted and Vaux's object was to evoke in the visitor a range of emotions, from tranquility and deliberation at the edge of

The Lake, to excitement and rapture in the midst of The Ramble. The romantic place names complete the vision of an untrammeled world apart from the city's grid.

To achieve this vision required a massive reengineering of the site, carried out over 20 years. Existing rock was blasted out, and some of the rubble used to build other features. About 500,000 cubic feet of topsoil was brought in from New Jersey. Four million trees, shrubs, and plants were acquired. In the end, ten million cartloads of material had been hauled in or out. In her appreciative history of Central Park, Sara Cedar Miller (2003: 13) wrote,

> The 843-acre Park *seems* natural because it is composed of real soil, grass, trees, water, and flowers that need constant tending. In reality, however, it is naturalistic—an engineered environment that is closer in essence to scenes created in Hollywood than it is to the creation of Mother Nature.

The appeal of such naturalism is still strong. A century and a half later, and just a few miles away, it has taken contemporary form in the High Line. Before it became a celebrated public park, this abandoned rail line on the west side of Manhattan drew urban explorers onto its elevated decks, where an unexpected wilderness had emerged. Botanist Richard Stalter (2004) describes passing from an artist's loft, across an adjacent roof, then via ladder and rope to the train tracks, where he cataloged 161 species, more than half of them native, growing in a dry grassland punctuated by the occasional tree of heaven (*Ailanthus altissima*) (fig. I.1). Haunting photographs by Joel Sternfeld (2001) of the overgrown industrial infrastructure captured the public imagination, helped garner support for saving the space from demolition, and set the tone for the park that has emerged.

The converted High Line, by James Corner Field Operations, Diller Scofidio + Renfro, and planting designer Piet Oudolf, enthralls crowds with its offset walkways, clever details, and staccato views out over the Hudson River and below to city streets. Exuberant plantings grow between relaid steel tracks from gravel mulch meant to recall railroad ballast (fig. I.2). When the first section of the High Line opened in 2009, *New York Times* architecture critic Nicolai Ouroussoff noted the resonance between the new plantings and what grew naturally before:

> And those gardens have a wild, ragged look that echoes the character of the old abandoned track bed when it was covered with weeds, just a few years ago. Wildflowers and prairie grasses mix with Amelanchier, their bushes speckled with red berries. . . . On Saturday the gardens were swarming with bees, butterflies and birds. I half expected to see Bambi. (Ouroussoff 2009: C1)

Hollywood should be proud.

As at Central Park, creating such a peaceable kingdom on the High Line was an enormous undertaking. A total of $152 million was spent on the first two sections' few slender acres, to upgrade the infrastructure and make it safe for visitors, to design and mix specialty soils and lift them by the bagful onto the platform, and to procure and plant the thousands of grasses, flowers, and trees that evoke the spontaneous vegetation they replaced.

Two spectacular parks call on us to imagine unfettered nature, yet they took prodigious human

Figure I.1   Joel Sternfeld. *Looking East on 30th Street on a Late September Morning, 2000.* (©2000, Joel Sternfeld; image courtesy of the artist, Luhring Augustine, New York, and The Friends of the High Line, New York.)

effort to construct, not to mention the ongoing exertions needed for their maintenance. Let these parks represent conventional landscape design. We need not even think of the acres of aspirational suburban yards, the turf-filled office parks, and the windy municipal plazas. Conventional landscapes, both the masterpieces and the mass produced, are intended to accommodate human functions while achieving a certain look and evoking certain feelings. They rely on a designer's vision, the alteration of the site as necessary to achieve that vision, and an often lengthy period of maturation and care.

What if, instead of depicting nature, we allowed nature in? What if, instead of building and maintaining artistic creations, we worked to develop and manage living systems? What could we learn from the wild and pastoral landscapes that Central Park imitates, and from places such as the undeveloped High Line, about how nature works? Could we create landscapes that were more efficient, more connected, more effective, and ultimately more valuable? In other words, could we create ecological landscapes?

An ecological landscape is a designed landscape based on the science of ecology. To clarify one point immediately, when ecologists say "landscape" they mean an area comprising multiple

Figure I.2   The High Line, Section 1, July 2009. (Photo by Travis Beck.)

patches that differ from one another. An ecological landscape is a landscape in this sense, but typically in this book we will emphasize *designed* or *constructed* when we refer to landscapes, such as ecological landscapes, that are imagined and assembled by people. Ecological landscapes may abut or include natural ecosystems, but above all they are human creations. An ecological design may incorporate restoration of degraded ecosystems, but it does not principally seek to put things back the way they were. Ecological landscape design is for the growing number of areas where there is no going back to the way things were. It aims instead to go forward, to apply our knowledge of nature to create high-performing landscapes in which our design goals and natural processes go hand in hand.

The science of ecology offers our most rigorous and accurate understanding of how nature works at the scales most relevant to landscape designers. It is a growing understanding based on more than one hundred years of observation, experiment, and debate. The scientific side of this book draws from academic articles, both classic and recent, and aims to present an overall picture of the current state of knowledge. The state of ecological knowledge may surprise you. It does not describe webs of exquisite interconnectedness and balance, with every creature in its place. Rather, it outlines a world ruled by change and chance, in which life self-organizes and persists. This is the world we must deal with as designers and managers of landscapes.

The design side of this book applies ecological understanding to answer practical questions. How do we set up a planting so that it will thrive with a minimum of care? How many different species should we include, and how do we select them? What do we do with the animals that show up? In what ways should a project we are designing relate to what is around it? How can a constructed landscape live through a catastrophe and recover? Can the landscapes we design help us face the environmental challenges of the twenty-first century? In places the answers are speculative, suggesting strategies for a theoretical ecological landscape. Often, however, they are based on actual projects in a range of sizes from multiple regions of the United States.

Increasingly, landscape professionals are taking an ecological approach to their work. For instance, there has been a large shift toward more natural approaches to managing stormwater. Landscape architects and landscape designers have also explored ecological methods of plant community assembly and managing the changes in plant communities over time. Notably, the American Society of Landscape Architects has taken a lead role in developing the Sustainable Sites Initiative, which offers a set of guidelines and benchmarks for sustainable land development practices centered around the idea of providing ecosystem services (Sustainable Sites Initiative 2009a, 2009b).

To be sustainable means to perform these indispensable services while demanding fewer resources, which we might think of as doing more with less. The best way to do more with less is to harness ecological processes. An ecological landscape knits itself into the biosphere so that it both is sustained by natural processes and sustains life within its boundaries and beyond. It is not a duplicate of wild nature (that we must protect and restore where we can) but a complex system modeled after nature. Above all, to be sustainable is to continue functioning, come what may. An ecological landscape is based on self-organized patterns, which are more robust than patterns imposed according to some external conceit. It is flexible and adaptive and continually adjusts its patterns as conditions change and events unfold.

We know such systems are beautiful and arousing because we have been imitating them in our designed landscapes for so long. Now that humans have co-opted so much of the planet, the time has come to cease representation and to partner with nature instead in acts of vital co-creation.

1. Right Plant, Right Place: Biogeography and Plant Selection

It is often said that the secret to good horticulture is putting the right plant in the right place. By matching plants to their intended environment, a designer helps to ensure that the plants will be healthy, grow well, and need a minimum of care. Too often designers force plants into the wrong places, putting large trees that thrive in extensive floodplains into confining tree pits or planting roses that need full sun in spindliness-inducing shade. Or we try to create a generically "perfect" garden environment, with rich soils and regular moisture, for a wide-ranging collection of plants, some of which may actually prefer more stringent conditions. Whether we do these things from ignorance, in conformance with established practices, or because our focus is on aesthetic qualities or our associations with certain plants, the too common result is struggling plantings, ongoing horticultural effort, and the dominance of familiar generalist species.

An ecological approach to landscape design takes the fundamental horticultural precept—right plant, right place—and views it through a biogeographical lens. Where do plants grow, and why do they grow there? How many degrees of native are there? What are the relative roles of environmental adaptation and historical accident? Selecting plants according to biogeographical principles can help us create designed landscapes that will thrive and sustain themselves. Such landscapes celebrate their region and fit coherently into the larger environment. Of course, these landscapes can also be beautiful. Let us begin, then, with a fundamental ecological question: Why is this plant growing here?

PLANTS ARE ADAPTED TO DIFFERENT ENVIRONMENTS

Five hundred million years ago the earth's landmasses were devoid of life. Then, scientists speculate, ancestral relatives of today's mosses began to grow along moist ocean margins and eventually on land itself. To survive out of water, these primitive plants had to evolve structures to support themselves out of water, ways to avoid drying out, and the ability to tolerate a broader range of temperatures. As they evolved, plants diversified and spread into every imaginable habitat, from deserts to wetlands, and from the tropics to the Arctic. Today, there are more than 300,000 plant species on our planet (May 2000).

Plant diversity and the diversity of habitats on Earth are closely related. Natural landscapes are composed of heterogeneous patches, each of which presents a different environment (see chap. 9). At the largest scale are deserts and rainforests. At the smallest scale are warm, sunny spots and wet depressions. Charles Darwin proposed in *The Origin of Species* (1859: 145),

> The more diversified the descendants from any one species become in structure, constitution, and habits, by so much will they be better enabled to seize on many and widely diversified places in the polity of nature, and so be enabled to increase in numbers.

Plants have been able to move into so many different environments because they have developed many means of adapting. Consider plant adaptations to two critical environmental variables: temperature and the availability of water.

Temperature affects nearly all plant processes, including photosynthesis, respiration, transpiration, and growth. Very high temperatures can disrupt metabolism and denature proteins. Low temperatures can reduce photosynthesis and growth to perilously low levels and damage plant tissues as ice forms within and between cells. Plants that grow in high-temperature regions may have reflective leaves or leaves that orient themselves parallel to the sun's rays in order to not build up heat. Some use the alternate C4 photosynthetic pathway, which can continue to operate efficiently at high temperatures. Plants in cold regions have developed bud dormancy and may grow slowly over several seasons before producing seed. They have high concentrations of soluble sugars in their cells to act as natural antifreeze, and they are able to accommodate intercellular ice without experiencing damage.

Plants that are adapted to grow well in wet, moist, and dry conditions are called, respectively, hydrophytes, mesophytes, and xerophytes. Hydrophytes have to provide oxygen to their flooded roots, which they do through a variety of mechanisms, including by developing spongy, air-filled tissue between the stems and the roots or by growing structures like knees that bring oxygen directly to the roots (fig. 1.1). Many hydrophytes also have narrow, flexible leaves to avoid damage from moving water. Xerophytes, on the other hand, exhibit adaptations to lack of water such as small leaves, deep roots, water storage in their tissues, and use of an alternate photosynthetic pathway that allows them to open the stomata on their leaves only in the cool of night (fig. 1.2).

Because of 500 million years of evolution and the diversity of habitats open to colonization, the planet is now filled with plants adapted to nearly every combination of environmental variables.

CHOOSE PLANTS THAT ARE ADAPTED TO THE LOCAL ENVIRONMENT

Because plants exhibit such a wide range of natural adaptations, we need not struggle—expending both limited resources and our collective energy—against the environment we find ourselves in to make it a better home for ill-suited plants. Using biogeography as our guide, we can always identify plants ready-made for the conditions at hand.

Gardeners, nursery owners, and landscape designers have long recognized that plants ill-suited

Figure 1.1 Knees bring oxygen to the roots of some hydrophytes, such as these bald cypress (*Taxodium distichum*) growing in a swamp at the Lacassine National Wildlife Refuge in Louisiana. (Photo courtesy of the US Fish and Wildlife Service.)

Figure 1.2 Tree cholla (*Cylindropuntia imbricata*), a xerophyte native to the southwestern United States and northern Mexico, photosynthesizes with its stems, rather than with leaves, and stores water from periodic rainfall in succulent tissues protected with spines. (Photo by Gary Kramer, USDA Natural Resources Conservation Service.)

to the temperature extremes of the place where they are planted are unlikely to survive their first year in the ground. The US Department of Agriculture has codified this knowledge in a map of hardiness zones, which was updated in 2012 (fig. 1.3). Hardiness zones represent the average annual minimum temperature, that is, the coldest temperature a plant in that zone could expect to experience. There are thirteen hardiness zones, ranging from zone one in the interior of Alaska (experiencing staggering winter minimums of below –50°F) to zone thirteen on Puerto Rico (experiencing winter minimums of barely 60°F). Plants are rated as to the lowest zone in which they can survive. Balsam fir (*Abies balsamea*), for instance, is hardy to zone three. The hardiest species of *Bougainvillea* are hardy only to zone nine. Plants are sometimes given a range (e.g., zones three to six). Strictly speaking, hardiness refers only to ability to survive minimum temperatures, but the practice of indicating a range serves as shorthand for the overall temperatures in which a plant will grow. The American Horticultural Society (2012) has also prepared a map of heat zones for the United States, indicating the number of days above 86°F that a region experiences on average per year. Catalog descriptions of landscape plants may include reference to these heat zones and to the more common hardiness zones.

Given the wide acceptance of hardiness zones, it is somewhat surprising that similar thinking applied to water requirements for plants has developed only within the past few decades. Perhaps this is because of the ease of meeting the needs of some plants for more water with irrigation. Or perhaps it

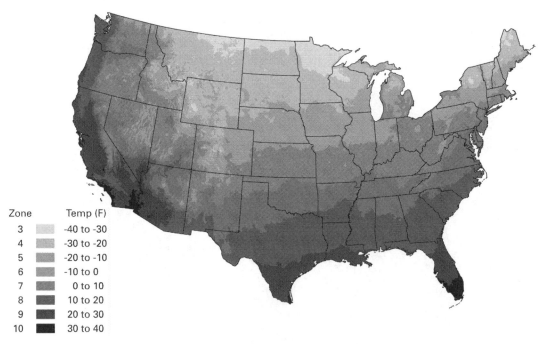

Zone	Temp (F)
3	-40 to -30
4	-30 to -20
5	-20 to -10
6	-10 to 0
7	0 to 10
8	10 to 20
9	20 to 30
10	30 to 40

Figure 1.3 The 2012 USDA Plant Hardiness Zone Map. Note the fairly regular progression of zones from north to south in the center of the continent and the irregular zone boundaries related to mountain ranges and the moderating effects of large bodies of water (including the Great Lakes) in the west and east. (US Department of Agriculture.)

is because of the deep influence of English gardening traditions in the United States and expectations of what a cultivated landscape should look like. Regardless of local conditions, our nationwide default residential landscape is water-hungry lawns and summer-flowering borders. Many regions of North America are in fact too dry, or receive precipitation too unevenly, to support this kind of designed landscape without major inputs of water. In San Diego, for example, more than half of all residential water is used to irrigate lawns and landscapes (Generoso 2002). Using water this way can deplete aquifers, damage habitat in areas from which water is drawn, decrease local agricultural production, and leave our landscapes vulnerable to desiccation when water restrictions go into effect.

The negative consequences of landscape irrigation and the countervailing benefits of water conservation motivated Denver Water (the water department in Denver, Colorado) to introduce xeriscaping in 1981. Xeriscaping, from the Greek word *xeros*, for "dry," emphasizes grouping plants in the landscape according to their water needs (Weinstein 1999). Not surprisingly, many xeriscapes feature xerophytes, plants with low water needs.

Denver exists in a semiarid environment, getting on average around 14 inches of precipitation a year, as compared to about 35 to 40 inches a year in most areas east of the Mississippi. Kentucky bluegrass (*Poa pratensis*) lawns, shade trees, and most common garden plants need additional water to survive. At their former home, Panayoti and Gwen Kelaidis ambitiously replaced their entire front lawn with plants well adapted to Denver's semiaridity. These include sulfur-flower buckwheat (*Eriogonum umbellatum*), soapweed (*Yucca glauca*), and partridge feather (*Tanacetum densum* ssp. *amani*). Today, 20 years later, these plants are still thriving with no supplemental irrigation (fig. 1.4).

Selecting plants that are adapted to the temperatures and available water of the environment in which they will be placed is a fundamental step in creating an ecological landscape.

BIOMES DESCRIBE THE BROAD CHARACTER OF A REGION'S VEGETATION

In late July 1799, Alexander von Humboldt, a German naturalist traveling aboard a Spanish vessel with French botanist Aimé Bonpland, came to the bow for his first glimpse of the shore of South America (Humboldt and Bonpland 1818: 175–76). He wrote,

> Our eyes were fixed on the groups of cocoa-trees that border the river, and the trunks of which, more than sixty feet high, towered over the landscape. The plain was covered with tufts of cassias, capers, and those arborescent mimosas, which, like the pine of Italy, extend their branches in the form of an umbrella. The pinnated leaves of the palms were conspicuous on the azure of a sky, the clearness of which was unsullied by any trace of vapors. The Sun was ascending rapidly toward the zenith. A dazzling light was spread through the air, along the whitish hills strewed with cylindric cactuses, and over a sea ever calm, the shores of which were peopled with alcatras, egrets, and flamingoes. The splendor of the day, the vivid coloring of the vegetable world, the forms of the plants, the varied plumage of the birds, everything announced the grand aspect of nature in the equinoctial regions.

For a couple of newly arrived Europeans, these were truly stunning sights. After 5 years of travel throughout Latin America, Humboldt (1805: 56) was able to organize some of his observations in

Figure 1.4   Xeriscape by Panayoti and Gwen Kelaidis, teeming with plants that need no supplemental irrigation, in Denver, Colorado. (Photo by Travis Beck.)

an essay on what he called "the geography of plants," a foundational work in the field we now know as biogeography:

> Plant forms closer to the equator are generally more majestic and imposing; the veneer of leaves is more brilliant, the tissue of the parenchyma more lax and succulent. The tallest trees are constantly adorned by larger, more beautiful and odoriferous flowers than in temperate zones. . . . However the tropics never offer our eyes the green expanse of prairies bordering rivers in the countries of the north: one hardly ever has the gentle sensation of spring awakening vegetation. Nature, beneficial to all beings, has reserved for each region particular gifts. A tissue of fibers more or less lax, vegetable colors more or less brash depending on the chemical mixture of elements and the stimulating strength of solar rays: these are just some of the causes that give each zone of the globe's vegetation its particular character.

What Humboldt recognized as the particular character of each zone of the globe's vegetation we today call a biome. Biomes are large geographic areas dominated by certain types of plant and animal life: rainforests in the wet tropics, for example, or prairies in drier temperate zones. Although today human impacts, particularly agriculture and urbanization, have somewhat obscured the nature and extent of biomes, underlying climatological realities still inform what will grow where. In fact, a simple graph uniting temperature and precipitation shows us what conditions give rise to what biomes (fig. 1.5). Where there are high temperatures and high levels of precipitation, tropical rainforests grow, capturing the sun's energy in the substantial biomass of large standing forests. At the opposite extreme, where temperature and precipitation are both low, we find arctic and alpine tundra full of slow-growing, diminutive plants. Thus, temperature and precipitation drive the adaptations of plants in each area and determine the character of the vegetation in different regions of the globe.

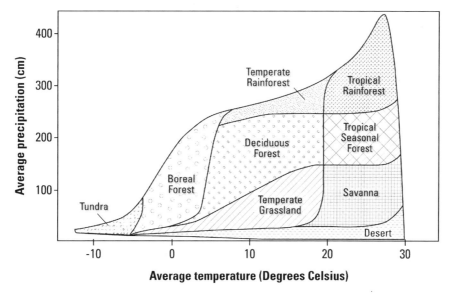

Figure 1.5 Graph of biomes in relation to precipitation and mean annual temperature. (Courtesy of http://www.thewildclassroom.com/biomes.)

DESIGN DIFFERENT LANDSCAPES FOR DIFFERENT BIOMES

Throughout the United States many cultivated landscapes are out of touch with their surroundings. Woodland trees line scrubland streets, and broad lawns hacked from forests pretend at grassland or pasture. An ecological landscape should respond to the same environmental realities that give rise to biomes. Areas of moderate temperature and moderate precipitation tend to be forest. Areas with less water tend to be grassland, desert, or in some cases chaparral. Designed landscapes that match their plants and the communities in which they are grown to the prevailing climate should take less effort to create and maintain. They will also be better able to provide habitat for local wildlife (see chap. 7), better connect to regional landscape networks (see chap. 9), and better bounce back after predictable disturbances such as fire, windstorms, or floods (see chap. 8).

In the rolling hills of northern Delaware, set between the formal gardens and the native forest of Mt. Cuba Center, the Woods Path is a landscape aptly suited to its biome (fig. 1.6). The moderate temperatures and rainfall in this region naturally give rise to a deciduous forest, the structure and feel of which the Woods Path captures in a subtly designed landscape. Tulip trees (*Liriodendron tulipifera*) provide an enclosing canopy and strong vertical architecture. Flowering dogwood (*Cornus florida*), hollies, and rhododendrons encroach gently on the meandering path. Herbaceous plants carpet the ground plane. This simple structure—canopy, understory, herbaceous groundcover—expresses the essence of a woodland. It also provides the cool, humid, partially shaded growing conditions to which many plants of the Appalachian Piedmont are adapted. The Woods Path is a designed garden that feels absolutely appropriate to its place.

Figure 1.6 Woods Path at Mt. Cuba Center, Delaware. Tulip trees, rhododendron, and herbaceous groundcovers create a three-story landscape that encloses the visitor. (Photo by Rick J. Lewandowski.)

Across the continent, at the base of southern California's San Gabriel Mountains, the coastal sage scrub community at Rancho Santa Ana Botanic Garden looks completely different (fig. 1.7). Here, before agriculture and development, the dry, warm climate supported an open scrub, also known as soft chaparral, intermixed with oak savannas and riparian woodlands. At Rancho Santa Ana an oak woodland provides a backdrop against which nestles a mix of loosely spaced drought-tolerant shrubs, including California sage (*Artemisia californica*), black sage (*Salvia mellifera*), and wild lilac (*Ceanothus*

Figure 1.7   Coastal sage scrub community at Rancho Santa Ana Botanic Garden, Claremont, California. An oak woodland forms a backdrop to California sage and flowering pinebush (*Ericameria pinifolia*). (Photo by Travis Beck.)

spp.). Living in a low-productivity environment, these shrubs discourage herbivory by filling their leaves with unpalatable aromatic compounds that give the landscape a pungent fragrance. Open ground in between the scrub is home to spring and summer wildflowers.

An ecological landscape need not be a slavish imitator of the biome in which it is situated, but the more carefully it responds to the regional climate, the more its structure and features are likely to express what Humboldt called that region's particular gifts (Darke 2002; Francis and Reimann 1999).

PLANTS ARE ADAPTED TO THE SEASONAL CYCLES OF THE CLIMATES WHERE THEY EVOLVED
It is not just the average temperature and the annual precipitation that determine the character of a biome, of course; it is also the seasonality of these factors. Compare the average monthly precipitation and low temperatures in Wilmington, Delaware and Claremont, California (fig. 1.8).

Wilmington demonstrates the characteristics of a humid temperate climate: regular, moderate amounts of precipitation and temperatures that cycle with the seasons. Claremont experiences a classic Mediterranean climate, with a cool, wet winter and a warm, dry summer. This is no travel brochure,

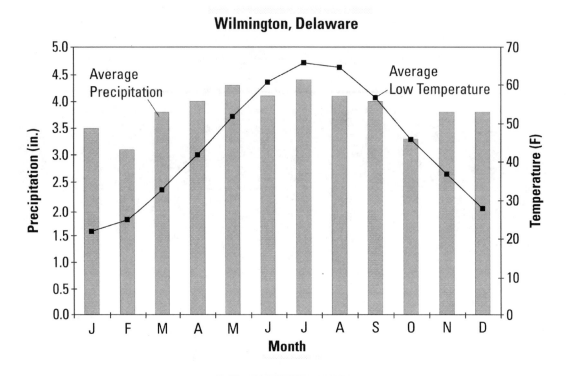

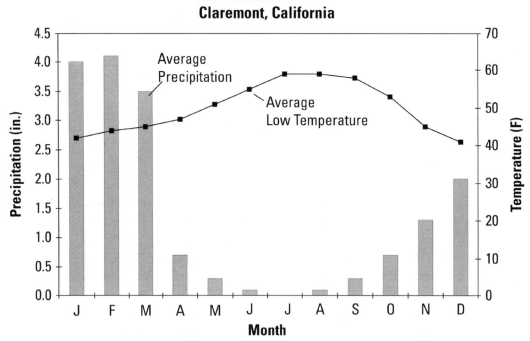

Figure 1.8 Average monthly precipitation and low temperature **(a)** in Wilmington, Delaware, near Mt. Cuba Center, and **(b)** in Claremont, California, the location of Rancho Santa Ana Botanic Garden.

however. Plants in both locations have to be prepared for the worst of these seasonal extremes: freezing cold winters in Wilmington and bone-dry (zero inches of precipitation in July!) summers in Claremont. The duration of stress—such as heat or cold—may be even more important than a one-time extreme.

Plants are adapted to climate extremes anatomically and physiologically, as we have already seen, but also through their phenology, the timing of events such as flowering, setting seed, leafing out, and going dormant. In deciduous forests, such as those found natively around Wilmington, as the days get shorter, signaling the onset of winter, trees and shrubs begin to drop their leaves. Evergreen plants such as American holly (*Ilex opaca*) and Christmas fern (*Polystichum acrostichoides*) have thicker leaves with a waxy coating and cell physiology that allows them to survive the winter. Most herbaceous plants survive the coldest months underground, either in perennial roots or as seed.

Interestingly, plants from the Mediterranean climate of California exhibit some of the same adaptations, only timed differently to handle the stress of summer drought. A few plants, such as California buckeye (*Aesculus californica*), are deciduous and drop their leaves during the summer drought. Many more plants, such as coast live oak (*Quercus agrifolia*) and manzanitas (*Arctostaphylos* spp.) have tough, leathery leaves (sclerophyll foliage) that they can keep year-round, even during a month with no rain. Many California wildflowers (such as California poppy [*Eschscholzia californica*]) are annuals, which bloom and set seed during the warm, moist spring and then die as the summer drought progresses, surviving underground as seeds until spring returns. The seasonal life cycles of plants are part of what create the character of each biome.

CREATE SEASONAL INTEREST BY SHOWCASING PLANT ADAPTATIONS TO CLIMATE

Designers are forever striving to create, and clients are ever clamoring for, year-round interest in the landscape. Nurseries have answered the call with spring-, summer-, and fall-flowering bulbs and perennials, ornamental evergreens of every size and hue, and frost-tolerant pansies in crayon colors. In a more naturalistic aesthetic, such as that of Dutch designer Piet Oudolf, plants are allowed to grow and die back in their own time, offering, among other delights, gorgeous winter tableaux of frost-coated grasses. An ecological landscape can integrate all these elements. The key is simply to recognize the adaptations behind plants' seasonal displays and match them to the changing environmental conditions of a particular site throughout the year. This will ensure the maximum seasonal effect and reduce the inputs and effort needed to maintain plants that are out of sync with the cycles of the environment in which they are planted. By necessity, this will create different landscapes for different places.

Looking once again at the Woods Path at Mt. Cuba in Delaware and the coastal sage scrub at Rancho Santa Ana Botanic Garden in California, we see that both create seasonal interest by showcasing the life cycles of plants that are adapted to their different climates.

On the Woods Path, the highlight of the year is the appearance of the spring ephemerals (fig. 1.9). Called ephemerals because they seem to appear and disappear in a matter of weeks, flowers such as trillium and bloodroot (*Sanguinaria canadensis*) take advantage of an early-season window in the deciduous forest. When temperatures have risen sufficiently, but before the canopy trees have leafed out to shade the forest floor, these plants emerge, creating a spectacle of showy white, pink, yellow, and red flowers. Through summer, after the ephemerals have set seed and died back, the ground plane of

Figure 1.9 Before the canopy fully leafs out in the spring, along the Woods Path at Mt. Cuba Center, flowering dogwood, dwarf larkspur (*Delphinium tricorne*), and wild blue phlox (*Phlox divaricata*) capture the eye at a lower level. (Photo by Rick J. Lewandowski.)

the garden is a leafy, mostly green space. In autumn, the Woods Path turns shades of yellow, orange, and red as the trees of the eastern deciduous forest stop producing chlorophyll in their leaves before shedding them, exposing the other photosynthetic pigments left behind. Come winter, the trunks of the trees and the evergreen rhododendrons and hollies preside over a quiet, sometimes snow-covered ground plane as the herbaceous plants wait dormant for spring.

The seasonal cycle at Rancho Santa Ana is very different. In spring the wild lilacs and manzanitas and currants burst into flower, along with annual wildflowers (fig. 1.10). As temperatures soar and precipitation ceases, most plants go dormant, though the evergreen oaks and shrubs maintain their leaves. Seed heads dry on the sages and remain that way through autumn, when they are joined in display by the dramatic flowering of the pinebush. In winter the still green (or gray) oaks, lilacs, and sages soak up moisture and push new growth.

These two landscapes create very different spectacles of seasonal interest—spectacles based on the seasonal cycles of plants adapted to two very different climates.

Figure 1.10   In early spring at Rancho Santa Ana Botanic Garden, seedheads of pinebush shine alongside flowers of manzanita and currant. (Photo by Travis Beck.)

ENVIRONMENTAL DIFFERENCES AT SMALL SCALES CREATE MICROCLIMATES

So far we have looked at environmental heterogeneity at the broadest scale, that of biomes and climate. An individual plant grows in a particular biome, under a particular climatic regime, but what really matters to its survival are the conditions in its immediate environment. Small-scale variations in environmental conditions create what are called microclimates. A microclimate for a group of trillium could be the shade of a single forest maple; the microclimate for a redwood (*Sequoia sempervirens*) grove might be several square miles in a deep canyon with moister soils than the hillsides above. Every place in a landscape experiences a combination of environmental variations; thus, one way of understanding a landscape as a collection of heterogeneous patches is to view it as a mosaic of microclimates.

In the midst of the Illinois prairie, protected from fire by the Salt Fork of the Vermillion River, a 16-square-kilometer mixed mesophytic forest known as the Big Grove once grew. After settlement, much of this forest was chopped down for development, agriculture, and woodlots. Trelease Woods and Brownfield Woods are two remnant parcels of the Big Grove, each about 400 by 600 meters, surrounded variously by roads, farm fields, fences, and a prairie restoration project. These woods served as the study site for Sophia Gehlhausen and her colleagues (2000) to investigate microclimatic differences between forest edge and forest interior and the effect of those microclimates on understory vegetation.

Gehlhausen established linear transects from the north, east, south, and west edges of each forest to the interior. Along each transect she took measurements of relative humidity, air temperature, and soil moisture, and she sampled the herbaceous vegetation, shrubs, and saplings. Gehlhausen's results are complex, showing the interplay of numerous factors, and demonstrate a clear link between microclimate and vegetation. Moving from forest edge to interior, canopy openness declined, and soil moisture and relative humidity increased in most cases. The direction (aspect) each edge faced and what bordered it made an important difference in the results, especially by affecting the amount of sun and wind to which the edges were exposed (see chap. 9).

Vegetation too changed from edge to interior. Samples from the forest edges were least similar to samples from the forest interior, and samples became more similar the closer to the interior they were taken. Gehlhausen suggested that competition (see chap. 3) and disturbance played a role in these differences, but to a large extent vegetation was responding to microclimate. Some species such as wood nettle (*Laportea canadensis*) and great waterleaf (*Hydrophyllum appendiculatum*) increased in coverage as one approached the interior. Wood nettle did poorly in full light, and both plants thrive where soil moisture and relative humidity were higher. The more sun- and drought-tolerant black snakeroot (*Sanicula odorata*), on the other hand, decreased in cover toward the interior.

Gehlhausen's results demonstrate that even at the small scale governed by microclimates, environmental heterogeneity drives what plants grow where.

MATCH PLANTS TO MICROCLIMATES

The same factors that govern the distribution of herbaceous plants in Trelease and Brownfield Woods influence what plants will grow best in different areas of a designed landscape. Relative humidity, air temperature, soil moisture, available sunlight, and exposure to wind are all important factors for a plant's well-being, even when that plant is sufficiently cold hardy or heat tolerant and adapted to the natural precipitation of a region.

One of the most detailed efforts to test, observe, and describe the relation between small-scale environmental variables and the success of garden plants has been that undertaken by Richard Hansen and Friedrich Stahl in Germany. In their book *Perennials and Their Garden Habitats* (Hansen and Stahl 1993: 33) they wrote,

Those who have seen the effect of a particular perennial growing wild in its characteristic environment, and compared it with the same plant's sad destiny in some of our gardens, planted here and there according to some arbitrary conceit, will surely understand this attempt to place perennials in their correct garden habitat. . . . Conditions vary tremendously within a garden. The correct choice of plants for any given spot requires detailed investigation of the planting position and careful consideration of all possible candidates. If this is done well, then a stable and long-lasting plant community can develop, often requiring just a bare minimum of maintenance, yet forming a convincing feature in the garden design.

Hansen and Stahl began by defining the main garden habitats for their region: woodland, woodland edge, open ground, rock garden, border (traditional garden bed), water's edge and marsh, and water (fig. 1.11). These habitat classifications correspond to sets of microsite variables. Open ground is obviously sunnier than woodland, water's edge wetter than a rock garden. It is with their more specific classifications, however, that things get really interesting. Within woodland edge, for instance, some of the subcategories they identified are "perennials for shade and bright shade on moist, nutrient-rich soils," "perennials for sun or bright shade on an open woodland edge (moderately dry, loamy, alkaline soils)," and "perennials for cool, damp, sunny or lightly shaded sites." As Hansen and Stahl's experience shows, it is really the set of all these environmental variables for which plants are adapted and according to which they should be selected for each place within a landscape or garden.

Figure 1.11 An open, sunny woodland edge. (Adapted from Hansen, R., and F. Stahl. 1993. *Perennials and Their Garden Habitats*, translated by R. Ward. New York: Cambridge University Press.)

TAKE ADVANTAGE OF MICROCLIMATES IN THE BUILT ENVIRONMENT

In urban and suburban environments, constructed elements of the landscape can play a role as large as or larger than that of natural features in determining microclimates. For instance, a stand-alone building creates its own patterns of sun and shade, as influential for growing plants as the direction a woodland edge faces. Materials such as concrete, stone, and steel absorb the sun's energy and reradiate it, raising the temperature of their immediate environment (fig. 1.12). Areas that are surrounded or overhung by structures remain drier than they would if they were out in the open. The edges of roadways and impermeable parking lots, on the other hand, can have significantly higher soil moisture than the surrounding landscape.

Landscape designers must be attentive to these differences in microclimate when selecting and siting plants. We should also look at microclimatic differences as providing horticultural and design opportunities. Planting beds backed by south-facing walls will warm up earlier in the season and stay warmer longer, effectively lengthening the growing season. Paradoxically, marginally hardy plants that would be killed by midwinter soil warming and daily fluctuations in temperatures can be safer in the shade on the north side of a structure, where they will remain safely dormant until spring fully arrives. In semiarid and arid climates, the protection afforded by structures can create a sufficiently cooler and more humid microclimate on north and east exposures to allow plants to be grown that otherwise would not survive.

Of course, designers are also not limited to making use of microclimates provided accidentally by architects and engineers. Walls and landscape structures can be built in order to create warmer and cooler microclimates and to serve other functions. Small-scale contouring of the landscape can also

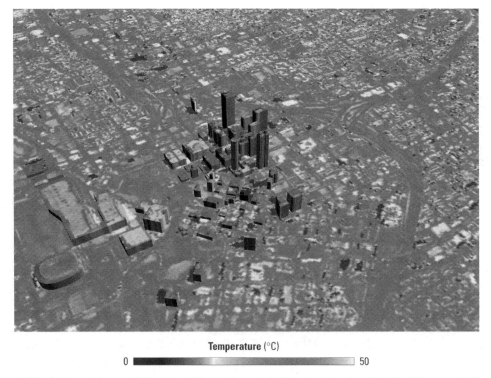

Temperature (°C)

0 ▬▬▬▬▬▬▬▬▬▬▬ 50

Figure 1.12 A thermal image of downtown Atlanta, Georgia in May reveals microclimatic differences in the built environment. Flat rooftops are scorching hot, whereas areas in the shade of buildings remain cool. (Image courtesy of NASA/Goddard Space Flight Center Scientific Visualization Studio.)

create drier mounds or wetter pockets where these are desired (see chap. 6). Because at a small scale it is the microenvironment that determines what will grow where, design of the physical site and planting design have to go hand in hand.

ECOTYPES ARE ADAPTED TO LOCAL ENVIRONMENTS

We have seen how plant species have evolved to grow in particular climatic and microclimatic environments. In fact, adaptation is even more site specific. In the late 1910s and early 1920s, Swedish botanist Göte Turesson noted that some plants, such as hawkweed (*Hieracium umbellatum*), have multiple forms. Where it grows in open woods, hawkweed is erect and broad-leaved. Where it grows in nearby sand dunes the same species is narrow-leaved and less erect. Turesson transplanted specimens of these different forms into a common garden, first at his house and later at the Institute of Genetics at Åkarp, Sweden. When these different forms persisted in the common garden, it was clear that they were not simply morphological changes caused by differences in the environment but true genetic differences. Turesson (1922) called these genetically distinct groups within a species, each adapted to its local environment, ecotypes.

In the 1940s a trio of scientists in California—Jens Clausen, David Keck, and William Hiesey—investigated ecotypes more thoroughly using common yarrow. Yarrow (*Achillea millefolium*) is one of the most widely distributed plants in the northern hemisphere. In California alone, it grows in nearly every conceivable environment, from seaside bluffs to the arid edges of the Great Basin. Where yarrow grows in the seasonally arid interior foothills it has thin leaves and gray foliage, and it goes dormant in summer. Where it grows in meadows amid conifers on the slopes of the Sierra Nevada, it is midsized with greener leaves, has winter dormancy, and is slow to mature. Where it grows above timberline it is short, frost-resistant, and early to flower after a long winter dormancy. Even when the researchers grew the different ecotypes of yarrow in a common garden at Stanford, these differences persisted (fig. 1.13).

Clausen, Keck, and Hiesey (1948) set out to find out what would happen to these ecotypes if they were each grown in the natural environment of the others. In addition to the garden at Stanford, which is located in a low valley between the inner and outer Coast Ranges of central California, they established a garden at Mather, near 1,400 meters in elevation on the western slope of the Sierra Nevada, and another garden they called Timberline, at 3,050 meters. The foothill ecotypes of yarrow developed and flowered quickly at Stanford but performed poorly in the mountain gardens. At Timberline the foothill plants were nearly all wiped out during the first winter of the experiment. The yarrow that were collected in the coniferous belt near Mather grew well at Stanford but reached a greater height and put out more stems at Mather, outperforming any of the other California ecotypes in that garden. At Timberline many of the Mather plants survived and grew, but none successfully set any seed. The extreme alpine ecotype of yarrow grew and flowered at Stanford and Mather but was tallest and best developed at Timberline. Taken together, the results of these experiments demonstrate that in yarrow the adaptations of each ecotype to its local environment increase its growth, reproduction, and overall fitness in that environment, relative even to other plants of the same species. The best-performing plants in each of the test gardens were those collected locally.

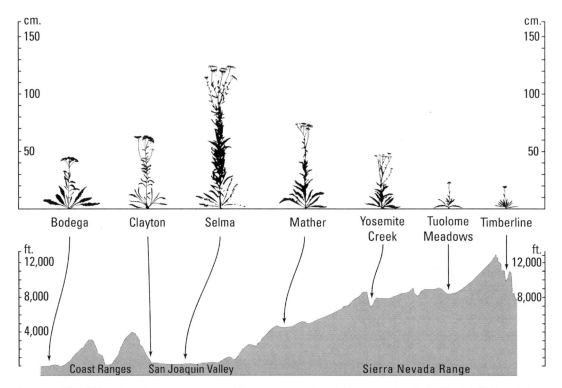

Figure 1.13   Different ecotypes of yarrow and the environments in which they grow in California. (Adapted from Clausen, J., D. Keck, and W. Hiesey. 1948. *Experimental Studies on the Nature of Species III. Environmental Responses of Climatic Races of* Achillea. Publication 581. Washington, DC: Carnegie Institute of Washington.)

USE LOCAL ECOTYPES WHERE POSSIBLE

Horticulturists have long been aware of the importance of provenance, or the ultimate source of plant material. Especially in wide-ranging species (such as yarrow), the origin of the seed from which plants are grown and even the environment in which they are propagated can make a difference in the establishment and success of the plants. If you are planting in hardiness zone three, for instance, you want to use plants whose provenance is from an equally cold area; otherwise those plants might not survive the winter, even if other members of their species do. Savvy gardeners know that choosing sources with conditions similar to where the plants will ultimately reside increases the odds that these plants will perform well in their new environment. Sourcing plants by ecotype takes this approach to another level of specificity.

On the edge of Freshkills Park (the former Fresh Kills Landfill) on Staten Island in New York Harbor, a tidy collection of buildings, greenhouses, and nursery fields houses the Greenbelt Native Plant Center, a project of the New York City Department of Parks and Recreation (fig. 1.14). Greenbelt is committed to growing local plant ecotypes for use in restoration and management projects throughout the city.

Ed Toth, Greenbelt's director, began his work with the production of native plants back in the 1980s for a revegetation project at Prospect Park in Brooklyn. As Toth continued his work, his definition of

Figure 1.14 Plots of ecotypic plants being grown at the Greenbelt Native Plant Center. (Photo courtesy of NYC Parks.)

native became more and more stringent as he realized that the genetics of local plant populations represent thousands of years of adaptation to particular sites. From a conservation standpoint, these are irreplaceable resources and form the basis for the future evolution of the species. From a restoration standpoint, local ecotypes can give the best assurance of success because of how well they are matched to site conditions.

To propagate local ecotypes, Greenbelt collectors identify existing, healthy populations of native plant species in natural areas throughout the five boroughs of New York City and, in the case of plants that have been extirpated within the city limits, in nearby New Jersey, Connecticut, Long Island, and upstate New York. Where possible they collect from populations with at least fifty individual plants, in order to capture the local range of genetic traits (see chap. 2). Collectors record local environmental information, such as the type of soil the plants are growing in, the slope and aspect of the site, whether the site is disturbed, and what other plants are growing nearby. Then they visit the site multiple times and collect seed from randomly selected plants. Some seeds are stored in a midterm seedbank; others are sown to produce live plants. At any one time, Greenbelt has 400,000 to 500,000 plants in production, representing more than three hundred species.

When asked what one should do if one is seeking plants for a project and there is no such careful nursery nearby, Toth points out, "There wasn't one here before either!" He acknowledges that we all have to make pragmatic choices to get projects done. The best source of seeds and plants, he suggests, is the site itself, and then one should search outward from there. Under Toth's leadership, Greenbelt has joined with the Bureau of Land Management, other government agencies, botanic gardens, and nonprofit organizations to support the Seeds of Success program (www.nps.gov/plants/sos). Seeds of Success aims to collect seed from every plant taxon native to the United States and to identify the thousand species most important for restoration and produce multiple ecotypic releases of seed for each of those species to support local restoration efforts throughout the country.

PLANTS FROM DISTANT REGIONS MAY HAVE SIMILAR ADAPTATIONS

While ecotypes of plants are finely adapted to their local environment, in some cases plants from distant corners of the globe have much in common.

Since the first botanical expeditions to Japan and China, western botanists have noted the striking similarity between the floras of eastern Asia and eastern North America. Numerous genera occur in these two regions only, with distinct species on the separate continents. Examples include *Magnolia*, *Wisteria*, *Pachysandra*, hickories (*Carya*), witch hazels (*Hamamelis*), and mayapples (*Podophyllum*) (figs. 1.15, 1.16) (Li 1952). These genera are said to be disjunct.

Figure 1.15 (left)   The North American mayapple, *Podophyllum peltatum*.
Figure 1.16 (right)   The Chinese mayapple, *Podophyllum pleianthum*.

Tens of millions of years ago, in the Tertiary period, a mesophytic deciduous forest spanned the two continents. Broadleaf trees and shrubs spread a dense canopy over rich, moist soils across a terrain of hills, mountains, and lowlands. In their shade grew herbaceous groundcovering perennials, and up their branches clambered aggressive vines. At the end of the Tertiary period, however, global cooling made the northern reaches of the continents uninhabitable for these forest plants, and they became separated on the two continents. There were probably several episodes of separation and reconnection across the Bering land bridge between what is now Russia and Alaska. Isolated on distant continents, the species continued to evolve, a process known as vicariance, which has created the separate but related species we know today.

Recent studies of the phylogenetic relationships of these plants have complicated this picture, however (Wen 1999). Some of the presumed sister species pairings based on morphological similarities between east Asian and eastern North American species (e.g., in the genus *Aralia*, the genus *Hamamelis*, and the *Magnolia* section *Rhytidospermum*) have not been confirmed genetically. Although the species are indeed distantly related, the morphological similarities may be seen as examples of convergent evolution.

In many cases plants and animals of different genetic origins growing in similar habitats develop similar adaptations. The most famous example of convergent evolution in plants is probably that of the Old World euphorbia family and the New World cactus family, both of which show reduced leaf area and store scarce water in fleshy stems that they protect from herbivores with sharp spines. In the case of woodland herbaceous plants, very broad, thin green leaves that can collect light under a shady canopy have been selected for across many disparate genera and families. This adaptation is shared by the unrelated Asian endemic Japanese wood poppy (*Glaucidium palmatum*) and the North American endemic hairy alumroot (*Heuchera villosa*), for example.

Whether because of disjunction and vicariance or convergent evolution, plants are sometimes well adapted to grow in distant but environmentally similar regions.

PLANTS FROM OTHER REGIONS CAN BE INCLUDED IN AN ECOLOGICAL LANDSCAPE

Disjunct taxa and convergent evolution pose a puzzle for the ecological designer: Is it ecologically justifiable to use well-adapted plants from other regions of the globe? Many aspects of this question are discussed later in the book, including what makes a plant community, ecosystem function, specific plant–animal relationships, the importance of diversity, the threat posed by invasive species, and the consequences of global change. At the level of choosing plants that are suited to their environment, however, it is clear that for every region there are plants from other regions that will grow with a minimum of care. Some of these plants are related to our natives, and once they even may have coexisted. Some have developed similar adaptations from evolving in similar climatic regimes on other parts of the planet.

The Asian Woods at Chanticleer Garden in Wayne, Pennsylvania demonstrates how well plants from other regions can grow alongside natives (fig. 1.17). Beneath a canopy of red maple and other trees native to the eastern North American deciduous forest, the gardeners at Chanticleer have created a woodland garden filled with plants from China, Japan, and Korea.

The structure of the Asian Woods is similar to the Woods Path at the nearby Mt. Cuba Center, with canopy, understory, and an herbaceous ground plane. Only here, among other substitutions, the east Asian kousa dogwood (*Cornus kousa*) takes the place of the native flowering dogwood. The seasonal spectacle of early spring flowers and intense autumn color is similar as well. Instead of the native trillium emerging through the leaf litter, though, the garden is graced by the early flowers of the Asian buttercup (*Adonis amurensis*).

One would not mistake the Asian Woods for a native landscape. Even without the Asian-inspired ar-

Figure 1.17 Asian Woods at Chanticleer Garden, Wayne, Pennsylvania. (Photo by Travis Beck.)

chitecture and site furnishings, the bamboo and broad-leafed hostas give the garden a decidedly Asian feel. But it is equally a celebration of the temperate deciduous forest, filled with plants well suited to their environment. If one is tempted to cringe at the use to which a remnant Pennsylvania woodland was put, consider that before the Asian Woods was created, this area was overrun by the native trouble-maker poison ivy (*Toxicodendron radicans*) and a truly invasive Asian honeysuckle.

In the right circumstances, adapted nonnative plants can be useful plants to include in an eco-logical landscape, whether for their toughness in urban conditions, their resistance to disease, their ability to perform needed functions (see chap. 4), or their aesthetic appeal. Several of the plants included in the yard of Panayoti and Gwen Kelaidis, for example, are not Colorado or even North American natives. It may not be desirable, or even possible, to grow pure communities of native plants in every landscape situation (see chap. 10). Consider, for instance, the work of the American Chestnut Foundation (2012), which is close to being able to reintroduce chestnuts that are resis-tant to the Asian fungus that decimated their stands in Appalachian forests, thanks to a breeding program using genes from the Chinese chestnut (*Castanea mollissima*). Both the cause of and the likeliest solution to chestnut blight stem from the close relation between eastern North American and east Asian forests.

HISTORY OF DISPERSAL AFFECTS BIOGEOGRAPHY

As the last section suggests, what plants grow where is not simply a matter of adaptation to the environment. Geologic and landscape history play roles as well. It is well understood that North America has experienced a series of massive glaciations in recent geologic history. We saw how these glaciations separated plants from a once-extensive mesophytic temperate forest into disjunct eastern Asian and eastern North American groups. The most recent glaciation was the Wisconsin, which reached its maximum about 18,000–20,000 years ago. As the massive glacier retreated over the course of a few thousand years, it left in its wake familiar features such as the terminal moraine we know as Long Island and the giant pools of meltwater called the Great Lakes.

Less well understood is the instability that the retreat of the glacier has caused in the vegetation of the region. Margaret Davis has made a career of studying changes in northeastern forests. She has gained insight into the history of these forests by examining grains of pollen trapped in layers of sediment at the bottom of lakes. Year after year the pollen of whatever wind-dispersed plant species are nearby drifts onto the surface of a lake, sinks to the bottom, and becomes trapped in the accumulating mud. By taking deep cores of this sediment, radiocarbon dating the layers, and counting the pollen grains of different species found in each layer, Davis and other researchers can identify the shifting abundance of different species.

One might imagine that as the glaciers retreated, bands of tundra, boreal, and temperate forests would follow the improving climate north. In fact, however, individual species migrated by different paths and at different rates (Davis 1981). Hickory and beech (*Fagus grandifolia*), which grow together in eastern North American hardwood forests today, appear to have survived the last glaciation in the lower Mississippi valley. From there hickory migrated quickly through the Midwest, reaching areas of Minnesota and Michigan as early as 10,000 years ago, but took another 5,000 years to penetrate New England. Beech, on the other hand, migrated east of the Appalachian mountains and arrived in Upper Michigan only 3,500 years ago (see fig. 1.18). Davis (1981: 152) concluded,

> Much of the time the rate of spread [of tree species] was not controlled by climate, and the geographic distributions of many species were not in equilibrium with climate, depending instead on the availability of propagules and the ability of seedlings to survive in competition with plants already growing on the site.

In other words, the distribution of plants is affected not only by climate but by the history of their dispersal.

Dispersal is simply the expansion of the geographic range of a species as individuals move into new areas. Biogeographers recognize several types of dispersal (Morrone 2009). Geodispersal is the simultaneous movement of many species brought about by the removal of a geographic barrier, followed by the emergence of a new barrier that creates vicariance. Geodispersal was involved in the evolution of the eastern Asian and eastern North American forests. Diffusion is the gradual movement of a species into suitable habitats over several generations. The migration of tree species after the Wisconsin glaciation is an example of diffusion. Jump dispersal was promoted by Darwin, among others. It is the random overcoming of a geographic barrier, as when a seed washes up on an island. Together with vicariance, dispersal helps explain the historical aspects of why plants grow where they do.

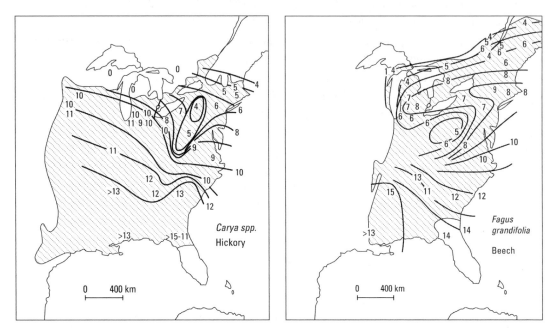

Figure 1.18 Migration of **(a)** hickory and **(b)** beech from the lower Mississippi Valley after the retreat of the Wisconsin glaciation. Hatching indicates the species' current range. Lines show extent of range at different times. Numbers indicate thousands of years ago. Hickory reached the upper Midwest 10,000 years ago but extended into New England only 5,000 years ago. Beech migrated east of the Appalachians and reached Upper Michigan only 3,500 years ago. (Redrawn from figs. 10.12 and 10.13 from Davis, M. B. ©1981. Quaternary history and the stability of forest communities. In *Forest Succession: Concepts and Applications*, edited by D. C. West, H. H. Shugart, and D. B. Botkin, 132–153. New York: Springer Verlag. With kind permission of Springer Science+Business Media.)

BE A MINDFUL AGENT OF PLANT DISPERSAL

Throughout this chapter we have discussed the importance of matching the adaptations of selected plants to their intended environment. As Davis's research showed, however, the natural distribution of plants does not represent a perfect balance between climate and adaptations. Instead, it is the result of interacting factors (availability of propagules, chance dispersal, ability to establish, competition) taking place in a changing space.

Before an adapted plant can grow and reproduce somewhere, it has to be brought to that location, whether by the forces of gravity, wind, or water or with the help of animals. Animals of all sorts, from birds with berries in their guts to bears with burrs on their legs, are responsible for dispersing plants (see chap. 7). Every time we humans select plants for a landscape or garden and decide where to get these plants and where to plant them out, we are also acting as agents of plant dispersal.

In some cases, we can use the built landscape to support and direct the diffusion of desired plant populations. In restoration plantings designers often reintroduce native plant species that were historically present on a site or species that are currently present in a reference site (see chap. 10). This type of dispersal can knit together disconnected populations and help create continuous corridors of habitat (see chap. 9). In these types of plantings, where it is anticipated that new plants will actively interbreed with surrounding populations, attention to plant genetics is especially important. In addition to filling gaps in species' ranges, one also might attempt to expand the edges of a species' current range, to see whether it could be done for horticultural or design purposes or in anticipation of climate change (see chap. 10). Planting out nonnative garden and landscape plants with a long and innocuous history in a region is another example of diffusion dispersal, one that simply further establishes populations of these plants in the built environment.

In other cases, planting a site involves the jump dispersal of exotic plants, whether these are continentally native plants that are not locally present or, as we discussed in the last section, adapted plants from other regions of the globe. Ecologically, this is a more uncertain form of dispersal, both because it is less clear how well an exotic plant will integrate with the flora and fauna of a local area (see chap. 7) and because of the threat of invasiveness (see chap. 5). For newer introductions, it pays to do one's homework and to consider limited introductions at first into a controlled setting.

Dispersing plants is an ecological act, one performed by humans for millennia with various consequences, from spreading useful plants across the globe to introducing diseases that wipe out native species. It is an act worth reflecting on fully when selecting plants for an ecological landscape. We should neither disperse plants blithely nor be afraid to try anything new.

CONCLUSION

Biogeography gives us a first lens through which to view landscapes ecologically. Plants in nature grow where they do for a variety of reasons, yet they all grow where they do without us needing to care for them. They accomplish this because, through various adaptations, they are suited to the environmental conditions of the regional climate and the local microclimate. They grow and senesce, flower and set seed, tough out winter and drought with durable leaves, or go dormant and reemerge in concert with the cycles of their area. When we design in harmony with the environment, we take advantage of these adaptations in our plant selection, creating landscapes that are in keeping with the character of an area not from specific design intent but because we are following the same rules as nature. Following nature's rules can only make our job as caretakers easier.

On one hand, we should maximize our use of local adaptations by planting local ecotypes where possible. On the other hand, we should recognize that not all the plants that could grow well in our particular environment currently do, that what is native to a given locale changes over time, and that dispersal is a natural process. Using adapted exotic plants in a thoughtful manner can be compatible with an ecological approach to design.

2. Beyond Massing: Working with Plant Populations and Communities

So far we have discussed how factors such as climate, microclimate, and place of origin influence why individual plants grow where they do in nature and how those factors should influence our selection of plants for the landscape. Of course, in nature and in the built environment plants rarely grow alone. They grow with other plants, both from their own species and from others.

Traditionally, in landscape and garden design, we call a substantial group of the same species a *mass* and the selection of plant species and varieties brought together for a project a *plant palette*. These terms reveal the aesthetic basis of how plants are conventionally grouped: to occupy a space, as a mass, and to work together harmoniously, as the colors chosen and mixed on a painter's palette. There is more to grouping plants than aesthetics, however. The demographic lens through which ecologists view assemblages of plants offers practical insights into how plants grow together and how we can group them in our designs.

In ecology, a group of individuals of a species living together in an area is called a population (Silvertown and Charlesworth 2001). An area is usually arbitrarily defined by the ecologist studying the population; it could be a measured research plot, an identifiable patch of habitat such as a meadow or copse of trees, or an entire watershed. However an area is defined, the individuals of a plant population within it are likely to interact—to interbreed, to compete for localized resources, in some cases to share resources via root grafting, even to communicate when attacked by pests. Plant populations, ecologists tell us, have a variety of characteristic structures: spatial structure, genetic structure, size structure, and age structure (Hitchens 1997). These structures are not stable but shift over time. In an ecological landscape design, we seek to bring ecologists' understanding of how plant populations are structured, and how they change, to the selection and placement of plants in the built landscape in order to set up landscapes with internal dynamics that don't require regular high levels of maintenance in order to remain full and healthy.

A community, in ecology, consists of populations of different species coexisting in a common environment. We can all think of recognizable groupings of plants in recognizable habitats: Atlantic coastal sand dune communities, for instance, with their beach grass (*Ammophila breviligulata*), beach pea (*Lathyrus japonicas maritimus*), beach plum (*Prunus maritima*), and seaside goldenrods (*Solidago sempervirens*). Even the names suggest these plants grow together in the same place. The concept of plant communities is intuitive yet hard to pin down scientifically. Still, it is one of the most fruitful areas for landscape designers to explore, whether we seek inspiration from communities observed in nature or attempt to make novel use of the principles that govern the commingling of plants. We can be guided in these efforts by the findings of ecologists regarding the number of species that occur in communities and the numbers of individuals within each species' population, and more importantly, by the mechanisms behind these numbers.

For our designs to function as ecological landscapes, we have to look beyond the sculptural and visual qualities of plants to the ways in which they grow together. When we design, we have the opportunity to set up self-perpetuating groups of plants that respond to a site, to each other, and to changes that take place over time. To accomplish this, however, we have to understand the factors that drive the locations, sizes, genetics, numbers, and proportions of different plants. In other words, we have to see plant groupings as populations and communities.

PLANT POPULATIONS HAVE A SPATIAL STRUCTURE

Naturally occurring plant populations are often arranged in striking ways: the dense blanket of color of a field of bluebonnets (*Lupinus texensis*), for instance, or the regular trunks of a stand of pitch pine (*Pinus rigida*), or the sweeps of grasses in a meadow (fig. 2.1). What explains these spatial patterns?

As we have seen, small-scale environmental differences play a significant role in determining what plants grow where. Patches of certain plants may grow on dry mounds, in wet depressions, or in areas of greater soil depth, creating a spatial structure that reflects environmental differences. Scattered plants may establish and mature only where safe sites exist, creating a dotted pattern (see chap. 8).

Layered on top of this environmental control of plant distribution are other factors, such as the location of parent plants and their means of spread (Greig-Smith 1979; Kershaw and Looney 1985). Seedlings from parent plants occur most frequently near the parent. When a plant dies, therefore, the most likely plant to take its spot is one of its own offspring, or offspring from a neighbor. Many plants also spread vegetatively. For instance, stoloniferous redtwig dogwoods (*Cornus sericea*) grow to create dense patches. Suckering plants such as beeches and redwoods create groves. Plants such as clover may spread more loosely, popping up between other plants. Taken together, these phenomena help explain the clustered patterns of many plant populations.

Other factors that affect the spatial structure of plant populations include competition (see chap. 3), the activities of animals (see chap. 7), and patterns of disturbance (see chap. 8). In all cases, the spatial pattern of a plant population is a reflection of underlying ecological processes.

DEVELOP PLANTING PATTERNS IN CONCERT WITH ECOLOGICAL PROCESSES

In the Meadow at Longwood Gardens in Pennsylvania, plants are managed as populations, and their spatial patterning reflects the myriad ecological processes that act on them, as well as human intention.

Figure 2.1 Populations of grasses, rushes, and other herbaceous plants form evident spatial patterns in the foreground of this wet meadow in Roxborough State Park, Colorado. (Photo by Travis Beck.)

First of all, the populations of the various plant species reflect the environmental heterogeneity of the site. The hillside on which the Meadow grows creates a range of conditions, from drier, less fertile areas at the top of the south-facing slopes to wetter, richer conditions at the bottom. In the richer areas, plants such as joe-pye weed (*Eutrochium maculatum*) have established strong masses. In the drier areas grow plants such as butterfly weed (*Asclepias tuberosa*) and the locally rare Elliott's broomsedge (*Andropogon gyrans*).

Plants' means of spread is another important factor. Joe-pye weed forms solid masses by means of aggressively spreading underground rhizomes. Seeds from little bluestem grass (*Schizachyrium scoparium*) can spread short distances on the wind, thereby pushing out the edges of existing masses, if conditions allow. The sawtooth sunflower (*Helianthus grosseserratus*) spreads so aggressively from seed that Longwood's land managers have had to use herbicide to knock it back.

Longwood's management of the site also affects spatial patterning. Various species have been introduced to the Meadow over time, both from seeds and from plugs (small rooted plants). Where they established well, their presence reflects human intention. Rotational burning of the Meadow favors certain species, such as Canada goldenrod (*Solidago canadensis*), in recently burned areas. Where land managers remove invasive species, they replant, so the latest plantings reflect the spatial patterns of invasive species establishment but with more appropriate plants.

The combination of all these factors has resulted in a diverse community in which clear bands and masses of plant populations are discernible. The spatial patterns that have emerged reflect natural processes layered with a history of human interventions. They are both highly ecological and aesthetically striking (fig. 2.2).

Figure 2.2   Populations of switchgrass (*Panicum virgatum*) and little bluestem form distinct spatial patterns in the Meadow at Longwood Gardens. (Photo by Travis Beck.)

PLANT POPULATIONS ARE GENETICALLY DIVERSE

Plant populations are made up of individual plants of the same species, from dozens to thousands of them, each with its own characteristics. Every individual in a population differs from the others in any number of ways—age, size, timing of flowering, tolerance of heat and cold, resistance to disease, just to name a few. Just as local ecotypes can be found within a species, within a population individual variation can be seen. To the extent that this variation has a genetic basis, it is a fundamental basis of plant biodiversity (see chap. 5).

Genetic diversity is maintained most apparently in populations through sexual outcrossing. When one plant in a population exchanges pollen with another plant to create a fertilized embryo within a seed, the genes the two plants carry are shuffled together. The offspring that result from this and similar outcrossings are then slightly genetically different from either of their parents.

Interestingly, however, diversity within plant species persists despite the fact that many plants produce genetically identical or closely related offspring and many others spread clonally (fig. 2.3). Dandelions (*Taraxacum officinale*) often use apomixis (in which embryos develop without fertilization having occurred) to produce seeds that are genetically identical to the parent. Self-fertilization, which produces seeds containing genes from only one parent, is most common in annuals such as the weedy common groundsel (*Senecio vulgaris*). Aspen (*Populus tremuloides*) suckers from its roots to create large stands of trees, as is evident in the fall when all the trees of a single clone turn color simultaneously. In all these cases genetically identical or closely related plants can spread quickly through an open area to which the parent plant has already proved to be adapted (Harper 1977).

Figure 2.3 Aspens sucker to create stands of genetically identical trees. Several such stands together form an aspen population of moderate diversity. (Photo by Mark Muir, US Forest Service.)

Ecologists have found that even in cases of asexually reproducing plants such as aspen and dandelion, local populations contain intermediate levels of genetic diversity (Ellstrand and Roose 1987). In these populations all the individuals that share the same genes are called a genet. Each physically separate individual of a genet is a ramet. Populations of asexually reproducing plants achieve intermediate levels of diversity by consisting of several co-occuring genets. Thus, a population of strawberries, for instance, might consist of seven hundred separate plants, one hundred ramets of each of seven genets. Whether working on sexually or asexually reproducing plants, then, natural selection seems to maintain genetic diversity in local populations.

There are several advantages to genetic diversity (Falk et al. 2006). One is that heterozygous plants (those with different alleles for a given trait) tend to perform better. Diverse populations avoid the effects of inbreeding depression, where negative mutations are more commonly expressed. Also, in diverse populations there is a subtle differentiation of adaptations down to the level of individual plants. This allows the population to take advantage of the smallest environmental variations on the site and slight differences in the ability to coexist with other species. This diversity can be especially important if environmental variables fluctuate or change directionally on a site over the lifetime of a generation of plants, which is perhaps why most longer-lived woody plant species reproduce through outcrossing. Finally, diverse populations are able to better withstand pressure from pests and pathogens. The population presents a more varied target, and resistant individuals may be able to spread their genes more widely in future generations (see chap. 7). In sum, genetic diversity helps a plant population on a given site survive, adapt, and persist through time.

CREATE DIVERSE POPULATIONS

For long-term stability in the face of environmental fluctuations, broad-scale resistance to pests and pathogens, and ability to continue to evolve, genetic diversity in a plant population is essential. This is as true in the constructed landscape as it is in nature. To benefit from these advantages of intraspecific diversity, designers should use cultivated varieties selectively, consider developing regional or site-specific landraces, and insist on broad-based collection of seed for the production of straight species for landscape use.

Plant breeders have selected, developed, and named a wide array of cultivated varieties of many popular landscape plants. Consider the coneflowers. In addition to the standard North American native *Echinacea purpurea* we now have *E. purpurea* 'Magnus,' 'Little Magnus,' 'Kim's Knee High,' 'Kim's Mophead,' 'Ruby Giant,' 'Vintage Wine,' 'Double Decker,' 'Fatal Attraction,' 'Pink Shuttles,' and 'Pink Poodle,' to name just a few. The goal of the cultivated variety is to reduce variability and produce uniformity of certain traits. Take *E. purpurea* 'Magnus,' for example. Whether propagated sexually by seed or asexually by root cuttings, the result is a plant with a strong, deep pink flower color and wide petals in a flat disk. This artificial selection greatly reduces the natural genetic variation found in a sexually reproducing population of the straight species.

Some of the more colorful coneflower cultivars are produced by hybridizing purple coneflower with the yellow *Echinacea paradoxa*. Offspring of these crosses are then themselves crossed, to produce plants such as *Echinacea* 'Sunrise,' 'Sun Down,' 'Summer Sky,' 'Twilight,' and 'Harvest Moon.' Crossing plants in this way can create genotypes with so-called hybrid vigor, resulting from a new combination of beneficial dominant genes. Once a promising offspring of the cross is identified and selected for release, however, it is reproduced asexually through divisions, cuttings, or micropropagation, which means each plant is genetically identical to the original parent.

Certainly there are advantages to the use of cultivars. Uniformity of size, shape, and color can help achieve design intent. Many cultivars are selected for their disease resistance, which can help plantings avoid or survive infection. Asexual annual weeds such as dandelion and suckering early-successional plants such as aspen suggest that in the right situation there are ecological advantages to using clones.

In a uniform site where a particular plant is known to do well, a fast-growing cultivar can provide quick, reliable coverage. Even in these situations, however, ecological designers would do well to create multiclonal populations of several related cultivars, to achieve the intermediate level of diversity found in natural populations of clonal plants.

Intermediate levels of diversity in a population can also be created by applying the agricultural concept of a landrace. Landraces are less formalized breeds of animals or varieties of plants that are adapted to local environmental and cultural conditions. They are distinctive in some manner, such as being early or late fruiting, but because selection is less rigorous than in the development of a modern named variety, landraces contain a higher level of genetic variability. Landraces of ornamental plants are not readily available but can be created by any land manager in one of two ways. One can select from an existing population of a species on the basis of flower size, disease resistance, or whatever characteristics one chooses and only allow certain plants to reproduce. Alternatively, one can plant multiple cultivars, or a cultivar and the straight species from which it is derived, and allow them to interbreed and again select the preferred plants to continue the experiment. The landrace approach allows the manager of a population of plants over time to combine the benefits of local adaptation and genetic variability with selection for particular characteristics.

To achieve high levels of genetic diversity within a population, however, it is necessary to use straight species rather than cultivars or landraces. It is also important that these plants be propagated by seed, rather than vegetative methods, to allow for sexual outcrossing and the accompanying genetic shuffling to occur. Beyond that, it is important to know how the seeds from which these plants are produced were collected (fig. 2.4). Growers often take many seeds from a single notable parent plant

Figure 2.4 Collecting seeds from brownfoot (*Acourtia wrightii*) in Arizona. Randomized collection over a period of time increases the genetic diversity of propagated plant material. (Courtesy of BLM/UAH, Seeds of Success.)

and then increase their stock from this limited initial collection. Where a small number of specimen plants are needed, selection from notable individuals can be appropriate. To achieve diversity, however, broader collection is necessary. Geneticists now recommend collection techniques such as randomized sampling over a period of time in order to capture 95 percent of the genetic diversity of local populations (Guarino, Ramanatha Rao, and Reid 1995). Only when all these methods are applied can the plant populations of our constructed landscapes approach the beneficial levels of diversity found in natural plant populations.

POPULATIONS INCLUDE INDIVIDUALS OF DIFFERENT SIZES AND AGES

In designed landscapes, plants of the same species are often the same size. In some cases this is simply a byproduct of redoing an entire area at one time, as when all the trees in a new park are planted the same year. In other cases it is an intentional part of the design, an attempt to create uniformity through repetition of a single element. Designers often further increase uniformity by specifying genetically identical cultivars.

Natural plant populations, on the other hand, contain individual plants of different sizes. Size is important in the plant kingdom. Because larger plants claim the resources of a larger area and tend to be more successful reproductively, which individual plants are able to grow larger influences the evolutionary direction of a plant population. Larger plants are able to better survive some disturbances, such as fire, and less able to survive others, such as windstorms. A diverse size structure presents a diverse defensive front to pathogens and herbivores. The ultimate size each plant attains is the product of its genetic makeup, the microenvironment in which it finds itself, and the events it experiences over its lifetime.

An example of the structure that the interaction between genetics and the environment creates in a plant population can be seen in a study by Charles Mohler, Peter Marks, and Douglas Sprugel (1978) of the balsam fir that grows in nearly pure stands below timberline on Whiteface Mountain in upstate New York. Here an interesting phenomenon can be observed: The forest is striped with lines of dead trees. These dead trees are the advancing edge of what is known as a fir wave. Behind the dead trees fir seedlings sprout, behind the seedlings saplings grow, and farther back mature trees, until at the very back of the wave the tallest trees are found. These tall trees are exposed to strong winds and winter rime-ice that lead to their death and the continuation of the wave. Fir waves move in the direction of the prevailing wind at a speed of 1 to 3 meters a year, the entire cycle taking about 60 years. Because of the regular nature of the waves, they are composed of even-aged stands of fir and provide a snapshot of the development of such stands over time.

Mohler, Marks, and Sprugel found that, as seedlings, most of the fir trees were of a similar size (small) as measured by trunk diameter (fig. 2.5). In the 19-year old stand, however, while most of the individuals were still small, some were clearly larger than others, and the range of sizes had increased greatly. In the oldest (54- and 59-year-old) stands, individuals displayed a broad, almost symmetrically distributed range of sizes.

As with the old "nature versus nurture" debate, size differences are determined in part by the genetics of each individual and in part by the circumstances under which it has grown. Spruce trees that spring from larger seeds will have an early advantage. Those that germinate in a particularly favorable

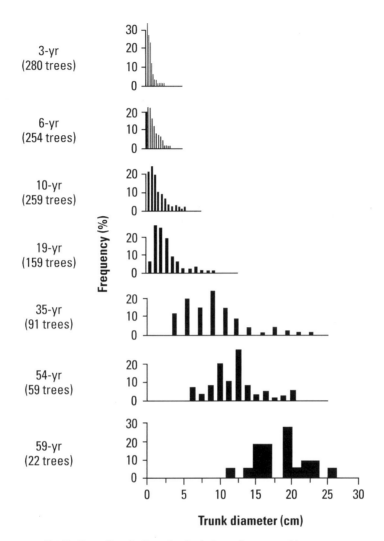

Figure 2.5 Frequency distribution of trunk diameter for balsam fir arranged in an age sequence. In younger stands, most of the plants were of a similar small size. In older stands, a nearly symmetrically distributed range of sizes emerged. Variation in size is normal in natural plant populations and enhances ecological function. (From Mohler, C. L., P. L. Marks, and D. G. Sprugel. Copyright ©1978 Blackwell Scientific Publications. Stand structure and allometry of trees during self-thinning of pure stands. *Journal of Ecology* 66:599–614. Reproduced with permission of John Wiley and Sons, Inc.)

spot will also have an advantage. As the plants mature, the larger ones are able to assimilate more resources and grow even larger, magnifying these early differences. Any plants damaged by storms or attacked by insects will be set back relative to their fellows.

Mohler, Marks, and Sprugel's study illuminates the processes that create a varied size structure within an even-aged stand. The size structure of most natural populations also stems from the inclusion of different age classes of plants. Large, mature trees play a very different role from tiny seedlings. Yet these seedlings and the saplings they grow into represent the future of a population. Where they are abundant, they portend a potential increase in local abundance of that species. Where recruitment has declined, as can happen during succession, the opposite is true (see chap. 8).

The range and proportions of individuals of different sizes and ages influence many of the ecological functions of natural plant populations. For instance, the ratio of large trees to saplings affects how nutrients and carbon are stored and cycled in a forest ecosystem (see chap. 4). It also affects the habitat value of the forest for insects, birds, and other animals (see chap. 7).

DEVELOP POPULATIONS WITH VARIED SIZE AND AGE STRUCTURES

Ecological landscapes should aim to develop populations with varied size and age structures for greater resilience and broader ecological function. As just discussed, genetic diversity makes a population better able to face varying environmental pressures and provides a basis for the beneficial evolution of that population. Similarly, a varied size structure, which is an expression of genetic diversity in the environment, and a varied age structure both promote the resilience of that population in the face of insect pests and disturbance. Variation in sizes also stabilizes ecological functioning and creates the complex habitat on which many other ecological interactions are based. One of the places that size structure can be discerned most easily in the built environment is in urban forests.

Not far from the fir waves of Whiteface Mountain lies the city of Syracuse, New York. Syracuse is located on the shores of Onondaga Lake, one of New York's Finger Lakes, and is recognized by the Arbor Day Foundation as a Tree City USA. In 2001 a broad cooperative effort led to the publication of an urban forest master plan for Syracuse (Nowak and O'Connor 2001). The master plan was based on a comprehensive assessment of the city's existing urban forest, during which all 34,000 street trees and more than 9,000 park trees were inventoried, and data were collected on two hundred random plots that cover both public and private property. Among the data collected was information on the diameter at breast height (DBH) of trees in the city (fig. 2.6). More than half of Syracuse's trees had a DBH of 6 inches or less. The shape of the distribution of tree sizes in Syracuse much resembled Mohler and his colleagues' graphs of the 6- or 10-year distribution of sizes of fir trees on Whiteface. That is to say, it represented a young population with a poorly developed size distribution.

There are numerous advantages to having more trees in the larger size classes. Among these, as the master plan reported, trees with DBHs of 33 inches or more remove about fifty times more airborne pollutants and about seventy times more carbon per year than trees with DBHs of less than 3 inches. To the extent that tree sizes reflect the microenvironments in which trees are grown, having larger trees represented in the distribution indicates that at least some trees are establishing and growing well where they are planted. However, the goal of a healthy urban forest is not just to have larger trees but to have a broader range of tree sizes within the populations of each species. Trees of different sizes react differently to droughts, storms, and pests, reducing the potential for catastrophic losses. To the extent that tree sizes reflect tree ages, a broader size structure within a population supports a more regular replacement of trees over time. This means maintenance budgets can be more even and predictable from year to year.

By comparison, in 2009 the city of Ann Arbor, Michigan, also a Tree City USA, completed an inven-

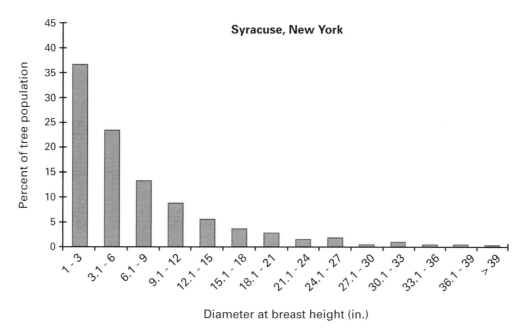

Figure 2.6 Size distribution of trees in Syracuse, New York. (From Nowak, D. J., and P. R. O'Connor. 2001. *Syracuse Urban Forest Master Plan: Guiding the City's Forest Resource into the 21st Century*. Newtown Square, PA: USDA Forest Service.)

tory of the more than 47,000 street and park trees in their urban forest (Davey Resource Group 2009). Although the size classes recorded differed from those of Syracuse, the number of trees of larger sizes was clearly greater, and trees were more evenly distributed across size classes than in Syracuse (fig. 2.7). This is a sign of a healthy urban forest, in which trees are attaining good sizes and in which re-moval of overmature trees and planting of new trees can happen in a regular, noncatastrophic fashion.

Creating populations with varied size and age structures is most easily done through long-term stewardship of a site. When installing new landscapes, however, we can jumpstart the process by planting individual plants of the same species at different sizes. We can even map this size distribu-tion onto the landscape in imitation or anticipation of environmental outcomes. We can plant larger specimens in the most favorable sites (where they are most likely to thrive in any case) and smaller, less expensive individuals in more marginal areas, where their success is less assured. Planting over several years instead of all at once can begin to create a diverse age structure. We should also allow populations to begin to replace themselves on site as soon as they reach reproductive maturity. Where their age structure comes to reflect an inability to do so, we should plan on their eventual replacement by a population of another, more suited species.

PLANT MASSES HAVE ECOLOGICAL LIMITS
As we have seen, habitat suitability, patterns of seed dispersal, and patterns of growth often lead to plants of a single species growing together in masses. The more plants of a single species grow

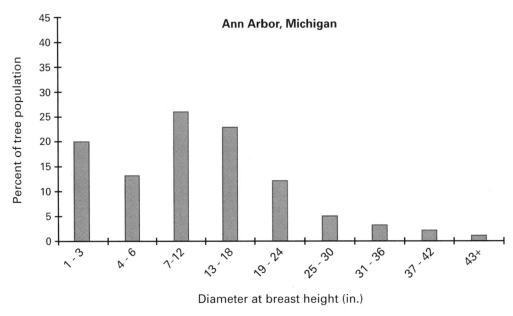

Figure 2.7 Size distribution of street and park trees in Ann Arbor, Michigan. (Courtesy of Davey Resource Group, a Division of the Davey Tree Expert Company.)

together in an area, the more they are subject to certain pressures. Diseases, such as the fungus that causes damping off in seedlings, are more prevalent in such dense populations. Seed predators and herbivores are also more active in dense stands. And competition between individual plants becomes more intense. These density-dependent factors place ecological limits on masses in the natural landscape.

Dense masses of a single plant species in the built landscape are also subject to these density-dependent factors. Especially where genetic variation is low, such populations may experience high rates of disease and pest problems. Even without raising concerns of visual interest and biodiversity, these issues suggest the importance of avoiding monocultures by including populations of more than one species on a site.

Density-dependent factors are influenced by plant spacing. Planting designers are often caught between a need to create immediate impact and a desire to leave sufficient room for plants at maturity. Conventional planting design advice is to set plants at such a spacing that they will just touch their neighbors at maturity. From the beginning, each plant is awarded a generous share of space in the landscape. This is essentially an agricultural model, in which plants are placed not so far apart that space is wasted and not so close that they suppress each other's growth. The difficulty is that until each plant reaches maturity, the design can feel underwhelming or incomplete, and large open areas are subject to weed invasion. If some plants do not make it, they have to be replaced, or their space is left empty; either way, the consistency of a designed mass is lost. Designs that provide immediate impact, on the other hand, can quickly appear overgrown and become subject to density-dependent disease problems. Frederick Law Olmsted's famous dictum "Plant thick, thin quick" offers one approach. Too often, however, designers are unable to communicate long-term removal plans to the people responsible for maintenance.

TRY SELF-THINNING

In natural populations, size structure and plant spacing are closely related. In the older stands of balsam fir studied by Mohler, Marks, and Sprugel (1978), the individual fir trees not only were larger but were fewer in number. In the 3-year-old stand Mohler and colleagues counted 280 individuals. In the 19-year-old stand they found 159 individuals. And in the 59-year-old stand there were just 22 individuals. This can be expressed graphically on a logarithmic scale as a relationship between the average weight of a plant in a study plot and the plant density (number per square meter) in that plot (fig. 2.8). An apparent limit line emerges. If there are many plants in a limited area, they must have a small average weight. If plants are large, there can only be few of them. This has an intuitive logic when we

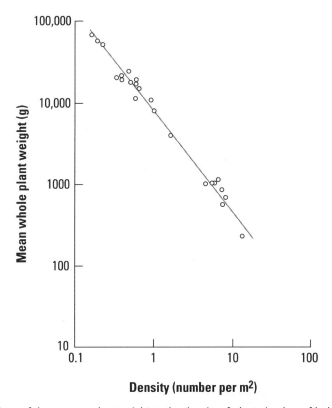

Figure 2.8 Comparison of the average plant weight to the density of plants in plots of balsam fir, showing that as plant weight increased in older stands, density decreased. This process is known as self-thinning. (From Mohler, C. L., P. L. Marks, and D. G. Sprugel. Copyright ©1978 Blackwell Scientific Publications. Stand structure and allometry of trees during self-thinning of pure stands. *Journal of Ecology* 66:599–614. Reproduced with permission of John Wiley and Sons, Inc.)

imagine the amount of space plants of different sizes take up. The interesting element is that the same populations that begin as many small plants end up as few large plants. A process of self-thinning occurs in which at every stage some plants die and others continue to grow. The plants that die tend to be the smaller plants, and the plants that continue to grow are the larger plants that have outcompeted their fellows. Kyoji Yoda and colleagues (1963) performed some of the earliest studies of self-thinning in agricultural plants in cultivated fields and roadside weeds in natural stands. The principle has been demonstrated many times since in a variety of plant populations.

A little-explored ecological approach to designed plantings is to allow self-thinning to maintain the balance between plant density and plant size. Applying self-thinning principles, the number of plants to include depends not on the ultimate number desired but on the size at which they are planted—either fewer larger plants or more smaller plants. In either case, plants should be planted in numbers necessary to fill the desired area, at such spacing that as soon as they are established, they face intraspecific competition (see chap. 3). Setting plants at high densities immediately crowds out weeds, as desired plants claim all the resources of the site. Where species selection or environmental conditions create the possibility that density-dependent diseases such as fungal pathogens will infect such a densely spaced mass, however, it might be wise to increase spacing.

Self-thinning can be a particularly good strategy with herbaceous groundcovers. As Mohler et al.'s research showed, however, the principle applies equally to trees and shrubs, for which it can also have aesthetic and maintenance benefits. Trees evolved in forests, and it is branches' competition for light that results in the upright mature forms of most trees. When landscape trees are planted as isolated "specimens," never competing for light, they tend to have spherical rather than tall, arching canopies. They develop larger branches lower on the trunk and can require more pruning.

As individual plants grow as part of a self-thinning mass, those with favored genetics, or in a slightly better location, or with an initial slight advantage of size will persist, and others will perish, all the while maintaining the balance between the number of individuals and their size. In the ultimate mature landscape, plants will be properly spaced, and although they might not be in the exact spots where a designer would have placed them, they will be well established there, having emerged triumphant from the self-thinning process.

POPULATIONS ARE DYNAMIC

Self-thinning is just one aspect of the changes that take place in a population over time. A population can exponentially increase in number of individuals, fluctuate in size, or go extinct.

Ola Inghe and Carl Olaf Tamm published a remarkable study in 1985, tracking the fates of individual plants within populations of hepatica (*Anemone hepatica*) and sanicle (*Sanicula europaea*) in Sweden over 38 years. In 1943 Tamm established several permanent 1-square-meter plots in a former hay meadow with scattered trees and in a nearby spruce forest. Over most of the intervening years, Tamm revisited these plots during early summer flowering. With the help of a frame with a wire grid, he was able to map individual plants and follow them over time. Overall, there was a fair degree of stability in the species composition and abundance of other plants in the study plots. Apart from summer mowing of the meadows, the plots were relatively undisturbed.

One of the hepatica populations in the forest provides a fair representation of the overall trends Inghe and Tamm observed. Recruitment of new hepatica seedlings occurred in bursts. In some years many seedlings germinated. In others few or no seedlings germinated. This was not clearly related to the flowering that had occurred in the previous year; it seems to have been more closely connected with the weather. In all years, mortality was highest among the youngest plants. Summer drought was a key factor. In the late 1950s, when summer rains were plentiful, young plants established more successfully. The high juvenile mortality can also be considered an example of self-thinning in each generation. After establishment, plants took different lengths of time to reach flowering maturity. Flowering too appeared to be linked to environmental conditions. Individual plants divided either because of damage to the growing tip or because of the apparent strength of the plant. Inghe and Tamm referred to the plants that were first observed in 1943 as "the old guard." In the last decade of the study, these plants appeared to be weakening, as they flowered and divided less than before. Inghe and Tamm attributed this weakening to increased shade from the spruce forest.

All plant populations experience similar dynamics of growth or decline based on the fates of their individual members in response to changing environmental conditions. Of course, few populations grow by themselves. The population dynamics of one species in an area are related to the dynamics of others. Nigel Dunnett and Arthur Willis (2000) reported on another long-term plant population dataset, this one taken from a plot of roadside grassland near Bibury, Gloucestershire, England. Every summer since 1959 researchers have estimated the aboveground biomass of each species present in the plot. The focus of this report was on a patch of willowherb (*Chamerion angustifolium*) that probably spread clonally from a single individual that established after a major disturbance such as a fire or a vehicle driving on the verge. From this lone ramet, the willowherb spread to make up more than a third of the biomass of the entire plot, before the clump broke apart and declined (fig. 2.9). Dunnett and Willis attributed the decline of the willowherb to a series of dry years in the mid-1970s, perhaps in combination with locking up nutrients in its own biomass.

Several less abundant species in the plot, including hedge woundwort (*Stachys sylvatica*), followed the same progression as the willowherb, perhaps in response to the same changing environmental conditions. The tall oatgrass (*Arrhenatherum elatius*), which otherwise dominates the roadsides in this area, however, exhibited the opposite trend, declining during the period of the willowherb's greatest growth and rebounding immediately after. Dunnett and Willis attributed the switches in dominance between the willowherb and the tall oatgrass to competition, interacting with disturbance and weather. This sort of dominance switching between dynamic populations is one of the means by which diverse ecosystems maintain high levels of function across time (see chap. 5).

ALLOW POPULATIONS TO CHANGE OVER TIME
All gardeners know that a landscape never stays the same as the day it was planted, though some like to imagine that it will. The precious plant you just had to include limps along for a number of years and then expires. Meanwhile, the groundcover that came in from the adjacent property takes over. One year the such-and-such flowers spectacularly; the next you barely notice it. Viewed from an ecological perspective, these are all examples of population dynamics.

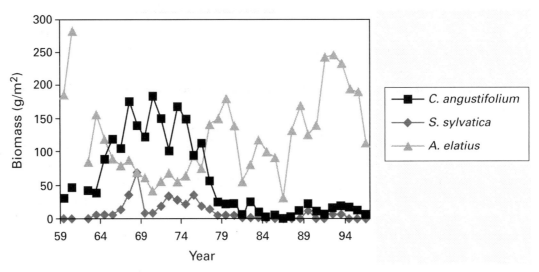

Figure 2.9 Midsummer biomass of 3 species in a plot of roadside grassland, 1959–1996. No measurements were taken in 1961. (From Dunnett, N. P., and A. J. Willis. 2000. Dynamics of *Chamerion angustifolium* in grassland vegetation over a thirty-nine year period. *Plant Ecology* 148(1):43–50.)

The goal of conventional horticultural practices is to establish a good environment for plant growth and display at all times and to keep the balance between green bullies and shrinking violets. An ecological approach is to allow plant populations to respond to environmental variation and to shifting competitive relationships in a dynamic way.

Inghe and Tamm's research showed the impact of weather on seedling establishment, plant growth, and flowering. Simply put, some years are better than others. For existing populations, we should anticipate good display and expansion of the population in good years (as defined by that species) and poor display and population decline after one or more bad years. Plant populations that are allowed to ebb and flow in this manner will naturally convey a sense of place, reflecting a particular environment at a particular time.

Competitive relationships also affect the dynamics of plant populations. As Dunnett and Willis demonstrated, environmental fluctuation and competitive relationships are related. A weather event such as a period of unusually dry weather can weaken one population and create an opportunity for another population to expand. The key to the success of a landscape design that allows for population dynamics to play themselves out is to include a mix of species that can fluctuate complementarily. These plants will need to have overlapping environmental tolerances but distinct competitive maxima (see chap. 3). In some years certain species will come to the fore; in other years, others will. Including populations of multiple species can also help keep a planting full if insects or disease ravage one particular species.

The trends of multispecies dynamics will not necessarily oscillate regularly. As Inghe and Tamm discovered, a changing environment can weaken an entire population. Or, when events allow one species to gain a competitive advantage, the balance of populations on a site may shift for good. We must also be prepared for our plantings to change in these ways over time (see chap. 8).

PLANTS FORM COMMUNITIES

When we consider multiple plant populations and their interactions, we are dealing with something new: a plant community. One of the early goals of ecologists was to identify, classify, and explain plant communities. In Europe, these efforts were led by botanist Josias Braun-Blanquet under the banner of phytosociology. In his 1932 magnum opus *Plant Sociology: The Study of Plant Communities*, Braun-Blanquet distinguished between the association (what we would now call a community) and the stand. The association is the general abstract type, of which the stand is the individual example. It is important to keep this abstract quality of plant communities in mind, especially when we consider criticisms of the concept. Braun-Blanquet noted that communities of plants come about because of dependent and commensal unions. In dependent unions, one plant literally depends on another: for sustenance (as in the case of parasitic plants such as dodder), for support (epiphytes such as Spanish moss [*Tillandsia usneoides*]), or for physical protection (shade plants growing beneath canopy trees). Much more decisive, Braun-Blanquet declared, are commensal unions, in which plants come together as *compagnons de table*, sharing or jostling for the same space and resources.

In North America, pioneering ecologist Frederic Clements explained plant communities in somewhat different terms. The centerpiece of Clements's theories was the climax, a unified and stable community of plants, inseparably connected with its climate, that is the endpoint of successional change (Clements 1936) (see chap. 8). In Clements's description, climax communities range in scale from continental (like a biome) to site-specific. At all scales, they are recognizable because of the unity provided by their dominant species. Tallgrass prairie, for instance, is unified by its tall grasses. Climax communities, Clements proposed, are perfectly adapted to their climate. They are stable because seasonal changes and changes from year to year "are superficial, fleeting or periodic and leave no permanent impress" (1936: 256). They are further stable, Clements asserted, because unless disturbed, they will maintain themselves indefinitely, and if disturbed, they will return to their current condition. This presumed stability led Clements, in his most far-reaching claim, to liken the climax to a self-regulating organism (see chap. 4).

The community is a powerful concept in plant ecology, one that has organized much of the research of the last century. Although, as we will see, much of Braun-Blanquet's and Clements's thinking has been set aside by contemporary ecologists, the fundamental idea of the community continues to shape how we understand the relationship of plants to each other and to their environment.

DESIGN PLANTINGS MODELED ON NATURAL COMMUNITIES

As we look to combine populations of different plants in the landscape, natural communities offer obvious models. We can learn about the plants that grow together in native plant communities by visiting them ourselves and by consulting plant lists for natural areas, such as those created by native plant societies, as well as historical accounts by early botanists. The *Landscape Restoration Handbook* (Harker et al. 1999) offers an encyclopedic reference for native plant communities across North America.

The Charles Anderson Landscape Architecture (CALA) planting design for the Olympic Sculpture Park in Seattle imitates natural communities and taps principal Charles Anderson's 20 years of experience with what he calls "eco-urbanism." The Olympic Sculpture Park makes a sharp *Z* in its descent of a remnant bluff from the Belltown neighborhood, across the busy Elliott Avenue and a set of railroad tracks to the Puget Sound waterfront. CALA used this framework to create planting areas that echo the natural plant communities found in Washington State from the mountains to the sound (Anderson 2007), from a mountain forest of larches (*Larix occidentalis*) and Douglas fir (*Pseudotsuga menziesii*) by the high pavilion, down through an aspen grove and meadows, to shore plantings along the board-walk and, finally, a pocket beach, the only place on the Seattle waterfront where the public can wet their feet in the cold salt water.

The beach planting looks and feels remarkably like a natural section of Washington beach (fig. 2.10). Riprap was removed to create an opening to the water. The offshore portion of the site was terraced to create habitat benches for kelp and marine life. The beach was sloped steeply in its lower reaches and then more gently to meet existing grade above the high tide line. At the crest of the slope, lines of driftwood naturalistically flank a gravel path that merges into the beach and, upslope of the path, retain a sandy soil colonized at its edge by dune grass (*Leymus mollis*), Puget Sound gumweed (*Grindelia integrifolia*), hairy manzanita (*Arctostaphylos columbiana*), salal (*Gaultheria shallon*), and beach strawberry (*Fragaria chiloensis*). A few feet further back, Nootka rose (*Rosa nutkana*), snowberry (*Symphoricarpos albus*), and evergreen huckleberry (*Vaccinium ovatum*) are gathered beneath red alder (*Alnus rubra*) and shore pine (*Pinus contorta* var. *contorta*).

Figure 2.10 Pocket Beach planting at Olympic Sculpture Park, a community modeled on natural shoreline communities of Washington State. (Photo by Travis Beck.)

The plant list for the pocket beach was derived not from a particular site but from Charles Anderson's recollection of Washington's coastal plant communities and his years of experience designing similar plantings. In Braun-Blanquet's terminology, it is very much an individual stand, reflecting an abstract association. Anderson does not claim that the plantings in the park are native plant communities. He calls them "likenesses."

Anderson's method is to plant the entire community at once, including both proven diehard plants and more delicate plants in protected locations. Then he likes to let the community adapt to its site, losing individuals that are not well situated and gaining new seedlings from within and off the site. In the case of the pocket beach, shore pine is already reproducing itself and common rush (*Juncus effusus*) has established itself as a new member of the community. This adaptive process results in a plant community that is ecological both in its inspiration and in its relation with its site and surroundings.

THE EVIDENCE FOR INDIVIDUALISM IN PLANT COMMUNITIES

Even as Braun-Blanquet and Clements were formalizing their detailed classifications of plant communities, a countervailing line of theory emerged. In a seminal 1926 article, Henry Gleason proposed an "individualistic concept of the plant association." No doubt plant communities exist and can be observed, Gleason suggested, but "precise structural uniformity of vegetation does not exist" (1926: 10). On similar sites, different species and proportions of plants may be present, including dominants from other communities. In areas where environmental transitions are broad, such as along the banks of the Mississippi River as it flows from north to south, the boundaries between communities can be very fuzzy. Because of difficulties such as these, Gleason asked, should we not conclude that "an association is not an organism, scarcely even a vegetational unit, but merely a *coincidence*?" (1926: 16).

Instead, Gleason proposed, we should think in terms of the individual plants that make up a community. They grow where they grow because they came from a parent in the area and their propagule landed in a favorable environment. No association is typical, and associations therefore cannot be classified. Each has come into being independently as a result of this process of migration and environmental sorting.

The revolutionary simplicity of Gleason's individualistic theory of plant communities was largely ignored for decades, until it received empirical support from the next generation of ecologists. In 1956, Robert Whittaker published a monograph on the vegetation of the Great Smoky Mountains along the border of Tennessee and North Carolina. In order to understand the complex vegetation patterns in this region, Whittaker compared the groups of plants growing at various points along environmental gradients. If plant communities exist in nature, Whittaker reasoned, we should see distinct groupings of plants, all of which have their boundaries at similar points along the environmental gradient. Where the dominant species of a plant community reach their limits, so should the associated species. When Whittaker assembled his data into tables and graphs, however, he found that plant species in the Great Smokies have rounded and tapered distributions and that the centers of these distributions are scattered along the environmental gradients and overlap greatly, creating a gradual change in community composition from one end of a gradient to the other (fig. 2.11). Based on this evidence, Whittaker concluded that species populations are distributed individualistically, as Gleason

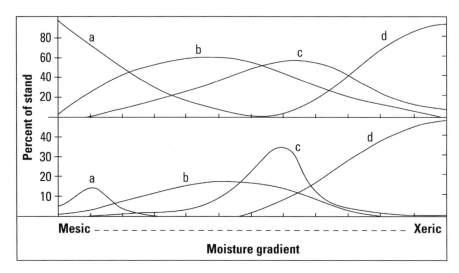

Figure 2.11 *Top:* Percentage of sampled stands composed of trees from **(a)** mesic, **(b)** submesic, **(c)** subxeric, and **(d)** xeric classes across the continuum of mesic to xeric habitats between 1,500 and 2,500 feet in elevation in the Great Smoky Mountains. There are no abrupt transitions in community composition but instead a blending from one class to the next across the continuum. *Bottom:* The same blending is observed with individual species: **(a)** yellow birch (*Betula alleghaniensis*), **(b)** flowering dogwood, **(c)** chestnut oak (*Quercus montana*), and **(d)** Virginia pine (*Pinus virginiana*). (From Whittaker, R. Copyright ©1956, Ecological Society of America. Vegetation of the Great Smoky Mountains. *Ecological Monographs* 26:2–80. With permission from the Ecological Society of America.)

proposed, and that, "in general, community-units are more 'arbitrary' products of classification than 'natural' units clearly defined in the field" (Whittaker 1956: 24). Instead of consisting of a series of interlocking communities, Whittaker (1956: 32) suggested, "vegetation forms a *complex population pattern* in relation to environment. In this pattern species (of green plants, at least) distribute themselves 'individualistically'; they occur together wherever their distributions overlap, and associate and dissociate freely in evolutionary time."

MIMIC THE STRUCTURE OF NATURAL COMMUNITIES WHILE SUBSTITUTING SPECIES

If plant communities are individualistic, as Gleason proposed and Whittaker substantiated, then eco-logical designers can take a flexible approach to their composition of plant communities, bringing together plants that might not grow side by side in nature. Of course, neither Gleason nor Whittaker claimed that plant communities were entirely coincidental, such that any collection of plants could grow together anywhere in the world. Environmental suitability, processes of plant establishment, and competitive relationships all come into play. The farther away we step from natural models, the more likely we are to run afoul of these factors and to create communities that require us to work to main-tain them rather than their being able to function by themselves. This is the trouble with combining plants primarily on the basis of form and color, as in any mixed planting bed. The advantage of using a natural community as a model, however arbitrarily delineated it may be, is that the relations between plants have been already worked out; the *compagnons de table* have already found their places, so to speak. In a designed landscape, we can preserve some of the demonstrated functionality of native plant communities while allowing ourselves more design freedom by keeping the structure of a natural plant community as a model but substituting individual species. This is the approach taken in the Asian Woods at Chanticleer (see chap. 1). It is also the philosophy behind forest gardening.

Forest gardens are collections of useful trees, shrubs, vines, and herbaceous plants that provide food, fiber, and medicine for their caretakers (Jacke and Toensmeier 2005). They are modeled after natural forests, not so much in their species composition (which is weighted toward useful species) but in their architecture. Researchers have shown that traditional tropical agroforestry systems from the humid lowlands of southeastern Mexico to Sri Lanka and Indonesia mimic the structure, and many of the functions, of their surrounding natural forests. Geneviève Michon and her co-authors (1983: 123) wondered about the origins of village agroforests in West Java:

Are they a gradual transformation of the native ecosystem, with a replacement tree by tree, selection and domestication of useful species, elimination of useless species, introduction of new species, or were they established on a bare soil following the very structure of the surrounding forest ecosystem?

We know more about the origins of agroforestry in temperate climates. Forest gardening was pioneered by Robert Hart in Shropshire, England. Hart (1996) described natural temperate forests as consisting of seven layers of vegetation: canopy trees, understory trees, shrubs, an upright herbaceous layer, a ground-covering herbaceous layer, the root layer, and vines. These are the same layers he included in his forest garden, only instead of native hawthorns (*Crataegus monogyna*) as understory trees, Hart used plums; in place of buckthorns (*Rhamnus cathartica*) or viburnums as shrubs, Hart used black currants (*Ribes nigrum*) and gooseberries (*Ribes uva-crispa*); and his herbaceous layer was filled with strawberries, mint, and other edible greens (fig. 2.12). Mimicking the architecture of a natural forest helps ensure that the various plants included in a forest garden will grow well together and sets up the conditions necessary for many natural ecological processes.

SPECIES RICHNESS INCREASES WITH AREA

As we design plant communities for the built environment, ecologists' studies of natural communities can provide guidance as to how different populations of plants fit together into communities. Again, we need not copy natural communities note for note, but we should strive to understand the factors and processes that underlie them, because these factors and processes will affect our designed plantings. Among the key questions ecologists can help us answer are, "How many different species should we include, and in what proportions?"

Ecologists use the term *species richness* to describe the number of species found in a particular area. What determines the species richness of a community? As a rule, the larger an area, the more species it will contain.

Figure 2.12 A section of the Central Rocky Mountain Permaculture Institute's forest garden. (Photo by Travis Beck.)

Mick Crawley and Josie Harral (2001) studied species richness at different scales in the county of Berkshire in southeast England. In the natural parkland of Imperial College's Silwood Park campus and in the surrounding Berkshire countryside they counted the number of species in quadrats ranging in size from 1 square centimeter to 100 square kilometers.

Ecologists often show the relationship between number of species and area using a curve described by the equation $S = cA^z$, where S is the number of species, c is a constant, A is the area, and z is an exponent (fig. 2.13a). Transformed logarithmically, the species–area curve is a straight line with a slope of z (fig. 2.13b). As area increases, so does the number of species found. Different sites have different curves because either the constant c is different (e.g., lower-latitude sites have more species than higher-latitude sites) or the slope z is different.

Crawley and Harral found that the slope z varied across scales. At the smallest scales (1 square

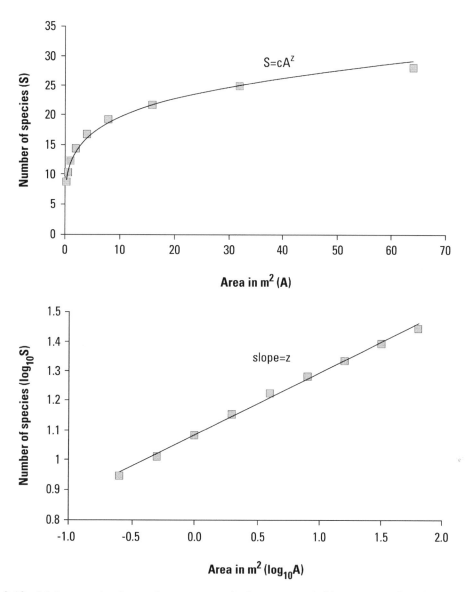

Figure 2.13 **(a)** An example of a species–area curve. As the area sampled increases, so does the number of species found. **(b)** The species–area curve transformed logarithmically. As the log area increases, so does the log number of species, along a line with slope z.

centimeter to 100 square meters) the slope was low (0.1 to 0.2). At intermediate scales (1 hectare to 10 square kilometers) the slope was high (0.4 to 0.5). At the largest scales (East Berkshire to all of Berkshire) the slope was low again (0.1 to 0.2).

Crawley and Harral deduced several factors underlying these changes in slope. At the smallest scales, the question was simply how many different species can be physically packed into a given area.

Also, the interactions between individual plants were very important at this end of the continuum. In an area dominated by one species, species richness increased little, even as the size of the plots sampled grew. This was especially true if the area was rarely disturbed (see chap. 8).

At intermediate scales, species richness increased rapidly with area as more populations could be fit together and as different habitat types were included. At the largest scales, species richness was limited by the size of the species pool of the entire region.

Thus the species richness of a community is governed not simply by its area but by the overall richness of the region, the number of different habitats included, the interactions between plants, and the frequency of disturbance.

MATCH SPECIES RICHNESS TO AREA AND DIVERSITY OF HABITATS

When composing plant communities, whether based closely on natural models or created anew, a designer has to consider how many different species to include. We know for a fact that species richness will increase with an increase in area. To give a sense of appropriate species richness at different scales for a temperate site, Crawley and Harral found an average of roughly ten species in a 10-square-meter area, thirty-five species in a 1,000-square-meter (1/4 acre) area, and 165 species in a 4-hectare (10-acre) plot. Species richness will differ in different places in the world given changes in climate, altitude, and other factors. A planting in subtropical Florida, for instance, should probably include more species than a planting of similar size in Anchorage, Alaska.

Crawley and Harral's findings on the causes of changes in the slope of the species–area curve are equally relevant. At the smallest (garden and small landscape) scales, the determining factor was how many species could actually be packed into the area. Species richness will be highest, then, where the individual plants are small (e.g., an herbaceous bed, as opposed to a shrub massing). Note, however, that Crawley and Harral's research plots were contiguous with the surrounding landscape. Therefore, individuals were tied to larger populations beyond the plot boundaries. In a small, isolated landscape, where an ecological designer is striving for self-maintaining populations, the number of species might have to be smaller (see chap. 9). Species richness is also influenced by management practices. It may decline where one species competitively excludes others (see chap. 3) or where we neither permit nor create periodic disturbances (see chap. 8).

In more expansive landscapes, species richness increases more rapidly with area as different habitat types are included. Knowing that this is a driving mechanism, if we want to increase diversity, we can intentionally increase the diversity of microhabitats. If a larger site is similar across its length and breadth, we may either keep species richness lower or create checkerboarded areas of different communities (see chap. 3).

SPECIES RICHNESS IS HIGHEST WHERE PRODUCTIVITY IS MODERATELY LOW

In addition to his work on the species–area relationship, Mick Crawley has also written about one of the most revealing experiments on community diversity, which has been running for more than 150 years at the Rothamsted Research Centre in England, not far from Silwood Park. Rothamsted is a former country estate whose owner, Sir John Lawes, and a chemist, Sir Joseph Gilbert, began the so-called Park Grass

Experiment in 1856 (Rothamsted Research 2006). They divided a long-established pasture adjacent to the manor house into a series of research plots to demonstrate the effect of manure and inorganic fertilizers on hay yields. Within just a few years it became clear that in addition to affecting hay yields, fertilization was affecting the botanical composition of the plots. Beginning in the early 1900s lime was added to portions of the plots to separate out the acidifying effects of fertilization.

Mick Crawley and a team of researchers (2005) analyzed the species richness of the various plots of the Park Grass Experiment using data collected between 1991 and 2000. Diversity was highest (up to forty-four species) in the unfertilized control plots. As phosphorus and nitrogen were added to the plots, biomass (hay yield) increased and diversity decreased. Where nitrogen was added in the form of ammonium sulfate, which acidifies the soil, diversity was lowest (as low as three species). The effect of fertilization was therefore twofold: As some species (grasses) were allowed to grow vigorously, other species were crowded out, and where the soil was acidified, fewer species were adapted to grow in those conditions.

These results are in keeping with a hump-backed curve for species richness in relation to productivity first proposed by a group of ecologists from the University of Sheffield, England. Al-Mufti and colleagues (1977) sampled the herbaceous biomass (standing crop plus organic litter) throughout the growing season in established woodland floor, grassland, and tall herbaceous (e.g., a patch of stinging nettle [Urtica dioica]) communities. When they compared the number of species found in each community with the maximum biomass produced, the greatest species richness was found at sites that fell within a certain corridor of productivity (fig. 2.14). The reasons for this hump-backed curve are two, they propose. First, few species are adapted to the stresses of life in a low-productivity environment. Second, at higher levels of productivity, competitive exclusion occurs.

The most diverse communities, then, are those with moderate or even moderately low fertility and productivity. As productivity increases above these levels (or is increased with fertilization), vigorous species exclude others and reduce species richness.

MATCH SPECIES RICHNESS TO PRODUCTIVITY

When determining the number of species to include in a designed plant community, an ecological designer should consider not just the size but also the fertility of the site. The hump-backed curve suggests something that may be counterintuitive to gardeners—that the sites with the best soil may not be suited to planting the greatest number of species. In a typical landscape bed that is prepared with good-quality topsoil and compost and is fertilized regularly, we should expect that the plants that are able to most quickly turn the available nutrients into biomass will overrun the others. In fact, this often happens, at least where aggressors are not cut back or pulled out when they move beyond their allotted space. As in so many other cases, designing at cross purposes with ecology creates more work.

As a point of reference, the >100-square-meter plots in the Park Grass experiment contained as few as three species and as many as forty-four. In what situations would it be appropriate to use as few as three species in a planting of similar size, and in what situations as many as forty-four? Where growth and coverage are the most important goals, pairing a high-fertility soil with a low-diversity community is a very appropriate treatment. An example of such a site would be a planting at a parking lot

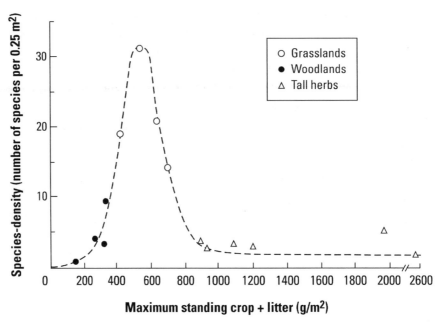

Figure 2.14 The humped curve for species richness. The greatest numbers of species are found in communities with maximum biomass production of 350–750 g/m². (Adapted from Al-Mufti, M. M., C. L. Sydes, S. B. Furness, J. P. Grime, and S. R. Band. Copyright ©1977 Blackwell Scientific Publications. A quantitative analysis of shoot phenology and dominance in herbaceous vegetation. *Journal of Ecology* 65:759–91. Reproduced with permission of John Wiley and Sons, Inc.)

entrance, which needs to look good quickly, receives maintenance attention (to remove weeds taking early advantage of the available nutrients), and is mostly viewed quickly in passing. At the other end of the spectrum, a meadow lawn could be a candidate for lower fertility and greater diversity. If preexisting turf and some portion of the topsoil are stripped off and the site is seeded without further soil preparation, such a meadow could have species richness toward the upper end of the range. However, it is important to note that the moderately low fertility of the most species-rich communities means that fast-growing plants will probably persist in a suppressed condition. Depending on one's point of view, such plants could be seen as not looking their best.

An ecological designer has to consider together the design goals, the size and location of the site, and the productivity of the soils in order to create a plant community with the appropriate species richness. In general, the larger the site, the greater the diversity of habitats, and the less rich the soil, the more species can be included.

WITHIN COMMUNITIES, SPECIES VARY IN ABUNDANCE

Once an ecological landscape designer has developed an appropriately diverse list of plants for a project, the question then becomes how many individuals of each species to include. If you were to go into a natural community and count all the individual plants of each species, you would discover something interesting. A few species account for most individuals in a community. The majority of species are represented by far fewer individuals (Keddy 2005). The number of individuals of a given species as a proportion of the number of individuals in the community as a whole is known as the relative abundance of that species. Look side by side at the relative abundance of all of the species in a community and you see the relative abundance distribution. Ecologists describe communities in which a higher number of species are represented by substantial populations as having a more even distribution.

Scott Collins and Susan Glenn (1990) investigated the relative abundance distributions of tallgrass prairie communities at three locations in the Midwest, including the Konza Prairie in northeast Kansas. The Konza Prairie is a native prairie located on the Flint Hills whose land, as its name suggests, is rocky and hilly and therefore was mostly never plowed. Its grassy slopes are divided by watersheds into experimental communities to investigate the effects of grazing, fire, and climate on grasslands. Although Collins and Glenn could not count every plant in each of the communities within the Konza, they did look at which species were present in each of the 10- × 10-meter research plots in each watershed. They then graphed how many species were present in 1–10 percent, 11–20 percent, . . . , and 91–100 percent of the plots. The results showed that in the communities studied, there were many infrequent species, a few species of intermediate frequency, and a few or, in some cases, several frequent species (fig. 2.15). This bimodal distribution has been found elsewhere but not in all cases.

To describe the exact shape of relative abundance distributions and the curve from many infrequent to few frequent species, ecologists have proposed several models, which vary from the prosaically to

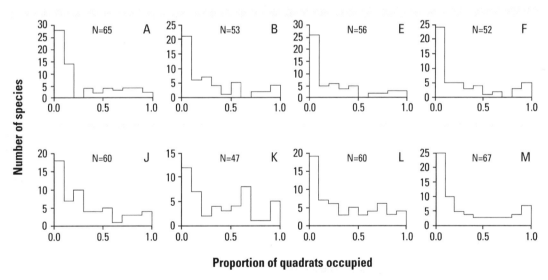

Proportion of quadrats occupied

Figure 2.15 Distribution of the frequency with which species appeared in quadrats within each watershed community of the Konza Prairie, ranging from sparse (1–10%) to widespread (91–100%). Most species are found infrequently. Bimodal distribution is evident in some communities. (From Collins, S. L., and S. M. Glenn. ©1990 by The University of Chicago. A hierarchical analysis of species' abundance patterns in grassland vegetation. *American Naturalist* 135:633–48. With permission from the University of Chicago Press.)

the colorfully named, including "broken stick," geometric, lognormal, and Zipf–Mandelbrot. Different datasets at different scales support each of the models. It is possible that relative abundance distributions are as individualistic as the communities they measure (Wilson et al. 1996).

The mechanisms that may be at work are also not entirely clear. Generalist species that can grow in a broad range of conditions are often among the most abundant species, for obvious reasons, as are tall plants that overshadow their neighbors and plants that spread aggressively from rhizomes. At a certain point the question becomes not "Why are some plants so abundant?" but "How do all the less abundant plants persist as members of the community?" (Silvertown 2005). That question and all its implications are the subject of our next chapter.

INCLUDE LARGE POPULATIONS OF A FEW SPECIES AND SMALL POPULATIONS OF OTHERS

Determining relative abundance in designed plant communities is important for both aesthetic and ecological reasons. The plants that are most abundant determine the character and color of an entire planting. The plants that are less abundant serve as accents or specimens or, if poorly placed, are hardly noticeable. The repetition and massing of each of these constituents is the designer's traditional art. Ecologists' findings suggest that there is a natural curve of relative abundance, with a few plants making up most of a community and many others making up the rest.

A balance of aesthetics, ecology, and practicality is evident in the seed mixes Neil Diboll of Prairie Nursery in Wisconsin produces for landscaping and restoration. Diboll's work is rooted in ecological restoration, and his seed mixes are modeled after natural communities. In addition to his own familiarity with remnant prairies, Diboll is fortunate to be able to refer to John Curtis's *The Vegetation of Wisconsin* (1959), which combined information from settlement-era surveys, a variety of studies and reports, and direct investigation of 1,420 stands of vegetation across the state to create lists of the prevalent species of various natural plant communities.

Diboll's published (1997) seed mix for a short prairie planting on dry sandy soil (table 2.1) provides an excellent example of the factors that determine the relative abundance of species in his designed prairies. One fact to note immediately is that Diboll's mix includes thirty-three species, whereas Curtis's list of species of dry prairies includes forty-seven species. Diboll acknowledges that he intentionally reduces the number of species in his mixes. One reason makes immediate sense based on ecologists' findings about relative abundance distributions: Many of the species in a natural community are infrequent. Diboll leaves out infrequent species that are not particularly good-looking or from which it is uneconomical to collect seed. Although these may sound like callous slashes at diversity, they are based on a hard-won sense of what it takes to market and install prairie plantings. Also note that his percentages are based on the number of seeds, which when multiplied by expected germination rates produces the actual number of individual plants that will be introduced to the community. Mixes by seed weight alone are not reliable because seed size varies dramatically across the species involved.

In Diboll's short prairie mix just three species, all grasses, are introduced at a proportion of 10 percent or above. Twenty-seven of the thirty-three species are introduced at a proportion of 3 percent or less. This is consistent with ecologists' findings about the prevalence of just a few species and the scarcity of the majority of species in natural communities. Diboll proportions his mixes across families

Table 2.1   Seed Mix for a Short Prairie Planting on Dry, Sandy Soil

Species	Common Name	Family	Percentage of Mix
Grasses			
Bouteloua curtipendula	Side-oats grama	Poaceae	10
Koeleria macrantha	June grass	Poaceae	5
Schizachyrium scoparium	Little bluestem	Poaceae	15
Sporobolus heterolepis	Prairie dropseed	Poaceae	10
4 total grasses			40
Forbs			
Amorpha canescens	Lead plant	Fabaceae	1
Anemone cylindrica	Thimbleweed	Ranunculaceae	1
Asclepias tuberosa	Butterfly weed	Asclepiadaceae	1
Asclepias verticillata	Whorled milkweed	Asclepiadaceae	1
Astragalus canadensis	Canadian milk vetch	Fabaceae	2
Campanula rotundifolia	Harebell	Campanulaceae	2
Dalea candida	White prairie clover	Fabaceae	2
Dalea purpurea	Purple prairie clover	Fabaceae	3
Echinacea pallida	Pale purple coneflower	Asteraceae	2
Euphorbia corollata	Flowering spurge	Euphorbiaceae	2
Helianthus occidentalis	Western sunflower	Asteraceae	1
Helianthus pauciflorus	Showy sunflower	Asteraceae	1
Lespedeza capitata	Round-headed bush clover	Fabaceae	2
Liatris aspera	Rough blazing star	Asteraceae	3
Lupinus perennis var. *occidentalis*	Lupine	Fabaceae	1
Monarda punctata	Spotted bee balm	Lamiaceae	3
Penstemon grandiflorus	Large-flowered beard tongue	Scrophulariaceae	3
Ranunculus rhomboideus	Prairie buttercup	Ranunculaceae	2
Rudbeckia hirta	Black-eyed Susan	Asteraceae	4
Ruellia humilis	Hairy ruellia	Acanthaceae	1
Solidago nemoralis	Old-field goldenrod	Asteraceae	1
Solidago ptarmicoides	White upland aster	Asteraceae	2
Solidago rigida	Stiff goldenrod	Asteraceae	3
Solidago speciosa	Showy goldenrod	Asteraceae	4
Symphyotrichum ericoides	Heath aster	Asteraceae	1
Symphyotrichum laeve	Smooth blue aster	Asteraceae	2
Symphyotrichum oolentangiense	Azure aster	Asteraceae	3
Tradescantia ohiensis	Common spiderwort	Commelinaceae	3
Verbena stricta	Hoary vervain	Verbenaceae	3
29 total forbs			**60**
33 total grasses and forbs			**100**

Scientific names updated.

Source: From *The Tallgrass Restoration Handbook*, edited by Stephen Packard and Cornelia F. Mutel. Copyright © 1997 Society for Ecological Restoration. Reproduced by permission of Island Press, Washington, D.C.

Figure 2.16 Third year of a dry sand prairie seed mix designed by Neil Diboll. (Photo by Neil Diboll, Prairie Nursery, Inc., Westfield, WI.)

based on natural models. The short prairie mix is made up of 40 percent grasses, 27 percent asters, and 11 percent legumes, the three predominant families in the natural prairie.

Horticultural considerations also come into play in determining the relative proportions of each species. In Diboll's mix the smaller-seeded showy goldenrod is included at a higher rate (4 percent) than its companion, stiff goldenrod (3 percent), because in Diboll's experience small seeds tend to get lost in the shuffle. Diboll also emphasizes showy species that will help win popular acceptance of prairie plantings. This is, no doubt, also a factor behind the abundance of asters in his mix.

Diboll's seed mixes provide an excellent example of how it is possible to combine ecologists' understanding of the relative abundance of species with practical and aesthetic considerations to achieve a successful and beautiful designed community (fig. 2.16).

CONCLUSION

Looking at groups of plants as populations and communities provides insights that should increase both the immediate success and the long-term sustainability of the landscapes we design.

A group of plants of a single species is not just a mass of one element repeated as many times as necessary to fill a space. It is a population of individual plants that interact with one another, with the surrounding environment, and with other species in the community. The arrangement of a population in space is the product of all those interactions. The more diverse we can make that population—in terms of genetics, sizes, and ages—the more likely it will be to persist as part of our planting through the many ups and downs the years will bring.

The plant species we choose to include as populations are not just blobs taken from a metaphorical palette but members of a community that must somehow coexist. Real mechanisms govern the number of species that grow together in communities and their relative abundances and will probably adjust our designed communities for us if we do not heed them from the start. Chief among these mechanisms is competition, to which we will now turn our attention.

3. The Struggle for Coexistence: On Competition and Assembling Tight Communities

How do you combine plants in a designed landscape?

From an aesthetic standpoint, the criteria are familiar. In *Perennial Companions: 100 Dazzling Plant Combinations for Every Season*, Tom Fischer (2009: 9) reviewed the conventional approach: "One of the greatest pleasures—and challenges—of gardening is combining plants to form pleasing juxtapositions of color, form, and texture."

Examined from an ecological angle, the question becomes very different. In order to put different populations of plants together in a designed community, we have to understand competition. Paul Keddy (2001) defines competition as the negative effect that one organism has on another by consuming or controlling access to limited resources. In order to live, grow, and reproduce, plants depend on resources such as light, water, mineral nutrients, and air. Plants will continue to grow until they reach their genetic limits or until one of these resources becomes limiting. Agricultural crops grow when given synthetic fertilizers because they are released from the limits to growth imposed by lower levels of macronutrients in the soil (see chap. 6). When released from one limiting factor, such as macronutrients, plants will continue to grow until another resource, such as water, becomes limiting. In different environments, different resources are limiting. In arid environments, the limiting resource is usually water. Underneath the rainforest canopy, light is a limiting resource. Because plants are almost always growing in the company of other plants and under the constraint of a limiting resource, plants almost always face competition.

The negative effects of competition are very real. Ecologists have often studied competition in the field through removal experiments. If you physically remove one species from a community, or all of the neighbors from an individual plant, what effect does this have on the other species or plant? In particular, how much more biomass can the other species or plant produce in the absence of competitors? In 1992 Jessica Gurevitch and her colleagues published a meta-analysis of competition studies from the previous decade. Reviewing all these studies, they found that in primary producers such as plants, removing a competitor increased growth by an average of 34 percent compared with the control group. They conclude that competition has a real, if moderate, effect on the growth of plants in natural communities.

Fertilization is one of the ways that conventional horticulture aims to reduce the effects of competition. If there are enough nutrients to go around, plants won't have to compete for them, and they can all grow big and lush. Spacing plants is another conventional response to the pressures of competition. There is a negative correlation between the number of plants in a given area and each plant's biomass. As some plants in a population grow bigger, they claim more resources, leading to a decline in growth, and ultimately the death, of smaller plants nearby (see chap. 2). Such self-thinning in a population is a case of intraspecific competition, or competition between individuals of the same species. Wherever plants grow alongside members of their own species, they face intraspecific competition. When we consider communities of plants, in which populations of multiple species live together, we also have to consider interspecific competition, or competition between species.

As we might imagine, interspecific competition is not always fair. In cases of symmetric competition, two species suppress each others' growth equally. In cases of asymmetric competition, one species has a much more profound effect on the other. Asymmetric competition drives many of the patterns we can observe in natural plant communities and in the designed landscape.

One fundamental premise of community ecology is that two species can coexist only when intraspecific competition is greater than interspecific competition. Plants have evolved and arrange themselves in natural communities in ways that reduce the amount of interspecific competition they face. Thus, this chapter is as much about coexistence as it is about competition.

The goal of an ecological landscape is not to eliminate the negative effects of competition but to have these effects play out in a way that supports our design intent. We can take advantage of natural means of coexistence to create tightly knit communities that fully use available resources and resist invasion. Considering competition offers a rigorous complement to conventional advice on the pleasures and challenges of combining plants.

ONE CLOSE COMPETITOR EXCLUDES ANOTHER

In a 1934 book titled *The Struggle for Existence*, Russian biologist Georgii F. Gause documented his mathematical and experimental investigation of competition. In his best-known experiment, Gause sought to determine how two competing populations of paramecia would divide the available energy of a nutrient-laced test tube between themselves (Gause 1934). When grown independently and provided with a steady level of nutrients (in the form of bacteria) every day, both populations had an s-shaped growth curve, accelerating exponentially when they were first introduced to the medium, then leveling off at an equilibrium population. When grown together, both populations grew exponentially until the point at which their combined biomass equaled the total biomass of a single equilibrium population. That is, they grew until all the available energy of the test tube had been allocated. As Gause drew off a portion of the community each day for sampling and added back in the nutrient solution, the two populations competed directly to fill the void. Day by day *Paramecium aurelia*, the better competitor, took over more of the available energy, until it had driven *P. caudatum* out of existence (fig. 3.1). The principle of com-

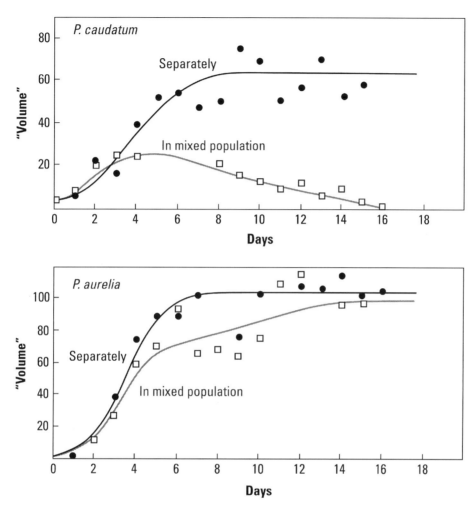

Figure 3.1 Grown separately, *Paramecium caudatum* and *P. aurelia* both increase in biomass to an equilibrium level. When grown together, however, *P. aurelia* outcompetes *P. caudatum* for the available nutrients and eliminates the other population completely. (From Gause, G. F. *The Struggle for Existence.* ©1934 Williams and Wilkins.)

petitive exclusion, otherwise known as Gause's Law, states that when populations of two species compete for identical resources in a stable environment, one will inevitably drive the other out of existence.

Around the same time, two scientists working for the U.S. Department of Agriculture conducted a similar experiment using plots of barley grown at experiment stations across the country. H. V. Harlan and M. L. Martini (1938) assembled a seed mix of equal portions of eleven varieties of barley that had nearly identical needs for water and nutrients. This seed mix was sent to the different experiment stations and grown for 4 and 12 years. At the end of each year the barley was harvested, enough seed was saved to sow the plot the next year, and a sample was sent in for analysis. By growing out the samples and identifying the plants, Harlan and Martini were able to track the changes in population levels of the different varieties over time. At all the stations, the less well-adapted varieties were rapidly eliminated. At several of the stations, one of the varieties quickly dominated. At other stations changes occurred more slowly, and several varieties remained present at the end of the trial. The dominant varieties differed from station to station, depending on climate. Though Harlan and Martini observed fluctuations in population levels caused by changing environmental conditions (see chap. 2), curves showing the trajectory of each population indicated which was likely to competitively exclude the others in the long run. Harlan and Martini's study demonstrated that competitive exclusion operates outside the laboratory in larger communities of plants, and which plants prevail is related to adaptation to the local environment.

COMPETITIVELY EXCLUDE WEEDS

Competitive exclusion is a double-edged sword. It can drive desirable species to extinction but can also prevent undesirable species from gaining a toehold. When invasive honeysuckle swarms through a woodland, we are desperate bystanders witnessing competitive exclusion in action. When established groundcovers keep weeding to a minimum, we are relieved to see the same competitive exclusion.

The plants that are most successful at competitive exclusion are thugs. Many gardeners have experience with aggressive plants that they would never plant again. However, there are situations in which an aggressive plant can be an appropriate selection. In a contained planting bed that is unlikely to be frequently weeded, let bishop's weed (*Aegopodium podagraria*), English ivy (*Hedera helix*), Louisiana wormwood (*Artemesia ludoviciana*), or cotoneaster take over and exclude all other plants, including weeds (fig. 3.2). These thuggish plants can be invasive and should not be planted in areas from which they are likely to spread.

In the rest of the landscape, competitive exclusion can still be practiced in its gentler forms. Any time we plant shrubs or perennials densely enough that they fill in as a mass, we are practicing competitive exclusion. Our desired plant material preempts the resources of the area, most critically light. Less aggressive groundcovers can also be used to keep down weeds. Plants such as creeping veronica (*Veronica repens*) or stonecrop may not have the potency of the thugs mentioned earlier, but this allows them to play well with others in a mixed bed, simply filling in unused spaces and reducing opportunities for weeds.

Competitive exclusion operates only among plants that are trying to use the same resources at the same time. Tree seedlings can often come up through a groundcover bed because the seed contains enough resources to get the plant's leaves above the shade of, and its roots below the interference of, the groundcover. Shrubs can more effectively prevent the growth of tree seedlings. Early spring weeds can establish and set seed before nonevergreen groundcovers have regrown enough to interfere with them. When applied in its gentler forms, competitive exclusion can only facilitate, not replace, ongoing management.

ORGANISMS IN COMMUNITIES PARTITION RESOURCES

If one species drives another to extinction when they compete, how can multiple species coexist in communities? Robert MacArthur (1958) posed just this question when doing his doctoral research on five very similar species of warbler that are found together in northern forests. All five species—Cape

Figure 3.2 English ivy fills a planting bed at Bryant Park, New York City. Because of competitive exclusion, only limited weeding is needed, nor can anything be grown alongside the ivy, apart from the plane trees (*Platanus xhispanica*) and daffodils, which do not compete directly with the ivy. Trimming the ivy from climbing the trees keeps it from developing into the arborescent, fruiting form. (Photo by Travis Beck.)

May (*Setophaga tigrina*), yellow-rumped (*S. coronata*), black-throated green (*S. virens*), Blackburnian (*S. fusca*), and bay-breasted (*S. castanea*)—eat mainly insects and have a similar body size and shape. During the summers of 1956 and 1957 MacArthur observed these birds closely on their nesting grounds, principally in a plot of white spruce on Mt. Desert Island, Maine. In particular, he recorded the amount of time they spent feeding in different parts of the spruce trees. He also categorized the movement of the birds as they fed.

MacArthur found clear differences in the warblers' feeding behavior. For instance, the Cape May warbler fed consistently near the top of the tree and moves vertically in the outer shell of the tree. The yellow-rumped warbler had a widely distributed feeding zone, including substantial time spent on the ground gathering emerging crane flies. The bay-breasted warbler spent most of its time in the shady interior of the tree at a middle elevation (fig. 3.3). MacArthur found that the five warblers nested in the same zones of the tree in which they feed. Furthermore, he found that the feeding habits of the warblers in their winter feeding grounds in Central America and the West Indies were nearly the same as in their summer habits in the northern forests.

Here we must remember the first of the two conditions of competitive exclusion: The species in question must compete for identical resources. By feeding and nesting in different zones of the trees, MacArthur's warblers effectively divided the available resources, thereby reducing the competition between them and permitting their ongoing coexistence.

Resource partitioning begins to explain some of the patterns of biogeography we observed at the beginning of this book. By specializing for certain environments and microenvironments, plants reduce their competition from other species.

THE NICHE IS AN *N*-DIMENSIONAL HYPERVOLUME

Around the same time that Robert MacArthur was observing the behavior of warblers in northern forests, his thesis adviser at Yale, G. Evelyn Hutchinson, arrived at a formalized way of describing the partitioning of resources between species (Hutchinson 1957). If you consider the area of the tree in which a species of bird forages as one axis in a coordinate system, each of MacArthur's warblers occupies certain points. If the manner in which the birds move as they forage is a second axis, each species again occupies certain points. Looking at both axes together, a two-dimensional region is defined by the overlap between each species' position on the two axes. Continue this process through *n* axes, one for each characteristic of the environment or behavior, and you arrive at an *n*-dimensional hypervolume that defines the environment and biology of each species. This hypervolume is known as a species' niche. Hutchinson did not invent the term *niche*, but he gave it the definition that is still used to this day. It is because species such as MacArthur's warblers occupy different niches that they can coexist in ecological communities.

Niche differentiation in plants is less immediately clear than it is in the case of animals. Unlike animals—which can specialize to feed on any other animal, or any plant, or any part of any plant—plants all need the same essential resources, and their means of acquiring them are very similar. Stephen Hubbell (2001) suggested that in diverse communities such as the Panamanian rainforest, many plants are near ecological equivalents, and their observed differences are neutral to their evolutionary success. Such species can coexist because all are dispersal limited and no one species can occupy every site that becomes available. This is a smaller-scale version of the explanation for why cactus and euphorbia can coexist on opposite sides of the planet despite having evolved very similar forms and survival strategies (see chap. 1) and sets up the spatial segregation hypothesis that we will discuss later in this chapter. Hubbell (2010: 288) suggested that his neutral theory "provides a solid theoretical foundation on which to build a new non-neutral, niche-based theory of ecology" in which greater levels of realism are added by considering species differences.

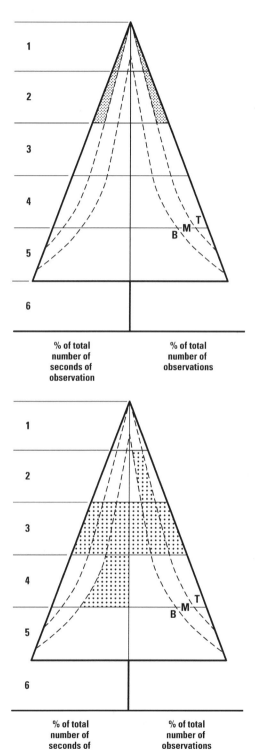

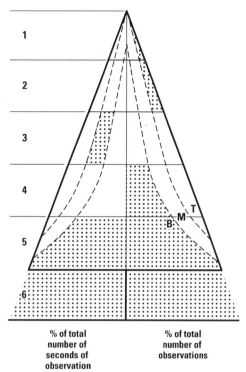

Figure 3.3 Feeding position of **(a)** Cape May warbler, **(b)** yellow-rumped warbler, and **(c)** bay-breasted warbler observed in conifers in New England. Numbered zones indicate 10-foot intervals measured from the top of the tree down. Base zones (B) are the bare base of branches. Middle zones (M) are the middle of branches with old needles. Terminal zones (T) cover new needles and buds. Hatched zones indicate those in which warblers of each species were most likely to occur, based on amount of time spent and number of observations. (From MacArthur, R. H. Copyright ©1958, Ecological Society of America. Population ecology of some warblers in northeastern coniferous forests. *Ecology* 39:599–619. With permission from the Ecological Society of America.)

Jonathan Silvertown (2004) reviewed several studies published between 1990 and 2003 that indicated that niche differentiation does indeed occur in plant communities. Among the niche axes Silvertown found are light gradients, canopy height, rooting depth, hydrologic gradients, exploitation of different sources of nitrogen, and association with different soil microbes (see chap. 6). The relative importance of any of these axes depended on the community and the environment in which it is located.

SELECT PLANTS WITH DIFFERENT NICHES TO GROW TOGETHER

When we bring plants together in a community, we overcome their dispersal limitations and so must plan for their coexistence based on other factors. One of the most effective ways to design a community of plants that will relate well and not eliminate one another through competitive exclusion is to select plants that partition the available resources and inhabit distinct niches. We can use niche differentiation along the gradient of light levels, for example, to design a multilayered woodland planting (fig. 3.4).

Canopy trees intercept the most sunlight. If we imagine a woodland planting in the Northeast, canopy trees might be oaks, beeches, and maples. In the wild, seedlings of these trees may persist in a suppressed state for many years until a canopy gap opens up into which they can quickly grow. Canopy trees will extend their limbs and grow leaves wherever bright sunlight is available, filling in such openings and leaving empty, shaded space beneath them.

Into this space we can plant understory trees and shrubs that grow with intermediate levels of light. Flowering dogwood, for instance, never grows as tall as canopy trees and therefore does not compete with mature canopy trees for light. Spicebush (*Lindera benzoin*) also flourishes beneath the shade of a forest canopy.

On the woodland floor, where light levels are lowest, shade-tolerant herbaceous plants such as ferns and foamflower (*Tiarella cordifolia*) will grow. These plants would not survive in the full sun to which the canopy trees are exposed. Another way of thinking about resource partitioning in this case is that each group of plants is effectively growing in a different microclimate, one created by the other plants in the community (see chap. 1).

A planting structured like this, with canopy, understory, and ground plane all filled, allows several different plants to coexist in a limited space without one excluding the other.

ASSEMBLY RULES GOVERN HOW COMMUNITIES COME TOGETHER

Birds on the islands that surround New Guinea led Jared Diamond to further insights in community ecology. Why is it, he asked, that nearby islands with similar habitats can have markedly different communities of birds? Diamond set out to examine the criteria that determine what species, out of all the species that live in the region, can come together to form a community. He called these criteria assembly rules.

Diamond found a clue to assembly rules in so-called checkerboard distributions, in which islands in an archipelago are occupied by one of two or more ecologically similar species but almost never by more than one. Here, it seems competitive exclusion is operating to prevent two species with similar niches from coexisting. However, sometimes in these checkerboard distributions there are empty squares, where neither species is present. This suggests that the determining factor is not simply one-

Figure 3.4 Spring in a multilayered woodland planting in the New York Botanical Garden's Native Plant Garden. Canopy oaks and maples are still leafing out. Flowering dogwood and spicebush occupy the understory. Foamflower and mayapple carpet the woodland floor. (Photo by Travis Beck.)

to-one competition but diffuse competition with other related species. A group of species competing for similar resources is called a guild.

Diamond examined the assembly rules of the fruit pigeon guild. Eighteen species of fruit pigeon live on New Guinea. The birds range in size from small (49 grams) to large (802 grams) and, based on examination of stomach contents, eat fruit of corresponding sizes. By measuring the frequency distribution of fruit sizes in the stomachs of birds of each species in a community and weighting those frequencies by the abundance of that species, Diamond was able to produce consumption curves for each community. Interestingly, consumption curves from similar habitats on different islands with different communities of fruit pigeons are similar. Diamond proposed that the actual consumption curves are matched to the production curves of fruit in each of these habitats. He suggested,

> Communities are assembled through selection of colonists, adjustment of their abundances, and compression of their niches, in part so as to match the resource consumption curve of the colonists to the resource production curve of the island. (Diamond 1975: 345)

The assembly process creates a stable community that is resistant to invasion, because no significant resources are left unused. Which species of a guild will come together in the community is somewhat up to chance, but the community as a whole fills out all available niche space.

ASSEMBLE COMMUNITIES TO FILL ALL AVAILABLE NICHE SPACE

Assembly rules can be thought of as the culmination of resource partitioning through niche differentiation. Resource partitioning suggests that species that inhabit different niches can live together. Assembly rules help us to imagine communities in which various resources are fully partitioned between guilds of species.

Mark Simmons is a restoration ecologist with the Lady Bird Johnson Wildflower Center outside of Austin, Texas, who is working to develop mixed native lawns that perform as well as or better than conventional lawn grasses. In central Texas the most widely used turfgrass is bermudagrass (*Cynodon dactylon*), an introduced species that is drought resistant, traffic resistant, and somewhat invasive. Simmons and colleagues (2011) compared bermudagrass with native grasses of the shortgrass prairie as monocultures and as low- and high-diversity mixes. The low-diversity native grass mix is a combination of the two dominants of the shortgrass prairie: buffalograss (*Bouteloua dactyloides*) and blue grama (*Bouteloua gracilis*). The high-diversity native grass mix adds another five species, each with slightly different characteristics (fig. 3.5).

Simmons found that the native mixes established more quickly and had a higher density of leaves in the spring than did the bermudagrass. By the end of summer, the density of bermudagrass was similar to that of the low-diversity mix but was exceeded by the high-diversity mix. The native mixes also suppressed weeds better than did bermudagrass. The high-diversity mix was the most effective at suppressing dandelion.

Simmons attributes the greater leaf coverage and weed suppression of the mixed lawns to the fact that in the mixes the available niche space is filled more completely. In a patch of thin lawn, certain light and soil resources go unused—until a weed begins to use them. In a properly diverse mix, these resources are captured by desired members of the community. In a designed community, Quigley (2003) found that mixing groundcover species was more effective in reducing summer weeds than planting just a single species. The fact that Simmons's native grass mixes are modeled on a natural community that has gone through the assembly process means that their niche relationships are especially tight.

In the next phase of the study, Simmons will test mixes in other regions of the country. He also intends to go beyond the grass guild and introduce forbs into the mix, including nitrogen fixers such as

Figure 3.5 Mixed native lawn test plots at the Lady Bird Johnson Wildflower Center. (Photo by Bruce Leander, Lady Bird Johnson Wildflower Center.)

clover, and some wildflowers. Ultimately, the native lawn could consist of representatives of multiple guilds, differentiated across the various niche axes of seasonality, height, rooting depth, and so on, fully assembled into a competitively tight community.

REGENERATION NICHE

Communities are structured not only by competition in the present but by the ghost of competition past—that which occurred between seeds and seedlings. In a classic 1977 article, Peter Grubb introduced the concept of the regeneration niche. Whenever one plant dies in a plant community, another replaces it. Grubb pointed out that the second plant will not necessarily be of the same species as the first. Numerous factors determine which plant will succeed, and this presents numerous opportunities for niche differentiation. Some species germinate in sun and some in shade. Some have seeds that travel far on the wind, others that fall close to the parent. Seeds of different species germinate at different times of the year. Grubb used the example of hairy willowherb (*Epilobium hirsutum*) and purple loosestrife (*Lythrum salicaria*) along river banks in England. When banks are scoured and patches of soil opened in the fall, willowherb establishes and prevents establishment of purple loosestrife. When banks are scoured in the spring, the opposite occurs. Perhaps there are lessons here for control of the invasive purple loosestrife in North America.

Variable environmental conditions interact with these evolved differences to determine which plant actually establishes. The various characteristics of an available gap—size, type of soil surface or litter, pathogens present—will favor certain seeds over others. Weather conditions will also influence the germination of seeds and the success of seedlings as they try to establish.

Once grown in, a plant may well be able to outcompete other comers, but the early interaction of evolutionary strategy with variable environmental conditions determines which plant will get that chance.

ESTABLISH PLANTS WITH FINESSE

The practical importance of the regeneration niche is reflected in the extent of effort that conventional horticulture devotes to plant establishment. Greenhouse operators and nursery managers have created an entire industry dedicated to shepherding plants through their most delicate life stages in carefully controlled environments. Landscapers and gardeners assiduously prepare a site to the liking of the plants that are intended for it and remove potential competitors. After planting, another round of heightened care begins. Many failed plantings can be explained by lack of attention to this critical moment in the competitive history of a plant community. If weed seeds germinate alongside seeds or seedlings of desired species, they can overwhelm the plants that were intended for that area. If rain does not come and no irrigation is provided, plants may die before they become established. Only once a planting is well grown in, the plants established and the competitors suppressed, do gardeners begin to relax.

Perhaps a more sophisticated understanding of the regeneration niche can suggest opportunities to reduce these efforts and still achieve good results. In an ideal scenario, we would plant our plants, then walk away and watch them grow. For this to happen, timing of plant establishment is critical. Different plant species need different sets of conditions (temperature, soil moisture, humidity) to establish. To the extent that we can adjust planting times to correspond to the arrival of favorable conditions, we will have greater success. This requires attention to both the calendar and the weather. As Grubb noted, certain times of year also favor the germination of certain weeds. If there is a particular species of concern, it can be worth timing planting so that desired plants are well established before the weeds emerge.

Rather than try to time the arrival of ideal conditions, we could introduce inexpensive propagules (seeds, plugs, or whips) over a period of weeks, or even years, and expect that only those that meet favorable conditions will actually establish. Or we could invest in the establishment of a nucleus from which propagation could occur naturally as conditions allow. Or we could plant several species with a range of tolerances and allow them to compete to establish based on the conditions that emerge.

Thinking about the regeneration niche can guide decisions about the most efficient propagule to use. If potential competitors are few, we can use seeds. Plants that grow vigorously can be safely planted from smaller containers or at plug size (fig. 3.6). Plants that are slow to establish or risk being overwhelmed by competitors may be worth bringing in at a larger size. Long-lived plants that structure a landscape justify a high level of investment and care. Short-lived plants whose next generation will have to fight for their spot ought to have adaptations that will enable them to regenerate on a chosen site with minimal intervention, or else we should not get too attached to their presence.

For the maintenance of an established plant community, we may wish to preload the next generation, planting eventual successors beneath mature plants or spreading seeds of desirable species before gaps even appear. We can also take advantage of good years for desirable species by timing removal of weeds or senescing plants to coincide with favorable conditions, or by allowing seedling volunteers to establish on their own and then moving them to other locations. In a healthy

Figure 3.6 Vigorous plants such as these American alumroot (*Heuchera americana* 'Dale's Strain') and Pennsylvania sedge (*Carex pensylvanica*) can grow quickly from small nursery containers to fill a space. (Photo by Travis Beck.)

community we might even just allow the interplay of available propagules and environmental conditions to determine which plants fill vacancies as they arrive without us having to lift a shovel or a watering can.

PLANTS HAVE DIFFERENT LIFE HISTORY STRATEGIES

The rule that underlies niche theory is that no organism can be a superior competitor at every point on every niche axis. Specialization leads to trade-offs. English ecologist J. Philip Grime (2001: 10) defined a trade-off as "an evolutionary dilemma whereby genetic change conferring increased fitness in one circumstance invariably involves sacrifice of fitness in another."

A classic trade-off is that between competition and colonization. Imagine a two-species plant community in which one species is the superior competitor at the adult stage. The inferior competitor can avoid exclusion if it focuses on the regeneration niche instead and devotes its resources to reproduction. Wherever they grow together, the competitively superior species displaces the colonizer. But wherever either species dies, the colonizer will appear first and reproduce before it is displaced.

Evolutionary trade-offs such as these are at the heart of Grime's theory of life history strategies. Based on close observation of the British flora and experimentation, Grime proposed that plant species fall into one of three functional types, depending largely on the habitats for which they have evolved: competitors, stress tolerators, and ruderal species. Each of these life history strategies turns on fundamental trade-offs between devoting energy to growth, storage, defense, and reproduction (fig. 3.7).

Competitors evolved in high-productivity environments with low frequency and intensity of disturbance (see chap. 8), such as floodplains. Competitors quickly exploit available resources through shoot and root growth, pushing their way above other vegetation. The invasive Japanese knotweed (*Reynoutria japonica*) is an example of a competitor, along with common elderberry (*Sambucus nigra*).

Stress tolerators are most common in low-productivity environments with low disturbance, such as rock outcrops. Stress tolerators are long-lived, slow-growing plants that flower infrequently and have a variety of mechanisms to reduce their palatability to herbivores. Sedum and olives are stress tolerators.

Ruderals appear in high-productivity environments with high disturbance. Ruderal (from the same root as *rubbish*, indicating the wastelands or disturbed areas where they thrive) species have short lifespans and immediately devote their energy to producing the next generation of seeds. These are the colonizer species in the competitor–colonizer trade-off. Common weeds such as lambsquarters (*Chenopodium album*) are ruderals, as are desert annuals such as California poppy.

Grime also recognized intermediate types that occur in habitats that do not fall quite to the extremes: competitive ruderals, stress-tolerant ruderals, stress-tolerant competitors, and even strategists that combine traits from all three camps.

Grimes' three- (or seven-) strategy classification offers a somewhat more explicit version of niche theory. Different plants compete in different ways, depending on the habitat they live in and the strategies they have evolved. These different strategies allow the coexistence of plants across the landscape.

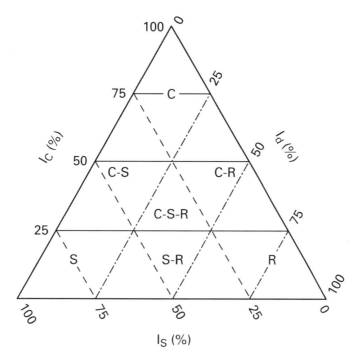

Figure 3.7 Grime's model for the relationship between characteristics of a habitat and plant life history strategies. I_c, I_d, and I_s indicate the relative importances of competition, disturbance, and stress in a habitat. C stands for competitors, S for stress tolerators, and R for ruderal species. Intermediate strategies are also possible. (From Grime, J. P. © 1977 The University of Chicago. Evidence for the existence of three primary strategies in plants and its relevance to ecological and evolutionary theory. *American Naturalist* 111(982):1169–94. The University of Chicago Press.)

CREATE A MIXED GARDEN USING PLANTS WITH DIFFERENT LIFE HISTORY STRATEGIES

Grimes's account of life history strategies emphasizes that the habitats to which plants are adapted cannot be fully understood by recognizing only their temperature and water requirements, or even their microclimatic preferences (see chap. 1). Soil fertility and the period of time between disturbances are also important axes in the *n*-dimensional hypervolume of plants' niches. By taking advantage of this niche differentiation, an ecological designer can create a mixed garden in which more desired species coexist and more undesired species are excluded.

Traditionally a mixed garden is regarded as one that includes woody trees and shrubs and herbaceous perennials, along with annuals and biennials. This definition emphasizes life cycle and suggests a mix based on the functional roles each group of plants plays in a garden's design: Woody plants provide year-round structure and often attain the largest sizes; perennials fill much of the area, provide color in waves, and maintain interesting foliage throughout the growing season; annuals provide summer-long color and fill in spaces between maturing plants. Larger landscapes often apply this same type of thinking, even where the plant types are segregated.

An ecological mixed garden or landscape would include plants with each of Grimes's life history strategies in their appropriate roles. Competitors will be best able to establish and thrive in rich soil. Their vigorous growth will fill in an area and outcompete weeds. They will probably overtop stress tolerators that are included and may bring about their demise. Stress tolerators are best planted in unenriched soils. These can be arid lands, rock outcrops, uplands, woodlands, sandy soils, or old meadows. Stress tolerators can also fill in spots where competitors begin to decline as nutrient levels drop off after a few years. They will be able to maintain their (albeit slower) growth and occupy a site without additional fertilization or care for many years. Ruderal species will perform best in frequently disturbed sites such as the edges of roads, where they can quickly regrow from seed after another season's snowplowing or weed-whipping. Recently disturbed sites such as newly exposed woodland edges are another candidate location for ruderal species. In both of these situations, fast-growing ruderals can help reduce weed problems. Every newly installed planting area is also a recently disturbed site and can potentially benefit from the inclusion of ruderal species.

Envision a planting to go along a new access road that has been cut through some woods. Underneath the established trees, where nutrient cycles are tight, we can plant a few stress tolerators to fill in gaps. Between the woods and the roadside verge, competitors, supplemented by ruderals in the first few seasons, grow in prepared soil, filling in the edge quickly and providing a lush display of foliage and flowers. Right along the road, ruderals will continue to grow where the competitors are knocked back by too-frequent disturbance. Their vigorous flowering and seed setting is lovely to watch and helps keep the balance in the design weighted toward desired species and away from weeds.

FUNDAMENTAL AND REALIZED NICHES DIFFER

We have seen how plants occupy niches in a community based on adaptations to certain sets of conditions or types of resources. Until now, we have assumed that where plants grow in nature indicates the environments for which their adaptations best suit them, or at least the set of places that their propagules were able to reach and get established. German ecologist Heinz Ellenberg (1953) showed in a famous experiment that this is not necessarily the case.

Ellenberg constructed a planter basin that increased in depth from one end to the other. In this basin he maintained a constant groundwater level, so that the plants at one end experienced groundwater at the surface and at the other end groundwater 150 centimeters below the surface. In this basin he sowed strips of six grasses, and a strip of a mix of all the grasses, so that each strip crossed all points in the moisture gradient.

When grown by themselves, all the species had their best growth at a water depth of between 20 and 35 centimeters—that is, in a well-watered but not overly soaked environment, with a well-aerated rooting zone. That was true for grasses typically considered hydrophytes (e.g., fowl bluegrass [*Poa palustrisis*]) and plants typically considered xerophytes (e.g., erect brome [*Bromus erectus*]). When they were grown together in a mix, however, the peak performance of each grass was shifted to another point on the continuum (fig. 3.8). Fowl bluegrass became most successful at the very wet end of the spectrum and erect brome toward the drier end. This is the niche compression to which Diamond referred when discussing assembly rules. Ellenberg called the point along the continuum where each species achieved its peak

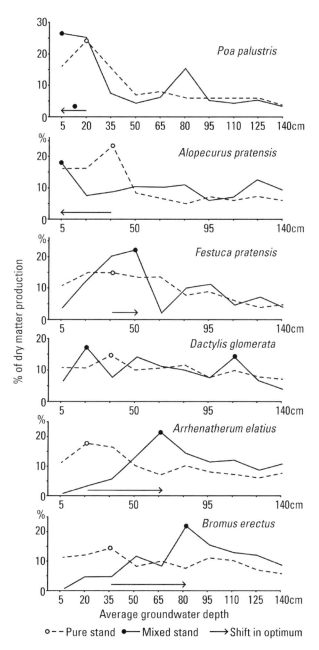

Figure 3.8 Percentage of overall dry matter produced by each species at 10 points along a continuum of groundwater depth in pure and mixed stands. Grasses grown alone in Ellenberg's experiment had similar physiological optima (open circles). When grown together in a mix, however, their ecological optima shifted to other points on the continuum (closed circles). Arrows indicate direction and extent of shift. (From Ellenberg, H. 1953. Physiologisches und ökologisches Verhalten derselben Pflanzenarten. *Bericht der Deutschene Botantischen Gesellschaft* 65:351–61.)

performance when grown alone its physiological optimum, and he called the high point when grown in a mix its ecological optimum. He concluded that only when we consider competitive relationships alongside environmental factors will we be able to understand plant communities causally.

Ellenberg's concepts of physiological and ecological optima are most commonly discussed today in terms of fundamental and realized niches. A species' fundamental niche is the full range of conditions in which a species is physiologically capable of growing. A species' realized niche is the actual set of conditions under which it appears in a community. A primary factor that restricts species' realized niches is competition.

WORK WITH REALIZED NICHES

The suitability of plants to the environment of a site is only one factor to consider in designing a community. Clearly, conditions have to be within plants' fundamental niche for them to grow there. What really matters in any given situation, however, are the plants' realized niches, based on the competitive environment in which they find themselves.

At Storm King Art Center in Mountainville, New York, Darrel Morrison has been converting former agricultural fields and lawns into simplified native grass communities since 1997. Over the years he has learned how the predominance of different grass species shifts depending on the interplay between environmental conditions and the mix of plants included in a community.

The first area planted under Morrison's direction was a wet field. Here Morrison used a mixture of Canada wildrye (*Elymus canadensis*), Indian grass (*Sorghastrum nutans*), and switchgrass. Canada wildrye is a short-lived grass and is intended to fade from the mixture as the other grasses fill in. What Morrison did not expect, however, was for Indian grass to also fade completely from the community under competitive pressure from switchgrass.

In 2003, Morrison specified a revised planting mix for a pair of drier mounds at Storm King, adding two additional native plants, little bluestem and partridge pea (*Chamaecrista fasiculata*). Partridge pea is a nitrogen-fixing legume and an annual. Like Canada wildrye, it is intended to be only a temporary member of the community. On this drier site switchgrass has come to dominate, but it has not excluded the Indian grass and little bluestem.

Having seen its dominance in his earlier plantings, when Morrison returned to the other half of the wet field in 2007, he left switchgrass out of the mix entirely. Instead he called for Indian grass, little bluestem, bluejoint grass (*Calamagrostis canadensis*, a native grass that grows well in wet conditions), Canada wildrye, and partridge pea. Without switchgrass, the community structure is very different. A more subtle patterning has emerged, with little bluestem dominant in some areas and Canada wildrye and partridge pea still abundant in others (fig. 3.9).

Morrison's experience at Storm King shows that the mix of plants included in a community, and the way that mix responds to different environmental conditions, will ultimately determine what grows where in a designed landscape. How these factors will play out may not be fully knowable in advance but will be part of the learning process on a site for any designer. Allowing niches to realize themselves in a given context and making adjustments based on observations of these adjustments is the ecological designer's art.

Figure 3.9 Two grass communities in a wet field at Storm King Art Center, October 2009. In the background an older planting is dominated by switchgrass. In the more recent planting in the foreground, little bluestem and Canada wildrye coexist. (Photograph by Travis Beck.)

PLANT COMMUNITIES ARE ARRANGED IN COMPETITIVE HIERARCHIES

To understand the dynamics by which some plants in mixed communities drive others to extinction, or at least into tighter realized niches, we need to better understand the mechanisms of competition in plants.

Paul Keddy and Bill Shipley (1989) examined eight studies in which plants that grow together in herbaceous communities were paired against each other in one-on-one pot-based competition experiments and the growth of each was measured. They found that in most of those pairings competition was asymmetric: One species suppressed the other (fig. 3.10). The primary mechanism, they suggested, is that the competitive dominant overtops the suppressed species, thereby acquiring more light for its own growth and keeping light from reaching its competitor at the same time (the strategy pursued by Grimes's competitive plants). Once a plant begins to gain dominance over its neighbors, the gains it makes are self-reinforcing.

In other cases, competition is about starving out competitors. David Tilman has examined the long-term success of plant populations that compete for limited nutrients in a patchwork of aban-

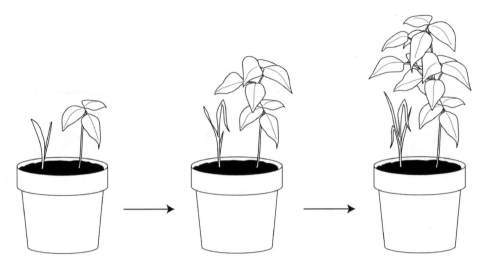

Figure 3.10 When two plants grow side by side, the one that grows larger and faster can suppress the other. This is one mechanism for competitive dominance.

doned fields at the Cedar Creek Ecosystem Science Reserve in Minnesota (Tilman 1982, 1997). Say two grass species, little bluestem and rough bent grass (*Agrostis scabra*), are growing together in an abandoned field where their growth is nitrogen limited. As the plants grow, they tie up nitrogen in their tissues and reduce the amount available in the soil. Both species have a minimum level of available nitrogen that they need in order to offset losses to herbivory, disturbance, and mortality. Tilman called this level a species' R*. As it happens, the R* for rough bent grass is 5.5 times higher than the R* for little bluestem. Consequently, as plant growth depletes soil nitrogen, little bluestem displaces rough bent grass because of its ability to survive at lower resource levels.

Whether competition is about quickly overtopping one's neighbors or starving them out in the long run, there are winners and there are losers. If we assemble the results of all the pairwise competition experiments within a community, a competitive hierarchy of plants in that community can be determined. Species A outcompetes species B. Species B outcompetes species C. Species A also outcompetes species C. This forms what Keddy and Shipley called a transitive path, meaning that the competitive relationships transfer in rank order. In the studies reviewed by Keddy and Shipley, transitive relationships were far more common than intransitive relationships, in which underdog species pull off upsets against species farther up the competitive hierarchy. Experimentally derived hierarchies such as these allow us to predict the outcome of competition between individual plants of different species within a community.

PLAN FOR DOMINANCE

Whenever we envision a mouth-watering combination of two plants, we also need to also consider the degree of symmetry or asymmetry in their competitive relationship. It is a shame to put two gorgeous plants together only to have one swallow the other. As we discussed previously, plants that occupy different niches, such as spring-flowering bulbs and warm-season grasses, can be combined successfully, because they do not compete directly. Where plants do compete, evenly matched pairings are excellent, although Keddy and Shipley's research showed asymmetry is much more common. Asymmetric combinations can sometimes be successful, as when a dominant prairie grass such as little bluestem reduces the growth of black-eyed Susan (*Rudbeckia hirta*) from galloping mass to thin fingers emerging through a grassy matrix (fig. 3.11).

Whenever we combine more than two species, we need to extend this sort of thinking in an attempt to understand the competitive hierarchy of the community we are creating. Earlier we discussed creating communities consisting of a few abundant species and a larger number of less frequent species (see chap. 2). The selection of which species will be the most abundant in any planned community cannot be arbitrary. It must be a species that is well suited to the conditions of the site and able to exert competitive dominance over other species that are present or may invade. If such a species is not picked as the most abundant initially, another such one will emerge over time, or else significant ongoing effort will be needed to keep the planting from failing. Experienced designers often have a sense of the relative competitive abilities of plants in different situations, but there is ample room for research in this area.

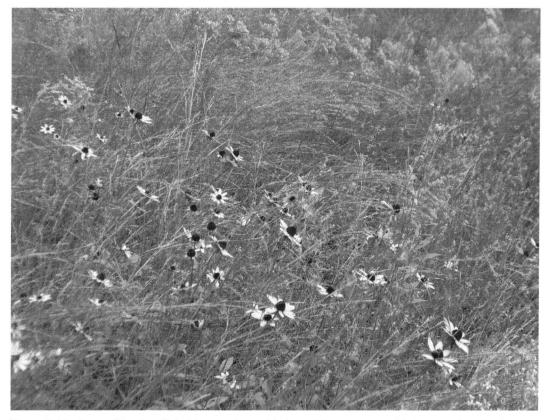

Figure 3.11 Competition from little bluestem keeps black-eyed Susan manageable in a meadow planting at Mt. Cuba Center, Delaware. (Photo by Travis Beck.)

COMPETITION AFFECTS SPATIAL PATTERNS

In addition to the importance of small-scale environmental differences and plants' means of dispersal in determining the spatial pattern of plant populations, we must now consider the effect of competitive hierarchies.

The competitive dominant in a community can occupy any site but is most likely to disperse to sites nearest its parents, leading to a somewhat clustered distribution. Because less competitive species can survive only in sites not occupied by the clustered dominants and are most likely to disperse to sites near parent plants, their distribution is increasingly aggregated. The exception to this rule is plants that emphasize the colonization side of the colonization–competition trade-off, which often have long-distance means of dispersal (e.g., airborne seed) and will be scattered throughout a community wherever openings occur.

The aggregating tendencies described earlier are balanced by the effects of local competition. While competition affects plant populations, it is experienced by individuals, primarily adjacent individuals. As we saw with self-thinning (see chap. 2), competition's effect is to push (surviving) individuals apart. This segregation effect is stronger the more directly individuals compete, which is why plants with different niches can live right on top of each other. Strong competition at the individual level can lead to weak competition at the community level as competitive species segregate themselves spatially. In other words, spatial segregation promotes coexistence.

Taken together, then, local dispersal and local competition lead to intraspecific spatial aggregation and interspecific spatial segregation. By reducing interspecific competition below intraspecific competition, this spatial segregation promotes coexistence. Stephen Pacala (1997) demonstrated this spatial segregation hypothesis using mathematical models. Recent empirical evidence has come from studies of Mediterranean shrubland in Spain (De Luis et al. 2008; Raventós et al. 2010). Researchers there established three 33- by 33-meter plots in a degraded pine forest that had been taken over by gorse (*Ulex parviflorus*). They burned the plots to initiate the study, then 2 months later they applied a simulated torrential rainfall in subplots within each plot. Then they mapped all the seedlings that emerged and tracked their fates over the next 9 years. When they analyzed the locations of the four dominant species, they observed clustering of plants from the same species and segregation of plants from different species. Furthermore, by looking at the nearest neighbors of dead plants, they were able to determine that intraspecific interactions were more important than interspecific interactions, lending support to the spatial segregation hypothesis.

ARRANGE PLANTS IN PATTERNS THAT ACCOUNT FOR COMPETITION

The layout of designed plant communities should take into consideration the competitive relationships of plants. If we plant competitive dominants right next to or mixed with less competitive plants, we will lose the less competitive species. We have already seen how plants distribute themselves vertically in a forest to partition light resources. Horizontally segregating the plants that compete more directly can allow us to maintain diverse plantings. In a way this is just a matter of giving spatial expression to the competitive hierarchy.

At a private residence along New York's Hudson River, landscape designer Larry Weaner created a shady woodland garden in which he used his knowledge of the relative competitive abilities of indigenous plants to guide the layout. Before Weaner began work on the site, the understory of the wooded backyard was dominated by a shrubby layer of spicebush and invasive Siebold viburnum (*Viburnum sieboldii*), along with some Japanese knotweed. Weaner removed all these plants except for selected spicebush and put in their place a selection of native trees and shrubs underplanted with a mix of native herbaceous plants. To prevent the resurgence of the undesirable plants, these plants had to grow together quickly and strongly. The herbaceous species Weaner used include ferns, Solomon's seal (*Polygonatum biflorum*), Jacob's ladder (*Polemonium reptans*), golden groundsel (*Packera aurea*), black cohosh (*Actaea racemosa*), and wild geranium (*Geranium maculatum*) (fig. 3.12). Weaner planted with

Figure 3.12   Golden groundsel, mayapple, and black cohosh form part of a dense competitive herbaceous layer in a woodland planting. (Photo by Larry Weaner.)

a tight spacing initially, allowed the natives to proliferate rapidly, and insisted on fastidious mainte-nance during the establishment period to remove any weeds that appeared. The result is a dense and commingled layer of native plants and no resurgent knotweed or viburnum.

The trouble with commingled plantings such as these, Weaner has found, is that they can be some-what illegible. In order to call attention to spots of interest within the landscape and to give the eye a place to rest, he placed small patches of single species. To hold their own against the competitive mix, the single species have to be aggressive. Lady fern (*Athyrium filix-femina*) and mayapple, for instance, are sufficiently strong competitors that they can be used in this way.

Weaner has completely segregated the most delicate species in a planting bed, separated from the rest of the landscape by a retaining wall and stone paving. Here ephemerals such as trillium and twinleaf (*Jeffersonia diphylla*) can be easily appreciated and can grow without interference from the more competitive species used elsewhere in the landscape.

By recognizing the competitive abilities of the plants used, using each where it is appropriate, and segregating plants in the landscape based on their place in the competitive hierarchy, Weaner has been able to both competitively exclude undesirable species and maintain populations of delicate woodland wildflowers.

CONCLUSION

How do we combine plants in a designed landscape? We begin by recognizing that when two popula-tions need identical resources, they will compete intensely. We bring together plants that have different niches and assemble communities that fill up all the available niche space. We use plants that have different life history strategies, each in their appropriate role. We recognize that plants will shove each other into tighter realized niches and monitor closely how this process plays out. We pay attention to which plants are more competitive than others and place equally competitive plants side by side and less competitive plants out of harm's way.

Competition is a structuring force in plant communities. By using competition intentionally, we can structure the plant communities we design to resist invasion and to include a diverse mix of coexisting plants that can then display all the delightful colors, forms, and textures we desire.

4. Complex Creations: Designing and Managing Ecosystems

A dragonfly flits over the sun-mirrored surface of a pond, snapping at hatching mosquitoes before coming to rest on an overhanging rush. This is an ecosystem: animals, plants, and their physical environment linked together in the exchange of energy and materials. If this were our pond, our ecosystem, we would have it all: a beautiful landscape feature, enlivened by creatures we never had to care for, and hassle-free pest control.

Ecosystems like this pond do quiet, crucial work, keeping alive the biosphere of which we are a part. Where such a natural pond, or a forest or floodplain, exists, it behooves us to protect it. Where one has been degraded, we would be well served to restore it (see chap. 10). But where such ecosystems have been plowed under or paved over, we can endeavor to replace them by filling the built environment not just with lawns and plazas and fountains but with ecosystems.

An ecosystem consists of all of the living organisms in an area along with their physical environment, and its properties arise from the interactions between these components. An ocean bay is an ecosystem, as is an alpine meadow or a green roof. Perhaps because of their clear boundaries, lakes and streams were important objects of study in the development of ecosystem ecology. Where boundaries are less distinct, the limits of an ecosystem can be defined, even arbitrarily, based on the question an ecologist is studying or the boundaries of a designer's site.

Designed landscapes already bring together a manipulated physical environment and living organisms. They do not necessarily function as natural ecosystems do, however. They are disconnected, too often wasteful and demanding, or else they simply fail to thrive. When we succeed in creating integrated ecosystems, the results can be remarkable. Life can spring forth, almost unbidden. Wastes can be transformed into resources. The various members of a living community can reach a tentative balance. The built environment can purify water, protect us from floods, and strengthen our sense of well-being.

THE ECOSYSTEM CONCEPT

The idea that plants and animals and their environment form an integrated whole is at the root of the discipline of ecology, although it took decades to articulate in its modern form. In 1887, in an address to the Peoria Scientific Association, Stephen Forbes described the lake as "a microcosm." In order for a scientist to understand any one species, he argued,

> He must evidently study also the species upon which it depends for its existence, and the various conditions upon which *these* depend. He must likewise study the species with which it comes in competition, and the entire system of conditions affecting their prosperity; and by the time he has studied all these sufficiently he will find that he has run through the whole complicated mechanism of the aquatic life of the locality, both animal and vegetable, of which his species forms but a single element. (Forbes 1887: 537)

The term *microcosm* did not enter into wider ecological use. However, the idea of many organisms forming a larger entity gained expression in the turn-of-the-century concept of the climax community (see chap. 2). This concept was singled out by British ecologist Arthur Tansley in a 1935 article provocatively titled "The Use and Abuse of Vegetational Concepts and Terms." The abuse to which he referred was the insistence of Clements and other ecologists on applying the term *organism* to the climax community. "There is no need to weary the reader," he wrote, "with a list of the points in which the biotic community does *not* resemble the single animal or plant" (Tansley 1935: 290). However, he did not hold back from mentioning that a community's process of development is very different from the life cycle of animals and plants. At best, Tansley offered, vegetation might resemble a "quasi-organism," though one not nearly so well integrated as a human society or a hive of bees. This acceptance of a quasi-organismal status for communities differentiates Tansley's criticism of Clementsian ecology from Gleason's purely individualistic focus. There is a certain truth to the idea of the climax community being well integrated and self-regulating, Tansley argued, but it could be stated more accurately another way.

Tansley preferred to think in terms of integrated systems. His notion of systems was borrowed from the physical sciences. "These *ecosystems*, as we may call them," he wrote, "are of the most various kinds and sizes. They form one category of the multitudinous physical systems of the universe, which range from the universe as a whole down to the atom" (Tansley 1935: 299). An essential part of Tansley's description of the ecosystem is that he included in it not only all of the plants and animals and other living things in a given "web of life" but also the entirety of the physical components of their environment, such as soil, sunlight, and water.

CREATE ECOSYSTEMS

Built landscapes also have physical and biological components: crudely, in industry terms, hardscape and softscape. Too often, these components are far from integrated. The hardscape is set in response to programmatic needs, and plants are tucked into the remaining spaces. If the physical environment is not right for the biological components, then it is altered, by providing irrigation, for instance (see chap. 1).

Consider a typical landscape pond. An estate owner might pay a contractor to clear an area, excavate a hole, line it, fill it full of water from a well, and trim the whole setup neatly with rocks or lawn and perhaps a few aquatic plants on a planting shelf. As water evaporates from the unshaded pond, the well pump kicks in and tops off the pond. Even suburban homeowners want their own ponds and waterfalls, full of municipal water and lined with dwarf conifers or Japanese iris (*Iris ensata*) sitting like rocky puzzle pieces on their lawns. These systems are fully artificial, rely on supplemental water, and often require filtration or even sterilization to remain aesthetically acceptable. Physical and biological elements are divorced from each other and from their surroundings.

By contrast, a pond that is conceived of as an ecosystem fuses physical and biological elements into a whole that integrates with, rather than sits apart from, the processes of the surrounding environment. Landscape architects Andropogon Associates created such a pond on a property in Greenwich, Connecticut. Naturally, throughout New England's forests, in the spring small depressions in the landscape fill with water, which infiltrates as groundwater levels drop in the summer. These vernal pools provide important habitat for amphibians such as salamanders and frogs. On this property such a depression existed, set against a granitic outcrop, only it had long been filled with branches, leaves, and other green waste by generations of gardeners. When Colin Franklin, founding principal at Andropogon, discovered the rocky dell and the small spring at its base, he saw an opportunity. Andropogon Associates' design philosophy has long been to build "dynamic, holistic systems," that is, ecosystems.

Franklin's approach was to line the center of the depression in order to maintain a minimum water level but leave the edges unlined. Water from the spring is collected in a sump beneath the pond and pumped via a slender waterfall off the rock outcrop and into the pond. In spring the pond overflows, recharging groundwater in the area (fig. 4.1). The margins are planted with trees and other plants that are adapted to this seasonal flooding. Between the open water, the planted wetland at the pond's edge, and the seasonal wetland beyond, the design provides diverse habitat (see chap. 7). When water levels drop to the level of the liner, the wetted margins dry, mimicking the cycle of vernal pools. If water levels drop further, the sump pump and waterfall can make up the difference from the recharged groundwater. Because the pond is in the forest, however, evaporation and the need for makeup water are minimal.

This forested pond is now a hub of life and the center of the entire landscape. Rather than create a sterile water feature of dissociated elements, Andropogon created an ecosystem, with natural physical cycles and plants and animals adapted to them.

ECOSYSTEMS ARE COMPLEX ADAPTIVE SYSTEMS

Ecologists' understanding of the multitudinous systems of the universe has evolved since Tansley wrote his critique of Clements in 1935. Most recently, ecosystems have been regarded as complex adaptive systems. Simon Levin (1998, 1999), a biologist at Princeton, is a chief proponent of this view. In complex adaptive systems, as explained by Levin, heterogeneous individual agents interact locally to create larger patterns, and the outcome of those local interactions affects the further development of the system (fig. 4.2). It is easy to see how this applies to ecosystems. The plants and animals, rocks and water and detritus that make up a pond are all different, yet they interact to create a recognizable

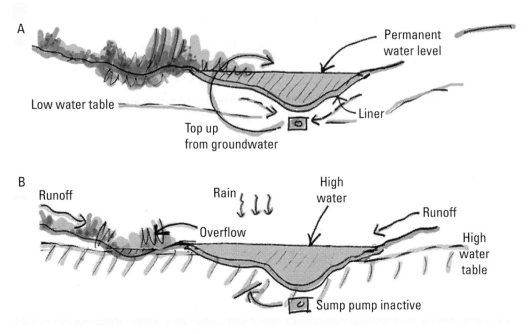

Figure 4.1 Schematic design of the Andropogon-designed pond ecosystem. During normal dry weather conditions **(a)** a liner and groundwater pump maintain a permanent water level. During normal wet season conditions **(b)** overflow enters peripheral seasonal wetlands and recharges groundwater. (Drawing by Colin Franklin.)

system with properties of its own. If a plant that produces more biomass competitively excludes others along the pond's margins, then the accumulation of detritus in the pond, the populations of bottom feeders, and other ecosystem properties will all be affected.

Levin further described four characteristics of complex adaptive systems. They are diverse, aggregated, nonlinear, and connected by flows. Ecosystems include individual organisms with diverse characteristics. Through their interactions, the individual agents in an ecosystem become grouped into larger organizational entities. For example, populations are groups of interacting individuals of the same species (see chap. 2). The most accurate way to view aggregation is through the composition of a hierarchy (see chap. 9). Nonlinearity means that small changes in an ecosystem can lead to outsized effects. Removal of a single keystone species, for instance, can change the composition of an entire community (see chap. 7). Nonlinearity also refers to the fact that ecosystems are affected by history as much as by present conditions. Finally, as we shall see in the following sections, ecosystems clearly exhibit flows of energy and materials that connect all their individual parts.

LET CONSTRUCTED ECOSYSTEMS SELF-DESIGN

If ecosystems are complex adaptive systems that develop from the interaction of their components and the events of history, then successful ecosystems are unlikely to spring forth from our heads fully formed but should emerge instead through a process we might call self-design.

Figure 4.2 Turing patterns, like this one, are an example of a complex system formed from local interactions. In this case, each pixel's color is determined by the color of the surrounding pixels according to a computer algorithm. Starting from a random initial state, the pattern continues to evolve. (Image by Jonathan McCabe, under Creative Commons 2.0 Generic License.)

Bill Mitsch and his colleagues explored self-design at the Wilma H. Schiermeier Olentangy River Wetland Research Park in Columbus, Ohio (Mitsch et al. 1998). They intentionally left one of two basins in their newly created experimental oxbow unvegetated. They knew that wind, water, and animals would bring in new plants soon enough, and they wanted to see how closely the unplanted wetland would resemble the one they planted. Within 3 years, the two wetlands were remarkably similar in terms of vegetative cover, diversity of plants, water chemistry, and several other measures of ecological function (fig. 4.3). This congruence results not simply from the unplanted wetland coming to resemble the planted one but from both wetlands changing to reflect site conditions and migrations. Of the thirteen original species in the planted wetland, four died off. The surviving species were joined by an additional fifty-two unplanted species. Because the wetlands were connected hydrologically to the nearby Olentangy River, the natural inflow of species had a much greater influence on the makeup of the plant communities in the two wetlands than did the initial planting of one basin.

The success of the two basins as self-designed ecosystems is indicated by the Olentangy River Wetland's designation under the Ramsar Convention as a Wetland of International Importance.

Figure 4.3   Aerial view of the two Olentangy River Wetlands. (Courtesy of William J. Mitsch, Wilma H. Schiermeier Olentangy River Wetland Research Park.)

ECOSYSTEMS ARE ORGANIZED IN TROPHIC LEVELS

As complex adaptive systems, ecosystems are animated by the interactions between their constituent parts and the flows that connect them. In the 1940s a young American ecologist, Raymond Lindeman, suggested a way of analyzing ecosystems in terms of energy flow. As with Forbes before him, Lindeman's focus was on lakes. After 5 years of field work on the small Cedar Bog Lake near the University of Minnesota, Lindeman signed up for a postdoctoral year at Yale University with G. Evelyn Hutchinson (who later advised Robert MacArthur on his study of resource partitioning in warblers) (see chap. 3). During that year he and Hutchinson worked on the article that was to become "The Trophic-Dynamic Aspect of Ecology" (Lindeman 1942). Tragically, Lindeman died at the age of 27, a few months before his article, which was initially rejected as being too theoretical, was finally published in the flagship journal of the Ecological Society of America. The ideas he put forth have had a lasting impact on the field of ecosystem ecology.

Lindeman's focus was on the trophic, or "energy-availing," relationships within an ecosystem. Borrowing from German limnologist August Thienemann, he abstracted the familiar food webs that naturalists and ecologists had produced for lakes and other systems into trophic levels: Producers are organisms such as plants and phytoplankton that obtain their energy from the sun, consumers are organisms such as zooplankton and fish that obtain their energy from eating producers, and decomposers are the bacteria and fungi that obtain their energy from breaking down the organic substances in the wastes and remains of other organisms. By abstracting an ecosystem to trophic levels, Lindeman sacrificed a certain amount of biological reality. He also created the problem of how to classify organisms that eat both producers and consumers. There can be several levels of consumers in an ecosystem, although earlier ecologists had noted that rarely are there more than five trophic levels in total. Lindeman's analysis explained this phenomenon.

Unlike the chemical elements, which can cycle indefinitely in an ecosystem (see chap. 6), energy flows through an ecosystem in one direction only: from the sun to producers to consumers to secondary consumers to decomposers. At each transfer of energy between trophic levels, Lindeman noted, a certain amount is lost (fig. 4.4). Primary consumers such as browsing snails expend a certain amount of energy just living and finding producers to eat. Some of them die before they are eaten by benthic predators. Some of the energy contained in the bodies of those that are eaten is tied up in tissues such

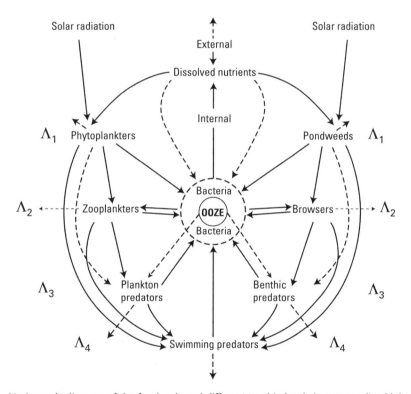

Figure 4.4 Lindeman's diagram of the food web and different trophic levels in a generalized lake. Energy and nutrients enter the system from the outside. These are captured and transformed by both microscopic and macroscopic producers (phytoplankters and pondweeds, Λ_1). Primary consumers (zooplankters and browsers, Λ_2) eat the producers and in turn are eaten by secondary consumers (plankton predators and benthic predators, Λ_3). Tertiary consumers (plankton predators and benthic predators, Λ_4) are at the top of the food chain. All the organic matter in the system ultimately cycles through the bacterial decomposers in the ooze at the bottom of the lake, which in turn feeds zooplankters and browsers. (From Lindeman, R. L. Copyright ©1942, Ecological Society of America. The trophic–dynamic aspect of ecology. *Ecology* 23:399–417. With permission from the Ecological Society of America.)

as shells that are difficult to digest and whose energy is not passed along. The available energy in each trophic level, then, is less than that in the preceding level. Lindeman expressed this relationship using the productivity symbol lambda (λ):

$$\lambda_0 > \lambda_1 > \lambda_2 \ldots > \lambda_n.$$

As we move to higher and higher trophic levels, less and less energy is available. Because higher-order consumers also need ever-greater levels of energy to seek out their prey, at some point in every ecosystem, there is no longer sufficient energy to support another trophic level.

Lindeman calculated the productivity and efficiency of energy transfer between trophic levels for several lakes for which he had data and drew some preliminary conclusions. This prefigured the more precise modeling of ecosystems that was to come in the next phase of ecosystem ecology.

INTEGRATE PRODUCERS, CONSUMERS, AND DECOMPOSERS

All ecosystems are governed by the rules of energy flow that Lindeman outlined. As we manage existing ecosystems and strive to create functioning ecosystems of our own, we need to be sure the different trophic levels are represented in their proper ratios. If a level is missing or there are too few organisms at that level, energy, in the form of organic matter, will accumulate as waste, or undesirable organisms may take advantage of the bounty. If there are too many levels or too many organisms, they will need supplemental inputs to survive, or else they will die or move away. Using an ecosystem approach, we can create a more balanced designed landscape in which various components support each other and produce little waste.

At El Monte Sagrado, an ecologically minded luxury resort in Taos, New Mexico, a linked series of carefully designed aquatic ecosystems provide wastewater treatment and an essential part of the landscape. The systems' ability to filter water depends on the integration of different trophic levels. At the heart of the wastewater filtration process is a Living Machine. Living Machines were originally developed by ecological designer John Todd in the 1970s and 1980s (Todd and Todd 1993). They have since been refined and are now designed and sold by Living Machine Systems. In the words of general manager Eric Lohan, one of the designers of the system at El Monte Sagrado, they work by taking natural ecosystem processes and "turbo-charging" them. In the wastewater system, much of the initial energy comes not from sunlight but from the waste products themselves, which are consumed by bacterial decomposers. Thus far the process resembles a conventional septic system, in which excess bacterial biomass settles out as sludge that eventually has to be removed. In the Living Machine, the bacteria that perform the initial decomposition are central to an entire ecosystem (just as bacteria are in Lindeman's diagram of a lake ecosystem), in which they are consumed by protozoans, microcrustaceans, and snails. Plants floating above the wastewater as it is treated take up a portion of the newly available nutrients and provide in their roots a living substrate for this diverse community.

After disinfection and final polishing in an outdoor wetland, the now clear water enters indoor display ponds and another aquatic ecosystem. Here producers include a variety of tropical plants, phytoplankton, and algae, and fish play the role of consumers. Resort guests also serve as consumers when they enjoy starfruit (*Averrhoa carambola*) and kumquat from the plants that are irrigated by the treated wastewater. By including all the trophic levels, this system fully uses the energy and nutrients present in the wastewater generated by resort guests, resulting in clear water and valuable end products rather than murky graywater and sewage sludge. On top of this, thanks to the efficient reuse of water that the aquatic ecosystems allow and their centrality to the overall design of the resort, even in the high desert El Monte Sagrado has a lush ambience that invites guests to relax and feel themselves a part of living processes (fig. 4.5).

Figure 4.5 Treated water from the Living Machine enters an indoor display pond at El Monte Sagrado resort in Taos, New Mexico. (Photo courtesy of Worrell Water Technologies.)

NEGATIVE FEEDBACK LOOPS HELP ECOSYSTEMS MAINTAIN STABILITY

One of the aspects of ecosystems that fascinated the early ecologists who studied them was that ecosystems can demonstrate, in Arthur Tansley's words, a "relatively stable dynamic equilibrium." Fifteen years after the publication of Lindeman's article on trophic dynamics, Howard Odum (1957) amassed large amounts of data into a much more exact picture of the surging dynamics behind such apparent stability.

The ecosystem Odum studied was the headwaters of Silver Springs, Florida. Since the nineteenth century Silver Springs has been a tourist attraction to which visitors flock to admire the crystal clear water, schools of fish, and waving freshwater eelgrass (*Sagittaria subulata*) (fig. 4.6). The glass-bottomed boat was invented at Silver Springs, in fact, and to this day one can take a boat ride around the three quarter miles of watery attractions with folksy names such as Fish Reception Hall. Silver Springs made

Figure 4.6 Research divers in main boil of Silver Springs hold herbivorous turtles amid algae-covered eelgrass. (From Odum, H. T. Copyright ©1957, Ecological Society of America. Trophic structure and productivity of Silver Springs, Florida. *Ecological Monographs* 27:55–112. With permission from the Ecological Society of America.)

an excellent natural laboratory for Odum because of the constancy of its flow, temperature, and chemical properties. Odum noted that the springs' "hydrographic climate" was at a steady state and that a long-standing climax community had resulted.

Odum and his team of researchers went to remarkable lengths to capture data on every aspect of the Silver Springs ecosystem. Bending over the bow of a motoring boat, they measured the temperature changes in water as it flowed out of the main boil and downstream. By harvesting and weighing samples of eelgrass and the algae that covered it, they determined the biomass of these producers. They grew snails in cages on the bottom of the stream and measured their increase in weight. They snuck up on quadrats marked in the eelgrass and parted the leaves to count a type of sunfish called stumpknockers (*Lepomis punctatus*) where they hid.

Cleverly, Odum and his team were able to measure the overall metabolism of the community by comparing oxygen levels in the water during the day and at night. The regular flow of Silver Springs carried all the "waste products" of the ecosystem past the measuring station three quarters of a mile downstream from the boil. At night all the organisms in the community respired, lowering oxygen levels to a point that reflected their cumulative metabolism. During the day, respiration continued, but the photosynthetic producers also gave off oxygen. The difference between daytime and nighttime oxygen levels, multiplied by the volume of the current, therefore provided a measure of the difference between photosynthesis and respiration, which is the ecosystem's net primary production.

Combining all these measurements, Odum was able to create a detailed description of the flow of energy in the entire ecosystem. This analysis also allowed him to explain how Silver Springs maintained itself in a seemingly unchanging state. Based on the ratio of community productivity to standing bio-mass, Odum estimated that the entire community turned over (died and was replaced) eight times per year. Clearly, smaller organisms turned over many times more than the average and larger longer-lived organisms less. Because of the different amount of sunlight reaching the primary producers in winter and summer, there was a natural pulse in production in the system. One might expect this burst of productivity to be reflected in a flush of new growth in the eelgrass or an increase in the population of primary consumers. In fact, standing biomass and population levels were stable throughout the year. Odum even reported an old boat captain asking him whether the eelgrass ever grew. Seasonal spikes in consumer reproduction seemed to be timed to match the increased productivity, and the extra young in one trophic level were quickly eaten by the extra young in the next, so that although more energy may have been flowing through, standing biomass in the ecosystem remained constant. Negative feedback loops such as an increase in consumption that absorbs an increase in production help ecosystems re-main stable. Where negative feedback loops meet a constant environment, as at Silver Springs, overall stability can be maintained for an extended period.

ECOSYSTEMS CAN EXIST IN ALTERNATIVE STABLE STATES

Stability is not entirely simple, however. Ecologists have demonstrated that ecosystems can have more than one stable form. Shallow lakes, for instance, possess two stable states. In one they are as clear as Silver Springs. In the other they are turbid, filled with the murk of algae and suspended sedi-ment. Marten Scheffer and colleagues (1993) explained how both states are self-reinforcing, because of feedback loops. In clear lakes vegetation reduces the resuspension of bottom sediments, takes up nutrients that would otherwise support algal growth, and provides a refuge from higher-level consumers for zooplankton that eat algae. Water clarity, in turn, encourages the growth of submerged aquatic veg-etation. In turbid lakes, sunlight cannot penetrate deeply into the water, so vegetation growth is limited to the shallows and turbidity increases, which makes it difficult for plants to grow.

Which state an ecosystem falls into can depend on its history. Scheffer and his co-authors de-scribed the case of Lake Krankesjön in Sweden, which changed from clear to turbid in the early 1970s after an increase in water level reduced the amount of aquatic vegetation. When in the mid-1980s a period of low water occurred, the lake switched back to a clear state with abundant vegetation. A common culprit in triggering the switch from the clear to the turbid state in lakes is nutrient pollution, especially by phosphorus (fig. 4.7). Phosphorus can trigger algal blooms, which kill off submerged

Figure 4.7 The addition of phosphorus to one half of this lake in Canada's Experimental Lakes Area tipped it into the alternative eutrophied state. (Photo courtesy of David Schindler.)

vegetation and much of the life that depends on that vegetation, in a process known as eutrophication. Because of the feedback loops involved, eutrophication can be difficult to reverse, even when nutrient pollution is reduced or ceases.

HELP ECOSYSTEMS REACH AND MAINTAIN DESIRED STABLE STATES

Managing ecosystems to achieve or maintain a desired stable state requires a delicate touch. Steve LaMere, owner of Adirondack Ecologists, LLC, is a professional lake manager who works mostly on the many natural lakes in the Adirondack region of New York. These lakes range in condition from crystal clear bodies of water to eutrophic lakes that are so thick with algae that they resemble pea soup. LaMere compares eutrophic lakes to patients with a chronic infection. They need regular doses of chemicals (LaMere uses alum, which binds with available phosphorus in the water column) just to reach acceptable water quality levels. In those lakes we are fighting feedback mechanisms. The key to keeping a clear-water lake clear, on the other hand, is to minimize perturbations and, when perturbations occur, to help the ecosystem recover its own balance.

One of the lakes LaMere manages is Schroon Lake, in the southeastern portion of Adirondack Park. Schroon Lake is approximately 4,000 acres in size and runs 9 miles from its northern to southern tips. As at Silver Springs, the clarity and water quality of Schroon Lake are excellent. Schroon Lake also has a healthy food web of wetland plants, thirty-three species of phytoplankton, thirteen species of zooplankton, and fish including lake trout (*Salvelinus namaycush*), largemouth bass (*Micropterus salmoides*), and northern pike (*Esox lucius*) (Schroon Lake Watershed Management Planning Committee 2010).

The very attractiveness of Schroon Lake brings challenges, however. Homeowners have developed properties along much of the lake's northwestern and southeastern shores. Hundreds of boaters put in during the summer. Faulty septic systems along the lake's shoreline contribute phosphorus to the water, as does runoff from fertilized lawns. Boaters have introduced two notable invasive aquatic species to the lake: Eurasian water milfoil (*Myriophyllum spicatum*) and curly-leaf pondweed (*Potamogeton crispus*). There are also larger watershed issues, including influxes of sediment-laden stormwater from roads, properties, and eroding streambanks.

"Lakes don't come with instruction manuals," LaMere jokes. One cannot know in advance exactly where the threshold lies at which a lake ecosystem will tip from one stable state into another. To maintain balance, you have to watch carefully. The earlier potential problems are identified, the less invasive, more environmentally sensitive, and more cost-effective the options for control are. For Schroon Lake, LaMere has recommended a program of monitoring and education so that residents can be aware of the state of the lake and work to reduce watershed inputs. He also pursues active physical removal of the two invasive aquatic plants he has found in the lake. Although eradication is impossible, he hopes to keep their populations below levels where they can affect the overall balance of the lake.

A promising approach to managing complex systems, about which we may have only an incomplete understanding, is adaptive management (Stankey et al. 2005). Adaptive management proposes a four-step process (fig. 4.8). First, we integrate existing information and our experience to propose possible approaches to a management problem. Then we test one or more of these approaches to a problem in a rigorous manner. Next, we evaluate the outcomes. Finally, we learn from our experiences to plan the next round of actions. Adaptive management can allow us to steward complex entities such as lake ecosystems that are themselves changing over time.

ECOSYSTEMS FUNCTION AS WHOLES

The organized complexity of ecosystems gives rise to emergent properties. These are the same properties that led Clements to describe the climax community as an organism. Ecosystems also capture solar energy and convert it into biomass, change the qualities of water that passes through them, and store or release materials such as carbon and nitrogen. These ecosystem functions become clear when we view the ecosystem not at the level of its intricate workings but as a whole.

In his studies of one important ecosystem function, net primary productivity, Howard Odum (1957: 87) characterized Silver Springs as "a giant flow-system respirator." In the 1960s a group of ecolo-

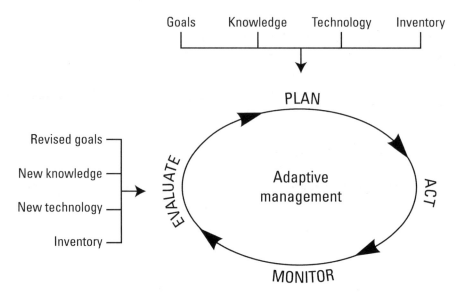

Figure 4.8 The adaptive management cycle. (From Stankey, Clark, and Bormann 2005.)

gists including Herbert Bormann and Gene Likens began using a similar approach to measure the flow of nutrients through forest ecosystems (Bormann and Likens 1967). The Hubbard Brook Ecosystem Study took advantage of the conditions in six small parallel watersheds in the White Mountains of New Hampshire. Here hardwoods and, at higher elevations, spruce and fir grow in forest soils over hard bedrock. These living and nonliving components of the ecosystem interact to produce a net effect that can be measured by comparing inputs and outputs (fig. 4.9). The rain and snow that fall on a watershed must leave the system through its central stream. By anchoring a weir to the bedrock at the bottom of the stream before it joins Hubbard Brook, the ecologists were able to measure not only the volume and rate of flow of water but also all the nutrients leaving the system. They could then compare their measurements with samples of precipitation to reveal the functions that these ecosystems, considered as a whole, perform.

In one experiment (Likens et al. 1970) the ecologists of the Hubbard Brook Ecosystem Study compared the functions of an undisturbed watershed with a watershed that had been clear-cut and in which vegetation had been prevented from regrowing by herbicide applications. They found that the amount of water running off the deforested watershed was much higher than that running off the forested control. Stream water temperatures were significantly higher in the deforested watershed than in the forested watershed in both the summer and the winter. Dissolved inorganic nutrient concentrations were much greater in the stream draining the deforested watershed. Nitrate nitrogen concentrations were more than forty times higher than that observed in the forested watershed. In sum, viewed macroscopically, the forested and deforested ecosystems had remarkably different levels of function. The watersheds at Hubbard Brook continue to be used to study the effects on ecosystem function of acid rain, ice storms, and climate change.

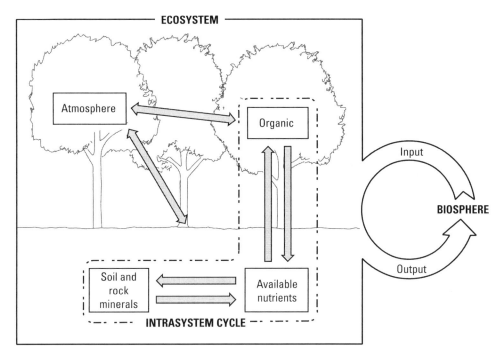

Figure 4.9 Bormann and Likens's model of a watershed ecosystem at Hubbard Brook. Nutrients cycle within the ecosystem, which can be considered as a whole in its exchanges with the biosphere. (From Bormann, F. H., and G. E. Likens. 1967. Nutrient cycling. *Science* 155(3761):424–29. Reprinted with permission from AAAS.)

ECOSYSTEMS PROVIDE VALUABLE SERVICES

As Bormann and Likens's clear-cutting experiment demonstrated, a functioning ecosystem such as the reference watershed at Hubbard Brook performs a lot of work. The watershed's forest ecosystem retains and cycles nutrients such as nitrate nitrogen, allowing for continuous plant growth and keeping them from becoming pollutants in downstream bodies of water. Many of the functions of ecosystems benefit humankind.

The Millennium Ecosystem Assessment (MA), an international scientific effort under the auspices of the United Nations, investigated in depth the links between ecological function and human well-being. The MA (2005) divided ecosystem services into four categories: provisioning, regulating, cultural, and supporting (fig. 4.10). Provisioning services include the production of food, timber, and clean water. Regulating services are such things as flood control by wetlands, breakdown of wastes, and control of pests. Cultural services include the recreational opportunities and aesthetic enjoyment that natural areas provide. Supporting services are such things as soil formation and the capture of solar energy by the phytoplankton that support fisheries.

In 1997 a group of ecological economists led by Robert Costanza synthesized a number of studies in order to place a dollar value on the services provided by the earth's ecosystems. Although such services rely on natural infrastructure, the ecological economists acknowledged that the value of that infrastructure is infinite and therefore do not include it in their calculations. Consider, for a moment, how much it would cost

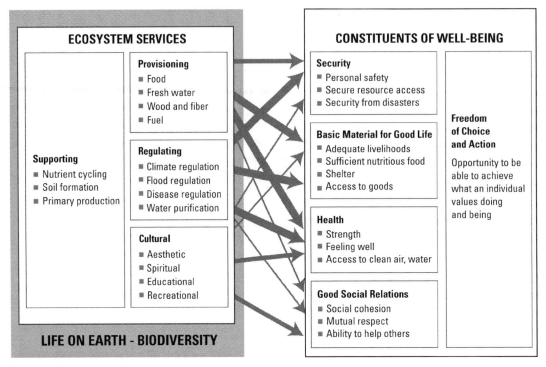

Figure 4.10 Ecosystem services, as categorized by the Millennium Ecosystem Assessment, contribute to human well-being. The width of an arrow indicates the strength of the linkage. (From Millennium Ecosystem Assessment. Copyright © 2005 World Resources Institute. *Ecosystems and Human Well-Being: Synthesis.* Reproduced by permission of Island Press, Washington, DC.)

to replace the atmosphere. Instead they focused on the marginal value of ecosystem services, or how the benefits or costs to human activities would change with a change in the current level of services. By multiplying the value of the multiple services that ecosystems provide by the global area of those ecosystems, they came up with an estimate of the total value of the earth's ecosystem services of US$33 trillion annually, or about 1.8 times the world's gross national product. They emphasized that, for several methodological reasons, their estimate was probably far lower than the actual value of the world's ecosystem services.

Both the MA and Costanza et al.'s report stressed that the earth's ecosystems have been degraded and their ability to continue providing services at historical rates is imperiled (see chap. 10). We are left to imagine how high the price of clean air or a livable climate might climb in a world where these are scarce commodities.

DESIGN LANDSCAPES TO PROVIDE ECOSYSTEM SERVICES

Although human activity has imperiled the ability of the earth's natural ecosystems to provide the services we depend on, human intelligence can design our built environment to perform many of those same services at some level.

An early step in any landscape planning process should be to identify the ecosystems that do or can exist on a site and the services they do or can perform. Like populations, ecosystems are arbitrarily defined units. In cases of smaller projects or uniform sites, property lines may define an ecosystem. However, it is probably most helpful to match up ecosystem boundaries with physical features such as a pond or a watershed. For functional planning purposes, we can consider these ecosystems, as the Hubbard Brook ecologists did, as black boxes with certain inputs and outputs. What are the physical, chemical, and biological elements that pass into and out of each ecosystem or the site ecosystem as a whole? Are some of the inputs elevated (e.g., concentrated stormwater from offsite or atmospheric pollution) or depressed (e.g., lack of nutrients entering a system because of the loss of large animals)? Do outputs need to fall within certain parameters, as with nutrient levels in water leaving a treatment wetland?

The Hubbard Brook clear-cutting experiment demonstrated incontrovertibly that how an ecosystem is structured affects how it functions. In other words, to achieve ecosystem function in the built landscape, design matters. When functional planning is done, we have to climb inside the black box.

In Philadelphia, Biohabitats, Inc. has used clever design details to address broad ecosystem services in their plan for Pier 53 and Washington Avenue Green. Pier 53 is one of the many piers built into the Delaware River in the mid-19th century. In 1965 a warehouse fire damaged the pier significantly, and the site was largely abandoned. The Delaware River Waterfront Corporation, with support from several other public and private entities, has initiated a revitalization of a 7-mile stretch of the river, beginning with the 1-acre site at the base of Pier 53.

The main objectives for the project were to provide public waterfront access, improve the ecological health of the Delaware River, and jumpstart redevelopment with a visible demonstration project. Barely 10 months passed between the request for proposals and the opening of a new park, Washington Avenue Green.

Biohabitats, Inc., the design–build firm selected for the project, created a plan that put their company philosophy of regenerative design into action. Along with the recreational, aesthetic, and spiritual benefits of the park, their plan offered ways to provide a number of tangible ecosystem services, including water quality improvement, soil regeneration, and habitat creation.

Before its rebirth as a park, much of the site had been covered with concrete and asphalt. Biohabitats, in collaboration with environmental artist Stacy Levy, used jackhammers and core drilling equipment to remove pieces of pavement in streamlike patterns. The resulting holes were filled with a bioretention soil mix and planted to create "dendritic decay gardens." This small intervention will accelerate the natural breakup and decay of the pavement and transforms an impermeable surface into a permeable filter that allows stormwater to sink in rather than being immediately shed into the river (see chap. 6). A rain garden at the mouth of the northern dendritic decay garden enhances the stormwater retention and filtration service provided by the feature.

As part of the Washington Avenue Green project, Biohabitats also piloted an approach to treating water in the Delaware River itself. In the sheltered area south of the pier, community volunteers installed floating wetlands. These wetlands gain their flotation from numerous plastic bottles that were collected during the cleanup of the site. The bottles are wrapped in fabric "socks" and coir fiber, then enclosed in mesh. Native wetland plants such as rose mallow (*Hibiscus moscheutos*) and cordgrass

(*Spartina pectinata*) were planted in the matrix. Their roots grow through this medium and down into the water itself, providing a measure of local water treatment and habitat for aquatic invertebrates and even fish. In Baltimore Harbor, where Biohabitats has also deployed floating wetlands, blue crabs (*Callinectes sapidus*) find refuge in these constructed features, and a pair of black-crowned night herons (*Nycticorax nycticorax*) have nested. When funded, the plan for Pier 53 itself calls for the installation of more of these floating wetlands and for the creation of more natural fringe wetlands at a collapsed pier edge (fig. 4.11). Together, these elements could improve local water quality and provide further habitat.

Even in its early incarnation as the Washington Avenue Green, the Biohabitats plan has converted a hard-edged industrial landscape into a living ecosystem. The new park improves water quality, speeds up soil regeneration on the site, and provides habitat for native plants, insects, fish, and birds. These are small-scale improvements, but they demonstrate techniques that could be applied all along the Delaware River and elsewhere to create built landscapes that provide ecosystem services.

Figure 4.11   Rendering of Pier 53 as it would look after redevelopment. (Courtesy of Biohabitats, Inc.)

CONCLUSION

Where Clements once saw an organism and Odum a tightly coupled self-regulating system, ecologists now see a complex adaptive system in which emergent properties develop from localized interactions. These emergent properties interest us greatly as human beings because they include services we depend on. It is no longer enough for designed landscapes to look good and to include spaces for the various activities we plan to pursue. They must function as ecosystems that provision and protect us and fill us with wonder.

To build such ecosystems, we have to marry physical and biological elements harmoniously. We have to include plants, animals, and microorganisms at different trophic levels. And we have to let these various elements interact, come to their own arrangements, and change over time. If we succeed, our ecosystems may reach and maintain a desirable stable state. Our work then becomes a matter of tweaking and nudging, trying to understand better, and looking for the key interactions to influence when necessary. Or we can just sit back and watch the dragonflies.

5. Maintaining the World as We Know It: Biodiversity for High-Functioning Landscapes

Consider the once great prairie. Ranging from the foothills of the Rocky Mountains to the ragged edge of the eastern deciduous forest, the American prairie encompassed an array of different communities and ecosystems, including shortgrass prairie, sand prairie, pothole wetlands, and oak savanna. Each of these ecosystems was filled with a panoply of plant and animal life (fig. 5.1). A recent 24-hour bioblitz on the American Prairie Preserve in Montana turned up 480 species, including 26 fungi and 76 birds (Billings Gazette 2011). Diverse prairies are found mostly in preserves these days or between the headstones of settlers' cemeteries. As the country pursued its manifest destiny, prairie gave way to farmlands, ranches, interstate highways, and sprawling subdivisions. Its interwoven plant communities became millions of acres of corn, wheat, sunflowers, and bluegrass lawns.

Since life began on Earth, species have come and gone. On average about one species per million has gone extinct each year. Where, for instance, are the dinosaurs and the armored fish of prehistoric seas? Species evolve into something else, or die out singly, or at several points in geologic history have been wiped out en masse by atmospheric change, shifting continents, global cooling, shrinking seas, and asteroid collision. Today we are in the midst of another mass extinction, this one driven by human beings. The loss of species began as humans spread across the planet, killing large wildlife such as wooly mammoths (*Mammuthus primigenius*) in Europe and North America and moa in New Zealand. We have also intentionally and accidentally introduced exotic animals and diseases that have devastated local species. Above all, since the advent of agriculture, we have transformed the global landscape, replacing diverse natural ecosystems with simplified, human-managed systems (see chap. 10). It is difficult to pinpoint the extent of extinctions going on today, in part because we are still identifying new species every day. In their 2003 assessment of global biodiversity, however, Rodolfo Dirzo and Peter Raven found evidence of species loss at rates 1,000 times higher than the geologic background rate. Given these figures, they concluded, "It is reasonable, although pessimistic, to envision the loss of two thirds of the species on Earth by the end of the twenty-first century" (2003: 164).

Figure 5.1   Prairies, such as this one at the Midewin National Tallgrass Prairie in Illinois, are home to hundreds of species. (Photo courtesy of the US Fish and Wildlife Service.)

Absolute loss of species tells only part of the story, however. *Biodiversity*, a shortened form of *biological diversity*, refers to the sum total of inherited variation in all the living organisms of a given area (Wilson 2010). It includes all scales of biological variation, from the biome to the population. A community that retains many species from only one or two families is arguably less diverse than a community that includes fewer species from more families. When local ecotypes of plants and animals are lost, biodiversity is reduced, even though the species live on.

The biological riches of this planet are still only partially explored, and they almost certainly contain untapped resources for medicine and agriculture. They also represent the product of hundreds of millions of years of evolution and have an intrinsic value for their rarity and irreplaceability. Crucially, the many species and populations, known and unknown, contribute to the functioning of ecosystems across the planet. Biodiversity, E. O. Wilson (2010: 15) concluded, "is the key to the maintenance of the world as we know it."

Ecologists distinguish between alpha, beta, and gamma diversity (Whittaker 1972). Alpha diversity is equivalent to the species richness within a community (see chap. 2). If two nearby ecosystems each have their own alpha diversity, beta diversity is a measure of how many species each has that are not present in the other. It quantifies the unique contribution that each ecosystem makes to overall diversity. Gamma diversity is the total number of species in the region or area being studied.

Regions with high gamma diversity have many different species organized in multiple contiguous ecosystems. Conservationists are especially concerned with endemic species, those that appear in one area and nowhere else. Areas that have large numbers of endemic species, and that are under development pressure, are known as biodiversity hotspots (Myers et al. 2000). In the United States, the California Floristic Province, stretching from southern Oregon to Baja, contains more than two thousand endemic plant species and is threatened by the expansion of agricultural and urban areas. Natural areas within biodiversity hotspots merit a high level of protection. Even where evolution has not produced endemic species, local ecotypes may be present and make an important contribution to overall biodiversity (see chap. 1).

From the perspective of a site designer interested in biodiversity conservation, whether working in a diversity hotspot or not, it is important to assess how the alpha diversity of the site contributes to the gamma diversity of the region. Does a site contain any locally rare species or recognized ecotypes? Is it a continuation of surrounding habitats, with low beta diversity, but allowing for increased population sizes and connectivity (see chap. 9)? Or is it a different ecosystem type, with high beta diversity? Are there opportunities to increase beta and gamma diversity by reintroducing locally extirpated species?

Ecologists also assess the evenness of species distribution in an area. As we saw before, within a community, some species are more abundant than others (see chap. 2). Is an area dominated by a single species, or are there good-sized populations of many different organisms? Reading tallies of biodiversity, you might come across mention of the Shannon–Wiener index, which is a common measurement that combines species richness with an assessment of evenness.

The richness and evenness of species in an ecosystem affect how that ecosystem functions, how well it converts sunlight to biomass, for instance, or cycles nitrogen, or provides habitat (see chap. 4). If a hypothetical ecosystem were made up of just one species, its functions would be exactly those of that species. If it were dominated by one species, even though others were present, the functions of the ecosystem would be largely those of that species. When multiple species combine and have large enough populations to play substantial roles, however, the functions of the ecosystem are derived from multiple sources. Ecologists have demonstrated that this increases ecosystem function, allows ecosystems to perform multiple functions more effectively, and keeps these functions stable over time and in the face of changing conditions.

Biodiversity is important for designers, then, not only because we have the potential to both disrupt and preserve natural biodiversity but because it influences the performance of the communities and ecosystems we design. If our designed communities are to persist and flourish, and if our constructed ecosystems are to provide ecosystem services, they must include appropriate levels of biodiversity. As designers, we need to understand how biodiversity works.

DESIGN THE BUILT ENVIRONMENT TO SUPPORT BIODIVERSITY

Although the conversion of natural ecosystems to plantations, agriculture, and urban development is largely responsible for the current extinction crisis, built landscapes harbor a considerable number of species and have the potential to play a more meaningful role in biodiversity conservation (fig. 5.2).

Attention to the conservation value of the built environment is especially high in Europe, perhaps

Figure 5.2 Even highly urbanized areas such as Manhattan host a surprising number of species, both native and introduced. But is this biodiversity ecologically significant? (Photo by Sarah Paulson.)

because of the longer history of development there. In Leicester, England, Jennifer Owen (2010) documented 474 species of plants, 1,997 species of insects, and 64 vertebrates over 30 years in her suburban garden. In samples taken across Berlin, Stefan Zerbe and his colleagues (2003) found as many as 513 plant species in a given 8-square-kilometer area. Both authors included native and nonnative species in their counts. Owen argued that the high species diversity of her garden resulted from her activity as a gardener, intentionally maintaining "contrived plant diversity" and "extreme structural heterogeneity." However, Zerbe found the highest levels of species diversity in areas that experienced the least intensive human management, including neglected yards and an abandoned railyard along the old Berlin Wall.

Built landscapes can help protect regional biodiversity. Landscapes that suit a biome will better maintain the life of that area than will generic lawns and trees (see chap. 1). Planting ecotypic plant material will help maintain those populations. Landscapes also have the potential to serve as ex situ conservation sites for plant species. The Center for Plant Conservation (http://www.centerforplantconservation.org) works with botanic gardens and arboreta to maintain living examples of endangered native plants in order to preserve them from extinction and to facilitate restoration efforts. Whereas the average property owner might not have the horticultural knowledge, long-term commitment, or concern for the genetic integrity of the species necessary to maintain rare plants, many avid gardeners would. Also, properly sited long-lived plants could easily persist in designed landscapes until a future time when they could provide pollen, seeds, or cuttings for restoration efforts. For example, the franklinia tree (*Franklinia alatamaha*) has been extinct in its wild home along the Altamaha River in Georgia since the early nineteenth century but persists in cultivation from specimens collected by early American botanists John and William Bartram.

The point of fostering biodiversity in the built environment is not simply to collect a large number of species or to pack our gardens with museum-like collections of endangered plants, however. Martin Quigley (2010) argued that the apparent biodiversity of urban areas is not ecologically meaningful, as most landscape plantings are small in scale, disconnected, taxonomically concentrated in a few families, ephemeral, and not structured to produce ecological function. For biodiversity to be ecologically meaningful in the built environment, it must become operative.

The biodiversity we plan and plant becomes operative when it supports a larger web of life than would a simplified landscape (see chap. 7). It becomes operative when it ties together the built environment and the remnants of native ecosystems (see chap. 9). It becomes operative when it permits the landscapes we install to evolve and adapt over time. Finally, and the idea we will examine through most of the remainder of the chapter, biodiversity becomes operative in the built environment when it helps us create ecosystems that function well and provide services that we need (see chap. 4).

INVASIVE SPECIES THREATEN BIODIVERSITY

Land development reduces biodiversity not only by converting and fragmenting habitat but also by promoting invasion by exotic species. Disturbance opens up patches of habitat (see chap. 8). Plants have different evolutionary strategies, and some are adapted to reproduce quickly in disturbed areas or to compete strongly in productive environments (see chap. 3). Dispersal is a critical factor in what plants grow where and become part of a community after disturbance (see chap. 1). Together these factors provide the ecological recipe for the widespread biological invasions we are experiencing today.

Even where humankind has not demolished natural ecosystems with bulldozers, we have altered their dynamics through fire suppression, overgrazing, pollution, and removal of keystone species. At the same time we have purposefully and inadvertently moved thousands of species of plants, animals, fungi, and microorganisms around the globe. Many of the species that have followed us closely are adapted to disturbance or are generalist species. These species have entered into regional species pools and become part of communities that are resorting themselves in the wake of both direct and indirect human disturbances (Hobbs 2000).

Invasive species can disrupt the functioning of native ecosystems (fig. 5.3). Purple loosestrife displaces native species in the wetlands it invades, and its dense stands reduce habitat for ducks and turtles. Cheatgrass (*Bromus tectorum*) can dominate rangelands in the Great Basin, reducing the growth of native grass and forb species. As a winter annual, it dries out midsummer and can make grasslands more fire susceptible. Increased fire frequency prevents the reestablishment and growth of indigenous shrubs. Cheatgrass-dominated communities can now be found over millions of acres in Idaho and Utah. Then there are introduced pathogens such as chestnut blight (*Cryphonectria para-*

Figure 5.3 Purple loosestrife can completely dominate wetlands it invades, such as this one in Boxborough, Massachusetts, reducing biodiversity. (Photo by Liz West, under Creative Commons Attribution 2.0 Generic license.)

sitica), which has eliminated the previously dominant chestnut tree (*Castanea dentata*) from eastern forests, and pests, such as the Asian longhorned beetle (*Anoplophora glabripennis*), which threatens hardwood trees across North America.

According to analysis done by David Pimentel, Rodolfo Zuniga, and Doug Morrison at Cornell University (2005), 42 percent of species on the endangered and threatened lists in the United States are threatened primarily by competition with or predation by invasive species. As humans degrade habitat and invasive species spread, we risk the extirpation of endemic species across the planet and the rise to dominance of global generalists. Science writer David Quammen (1998) called this scenario of proliferating cockroaches and gray squirrels, house sparrows, and cheatgrass the "Planet of Weeds."

Life on a planet of widely dispersed plant and animal species is not unremittingly grim, however. A few invasive plants fill unoccupied niches and do not directly affect native species. In some cases, exotic species have a facilitative effect on native animals and plants by serving as a food source, acting as pollinators or seed dispersers, providing nesting cover, or releasing native species from predation pressure. Often the interactions of exotic species with native ecosystems are complex, positively affecting some native species and ecosystem processes while negatively affecting others (Goodenough 2010). Above all, invasive exotic species are new members of the (often already disrupted) communities they have intruded on. They are both a further tear to the fabric of these communities and, in many cases, one of the threads that these communities will have to use to reweave themselves over time (see chap. 10).

ESCHEW INVASIVE SPECIES, INCLUDING THOSE NOT YET LISTED

Many of the worst invasive plants were intentionally planted for horticultural or restoration purposes. Cogongrass (*Imperata cylindrica*), originally from Asia, was planted in the southeastern United States as fodder and as an ornamental plant. It spreads from rhizomes and seeds to create dense mats that displace native vegetation and alter the fire ecology of invaded communities. Salt cedar (*Tamarix*) was used as an ornamental and for windbreaks before escaping to dominate riparian environments throughout the Southwest.

Given the economic costs and environmental problems of invasive species, the federal government and many state governments have listed the most notorious noxious weeds that are not permitted for importation or trade (US Department of Agriculture 2011). Additionally, numerous universities and environmental groups have prepared lists of invasive plants that are not recommended for planting in particular localities. The species on these lists are demonstrated nuisances and should not be propagated, planted, or allowed to establish themselves on project sites.

Of course, many of these plants are already established on public and private lands across the country. Landscape designers and land managers will probably encounter these plants as part of their projects and should plan for their management or eradication, particularly where restoration efforts can be made immediately.

The trickier question is how to identify the plants that are available now in the nursery trade but may cause problems in the future. There is often a lag time between introduction and invasion, so the problem species of the next several decades are probably already among us. Not every exotic plant will escape cultivation and become a noxious weed, though. Only a fraction of the alien plants introduced to our shores will appear spontaneously in the wild, only a fraction of these will develop self-sustaining populations, and only a fraction of these will run rampant over native ecosystems.

There are useful clues by which to judge the potential invasiveness of a plant one is considering for inclusion in a design. First, is the plant listed as invasive elsewhere? Butterfly bush (*Buddleja davidii*), for instance, is invasive in Great Britain and appears on Washington and Oregon state invasive lists, yet it can be easily found at garden centers in other parts of the United States. If one's area has a similar climate and environmental qualities to a place where a plant is listed as invasive, it might be best to stay away from it. Second, are close relatives of the plant listed? The fact that diffuse knapweed (*Centaurea diffusa*) is an incredibly noxious weed might cause one to think twice about the charming naturalizing habit of bachelor's button (*Centaurea cyanus*). Third, does the plant have traits that would allow it to expand and reproduce quickly, such as rapid growth, aggressive vegetative spread, and early reproductive maturity? Fourth, does the plant have effective means of long-distance dispersal, such as windborne or waterborne seeds, or fleshy fruits that would be attractive to birds? Other considerations include whether the species has close local relatives with which it is likely to hybridize, altering the genetics of a local population, whether it is difficult to control mechanically or chemically, and whether it has ecosystem engineering properties, such as a propensity to burn or a tight clumping architecture. Sarah Reichard and Clemant Hamilton (1997) analyzed the traits of invasive and noninvasive woody plants introduced to North America since 1930 and developed a decision-making tree that combines many of these considerations and can be used to analyze species for their invasive potential (fig. 5.4).

The context of a site is as important as the qualities of a plant when making these sorts of decisions. Plants are not uniformly invasive across all environments. Some places are also less suitable for questionable plants, such as along watercourses that could facilitate their spread, or adjacent to recently disturbed land. Making distinctions such as these about plant and context can allow us to take advantage of the diversity of the world's flora while minimizing the risk to native ecosystems.

BIODIVERSITY SUPPORTS ECOSYSTEM FUNCTIONING

Native North American prairies are diverse. In the Konza Prairie in Kansas, Scott Collins and Susan Glenn (1990) found that most of their 10- by 10-meter research plots contained fifty or sixty species each. Similarly, John Curtis (1959) listed forty-seven species of dry prairies in his survey of the vegetation of Wisconsin (see chap. 2). What are all these species doing? And, from the perspective of someone planning a prairie garden or other designed community, do we need to include so many species?

Looking for answers, David Tilman, David Wedin, and Johannes Knops (1996) set out to examine the link between biodiversity and ecosystem function in the grasslands of the Cedar Creek Ecosystem Science Reserve in Minnesota. This is the same site where Tilman performed his research on the mechanisms of plant competition (see chap. 3). The scientists seeded 147 thoroughly prepared plots with random mixtures of either one, two, four, six, eight, twelve, or twenty-four native prairie species. In August of the next year they calculated total percentage cover and available nitrate in the rooting zone of the plots. They found clearly that the greater the diversity of the plots, the higher their productivity and the greater their use of soil nitrogen. In other words, biodiversity was strongly related to two important ecosystem functions: the ability to capture energy from the sun and retain nutrients within the ecosystem.

A couple of mechanisms can explain the findings of Tilman and his colleagues. One is the so-called sampling mechanism. As more species are included, the better the odds are that a high-producing species will be included. The other is the complementarity mechanism. As more species are included, more niches are filled, allowing the community as a whole to take advantage of more of the available resources (see chap. 3). Whereas individual species may be less productive in a more diverse community than they would be if they grew by themselves, the community as a whole is more productive. Interestingly, the researchers at Cedar Creek found that increasing diversity from one to six species changed productivity and nitrogen use dramatically. Above that point, changes occurred more slowly, reaching an apparent saturation point where additional species did not markedly increase function.

The study by Tilman and his colleagues prompted a stormy debate. However, its findings have been demonstrated repeatedly elsewhere, and the underlying concepts are now generally accepted (Naeem et al. 2009). In a carefully worded 2005 consensus statement, a panel of distinguished ecologists concluded, "A long history of ecological experimentation and theory supports the postulate that ecosystem goods and services, and the ecosystem properties from which they are derived, depend on biodiversity, broadly defined" (Hooper et al. 2005: 24).

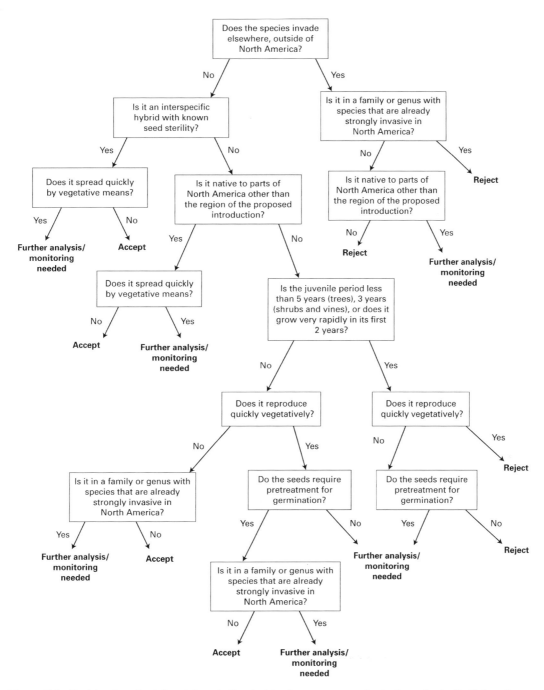

Figure 5.4 Decision tree for determining whether to introduce a new woody plant species to North America. (From Reichard, S. H., and C. W. Hamilton. Copyright ©1997 John Wiley and Sons. Predicting invasions of woody plants introduced into North America. *Conservation Biology* 11(1):193–203. Reproduced with Permission of John Wiley and Sons, Inc.)

So far we have accounted for the value of six or eight of the plant species in a prairie. What about the other forty or fifty? Although the effect of species richness on a single ecosystem function such as productivity saturates fairly quickly, ecosystems perform more than just one function, of course. Ecologists have theorized that ecosystems are able to pull off these multiple functions because they contain so many species. Because of evolutionary trade-offs, no small number of species can maximize performance on every function. For instance, it is impossible for any plant to be the most productive and the most stress tolerant. A diverse community builds on the qualities of different sets of species to achieve multiple functionality, however. In 2010 Erika Zavaleta and two fellow researchers, working with David Tilman on data derived from his long-term grassland diversity experiments at Cedar Creek (Tilman et al. 2006), found empirical support for these theories. They assessed the performance of plant communities at different levels of species richness for eight ecosystem functions, including aboveground productivity, insect species richness and abundance, and soil carbon storage. The researchers calculated how many of the plots at each level of species richness met a certain threshold (percentage of maximum function) for each of the ecosystem functions. Setting the threshold at 60 percent of maximum function, for instance, in the year 2000, far more plots with eight and sixteen species were able to perform two, three, and four ecosystem functions at the threshold level than were plots with just one, two, or four species (fig. 5.5). Above four functions, the proportion of all plots able to maintain multifunctionality declined dramatically. The researchers deduced that there are trade-offs not only between species but also between communities. They concluded that in order to achieve multiple ecosystem functions, diversity is necessary both within communities (alpha diversity) and between communities across a landscape (beta diversity).

In summary, ecologists have demonstrated that in order for grasslands to provide multiple ecosystem services, they need at least moderate levels of plant diversity.

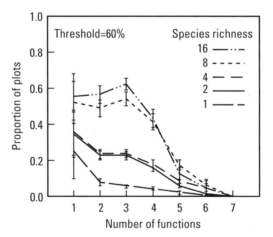

Figure 5.5 Diverse communities are able to sustain higher levels of more ecosystem functions simultaneously. (From Zavaleta, E. S., J. R. Pasari, K. B. Hulvey, and G. D. Tilman. 2010. Sustaining multiple ecosystem functions in grassland communities requires higher biodiversity. *Proceedings of the National Academy of Sciences* 107(4):1443–46.)

CREATE DIVERSE ECOSYSTEMS

If we are to create landscapes that perform ecosystem services, ecologists' findings inform us, they will have to be diverse. The Cedar Creek biodiversity experiments, and others like them, are especially relevant to landscape designers, because the scientists who conducted them built plant communities from scratch. Although these scientists drew conclusions about natural ecosystems and the dangers of species loss, their experiments tell us directly about the functional value of diversity in plant communities put together by people.

We know from agriculture that it is possible to create low-diversity environments that have a high level of an ecosystem function such as productivity. A field of F1 hybrid corn produces enormous amounts of biomass, more perhaps than the prairie it replaced. The field's productivity depends first on our selection of a highly productive plant (a corollary of the sampling effect). It also depends on high inputs of energy, fertilizer, and even water. When the corn field is turned into an office park lawn, the same practices are continued, only productivity in the landscape context means not bushels yielded but good growth, a healthy appearance, and reduced opportunities for weed invasion. Emphasizing

Figure 5.6 Diverse prairie plantings, like this 7-year-old dry prairie from seed designed and installed by Neil Diboll, are productive and attractive without high inputs. (Photo by Neil Diboll, Prairie Nursery, Inc., Westfield, WI.)

the complementarity mechanism, on the other hand, if we were to till up the lawn and replace it with a diverse planting such as a prairie garden, we could achieve similar levels of overall productivity by using each species' distinct and complementary evolutionary advantages (fig. 5.6). This ecological approach requires a different sort of management, based not on high-energy inputs but on knowledge: recognizing all the species involved, knowing their life cycles, and interceding in ways more subtle than mowing once a week.

Diverse ecosystems such as our prairie planting are also better at performing multiple functions. The corn field is fabulous at growing corn and the lawn at looking green, but both make lousy bird habitat and probably reduce, rather than improve, the quality of the water that passes through them. Because we need our landscapes to perform many functions simultaneously, we should make them at least moderately diverse. Where our sites are large and varied enough, we should also include multiple communities with their own sets of plants. This concurs with the findings of Crawley and Harral (2001) about species richness over larger areas and the importance of varied habitat (see chap. 2).

Within a community at a given point in time, Tilman and his colleagues' findings show, ecosystem function can be achieved with moderate numbers of species: six to sixteen, say, rather than fifty plus. We know from the sampling effect that including the right species is an important part of building ecosystem function. Given the variety of species available, how do we choose the right ones?

FUNCTIONAL BIODIVERSITY IS MORE IMPORTANT THAN NUMBER OF SPECIES

Biodiversity is not just a matter of the number of species in a community. The truly important measure, ecologists have realized, is diversity of functional traits. Functional traits describe a species' niche (see chap. 3). Some functional traits of plants are leaf area, height, light requirements, water requirements, whether a plant is woody or herbaceous, whether a plant is evergreen or deciduous, time of flowering, mutualisms (such as with nitrogen-fixing bacteria), photosynthetic pathway, and pathogen resistance. The totality of all the traits represented in a community is a measure of that community's functional diversity.

Increasingly, ecologists are recognizing that functional diversity is a better predictor of ecosystem function than species richness (Cadotte et al. 2011). One reason for functional diversity's predictive power is the potential for redundancy in communities. Redundancy helps explain Tilman et al.'s (1996) findings that ecosystem function reached a saturation point beyond which the inclusion of additional species had little effect. If several species perform similar functions, then adding more of those species to a community will not increase ecosystem function at a given point in time. Seen from the perspective of the biodiversity crisis, if species are lost from a community, redundancy allows other species with similar functional traits to compensate for the loss and maintain ecosystem function.

Assessing functional diversity can be tricky, however. One approach is to assign species to different functional groups. In grasslands, for instance, a plant could be categorized as a woody plant, C3 (cool season) grass, C4 (warm season) grass, nitrogen-fixing forb, or non–nitrogen-fixing forb (fig. 5.7). The fewer the groups, however, the greater the assumed similarity in function, which can distort biological reality; the more the groups, the closer this method becomes to actual species richness. There is greater explanatory power in identifying functional traits of importance and representing them in a continuous rather than a discrete way. In a grassland, again, we might look at plant height, leaf nitrogen

Figure 5.7 Native prairies, such as this remnant on the Waubay National Wildlife Refuge in South Dakota, include plants from different functional groups. Pictured here are the cool season green needlegrass (*Nassella viridula*), nitrogen-fixing leadplant (*Amorpha canescens*), and non–nitrogen-fixing narrow-leaf coneflower (*Echinacea angustifolia*). (Photo courtesy of the US Fish and Wildlife Service.)

percentage, root length and thickness, and whether a plant forms nitrogen-fixing nodules. The difficulty here is that we have to know in advance which functional traits are important. An emerging approach is to use the phylogenetic diversity of a community to represent its functional diversity. Phylogenetic diversity is a measure of the similarity of all the members of a community based on their ancestral relationships. This approach assumes that evolutionary distinctness corresponds to functional distinctness, which may not always be the case (think of convergent evolution). However, it has the advantage of being able to capture functional differences that we have not yet recognized. Phylogenetic diversity has proven to be an effective predictor of ecosystem function (Flynn et al. 2011).

Looking at evolutionary, that is to say genetic, differences of functional traits, ecologists are also finding important levels of variation within as well as between species. For example, individual grass plants reach different heights. It is the diversity of functional traits at all biological levels, not just the number of species, that truly determines ecosystem function.

INCLUDE FUNCTIONAL DIVERSITY

To maximize ecosystem function in designed communities, we need to maximize functional diversity. There are several approaches a designer can take to ensure functional diversity.

The simplest approach, though the least ecologically accurate, as we have seen, is to develop functional groups and be sure to include at least one species in every group. In a grassland community, for instance, we would want to include cool and warm season grasses, nitrogen-fixing plants, forbs, and perhaps a shrub or two. For an upper midwestern grassland, we might include Canada wildrye (*Elymus canadensis*) as a cool season grass, little bluestem (*Schizachyrium scoparium*) and Indian grass (*Sorghastrum nutans*) as warm season grasses, lead plant (*Amorpha canescens*) and round-headed bush clover (*Lespedeza capitata*) as nitrogen fixers, prairie tickseed (*Coreopsis palmata*), flowering spurge (*Euphorbia corollata*), and tall blazing star (*Liatris aspera*) as forbs, and prairie wild rose (*Rosa arkansana*) as a shrub. We could expect a community modeled after a natural community in this way to have reasonably tight niche relationships and fairly high function.

A more challenging approach is to identify functional traits of importance and include species along a range of values for each trait. In our grassland, again, we might want grasses at a range of heights and forbs with different life cycles (annual, biennial, and perennial). Adding low-growing June grass (*Koeleria macrantha*) and tall switchgrass (*Panicum virgatum*) to our mix will increase the range of heights represented, and including annual prairie sunflower (*Helianthus annuus*) and short-lived black-eyed Susan (*Rudbeckia hirta*) will increase the number of life cycles present.

Finally, we can work to maximize the phylogenetic diversity of our proposed community. Phylogenetic diversity alone is not enough to create highly functioning designed communities, as it would be possible to assemble some wacky combinations of distantly related plants, but it can serve as a tool to check and refine a proposed plant list developed from other principles. We can calculate the phylogenetic diversity formally using a method such as that followed by Flynn et al. (2011) or more informally by assessing the sum of branch lengths in a phylogeny for our community. Phylogenies for plant communities can be assembled online using Phylomatic, available at http://www.phylodiversity. net/phylomatic/phylomatic.html. To continue with our grassland example, we can see that adding field goldenrod (*Solidago nemoralis*) to our mix would increase the phylogenetic diversity of our community less than would adding prairie buttercup (*Ranunculus rhomboideus*) (fig. 5.8). This is because goldenrod, as a member of the aster family, has other close relatives already included in the community, whereas buttercup is a novel introduction, more distantly related to the other plants in the community than even other plants such as the prairie rose that are the sole included member of their family.

We might not immediately recognize the unique functional benefits that a plant such as prairie buttercup brings to our designed grassland. Perhaps they have to do with its spring bloom time, and the pollinator relationships that brings, or with its degree of moisture tolerance. To use phylogenetic diversity to guide our plant choices is to gracefully acknowledge our ignorance about the workings of complex natural systems. If we need to achieve particular functions, we could always test diverse combinations incrementally, as Mark Simmons has done with native lawns (see chap. 3). We need not take shots in the dark, however. Increasing the functional and phylogenetic diversity of a designed plant community will increase its ecosystem function more directly than will simply adding additional species.

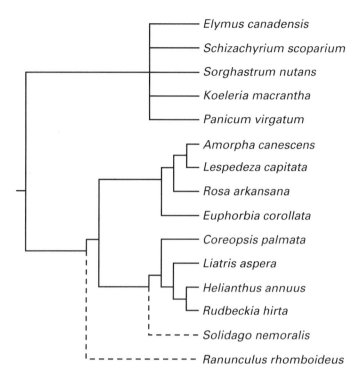

Elymus canadensis

Schizachyrium scoparium

Sorghastrum nutans

Koeleria macrantha

Panicum virgatum

Amorpha canescens

Lespedeza capitata

Rosa arkansana

Euphorbia corollata

Coreopsis palmata

Liatris aspera

Helianthus annuus

Rudbeckia hirta

Solidago nemoralis

Ranunculus rhomboideus

Figure 5.8 A phylogeny for a designed prairie community, prepared using Phylomatic. Branch lengths indicate degree of evolutionary relatedness.

BIODIVERSITY INCREASES STABILITY

Diverse communities have higher levels of ecosystem function and perform multiple functions better than simple communities, especially when they contain organisms with a range of functional traits. They are also able to maintain these functions over time, despite environmental fluctuations.

Continuing their work at the Cedar Creek grasslands in Minnesota, David Tilman and Johannes Knops, this time with Peter Reich (2006), seeded 168 plots with a random mix of either one, two, four, eight, or sixteen perennial grassland species, including C3 grasses, C4 grasses, legumes, nonlegume forbs, and woody species. For 2 years they allowed the plants to establish and begin to grow in. Each August for 10 years thereafter, they clipped the aboveground biomass of areas within each plot and calculated the annual productivity. Over the decade of their experiment the plots experienced widely different climatic conditions from year to year. Average high temperature during the growing season varied by almost 3°C, and precipitation varied more than twofold. These variations are reflected in the productivity of the low-diversity plots. In the high-diversity plots, however, productivity was much more consistent. The most diverse plots were 70 percent more stable than the monocultures tested.

As we have noted from the beginning, plant species have different environmental needs. These different needs allow them to coexist in communities. Even if a drought, for instance, stresses all the members of a grassland community, some will feel the effect sooner than others, and some will have their growth more curtailed. This asynchrony evens out the productivity of the entire community when there are more species. Just as mutual funds purchase multiple stocks in order to achieve more consistent yields, diverse plant communities achieve greater temporal stability because of a "portfolio effect." Although the individual populations within the community fluctuate in relative abundance and performance, overall ecosystem processes are maintained (fig. 5.9). Also, because diverse communities are more productive overall (an effect called overyielding), a loss of productivity of a set amount has less of a percentage effect on them than on a simpler, less productive community.

We know that not all species are equally abundant in communities (see chap. 2), however, and that even some infrequent species can have an outsized effect on community properties (see chap. 7). That is, not all species within a community are equal in terms of their impact on ecosystem function. Where one or a few species drive overall ecosystem function, the impact of environmental change on those species will affect overall community properties, even where diversity is present (Hillebrand et al. 2008). Communities with greater evenness, or where dominance can switch between several species depending on environmental conditions, will experience greater stabilizing effects from diversity.

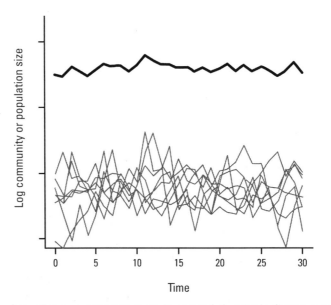

Figure 5.9 Because of asynchronous responses to environmental changes in diverse communities, even when individual populations (thin lines below) fluctuate in size, community size (thick line above), which is the sum of population sizes, remains stable. (From Loreau, M. 2010. Linking biodiversity and ecosystems: Towards a unifying ecological theory. *Philosophical Transactions of the Royal Society: Biological Sciences* 365:49–60.)

INCREASE STABILITY WITH GREATER DIVERSITY

No year of weather is quite like the last, or the next. Heat waves, hurricanes, droughts, and record snows come and go unpredictably. Even when we have chosen plants carefully for the conditions where they are planted, those conditions can change from one season to another. On top of this, global climate patterns that we and our plantings have grown accustomed to seem to be shifting (see chap. 10). Our landscapes have to live with these realities and maintain the high level of function we expect from them, whether that function is to produce lots of growth and look full, to filter stormwater, to provide food to migrating birds, or all of the above. Again, ecologists have demonstrated, diversity holds the key.

We have seen that for a designed plant community to function ecologically, it should include a diverse list of species, and that these species should represent a range of attributes on important functional traits. In order for the plant communities we install to be able to maintain the high levels of function we expect of them year after year, each cluster of functionally similar species must include plants with different responses to environmental change. We can think of this in somewhat the same way as we did with fundamental versus realized niches (see chap. 3). Although all of our fastest-growing grasses, to take an example, would prefer warm temperatures and moderate precipitation, one of them may still be able to grow reasonably well the summer it rains less. We need to be sure to include that grass in the mix, along with the one that can grow reasonably well the summer it is unusually cool. Incorporating a diverse mix of species ensures that our portfolio of plants can perform in all conditions. Recall too that functional trait diversity exists below the species level, within populations (see chap. 2). Planting genetically diverse populations creates a secondary stabilizing asynchrony.

Suddenly, when we add the dimension of time, our mix of six or twelve or sixteen species becomes a community of twenty-four or forty-eight. Not all these species need to be represented by large populations. Communities that maintain ecosystem function over time using diversity will fluctuate in their composition. During the year or series of years that are warm with moderate precipitation, one species may increase in biomass and relative abundance. During a drought, the first species may decline and another take its place. In communities of longer-lived plants, these effects may not become evident until years later. The designer's art in diverse communities is not to set the exact proportions and blends of different plants but to create a mix of plants that can respond dynamically to changing conditions.

CONCLUSION

So far, the transition to a human-dominated landscape has come at the cost of an epochal loss of global and local biodiversity. Habitat destruction and introduction of invasive species are two of the principal drivers of biodiversity loss for which landscape designers are partially responsible. Going forward, we need to find ways to use designed landscapes to meaningfully support and conserve biodiversity, especially of endemic species and locally adapted populations. We also need to adopt a mindful approach to the use of exotic species, working to control established invasives and being sure not to introduce new ones.

Creating landscapes that harbor diverse plant, animal, and microscopic life is not merely a matter of acting responsibly. Ecologists have proven that ecosystem function is tied to biodiversity. Even functions as basic as productivity and retaining nutrients—growing well and not needing constant fertilization—are improved in more diverse plantings. If we are to ask our built landscapes to provide more and more of the ecosystem services formerly provided by the natural environment, that is, to perform multiple functions consistently over time, we will need to build them as diverse ecosystems. The biodiversity of an ecological landscape is not a virtue but a necessity.

6. The Stuff of Life: Promoting Living Soils and Healthy Waters

One of the most incredible ecosystems has long remained invisible, though it is right beneath our feet. In the landscaping world there has been a tendency to treat soil as a crude substrate into which to stick plants, as if it were the chunk of foam at the base of a florist's creation. Most gardeners are taught to assess a few simple criteria: soil texture, pH, amount of organic matter, and nutrient levels. If a soil is in the proper range for all of these, it is good to go. If not, adjust as needed. This approach fails to recognize the complexity of the soil ecosystem and all the ways that, if we can keep that ecosystem humming, it will do important work for us.

Like every ecosystem, soil is an interconnected physical and biological system. The physical attributes of soils—such as their texture, structure, and vertical profile—reveal their history and influence how they hold or drain water and retain or leach nutrients. These attributes have been appreciated and described scientifically for many decades. The great revolution of recent years has been appreciating the vast intricacy of the biological component of soils. One gram of soil, filling perhaps a quarter of a teaspoon, can contain as many as one billion bacteria from as many as 20,000 species. Viruses far outnumber bacteria in the soil, and in many soils fungi have ten times the biomass of all other soil organisms combined (Sumner 2000). Soil organisms cover a range of sizes from the microscopic, such as bacteria and viruses, to the visible and familiar, such as earthworms and prairie dogs. They also include fantastical creatures such as water bears.

Water bears, or tardigrades, are between a tenth and a half of a millimeter in length and look like tiny chewy gummy bears or, on closer magnification, eight-legged rhinoceroses. They are consumers, and most species of water bear feed on plants or bacteria by sucking out the contents of cells. Most impressively, they are able to dehydrate and suspend their metabolism for years at a time. In this state they have even survived being exposed for days to the vacuum of space, after which, when rehydrated, they waddled off and laid eggs (Jönsson et al. 2008). Mostly, they just use this strategy to survive dry periods in the soil or to travel on the winds. Life in the soil can be wondrous strange.

Soil organisms, in their multiplicity, join in complex food webs (fig. 6.1). Many soil organisms are decomposers and thrive on fallen plant litter, excrement, and the dead bodies of other organisms. There are primary producers in the soil as well, though, notably plants, whose roots both are fed on by consumers and intentionally feed symbiotic microorganisms by leaking sugars or forming cellular structures where both cohabitate. Depending on the species, consumers such as nematodes (roundworms) can become pests on plant roots or can aid plants by eating the hyphae of pathogenic fungi (see chap.

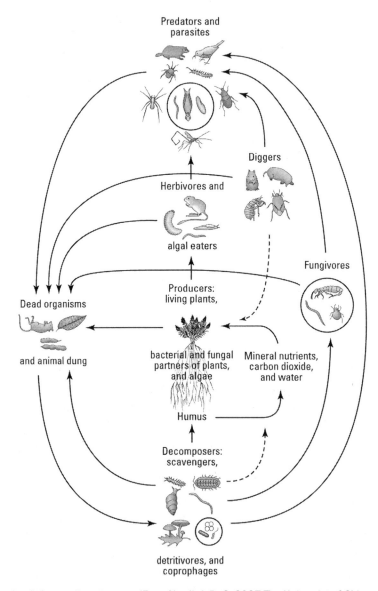

Figure 6.1 Food web for a soil ecosystem. (From Nardi, J. B. © 2007 The University of Chicago. *Life in the Soil: A Guide for Naturalists and Gardeners.* The University of Chicago Press.)

7). Higher-level consumers such as predatory mites and wolf spiders eat a variety of organisms and are themselves prey for shrews and garter snakes. Thus, as in all ecosystems, energy flows through the soil.

Thanks to gravity and the movement of water, the soil is the place where many materials cycle. Organic materials that come to rest on the surface of the soil are broken down by the actions of insects and fungi. Smaller particles are drawn down into the soil by earthworms, ants, and other creatures. Much of the carbon and nutrients these particles contain are incorporated into microbial biomass and, on the death of the microorganisms, made available again in the soil. The cycling and storage of materials is one of the essential ecosystem services that soils provide. We have long appreciated this service for its role in agriculture and our own sustenance. Only recently are we coming to understand the global significance of the carbon reservoir that soils provide (see chap. 10). A properly functioning soil ecosystem can hang on to materials and provide the fertility needed to grow adapted plants, without the need for introduced fertilizers, whether synthetic or organic.

Soils are also the point of interface between terrestrial life and water. Water contributes to soil formation, and the movement of water drives many soil processes. Soils also greatly influence water, how quickly it moves, how much is taken up by plants, and what its turbidity and chemistry are. These services affect the character and health not only of the immediate ecosystem but of aquatic and marine ecosystems downstream. Whenever we work with soils, we are also working with water. All grading and soil improvement work should be thought of in this dual way.

For a designed landscape to function ecologically, it must have a functioning soil ecosystem. Let's dig into this world beneath our feet.

SOIL TEXTURE AND STRUCTURE INFLUENCE ECOSYSTEM PROCESSES

The soil ecosystem is a three-dimensional maze of solid particles, water that adheres to these particles, and air (fig. 6.2). This physical structure affects soil life and belowground ecosystem processes.

Mineral soil particles fall into one of three classes—sand, silt, and clay—depending on their size. Despite our sense of the tininess of a grain of sand, sand is the largest class of particles. Silt, the intermediate particle size, is well known as the fertile result of annual flooding in river systems. Clay particles are the smallest. The texture of a soil is determined by its mix of particle sizes (fig. 6.3). A loam contains a fairly even mixture of the three particle sizes. Soils with more extreme concentrations of one particle bear the name of that particle. Texture influences how water and air move through a soil. Sand has very high porosity and drains water quickly. Clay soils tend to hold water and swell when wet, thus reducing the ability of air to diffuse through the soil. Texture also affects the availability of soil nutrients to plants. The smaller the particle, the higher the ratio of surface to volume, and the more likely nutrients are to be bound to the surface of the particle.

Soil particles are much more than different-sized pieces of rock, however. Another critical component of soils is organic matter, which is a general term for all the compounds that accumulate in the soil from the decay of plants and other once-living organisms. When organic matter has been fully broken down, it forms a dark and stable material known as humus. At a microscopic level, humus is coiled in intricate shapes that allow it to hold both water and nutrients.

In a healthy soil ecosystem, mineral particles join together with humus, plant roots, root exudates,

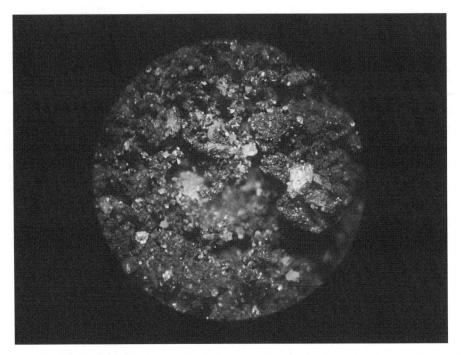

Figure 6.2 Soil (magnified here 30×) has a three-dimensional structure of particles, peds, and pores. (Photo by Joyce Arias.)

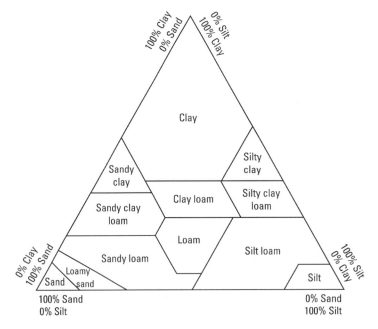

Figure 6.3 Soil texture is determined by the relative percentages of its three mineral components: sand, silt, and clay. Soils with a more even mix of particles are known as loams.

and microbial excretions to create larger aggregates known as peds. Peds form in different shapes, from the granular to the prismatic, and range in size from millimeters to centimeters. The arrangement of peds and the pores between them determines a soil's structure. Along with texture, soil structure also greatly affects the movement of water and air through a soil, as well as the movements of plant roots and macroinvertebrates.

When it rains, soil pores fill with water, driving out the air that filled those spaces. As water moves down through the soil it draws fresh air from the atmosphere into the soil. It is well understood that plants need water in order to survive and that their roots move through the soil in search of water and nutrients. However, it is easy to forget that the cells that make up plant roots also need air in order to respire. Although some plants have developed adaptations to hydric soils that bring air to their roots through plant tissues (see chap. 1), most rely on the air in soil pores to sustain their roots. Thus the life of roots and the plants they support is governed by the movement of water and air through the soil.

Soil bacteria are affected by the movement of water and air too. Aerobic bacteria predominate in well-drained soils and, like plants and people, use oxygen as the terminal electron acceptor in their respiration. Anaerobic bacteria, both obligate and facultative, use oxidized forms of other elements, such as iron, sulfur, and nitrogen. The fact that bacteria have reduced (stripped the oxygen from) iron oxides contributes to the grayish cast of hydric soils. Reduced sulfur creates the "rotten" smell of wetland soils. Reducing nitrogen releases it as a gas back into the atmosphere, which is why wetlands are so important in preventing nitrogen pollution. Populations of aerobic and anaerobic bacteria, and the respiratory pathway facultative anaerobes use, fluctuate in response to soil moisture levels.

Thus the physical properties of soil—its texture and structure—influence the movement of water and air through the soil, which in turn influence the survival and growth of plants, fluctuations in populations of soil organisms, and rates of denitrification.

PRESERVE AND ENHANCE SOIL STRUCTURE

Gardeners are very interested in soil texture because of its relation to the movement of soil water and air. If the soil around the roots of unadapted plants remains saturated, the roots can die. Disease-causing organisms such as *Phytophthora* also proliferate in wet soil. For these reasons, gardeners most often worry that their soil is too "heavy," meaning too full of clay. It can be tempting to try to improve the texture of a clay soil by adding sand. Consider the soil texture triangle, however. To change even a not-very-clay soil that is 50 percent clay, 30 percent silt, and 20 percent sand into a loam requires reversing the proportions of sand and clay. For every cubic yard of existing soil, you would have to add 1.05 cubic yards of sand and 0.3 cubic yards silt, more than doubling your soil volume. To add a lesser amount of sand to clay is the recipe for making bricks. Unless one has a ready supply of sand and room to grow, or is in the brick-making business, it is much easier to work with existing soil.

In a designed landscape, the true key to influencing the movement of water and air through a soil is to preserve and improve its structure. Compaction of a soil by vehicle or foot traffic collapses soil pores and breaks down peds. Once a soil is compacted, its structure can be very difficult to restore; therefore it is important to avoid compaction in the first place. Design landscapes to avoid affecting areas of healthy soil. During construction, fence off areas that will be planted to protect them from compaction. In finished landscapes, keep traffic to roads and paths. When it is necessary to bring vehicles or equipment onto a soil with good structure, give preference to low ground pressure machines or spread the load with mats or sheets of plywood. It is especially important to stay off soils when they are wet. Tilling a soil, whether by double-digging, rototilling, or using a plow, can also damage its structure by breaking up larger peds. There is a further danger of creating a compacted hardpan directly beneath the tilled soil.

Incorporating organic matter into a soil can improve its structure. The fastest way to do this is to till or dig compost into the top foot of the soil. Because of the dangers of tilling, however, this method is probably best reserved for already-compacted or new and unstructured soils. On existing soils that have or are developing structure, top-dressing with compost is a better option. Soil organisms will incorporate this material deeper into the soil without damaging its structure. Encouraging plant growth and leaving residues and trimmings in place also increases soil organic matter and structure over the years. This natural process can be accelerated by adding organic mulches, which additionally help protect a soil from surface compaction.

NATURAL SOILS HAVE A VERTICAL PROFILE

Natural soils are not uniform mixtures of peds and pores. They have a definite vertical structure known as a soil profile. The profile is formed by physical and biological processes that create distinguishable levels, or horizons, in the soil (fig. 6.4). Starting at the surface, soils commonly have an O horizon of mostly undecomposed organic matter that has accumulated from fallen leaves, branches, and so on. Beneath the O horizon is the A horizon. Here humus is mixed with mineral particles (sand, silt, and clay). This is the soil horizon of greatest biological activity and is commonly known as topsoil. Rainfall leaches small particles and nutrients out of the A horizon into the B horizon below. The B horizon contains little or no organic matter; it is commonly known as subsoil. Beneath the B horizon is the C horizon of mostly mineral soil (siliceous and calcareous soils of prehistoric biological origin are also included) little affected by the soil forming processes taking place above it. Plant roots and burrowing animals can reach into the C horizon. Beneath the C horizon is hard bedrock.

It is easy to think, as many practitioners do, that the most important properties of soil lie in just the topsoil. In fact, each of the soil horizons contributes to the overall properties of a soil, such as its fertility, water-holding capacity, drainage, and resistance to compaction. The C horizon serves as the long-term source of the mineral soil of a site and determines many of its characteristics. For instance, a soil with a limestone C horizon will probably remain alkaline despite repeated amendment. The C horizon also provides additional rooting volume for plants, helps determine how soils drain, and influences soil strength. The drainage properties of the B horizon have as much or more to do with water relations in the topsoil than the texture or structure of the topsoil itself. Plants that need or are adverse to well-drained soils will do best with the appropriate subsoil beneath them. B horizon soil also provides additional nutrients and offers a strong base for plants to root into and gain support. The organic matter in the O horizon protects the soil surface from erosion by wind and water, moderates soil surface temperatures, retains water, and returns nutrients to the soil below.

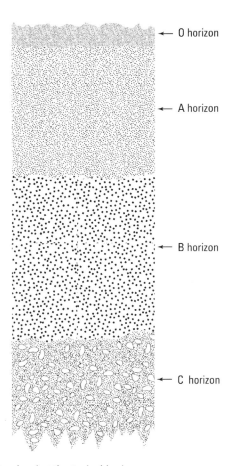

Figure 6.4 A generic soil profile, showing the typical horizons.

PRESERVE AND CREATE SOIL PROFILES

Careless yet common construction practices can devastate soil profiles. On large development projects, the site is often stripped of all vegetation, and the topsoil is removed and either stockpiled or sold. Subsoils are then used for regrading, with contours often being reshaped dramatically across lot lines. Subsoils and engineered fill are piled as backfill around structures. Finally, a thin layer of topsoil (whether from the stockpile, a commercial supplier, or another site) is then spread over the surface. The resulting soil profile scarcely resembles the preexisting profile or the profile of productive agricultural soils it is asked to imitate to grow lawns and beds of ornamental plants. Construction projects within existing landscapes often lead to mixing of the soil profile, with topsoil buried in trenches, subsoil brought to the surface, and strange agglomerations of the two spread as the new growing medium.

The best alternative to these destructive practices is to preserve existing healthy soils by siting buildings and roads carefully, minimizing grading, and tightly limiting the areas disturbed by construction. Where soils are disturbed, efforts should be made to re-create full soil profiles. Store topsoil and subsoil from excavations separately and replace in the proper sequence, to the same depth, and at the same bulk density as found in nearby undisturbed soil. In areas of fill, or when using manufactured soils, we should also create entire soil profiles and not just hide rubble beneath topsoil or lay deep topsoil with the idea that it will be better for plants. Building soil profiles can be more economical than using homogeneous fill. It also creates opportunities for the reuse of several different materials, whether from the site or brought in, including stones, subsoil, and organic debris. Many soil profiles include an O horizon. Plants accustomed to growing in soils with a thick O horizon will appreciate having this layer re-created in a landscape setting with organic mulch.

It is also important that the different horizons in the soil profile interface properly. Sharp discontinuities between layers can prevent water movement through a soil and can discourage roots from penetrating deeper horizons. When laying a soil profile, where two horizons meet, roughly mix a couple of inches of the two materials together before spreading the remainder of the upper horizon. The O horizon also needs to interface directly with the topsoil. The commercial practice of laying a fabric barrier between mulch and soil, in the mistaken belief that it will prevent weeds, interferes with the movement of air and water into the topsoil and cuts off the biological life of the soil from the organic matter it needs in the O horizon.

SOILS VARY BY REGION

Hans Jenny was an influential soil scientist who in 1941 proposed a simple yet powerful formula to explain the formation of soils:

$$s = f(cl, o, r, p, t),$$

meaning soils are the product of climate, organisms, topography, parent material, and time. As climate, organisms, and topography act on parent material over time, they create regionally distinct soil orders and local variations.

As we saw before, the simplest way to describe a climate is in terms of temperature and moisture (see chap. 1). Temperature and moisture both influence the development of soils. At higher temperatures, chemical reactions in the soil occur more quickly. In regions that are frozen for parts of the year, weathering is a much slower process. For example, Jenny produced evidence showing that among unglaciated soils in the eastern United States, soils in the north have significantly less clay (smaller, weathered particles) than similar soils in the warmer south. In humid regions, rainfall percolates through the soil and leaches dissolved materials along the way. This differentiates the A and B horizons, with the A horizon being leached of materials that accumulate in the B horizon. Higher rainfall also more thoroughly weathers material, creating more clay particles. In arid regions, on the other hand, most of the water that enters the soil through precipitation evaporates back out, leaving in place the dissolved materials. Jenny showed that arid soils contain higher concentrations of various nutrients.

Organisms are another factor in the development of soils. Plant roots penetrate the soil and, when they die, leave behind gaps and channels, contributing to soil structure. They also leave behind organic matter, as do the booms and busts of microbial populations. Because climate also determines the biota of a region, it can be difficult to tease apart the influences of climate and organisms on soil. Jenny succeeded in differentiating the two in the prairie–forest transition in the Midwest. Here, in a broad stretch of land with similar climate, some areas are covered in prairie and others in trees. Beneath the prairie, Jenny found, organic matter and total nitrogen were higher than in forest soils. In the forest, soil carbon was largely in the surface layer (O horizon). Leaching was also higher in the forest soil.

Because of the governing influence of climate and organisms, soil types are distributed across the earth's surface in much the same way as biomes (fig. 6.5). The different soils of different regions are identified by the widely applied US Department of Agriculture (USDA) Soil Taxonomy as soil orders (USDA 1999). The USDA taxonomy currently recognizes twelve major soil orders: alfisols, andisols, aridisols, entisols, gelisols, histosols, inceptisols, mollisols, oxisols, spodisols, ultisols, and vertisols. Ultisols are the red clay soils of the southeastern United States. Heavy precipitation has weathered these soils greatly and leached them of base ions such as calcium and magnesium. The resulting acidity supports forests of typical southeastern plants such as pines and azaleas, which in turn contribute moderate levels of organic matter to the soil. Mollisols form in grasslands. They are most notable for the thick A horizon, filled with organic matter left by generations of grass roots. Precipitation is adequate to move carbonates and clay particles from the A to the B horizon but not so great as to strongly leach the soil. These are the fabulously productive soils of the US corn belt. Aridisols form in dry regions such as the US Southwest that are incapable of supporting mesophytic vegetation. Lack of vegetation leads to low levels of soil organic matter. As Jenny observed, aridisols contain high levels of materials such as calcium carbonate that are leached from soils in more humid regions. In some cases this calcium

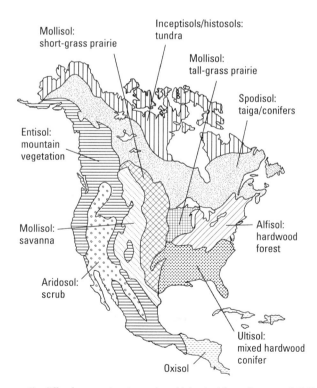

Figure 6.5 Like biomes, soils differ from region to region. (Adapted from Forman, R. T. T., and M. Godron. Copyright ©1986. *Landscape Ecology*. Reproduced with permission of John Wiley and Sons, Inc.)

carbonate hardens into an impermeable layer in the soil known as caliche. Although mineral nutrients are present, they may not be available because of the generally high pH (alkalinity) of aridisols.

WORK WITH REGIONAL SOILS

As we have seen, plants play a role in developing the soil profiles of each major order. In turn, plants are closely adapted to these types of soils. When we try to grow them in other soils, they can suffer. Nothing is sadder than an azalea planted not in the ultisols of the Southeast but in an alkaline aridisol. Miracid may fend off chlorosis for a little while, but the poor plant will never thrive. And yet people persist: If the soil isn't right, we'll fix it! The predominant influence on American horticulture of garden traditions carried from England to the eastern United States has left a default preference among gardeners for soils that are rich, loamy, and moist. This is an excellent description of a mollisol, but it does not fit the soil of many other regions. It is possible to recreate such soils in a small area of a garden or in a container, but to do so across an entire designed landscape is an enormous effort and kicks against the pricks of long-term soil-forming processes. We should instead adapt our choice of plants and our methods of soil preparation to the soils of our region and site.

David Salman, president and chief horticulturist at Santa Fe Greenhouses and High Country Gardens in New Mexico, is well aware of regional differences in soils. Over the course of his career, he has developed reliable methods for growing xeric plants beautifully in a garden and landscape setting, principally in the arid West. Among the keys to success, he says, are matching plants to the soils they are going into and preparing those soils properly. Whereas many of our favorite garden plants have persisted in cultivation in part because they are adaptable to a wide range of soil conditions, native plants can be more particular. If some of the natives that Salman sells are planted in a soil that is too rich, they may grow extravagantly for a season but never come back, effectively turning long-lived perennials into annual bedding plants. Plants such as the spectacular bush morning glory (Ipomoea leptophylla) need a well-drained, sandy soil. Others, such as poppy mallow (Callirhoe involucrata), do best on clay soils. Some xeric plants, such as wild four o'clock (Mirabilis multiflora), are more forgiving, as long as they do not get too much water (fig. 6.6). The High Country Gardens catalog (available at http://www.highcountrygardens.com) describes the most suitable soil for each plant.

Salman thinks that because we expect the plants in gardens to perform better than plants in a reclamation project, a little soil improvement is worthwhile. It will also help a plant make the transition from the nursery environment out into the landscape. If a plant is well suited to the soil it is going into, only moderate amendment is necessary. The goal is not to create a loamy garden soil, only to address any specific deficiencies of the existing soil. Compacted soils should be loosened. To address the low organic matter of most western soils, Salman recommends the addition of some amount of compost, depending on the preferences of the plant or plants going in. To increase available nutrients for plants and soil organisms, he suggests applying a low-level organic fertilizer and a rock dust high in trace minerals. Last, Salman advocates ensuring that plants have the allies they need by inoculating the soil with mycorrhizae.

Caliche, Salman notes, is a real problem in New Mexico. Shallow-rooted perennials and grasses are less affected, but for tap-rooted perennials, shrubs, and trees, caliche can be an impenetrable barrier.

Figure 6.6 Wild four o'clock growing well in a dry, gravelly soil. (Photo by highcountrygardens.com.)

Salman says it is necessary to physically break through caliche, where it is present, either by digging deeply enough to break it up or by piercing it in planting holes with a digging bar or auger.

These are apt examples of regional soil preparation advice.

SOILS CAN VARY ACROSS A SITE

Soils are not a uniform resource, even within a region. When flying over agricultural areas, such as the American Midwest, it is easy to see variations in the soil, which are evident in the different colors of plowed fields and in changes in vegetation. Patchiness of soils can occur from very small to large scales, depending on Jenny's other two factors of soil formation: parent material and topography.

Parent material in the C horizon varies with the geology of a region and can include everything from sandstone formed at the bottom of ancient lakes to relatively recent washout from retreating glaciers. Because soils are formed from the underlying parent material, geological discontinuities can lead to soil patchiness. Along faults, near exposed intrusions of igneous rock, or where geologic strata are exposed by uplift or folding, soils derived from different parent materials can be found in close proximity. Serpentine soils, to give one example, occur patchily where ultramafic rock (igneous rock high in magnesium and iron) from the earth's mantle is exposed at the edges of continental plates and in mountain ranges (for an example of how soil patchiness influences larger processes, see chap. 9).

Areas at the edges of long-disappeared glaciers can have large deposits of glacial till. Former stream-beds can be layered with gravel and sand.

Topography also influences soils on a local scale. In Jenny's explanation, a level soil is influenced by the precipitation that falls directly on it. An upland soil is influenced by the precipitation that falls on it, minus the amount that runs off. Soil in a depression is influenced by the precipitation that falls on it, plus the amount that runs onto it from surrounding areas. This effectively creates three different soil-forming regimes in close proximity. The result is average soil in level areas, thinner soils with less organic matter in the upland areas, and more developed, organic soils in the depressions. Depressions are also more likely to be saturated with groundwater and to develop hydric soils. Vegetation also responds to topography (see chap. 1) and will further affect the development of soils at different positions in the landscape (fig. 6.7).

In addition to the twelve orders of basic soil taxonomy, soils are further subdivided into suborders, groups, subgroups, families, and series (USDA 1999). Each soil series has the same narrow range

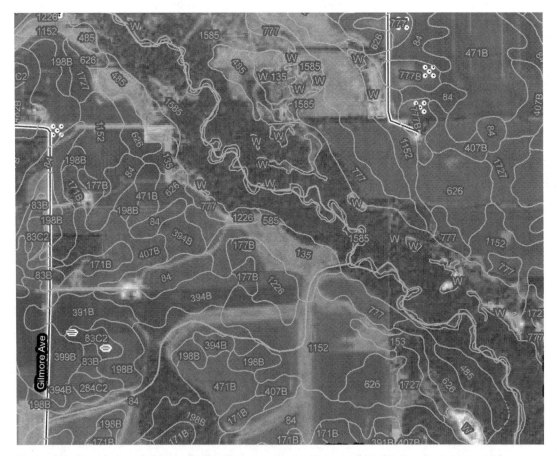

Figure 6.7 The relation of soils to topography is apparent in this map of local soil series in an area of Chickasaw County, Iowa from the web soil survey. (Courtesy of USDA Natural Resources Conservation Service.)

of characteristics, including color, texture, thickness, and pH. Soil series are named for a geographic feature near where they were first identified. For example, soils named Amarillo and Fargo identify their origins in northwestern Texas and eastern North Dakota, respectively.

KNOW YOUR SOIL

Planting plans that ignore the differences between soil patches may be doomed to failure—or, at least, to higher maintenance costs. Similarly, applying a one-size-fits-all approach to soil preparation across a site may not bring about the desired results.

Because of the patchiness of soils, it is essential when designing a landscape to examine the site's soils both by use of soil maps and by verification in the field. Although some areas of the United States remain unmapped, particularly in cities and in the mountain and desert West, detailed soil maps are available for much of the country from the Natural Resources Conservation Service (NRCS; http://websoilsurvey.nrcs.usda.gov). Field verification can be done systematically with gridded samples or, more informally, by walking the site and investigating the soil with a soil probe or by digging small pits in representative areas and at apparent transitions between soil patches (fig. 6.8). Soil samples can be sent out for testing to determine qualities that are not apparent in the field, such as pH.

Figure 6.8 Examining soils in the field is critical to understanding conditions across a site. (Photo by Jeff Vanuga, USDA Natural Resources Conservation Service.)

Ecological designers may choose to reflect and exploit soil patchiness in their plans. Large-scale soil patches can help organize different planting elements and even drive site planning. Variations in soil at a small scale can provide niches for plant species that are adapted to particular conditions. Soil preparation also must be tailored to each soil patch. For instance, upland and wetland soils are not in equal need of organic matter.

Just as with microclimates, attentiveness to variations in soil will create an appropriately diverse, and ultimately more successful, designed landscape.

SOILS IN THE BUILT ENVIRONMENT ARE LIKELY TO HAVE BEEN DISTURBED

Natural soils are the result of long-term processes: the physical breakdown of parent material, the movement of materials and water with topography, the effects of climate and vegetation to create horizons, and the development of soil aggregates and structure. Agricultural soils have been modified by humans through clearing of vegetation, tilling, amendment, and drainage. In urban and suburban areas, human impact on soils can be even more significant. Since it is in cities and suburbs that designers do much of their work, the qualities of soils in these areas are important to understand.

Suburbs are often built on agricultural land that was converted all at once. Despite these dual efforts at homogenization, the underlying soil series may still be relevant. Soils in cities are exceedingly heterogeneous, and for this reason, as well as their presumed uselessness for agriculture, they are not mapped by the NRCS soil survey. One may find anything from an undisturbed soil that has been in a park for decades or centuries to "made land" put together out of garbage and fill.

Soils in suburbs and cities have often experienced significant disruption of their physical structure (Craul 1992). Excavation and grading can bring B and C horizons to the surface or lead to uneven mixing of soil layers across a site. Imported fill and topsoil are often used. Urban soils may be contaminated with rubble, construction waste, or even footings, foundations, and paving from previous incarnations of the site (fig. 6.9). Urban soils are often compacted through construction, vehicle and foot traffic, and lack of biological activity. This compaction, along with a lack of vegetative cover and hydrocarbons from air pollution, can form a hydrophobic surface crust that prevents water penetration.

The chemistry of soils in the built environment can be affected by a number of factors. Leaching from concrete, bricks, and plaster can modify soil pH. Soils are also subject to runoff of petroleum products and salts from roads and to direct contamination with paints, solvents, detergents, and industrial waste. Air pollution can also bring high levels of heavy metals and other pollutants (see chap. 10).

Soils in developed areas are also subject to environmental conditions that affect soil formation. The urban heat island can elevate soil temperatures, particularly in soils directly adjacent to pavement and south- and west-facing structures (see chap. 1). Water may not move through altered soils as readily as it does through natural soils. Discontinuous horizons and interruptions by footings, retaining walls, and the like can lead to impoundment of water in certain areas and its dearth in others. Engineers' traditional concern for moving water away from buildings can leave urban and suburban soils, especially in small patches, dry or subject to alternating flash floods and drought, almost like desert soils.

All of these factors can make it difficult for urban and suburban soils to sustain the communities of plants, animals, and microorganisms that we would like to be present in an ecological landscape.

Figure 6.9 Soils in urban areas may scarcely resemble soils formed by natural processes. (Photo by Sarah Paulson.)

PLAN SOILS FOR THE BUILT ENVIRONMENT AND THE BUILT ENVIRONMENT FOR SOILS

When working in the built environment, our job is to restore and create soils so that they are well structured, functional, and full of life. The more highly impacted a site has been, the more important it is to get to know its soil. Historic maps can help us understand changes that have taken place on a site over time. Physical investigation with soil cores or test pits can help identify layers of fill and their boundaries. Test compaction levels in the field with a cone penetrometer. Beyond standard soil tests, testing for pollutants such as heavy metals and petroleum products can be worthwhile, especially where there is a history of industrial use on the site or nearby.

Depending on what is found during site analysis, soil work on developed sites can range from the minimal to the extreme. In older suburbs, decades of growth by lawns and trees may have developed acceptable A and B horizons. Even in cities, soil preserved around established trees may just need to have compaction alleviated, organic matter added, and the biological community stimulated. This can be accomplished with vertical mulching, using an auger or airspade to make a network of small-diameter holes under the canopy and filling them with compost and other soil amendments. In new suburbs it can be worth ignoring the initial paltry efforts at landscaping entirely, restripping the topsoil and building an appropriate soil profile from the B horizon up. In cities, areas that are largely filled with rubble or where the soil is contaminated may need to be completely excavated and replaced. In the case of heavy metal contamination, one alternative to complete excavation is phytoremediation, in which plants that are metal hyperaccumulators are grown to concentrate metals in more easily removable plant parts (Agricultural Research Service 2000).

In many high-profile urban landscape projects these days, soils are completely designed and manufactured for the site. Philip Craul (1999), a pioneer in the design of such soils, stated that the greatest challenge of such soils is to create a favorable structure. A designed soil may start with a mineral base of existing soil material or sand, which is leavened with organic matter and sometimes additional structural materials such as expanded shale. The hope is that proper soil structure will increase the likelihood of the biological community establishing itself successfully. When working on a project that requires designed soils, it is highly advisable to consult a soil scientist.

Site analysis of soils should also influence site and planting design. Areas of highly compacted or disturbed soil suggest preferred locations for buildings, paved surfaces, and other constructed elements. Where we want plants to grow, we should ensure that adequate soil volumes are present, not just for plant health but also for soil health and broader ecological function. Larger beds can somewhat reduce local heat island effects, more easily maintain populations of soil flora and fauna, allow air exchange and decomposition to take place at the soil surface, and receive and process larger volumes of water.

Where soils in the built environment differ substantially from their predevelopment condition and complete remediation is not an option, it may be difficult to reestablish communities of locally native plants. Rather than fight these soil conditions and see one's plantings taken over by invasive opportunists, it may be preferable to create communities that include adapted plants from a broader region, including cosmopolitan survivors that are long familiar in cultivation and in cities (see chap. 10).

SOILS CYCLE NUTRIENTS

There is a strong tendency to think of the fertility needs of our managed landscapes in agricultural terms. In modern industrial agriculture, the focus is on high yields. High yields translate to high nutrient needs, especially as plant biomass is removed from fields and traditional methods of nutrient management such as crop rotation and manuring have given way to fertilizing.

Fertilizers are accompanied by a host of environmental issues. The production of synthetic nitrogen fertilizer requires large amounts of fossil fuel energy. Phosphorus, potassium, and sulfur are obtained through damaging mining operations. Fertilizer runoff is a significant pollutant in streams, rivers, lakes, and even oceans, promoting eutrophication, algal blooms, and hypoxic dead zones such as the one that now appears each year in the Gulf of Mexico (fig. 6.10). The loss of vegetated stream buffers and draining of wetlands where denitrification can take place exacerbate the problem.

Along with agricultural lands, designed landscapes contribute to fertilizer runoff. Researchers in Maryland estimated that turf grass is the state's biggest crop, covering more than one million acres, including 23 percent of the state's Chesapeake Bay watershed, and receiving 86 million pounds of nitrogen fertilizer annually (Environment Maryland Research and Policy Center 2011). Much of this nitrogen enters waterways and, ultimately, the bay. Nutrient pollution has led to over 80 percent of the bay and

Figure 6.10 Nutrient-laden runoff carried from the agricultural Midwest down the Mississippi River leads to annual algal blooms and the creation of a hypoxic dead zone in the Gulf of Mexico. (Image courtesy of NASA/ Goddard Space Flight Center, Scientific Visualization Studio.)

its tidal tributaries becoming low-oxygen or no-oxygen zones in which most aquatic life cannot survive.

There are other, more ecological ways to manage nutrients in designed landscapes. Whereas energy flows through ecosystems in one direction only, nutrients and other materials such as carbon can cycle within an ecosystem as well as flow in and out (see chap. 4). Soils are the site where much of this cycling takes place, and the ability of soils to take nutrients from dead tissue and make them available for new growth is one of the key ecosystem services they provide. As the researchers at Hubbard Brook found, it is when this cycling breaks down that nutrients are lost downstream.

As nutrients cycle through the soil ecosystem they take several forms: living tissue, soil organic matter, and charged atoms and molecules. To jump into a cycle at an arbitrary point, nitrogen is contained in the proteins and DNA of all living creatures, including in short-lived fine plant roots. When these roots die, they become soil organic matter. Bacteria decompose this organic matter and incorporate a portion of the nitrogen into their own tissues. This nitrogen may return as soil organic matter when the bacteria die or may be assimilated by bacteria-eating nematodes and so on, up through the food chain. Thus the biological community in the soil forms a swarming reservoir of nutrients.

In the process of feeding on soil organic matter, the decomposing bacteria transform another portion of the nitrogen it contains into ammonium (NH_4^+). Some of this ammonium is taken up directly by growing plants. Some, because of its positive charge, is held by negatively charged clay particles and humus. Some is further transformed by soil bacteria into nitrate (NO_3^-). Because it is negatively charged, nitrate is not held by clay and enters into solution in the soil. From here it can be easily taken up by plants, or leached away, or broken down by denitrifying bacteria into nitrogen gas.

Positively charged atoms and molecules (such as ammonium) are called cations, which, as the example from the nitrogen cycle shows, can be held in the soil via electrostatic bonds they form with clay particles and humus. Soil tests often include a measure of the cation exchange capacity (CEC) as an indication of the soil's ability to hold nutrients. Plants do not absorb their nutrients directly from clay particles or pieces of organic matter, however, but from the solution that is formed as these nutrients dissolve in water in the soil. The soil solution is governed by rapid and dynamic chemical reactions, and how readily different nutrients enter the soil solution depends on its pH. While in solution, nutrients are available for uptake by plants but also susceptible to leaching away.

As with every ecosystem, nutrients also enter and leave the soil. Erosion of soil itself, leaching (as in oxisols), denitrification, and removal of plant biomass all take nutrients away. Nutrients enter the soil ecosystem through the weathering of parent material, importation of soil (as in floods), importation of organic matter (e.g., animal manure), transport in rainwater, or, in the case of nitrogen, biological fixation.

MEET PLANT FERTILITY NEEDS THROUGH NUTRIENT CYCLING

Instead of pouring on the fertilizer, we can provide plants with the fertility they need by promoting cycling of nutrients within the local ecosystem. The first step is to retain nutrients in the landscapes we manage by making use of grass clippings, leaves, and yard waste. We can leave these in place or process them on site into compost and mulch. If we need to increase nutrient levels, we can import compost and organic mulches. The most sustainable products, of course, are those made with local materials that would otherwise have gone to waste.

The organic matter we retain in our landscapes forms an important basis of the soil food web. As we have seen, as nutrients pass through this web, they are made periodically available to plants. In their informative book *Teaming with Microbes*, longtime Alaskan gardeners Jeff Lowenfels and Wayne Lewis (2010) make the astonishing claim that up to 80 percent of a plant's nitrogen needs are met by the wastes produced by bacteria- and fungi-consuming protozoa. In order to feed our plants, then, we need to build and nourish the biological community that inhabits the soil.

If we really want to supercharge our landscape with beneficial microbes, Lowenfels and Lewis advocate use of actively aerated compost teas. These easily applied concoctions come loaded with bacteria and fungi and can even be customized to introduce the organisms we are lacking most. If you were taken by their protozoa statistic, the authors also provide a recipe for growing protozoa: Soak grass clippings or hay in a bucket of nonchlorinated water and wait 3 or 4 days. When you can see the tiny organisms swimming around, your mix is ready; pour over mulch and let nature do the rest.

Cycling nutrients through the biotic and abiotic components of an active soil ecosystem is the most effective way to retain and make available the nutrients plants need to grow and to avoid the many environmental problems associated with fertilizer use.

PLANTS INTERACT WITH THE SOIL COMMUNITY

Even in the context of an active soil community, plants do not wait passively for nutrients to become available. Instead, they form complex mutualisms with a variety of soil organisms (see chap. 7).

The most well-known mutualism is between plants in the bean family (often still called legumes) and nitrogen-fixing bacteria in the genus *Rhizobium*. Different species of plants associate only with certain species of bacteria. The bacteria enter root cells, and as the plant forms a specialized nodule around them, they change shape and lose their motility, becoming what is known as bacteroids. Plants provide the bacteroids with sugars, up to 30 percent of their overall production. In these commodious surroundings, the bacteroids convert gaseous nitrogen (N_2) into ammonia (NH_3), which the plants use for their growth. Most legumes can fix nitrogen in this way. Some nonleguminous plants such as alder and bayberry (*Morella*) also form nodules with nitrogen-fixing *Frankia* bacteria.

Mycorrhizae are another common mutualism that occurs between plants and various fungi. Eighty percent of plant species surveyed in a recent study form mycorrhizal associations (Wang and Qiu 2006). Mycorrhizal fungi connect with plant roots via one of several types of structures and then extend their hyphae out beyond the plant's roots into the soil (fig. 6.11). The plant provides sugars to the

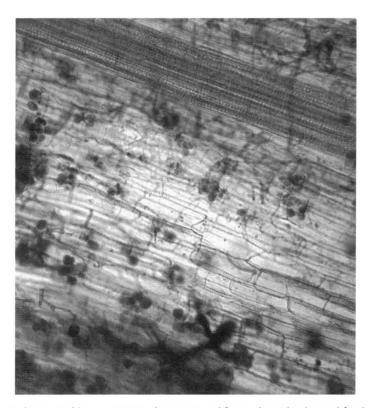

Figure 6.11 Arbuscular mycorrhizae penetrate plant roots and form arbuscules (named for their resemblance to trees), where exchanges of materials between the plant and the fungus take place. (Photo by M. S. Turmel, University of Manitoba, Plant Science Department.)

fungus, and the fungus returns nutrients such as phosphorus to the plant. Plants in association with mycorrhizae have also been shown to be more drought tolerant and more disease resistant than plants of the same species without mycorrhizae.

In recent years, plant physiologists and ecologists have come to realize that even beyond their specialized symbiotic partners, plant roots interact extensively with the soil microbial community (Walker et al. 2003). The area of soil immediately around plant roots is known as the rhizosphere, and it has different physical, chemical, and biological properties from the surrounding soil. Into the rhizosphere, roots release a variety of exudates, including mucilage, sugars, amino acids, phenolics, and various secondary metabolites. Root exudates can account for up to 20 percent of the carbon fixed by a plant, so, in evolutionary terms, they must be of value to the plant. Among their probable functions is communication with the microbial community of the rhizosphere. The microbial community in the rhizosphere of one species of plant differs from that in the surrounding soil and from that in the rhizosphere of other plant species. These favored associates may help protect plant roots against disease and may help make nutrients available in response to signals from the plant. These are complex interactions that ecologists are only now beginning to explore.

FACILITATE PLANT INTERACTIONS WITH THE SOIL COMMUNITY

In an ecological landscape, we can help plants develop relationships with their microbial associates to acquire the nutrients they need. As our understanding of the intricate relations between plant roots and the soil community develops, horticultural practices are evolving too. More and more plants are being grown in media that contain mycorrhizae. Commercial preparations of mycorrhizae and beneficial bacteria are also available for mixing into backfill at time of planting. To be sure that plants have the soil microbes they need, one can also inoculate plantings with small amounts of soil taken from around the roots of a nearby similar plant community that is already well established.

Microbes, as much as plants, need good soil structure to survive. Tilling or digging soils destroys networks of fungal hyphae. Compaction that reduces drainage and air movement through soil can decimate populations of beneficial bacteria. Once a living soil has been established, the best prescription is to leave it in place and let plants feed the soil community, both through surface litter and through their roots.

If we want to increase the amount of nitrogen cycling through our landscape ecosystem, one method is to use biological nitrogen fixation. This has been a long-standing part of traditional agriculture across the world. In Europe, farmers alternated leguminous plants such as clover or beans with other crops. In the Americas, one of the "three sisters" of interplanted crops, along with corn and squash, was nitrogen-fixing beans. In a landscape setting we can also interplant ornamental legumes and other nitrogen fixers, from herbaceous perennials to large trees. Clover makes a good addition to turfgrass lawns, for instance. Or nitrogen-fixing plants such as false indigo (*Baptisia australis*) or wild lilac (*Ceanothus* spp.) can be incorporated into a planting design. In order for nitrogen fixation to take place, soils may have to be inoculated with the appropriate strain of bacteria. Remember also that these plants are themselves incorporating all the nitrogen their bacteroids fix. The only way to make it available to other plants is by getting their biomass into the soil, through leaf drop, using their trimmings as mulch, or by eventually killing the plant and letting it (or at least its roots) decompose in situ.

ANIMALS INFLUENCE SOIL PROPERTIES

Animals, as well as microbes, have a tremendous effect on soil structure, on the movement of water and air in soils, and on nutrient cycling (Hole 1981). In any acre of ground, more animals probably live within the soil than above it. These include nematodes, mites, springtails, and our friends the tardigrades. Many other organisms, such as ants, ground-nesting wasps, and ground squirrels, spend part of their life or part of their life cycle in the soil and part above it. Even animals that live wholly above the soil, such as bison (*Bison bison*), can have a significant effect on it.

By seeking safety, shelter, and food, animals alter the physical structure of soil. Burrowing animals create voids ranging in size from bear dens to ant tunnels. Many animals backfill their tunnels, either with loosened soil (moles), their own excrement (earthworms), or plant and animal parts (ant refuse chambers, predatory wasps). The net effect of digging and loosening the soil, and incorporating organic matter, is to increase the soil volume. Charles Darwin's last book, and the one that sold the best during his lifetime, was *The Formation of Vegetable Mould through the Action of Worms with Observations on Their Habits*. Darwin (1881) carefully observed worms in the fields around his residence at Down House and performed clever experiments. In 1842, for example, Darwin spread a layer of broken chalk over one of his fields in order to track the amount of soil and castings that earthworms brought to the surface. When he dug a trench across the field 29 years later, he found the chalk still evident 7 inches beneath the surface. Darwin concluded,

> The plough is one of the most ancient and most valuable of man's inventions; but long before he existed the land was in fact regularly ploughed, and still continues to be thus ploughed by earthworms. (Darwin 1881: 313)

The plow is a poor metaphor for earthworms, however, because where a plow breaks down soil aggregates, earthworms help create them. Their castings are a mix of mineral and organic matter, coated in fluids and microbes from the worms' alimentary canals, forming fine granules. Do note, however, that about one third of the earthworm species present in North America today, and those with the greatest populations in most areas, are introduced species from Europe and Asia. The Eurasian worms accelerate the breakdown of surface organic matter in northern forests, which has led to reduced diversity in herbaceous plant communities.

All the physical activity of soil animals influences the movement of water and air through soils. Water may preferentially penetrate voids and channels created by animals or be held temporarily in the small depressions between animal-created mounds. Where tunnels, such as those made by pocket gophers, connect to the surface at more than one point, they form a conduit for moving air through the soil.

Animals, from small invertebrates to grazing cows, are also a key link in the cycling of nitrogen and other nutrients. Apart from humankind's creation of synthetic fertilizer, animals fix no nitrogen. They concentrate it in their tissues and in their waste, however. Urine and droppings from large animals provide bursts of nutrients to soil communities. The excretions of invertebrates are distributed at a finer scale. When animals of all sizes die, the decomposition of their bodies also returns nutrients to the soil.

Figure 6.12   Soil fauna, such as this patent leather beetle (*Odontotaenius disjunctus*) and millipede (*Narceus americanus*), help break down organic matter and cycle nutrients. (Photo by Sarah Paulson.)

Dung beetles and carrion-feeding insect larvae specialize on these foods and quickly make available their nutrients to the rest of the soil community. Soil-dwelling invertebrates such as millipedes mix and aerate plant litter, breaking it into smaller pieces and coating it with microbes as they pass it through their guts (fig. 6.12).

USE ANIMALS TO IMPROVE SOIL

A healthy living soil will include a diverse fauna, along with its microscopic flora. These animals can do much of a gardener's work to make sure that the soil develops and maintains good structure, it is adequately aerated, and organic matter gets broken down into forms that are more readily accessible to microorganisms. The gardener's work then becomes maintaining a diverse soil fauna and sufficient populations of key functional groups (see chap. 5). Because many desirable soil animals live in the O and A horizons and feed on organic matter, it is important to provide them with their habitat and food-stuffs. We should leave on, not rake off, fallen leaves and twigs, allow the aboveground biomass of last year's perennials to decompose in place, or trim it neatly and spread it as mulch. Where neatness is even more prized, we can substitute application of organic mulches. Again, inoculating a newly prepared area with small quantities of soil and duff from a healthy nearby area can help jumpstart a community.

Populations of soil-dwelling vertebrates such as ground squirrels can aerate soils and help them quickly infiltrate rainwater. However, these populations can become more of a hindrance than a help if they grow too large. The same strategies recommended for all herbivores will be effective in these cases (see chap. 7). It is also worth asking whether other sources of food in the area, such as bird feeders or trash cans, are supporting elevated populations and can be eliminated.

We can also increase the fertility of soils using animals. This is the basis of the age-old practice of spreading manure and is one of the advantages of rotational grazing systems (see chap. 8). Jerome Osentowski of the Central Rocky Mountain Permaculture Institute in Basalt, Colorado had developed a small-scale system that uses animals to greatly accelerate the delivery of nutrients to his food-producing landscape. Osentowski has built a chicken yard on a slope on the property, where his small flock of chickens spends most of every day under the shade of nitrogen-fixing Siberian pea shrubs (*Caragana arborescens*), whose nutrient-rich pods they love to eat. At the top of the slope, Osentowski throws in compostable kitchen scraps, along with garden waste and hay or straw. The chickens enthusiastically pick through this mix for seeds, insects, and edible bits, turning it over, adding their manure, and all the while kicking it downhill. Periodically Osentowski opens a gate at the bottom of the yard and collects what he calls his "value-added mulch." Osentowski spreads this mulch throughout his gardens, where worms quickly break down the rich mulch and make the nutrients it contains available to soil microbes and plants. Most landscapes will not need the high levels of fertility Osentowski's system provides. However, his system shows the potential of meeting even high fertility needs through active management of nutrient cycling combining plants, microbes, and animals.

DEVELOPMENT HAS ALTERED THE NATURAL MOVEMENT OF WATER

Water is an absolute requirement for life as we know it, and its movement drives many ecological processes. Plants absorb water through their roots and use it to transport nutrients and for photosynthesis before transpiring it to the atmosphere. The availability of water affects plant growth and survival, especially during establishment. The phenologies of plant communities and entire ecosystems are synchronized with annual cycles of precipitation (see chap. 1). Temporary pools after rain can bloom with life in both forest and desert ecosystems. Cycles of wetting and drying pull air into the soil and help drive the dynamics of microbial populations. This in turn affects decomposition rates of organic matter and conversion of nitrates to nitrogen gas.

Like nitrogen and carbon, water has a cycle that brings it in and through and out of ecosystems. As is familiar to every elementary school student, water vapor in the atmosphere condenses around particulate matter to fall to the earth as rain or, depending on the temperature, snow. Here it soaks into, or runs off, the soil, entering groundwater, streams, rivers, lakes, and, at the end of a long downhill journey, the ocean. Water molecules evaporate from all these bodies of water and from soils in arid regions, sublimate from ice and snow, and transpire from plants to form the water vapor in the atmosphere that begins the cycle again.

In every watershed, the combination of climate, topography, soils, and vegetation creates a hydrologic regime around which local ecosystems and ecosystem processes have formed. Urban development, agriculture, and other human activities can radically disrupt this regime (fig. 6.13). Across North

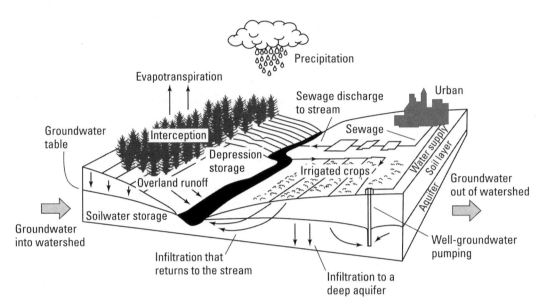

Figure 6.13 The hydrologic cycle, showing both natural processes (on the left) and alterations to the cycle resulting from development (on the right).

America, huge acreages of wetlands have been filled or drained. Dams directly alter the hydrology and ecology of streams and rivers. Wells can lower the water table, and septic systems discharge nutrients into groundwater. Land clearing reduces evapotranspiration. Soil compaction reduces infiltration. Impervious surfaces such as rooftops, parking lots, and roads keep water from soaking into the ground. Less subsurface flow of water reduces the base flow of streams. Instead, water flows quickly off hard surfaces during storms and concentrates in small waterways, incising banks and damaging habitat. In many cities buried storm drains have literally taken the place of small stream systems. Where stormwater systems are combined with sanitary sewers, even minor rain events can overwhelm the system, releasing untreated wastewater full of nutrients and chemicals into rivers, bays, and oceans.

USE GREEN INFRASTRUCTURE TO RESTORE PREDEVELOPMENT HYDROLOGY

In the past two decades a major shift has taken place in the civil engineering and landscape architecture professions' handling of stormwater, one that aims to counter the negative effects of conventional development and restore a measure of the hydrologic regime that existed previously. The newer approach emphasizes open spaces, vegetation, and living systems as key elements in stormwater management, all of which are called green infrastructure.

The Menomonee Valley Community Park, west of downtown Milwaukee, Wisconsin, provides an example of green infrastructure in action. The valley was once a wide estuary where the Menomonee River entered Lake Michigan (Gurda 2012). Cattails, rushes, and large expanses of wild rice grew, giving the valley its name, from the Algonquin word for wild rice, *menomin*. In the spring, fish and ducks bred in abundance in the marshland. As the city expanded, however, development encroached. Up to 22 feet of

Figure 6.14 A filtration basin planted with native species in Menomonee Valley Community Park, Milwaukee captures and treats runoff from an adjacent light industrial development. Smokestacks are a reminder of the Menomonee Valley's heavy industrial past. (Photo courtesy of Wenk Associates.)

fill (from surrounding bluffs and permissive dumping) was brought in, and the river was canalized and lined with rail spurs and docks. Agricultural processing industries, such as meat-packing plants, tanneries, and breweries, filled the valley floor, followed by heavy manufacturing of engines and rail cars. The waters that once teemed with wild rice and ducks churned instead with noxious waste.

As local industries declined or moved away, the valley grew more blighted, and several redevelopment efforts were made. In 1999 the Menomonee Valley Partners was formed to revitalize the valley economically, culturally, and ecologically. This combination can be seen in a project in the 100-plus-acre former Milwaukee Road Shops property that pairs a zone of light industrial development with the community park, providing public access to the river, recreational opportunities, and treatment of all the stormwater from the adjacent industrial area.

To capture and filter stormwater, landscape architects Wenk Associates designed a linked series of catchment basins (fig. 6.14). Stormwater piped from the industrial zone enters the park at several outfalls, where larger particles drop out in settling pools. Overflow from these pools spreads across shallow basins, where a clay cap on top of the contaminated fill prevents water from mixing with remaining hazardous substances, while an infiltration layer made of recycled concrete from the demolition of a nearby highway interchange allows the absorption of large volumes of stormwater. A planting soil profile was placed on top of the infiltration layer and seeded with native wet prairie species. The water infiltrated in the shallow basins drains to a swamp forest along the river's edge, where trees such as swamp white oak (*Quercus bicolor*) and tamarack (*Larix laricina*) provide further filtration and transpire a portion of the accumulated volume before it is released to the river itself.

This system has proven its ability to provide ecosystem services in practice (see chap. 4). When a hundred-year storm deluged the area in 2007, the stormwater basins were able to fully absorb the large volume of water and slowly release it to the river. Thanks to both physical and biological filtration, the water that entered the river and Lake Michigan beyond was far cleaner than it would have been if it had gone directly into a storm drain. No one would mistake the Menomonee Valley today for the wild rice marsh that existed before development, but the stormwater treatment system designed for the Community Park duplicates important aspects of the natural hydrology, allowing economic redevelopment of the brownfield site to go forward while improving water quality in the river and Lake Michigan.

MEET PLANT WATER NEEDS THROUGH CONTOURING AND DRAINAGE

Water is not merely something to be slowed, cleansed, and sent on its way. It is a resource that keeps alive every living thing on the planet. That is why we love fountains and pools in our landscapes. And it is why nearly every garden includes a source of water, if not an entire computer-controlled irrigation system. Water can also be a destructive force. It can erode hillsides, dig gullies, undermine paving and foundations, push over trees, and deposit mud, rocks, and debris in alarming places. Every designed landscape walks a balance between having too little water and too much.

If we have matched our plants to our climate, then what we grow should be able to survive on natural precipitation alone (see chap. 1). But within each biome live many different communities of plants, some in drier sites, others in wetter. Manipulating the flow of water with contouring and rainwater harvesting techniques can move water away from where it is a problem to where it is a resource, dissipate its destructive power, and create a range of conditions suitable to growing a variety of plants.

Where we do not want water, such as around the foundations of buildings, we can use grading and drainage channels to direct the water away. These areas then become places to plant more drought-tolerant plants, and the water directed away becomes a resource for other areas of the landscape. Just as Wenk Associates did at Menomonee Valley Community Park, slowing the water, spreading it out, and getting it to infiltrate recharges groundwater and keeps it available for local ecosystems. When this practice is carried out fully, dry springs can resume their flow, and once-ephemeral streams can become perennial. Although the best place to store water is in the ground, rain barrels and cisterns can also be used to capture seasonal surplus water that would otherwise leave a site and make it available during later dry spells.

Water drained from other areas of a landscape can help certain plants grow in regions where the annual precipitation figures make it seem as if they should not. Say, like Brad Lancaster of Tucson, Arizona, you wanted to grow a tree in the Sonoran Desert, the home of saguaro (*Carnegiea gigantea*) and cholla cacti. You would start by selecting a tree that is adapted to the climate, such as velvet mesquite (*Prosopis velutina*). Mesquite grows naturally on seasonally flooded terraces next to rivers and streams and along washes that concentrate rainwater from the surrounding area.

Lancaster (2008, 2012) took advantage of similarly concentrated flows of water on the impervious street beside his house. With all the appropriate permissions, Lancaster cut a series of openings in the curb that separated that street from the barren public right-of-way that ran along his and his brother's property. Behind each curb cut they dug a sunken infiltration basin and used the dirt from their excavations to build a meandering raised path through the right-of-way. Now when it rains, each basin fills with water, then overflows back into the street, sending water along to the next curb cut and basin. Lancaster also placed layers of organic mulch in each basin to keep the water that has infiltrated from evaporating away.

Thanks to these simple techniques, the previously sun-baked right-of-way is now shaded by maturing trees, without the need for extensive watering (fig. 6.15). Starting in 2010, the City of Tucson now requires all new commercial landscapes to provide 50 percent of their landscape water needs through rainwater harvesting, primarily passive techniques such as those demonstrated by Lancaster (City of Tucson 2009). Curb cuts and infiltration basins planted with trees have also been used in cities such as Portland, Oregon; these features are not for arid regions only.

A properly graded landscape will preserve built structures, create dry routes for access and circulation, and infiltrate rainwater in areas where it can recharge groundwater and nourish plants with higher

Figure 6.15   A verdant right-of-way in Tucson, irrigated with harvested rainwater. (Reprinted with permission from *Rainwater Harvesting for Drylands and Beyond*, Volume 1, 2nd Edition, 2012 by Brad Lancaster, www. HarvestingRainwater.com.)

relative water needs. The microtopography thus created opens opportunities to grow communities of plants with different water needs across a site.

CONCLUSION

Soils and water are critical components of terrestrial ecosystems and of designed landscapes. Healthy soils need good physical structure to move air and water through them and facilitate the growth of plants and the multitudinous organisms that make the soil their home. Because structure is so hard to create, we should preserve existing healthy soils wherever we can. Where we have to restore and build soils from scratch, there are many benefits to imitating natural soil profiles, recognizing that these profiles differ from region to region and that our working methods must as well. Soils also differ at small scales, especially where human activity has mixed and altered them. Success in an ecological landscape begins with an investigation of a site's soils and the tailoring of site plans, planting plans, and soil improvement plans to one's findings.

Soils are so much more than a physical medium for plant growth. They are ecosystems in their own right, full of microorganisms and animals with which plants interact, including in subtle ways we are only now beginning to recognize. As organic gardeners since Sir Albert Howard (1943) have propounded, the key to plant growth lies in the living soil. Rather than dosing the soil with fertilizers, we should encourage the natural cycling of nutrients and allow plants to seek what they need as they need it. Animals along with microbes play an important role in this cycling and in the creation and maintenance of soil structure. We should incorporate them into our soil management plans.

Water, interacting with soil, drives many ecosystem processes. We are learning how to create a built environment that imitates natural hydrology and incorporates these processes. We can also move water intentionally to minimize its destructive potential and maximize its use as a resource that gives life to the soil, to everything that inhabits it, and to the landscapes we create.

7. The Birds and the Bees: Integrating Other Organisms

Ecological landscapes are full of life. The myriad organisms that inhabit living soil are just the beginning. Spores settle on every leaf. Insects crawl along stems, while birds hop, strut, and chatter. Animals, like plants, have diversified to inhabit most every climate. They have further diversified to exploit different plants in each environment, and even different parts of those plants, and also other animals. This explains why, if we accept Robert May's (2000) estimates of the number of species on Earth, there are 300,000 plants and more than five million animals. Most of these animals are insects, and most of them have yet to be identified.

Animals are active, and by their activity they play important roles in ecosystem processes. They help cycle nutrients in the soil and affect hydrology (see chap. 6). They physically alter ecosystems by hunting and pecking, scratching and wallowing, traveling and finding shelter. Moreover, they constantly interact with other organisms. They court, compete, and, critically, eat. Herbivores eat plants, predators eat prey, and ultimately decomposers consume most everything that has lived (see chap. 4).

Animals and other organisms also engage in symbiotic relationships. Symbiosis is an intimate and long-lasting relationship between individuals of two different species. Mutualisms benefit both parties in the relationship. The relationship between plants and mycorrhizae is an excellent example of mutualism (see chap. 6). Commensalisms benefit one party while doing no harm to the other. In parasitism one species benefits and the other is harmed. Plant diseases of microbial origin and the laying of eggs in other insects by parasitoid wasps are examples of parasitism. Symbioses are not trivial curiosities, the stuff of late-night nature documentaries. They are the very fabric of life. Pollination links nearly a quarter million species of flowering plants with an equal number of insects and other animals, for instance (fig. 7.1). Intimate relationships such as these develop over evolutionary time and contribute to the diversity of life on this planet.

Plants and all the organisms living in a built landscape simultaneously experience competition, trophic interactions, and possibly all three types of symbiotic relationships. The complexity of these

Figure 7.1 A bay checkerspot butterfly (*Euphydryas editha bayensis*) feeding from, and pollinating, a tidy tips flower (*Layia platyglossa*). (Courtesy of US Fish and Wildlife Service.)

relationships makes their management difficult. But in that complexity lies the promise of an ecological approach to landscape design. We can manage organisms that act as pathogens and pests without resorting to harmful chemicals. We can work with animals' natural impulses to further our own design and management goals. The more organisms we can embrace in our landscapes, the more successful those landscapes will be.

CREATE REAL HABITAT

In order to embrace animals in the built environment, we have to provide them with the habitat they need. Habitat is simply a place that satisfies an organism's needs. In our rush to grow crops, graze cattle, lay interstates, and build box stores, we have destroyed mile after mile of habitat (see chap. 10). Among the important ecosystem services that the built environment can offer in partial compensation are living space, sustenance, and shelter for animals (see chap. 5).

Programs such as the National Wildlife Federation's (2012) Certified Wildlife Habitat initiative describe the basic requirements of creating habitat in the built environment. To function as a wildlife garden, a yard or school grounds must include food for wildlife, such as plants with edible fruit or nectar; water, as from a pond or birdbath; cover, such as a rock wall or thicket of shrubs; and a place to raise young, such as a dead snag or nesting box. The very generality of such guidelines can make them hard to translate into ecologically meaningful results, however. Many a bird and butterfly garden is a mockery of the rich natural habitat it supplants (fig. 7.2). To create real habitat entails identifying species of concern and understanding their biological needs.

Figure 7.2 Creating wildlife habitat takes more than installing a sign. (Photo by Travis Beck.)

In order to create effective habitat on a large agricultural property near Charlottesville, Virginia, Thomas Woltz of Nelson Byrd Woltz Landscape Architects enlisted the help of biologists from the State University of New York College of Environmental Science and Forestry and other universities. In the late spring of 2009, seventeen scientists joined Woltz's team of landscape architects on the property, called Oakencroft, for a 3-day "bioblitz." Specialists inventoried Oakencroft's vegetation, small mammals, birds, reptiles, amphibians, fish, aquatic invertebrates, butterflies, moths, bees, and beetles to gain an overall picture of the property's biodiversity and the conservation opportunities and challenges the property presented.

The overall goal for the property was to create a revenue-generating farm that combined sustainable agriculture with biodiversity conservation. The preliminary master plan for Oakencroft included a vineyard, a central native meadow surrounded by pastures for intensive cattle grazing, a restored riparian forest along the property's main stream, and improved connectivity between forest patches (see chap. 9). Woltz shared this master plan with the team of scientists and asked them not only to summarize the data they had collected and suggest a protocol for future monitoring but to make recommendations on how the master plan might be adjusted to benefit their species of concern.

Among the species identified at Oakencroft were the grasshopper sparrow and numerous native bees. The grasshopper sparrow (*Ammodramus savannarum*) is a small, furtive bird that builds its nest concealed on the ground in grasslands, including hayfields and old fields. Along with several other grassland birds, grasshopper sparrow populations in the region have declined by more than 95 percent. The species is identified by Partners in Flight as a conservation priority for the Mid-Atlantic Piedmont, which includes Virginia (Kearney 2003).

Writing in the *Northeastern Naturalist*, Benoît Jobin and Gilles Falardeau (2010) of the Canadian Wildlife Service reported on the habitat associations of the grasshopper sparrow in southern Québec. Grasshopper sparrows prefer grass-dominated fields with shallow litter and limited shrub cover. Studying thirty-two sites that display these characteristics, Jobin and Falardeau identified two other factors that influence grasshopper sparrow habitat preferences. Area was the most significant factor, with sites with sparrows present averaging twice the size of those where sparrows were absent. The smallest site where Jobin and Falardeau located grasshopper sparrows was 6.4 hectares. Surrounding land use was also important. Grasshopper sparrows were more likely to be present in sites surrounded by hayfields and pasture than in sites surrounded by forest. Jobin and Falardeau ended their article by calling for conservation of large remaining grasslands in southern Québec and for the promotion of farming practices that are consistent with the maintenance of breeding grasshopper sparrow populations.

Native bees also find habitat in agricultural as well as natural landscapes. However, development and landscape fragmentation, monocultural cropping, the use of pesticides, and diseases introduced through domestic honeybees have all led to dramatic declines in the populations of native bees. The familiar honeybee (*Apis mellifera*), which strongly shapes our image of how bees live, is actually an introduced species. Native North American bees are diverse in their taxonomy, behavior, nesting requirements, and food needs (Xerces Society 2011). Many are solitary, such as the mason bees, whereas some, such as bumble bees, are social. Seventy percent of native North American bees nest on the ground, in abandoned rodent burrows, or in patches of bare soil that are well drained and receive direct sunlight. The other 30 percent of native bees nest aboveground in tree cavities, for instance, or in beetle tunnels in dead wood, or inside reeds or the stems of other pithy plants. Native bees depend on nectar and pollen that they forage from flowering plants. Some species of bees are specialists, and they time their life cycle to coincide with the flowering of certain plant species. Many are generalists, however, able to forage from a wide range of flowers as long as something is blooming at all times when they are active. With colony collapse disorder threatening honeybee hives, native bees can provide important pollination services to farmers.

At Oakencroft, the blitzing ornithologists found the grasshopper sparrow at a quarter of the points they surveyed and estimated its density at 0.435 per hectare. They suggested that with proper conservation measures, the species could be increased to a density of 2.0 per hectare. Among their key recommendations was to increase birds' perception of there being a large, continuous grassland. This is in line with the findings of Jobin and Falardeau about the importance of area and surrounding land use. If the riparian forest could be converted to a riparian shrubland, the ornithologists suggested, and meadow continued on the other side, area-sensitive grassland birds such as the grasshopper sparrow would have a continuous line of sight and be more likely to nest on the property. The ornithologists also recommended specific management practices that would increase the habitat value of Oakencroft's meadow for grassland birds. They suggested that mowing be delayed until mid-July or early August to allow birds to complete their breeding. They proposed that the farm manager leave portions of the grassland unmowed to create refugia and that mowed areas be tackled from the center outward, allowing birds to escape to surrounding areas.

Entomologists collected 1,500 individual bees of forty-five species on one day of sampling at Oakencroft. They concluded that although there was no shortage of bees, only the most ubiquitous species were represented, and there was much room to increase the diversity of the native bee community on the property. The entomologists also emphasized the importance of the central grassland area on the property as providing important nesting sites for ground-dwelling bees. Like the ornithologists, they advocated removing many of the young trees along the streams or girdling them to create standing deadwood for bee nesting. In place of these trees they recommended planting low shrubs such as willow and buttonbush (*Cephalanthus occidentalis*), patches of wet meadow forbs such as bee balm (*Monarda didyma*), and ironweed (*Vernonia*). These are all excellent bee forage plants, and several have bee species that specialize on them. In the upper grassland areas, the entomologists suggested including late-season composites and other native forbs to draw in additional unrepresented bee species.

Woltz is passionate about the role of design in bringing together the realities of the site, the client's goals, and scientific analysis. Following the biologists' recommendations, the landscape architects revised their initial master plan to open up the center of the riparian corridor, using shrubs and wet meadow forbs in place of trees (fig. 7.3). They hope that future monitoring will show that they have created real habitat, with measurable increases in the local density of grasshopper sparrow and greater diversity of native bees.

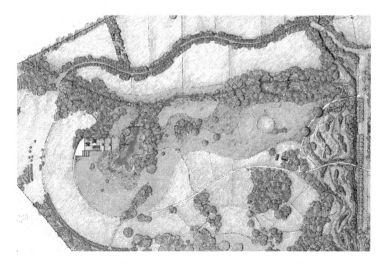

Figure 7.3 A portion of the master plan for Oakencroft shows the large meadow habitat connected visually via riparian plantings of shrubs and wet meadow forbs to pasture grasslands on the other side of the stream. (Courtesy of Nelson Byrd Woltz Landscape Architects.)

THE WEB OF LIFE IS MADE OF COEVOLUTIONARY RELATIONSHIPS

The habitat needs of species can go well beyond having fields of a certain size with a certain type of vegetation. They are likely to include particular relationships with other species. Many of the myriad relationships in the web of life are forged by coevolution, or evolutionary change induced in two or more species or populations by each other.

In the classic article on coevolution, Paul Ehrlich and Peter Raven (1964) of Stanford University discussed in detail the food preferences of different groups of butterflies. Monarch butterflies, to give a well-known example, are members of the butterfly subfamily *Danainae*, all of which are known to feed primarily on milkweeds and other members of the dogbane family. Milkweeds are named for their milky sap, which contains toxic alkaloids and glycosides. In order to consume these plants, monarchs have evolved the means to safely sequester the toxins in their tissues as they grow, thereby gaining access to a food resource that is not used by many herbivores and borrowing its chemical defenses for their own protection.

Ehrlich and Raven proposed that flowering plants and the butterflies that consume them demonstrate a series of mutual adaptations. Groups of plants such as milkweeds evolved toxic secondary chemicals to escape herbivory. A group of butterflies (the danaines) then evolved the ability to feed on the milkweeds. In this way, coevolution has led to adaptive radiation and helps explain the diversity of both plant and butterfly species. It has also led to specialized feeding relationships between butterflies and their specific plant hosts.

Recently ecologists have come to understand that coevolution is even more intricate than these classic species-to-species pairings (Thompson 2009). Species are often engaged in simultaneous coevolution with several other species. For instance, flowering plants are involved in mutualistic networks with multiple pollinators. Within these networks both highly specialized and generalized relationships can emerge. Species such as honeybees can evolve only when a sufficiently large web of mutualistic relationships is already in place. In this sense, they are not generalist pollinators but network specialists.

Coevolution does not take place only over long time spans but can occur rapidly and continually. Moreover, this change takes place not uniformly throughout species' ranges but in a geographic mosaic of locally interacting populations. In coevolutionary hotspots two populations will induce reciprocal change, but in other parts of the species' ranges populations may not interact in this way. As new traits appear and spread or are swamped by gene flow from non-coevolving populations, a shifting pattern is created of coevolution taking place before our eyes. Such dynamic evolutionary change is part of the endless adaptation of complex systems (see chap. 4). Interactions between local populations drive an upwelling of genetic change that helps renew biodiversity on Earth (see chap. 5).

DESIGN FOR SPECIES WITH COEVOLUTIONARY RELATIONSHIPS

The concept of coevolution has tremendous implications for any attempt to design a landscape as habitat. It suggests that it is not enough to conceive of the landscape ecosystem in terms of trophic levels and stock it with appropriate numbers of producers, consumers, and decomposers (see chap. 4). We must understand and replicate actual species-to-species, population-to-population, and network relationships. These are the relationships embodied in native ecosystems.

We can immediately grasp that a landscape designed to sustain monarch butterflies must include their host milkweeds. Research by Douglas Tallamy (2007) suggests that even butterflies whose larvae are considered generalist feeders grow best and in some cases survive only when reared on particular native plants with which they have an evolutionary relationship (fig. 7.4). When we use alien plants in our landscapes, the biomass of native insects declines. Because birds rely on protein-rich insects as food during the rearing of young, a decline in insect biomass has negative consequences up the food chain. When we create landscapes of locally native plants, on the other hand, they can immediately support a greater abundance and diversity of insect and bird life (Burghardt et al. 2008).

Pollination of plants by animals is another key coevolutionary relationship. If we want populations of animal-pollinated plant species to persist on site, their pollinators must be present. This can mean ensuring that nesting sites for bees, for instance, or food plants for butterfly larvae are incorporated into the design or are present in adjacent areas.

Habitat for animals and pollination for plants are not the only issues at stake. Although even simple built landscapes can provide a range of ecosystem services (see chap. 4), finely tuned ecosystems are built of species-to-species relationships based on shared evolutionary history. Where feeding relationships are disrupted, nutrient cycling is altered, which can change the soil community, and on and on.

Figure 7.4 A double-toothed prominent (*Nerice bidentata*) caterpillar feeding on the leaf of its host plant, the American elm (*Ulmus americana*). The evolution of the caterpillar to mimic the form of the elm's leaf margin is apparent. (Image by Doug Tallamy.)

This line of thinking should inject a note of caution when we consider creating novel communities (see chap. 10) and lends more support to the importance of preferring plant material propagated from local populations (see chap. 1).

In further research, Burghardt and colleagues (2010) found more Lepidoptera on close relatives of native plants than on alien plants with no local relatives. When creating a community by placing unusual plants in the architecture of a local natural community (see chap. 2), therefore, using plants that are of the same genus as the natives they replace will probably support intermediate levels of insect and bird life. Over a sufficient number of generations, evolution can catch up. For example, a population of insects may evolve to take advantage of the food resources presented by a heretofore uneaten alien plant. In the meantime, however, we may be missing opportunities to achieve the highest level of ecosystem function.

Truly supporting native biodiversity can be a wondrous experience. Imagine bringing children to witness a tiger swallowtail butterfly (*Papilio glaucus, P. rutulus*) emerge from its cocoon, or watching a yellow warbler (*Setophaga petechia*) glean insects busily off the young oak outside one's window. These sorts of experiences can be common in a landscape designed with coevolution in mind.

PLANTS ARE SUBJECT TO ATTACK BY PATHOGENS

The organisms with which plants interact and have coevolutionary relationships include numerous pathogens. These disease-causing organisms include animals such as nematodes, animal-like single celled flagellate protozoa, and species of fungi, bacteria, and viruses. When on the attack, they can break down cell walls, disrupt biochemical activity within cells, destroy plant tissues, reduce levels of photosynthesis, and reduce the absorption and distribution of water. Plants suffer from other diseases caused by environmental factors, such as excessive soil moisture, lack of nutrients, or air pollution, but here we speak of diseases that result from plants' interactions with other organisms.

In order for a disease to emerge, three elements need to be in place, which plant pathologists typically describe as the disease triangle (fig. 7.5). The first element is a susceptible host. Some pathogens attack only young plants, for instance. If only mature plants are present, no disease can break out.

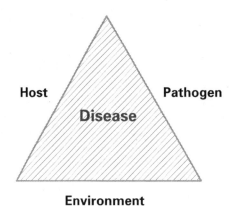

Figure 7.5 The disease triangle.

Also, healthy plants can better resist pathogens, whereas plants stressed by environmental conditions may be more susceptible to infection. The second element of the disease triangle is a virulent pathogen. If the pathogen is not present in the environment, obviously, no disease can occur. Pathogens may be abundant because of infection of other plants nearby or infrequent after a chance dispersal. Some pathogens will infect a wide range of plants, whereas others are limited to a single genus or species. Different strains of each pathogen species can be more or less virulent. The third element is environmental conditions conducive to the outbreak of disease. Most pathogens need a given range of temperature and moisture in order to grow, reproduce, and infect plants. The disease triangle also allows us to envision the likelihood of a disease outbreak. The more susceptible the host, the more virulent and widespread the pathogen, and the more conducive the environment, the longer each side of the disease triangle gets, and the larger it grows. Conversely, shrinking even one side of the triangle can reduce the likelihood of outbreak substantially.

Plants and their pathogens have coevolved in an unending arms race (Agrios 1997). Healthy plants display a general resistance to pathogens, which plant pathologists call horizontal resistance. They maintain a cuticle around their epidermal cells, for example, to prevent penetration by fungi and bacteria. They may produce compounds such as tannins and saponins in their cells that are toxic to pathogenic organisms. They may form abscission layers around the site of infection and slough off the dead tissue, or infected cells may die quickly, in both cases isolating the pathogens and preventing the infection from spreading. Or plants may produce antimicrobial toxins in infected cells. In order to be successful, plant pathogens have had to evolve ways around each of these defenses. They enter leaves through stomata, for instance, or detoxify a plant's chemical defenses. Plants may also display vertical resistance, which is complete resistance to a single strain of a pathogen species. Vertical resistance is understood to be conferred by a single plant gene (that prevents recognition of the host by the pathogen, for instance) corresponding to a single pathogen gene. Much plant breeding for disease resistance has concentrated on vertical resistance because it conveys complete resistance and because its limited genetic basis makes it easier to manipulate. The flip side is that a single mutation of the pathogen can completely undo vertical resistance.

USE ECOLOGICAL METHODS TO LIMIT THE IMPACT OF PLANT PATHOGENS

Plant pathogens such as wheat rust (*Puccinia graminis*), potato blight (*Phytophthora infestans*), and chestnut blight have caused major economic losses, famine, and ecological disruption, so it is no wonder that the conventional approach to plant disease is serious and aggressive. Conventional control of plant diseases begins with a focus on reducing the spread of pathogens through quarantine, inspections, crop rotation, and proper sanitation. It continues with the breeding and dissemination of resistant varieties of economically important species. And it culminates in the application of chemicals that kill plant pathogens directly. These approaches have been well developed for agricultural and important ornamental plants. Depending on the chemicals used, they are even compatible with organic production methods.

An ecological approach to plant pathogens focuses on limiting the spread of plant disease and mitigating its impacts on the overall plant community. Each side of the disease triangle presents opportunities for ecological control.

Susceptible host plants are those that are recognized by a specific strain of pathogen and are unable to ward off its attack. Recognition by a pathogen is largely a matter of chemical interactions on the surface of the plant, most of which have not been fully explained. Of the thousands of plant pathogens, only a limited number attack each species of plant. Even within plant species, different plant populations and individual plants show varying degrees of susceptibility to different strains of pathogens. Promoting genetic diversity in plant populations is therefore a first line of defense against the spread of disease (see chap. 2). A diverse population will also be able to continue to evolve to keep up in the arms race with plant pathogens. The many genes involved in horizontal resistance can be exchanged and amplified in a population over time. The use of resistant cultivated varieties, rather than a diverse population of outcrossed plants, can be sensible for species subject to likely attack by known pathogens, especially for long-lived species that will not evolve quickly. Even in these cases, however, using multiple resistant varieties can help reduce the number of susceptible hosts and slow the spread of disease.

We can also limit the abundance of virulent pathogens and their contact with susceptible hosts. Plant pathogens are organisms living in a community of other competing, predatory, and parasitic organisms. In a landscape with a healthy soil ecosystem (see chap. 6), microbial antagonisms can limit the growth of soilborne pathogens. Nonvirulent microbes growing on plant leaves can also limit infection by outcompeting or attacking pathogenic organisms. It is possible to promote the growth of nonvirulent microbes with direct inoculation or application of compost teas, but it is probably most important to simply not destroy them with broad-spectrum toxic chemicals. Dispersing susceptible plants among nonsusceptible plants in multispecies plantings can reduce the transmission of infections by keeping virulent pathogens away from their hosts. In diverse communities, the loss of one species to disease will also have less of an impact on overall ecosystem function (see chap. 5).

The most important thing we can do to reduce the environment side of the disease triangle is to not plant susceptible plants in conditions where pathogens are likely to thrive. Common lilacs (*Syringa vulgaris*), for instance, are relatives of olives and grow naturally on rocky hillsides in the Balkans. When grown in more humid climates, in the shade, or crowded together where air circulation is poor, they commonly suffer from powdery mildew and lilac bacterial blight.

Planting diverse populations of well-sited plants in diverse communities and integrated ecosystems may not eliminate disease, but it should reduce its incidence to levels that are tolerable in terms of both appearance and ecosystem function.

HERBIVORES CAN ALTER THE SPECIES COMPOSITION OF PLANT COMMUNITIES

From mammals to insects, birds to nematodes, animals both depend on the plant communities on which they feed and strongly influence the makeup of those communities. The effect of high white-tailed deer (*Odocoileus virginianus*) populations on forest communities in the eastern United States is a case in point (fig. 7.6). In a synthesis of the literature, David Augustine and Samuel McNaughton (1998) concluded that the effects of ungulate herbivores on a plant community depend on the joint mechanisms of herbivore selectivity and plant tolerance to herbivory.

Whereas insects are often specialized to feed on a narrow range of plants, or even one plant spe-

Figure 7.6 White-tailed deer have altered forest communities in the eastern United States. (Photo by Thomas J. Rawinski, US Forest Service.)

cies, most mammalian herbivores consume a wider range of plant material. Browsers eat mostly twigs, buds, and leaves of woody plants. Grazers eat mostly herbaceous grasses and forbs. Plant food is patchy in space and time, and herbivores are constantly selecting what it is most efficient and nutritious for them to consume. Deer will feed on herbaceous plants and the leaves of deciduous trees and shrubs in the spring and summer, favor fallen fruits and acorns in the fall, and browse on woody stems when food is scarce in the winter. Herbivores have both innate and learned feeding preferences, typically for palatable plants with lower levels of distasteful secondary chemicals.

Selective feeding can affect the species composition of a community. Augustine and McNaughton explained how selective browsing by white-tailed deer reduces the regeneration of more palatable species such as sugar maple (*Acer saccharum*) and pin cherry (*Prunus pensylvanica*) in forest gaps, thereby increasing the relative abundance of beech, birch, and striped maple (*Acer pensylvanicum*). Rawinski (2008) reported that deer eat many herbaceous species on the forest floor but avoid others, including natives such as Pennsylvania sedge and eastern hayscented fern (*Dennstaedtia punctilobula*). They seem to disproportionately avoid exotic invasives such as Japanese stilt-grass (*Microstegium vimineum*) and garlic mustard (*Alliaria petiolata*). The end result is forest floors dominated by a few unpalatable native species and invasive exotics.

Which plants are eaten most heavily is only half of the story, however. The other half is plant response to herbivory. In the right circumstances, plants that are eaten can regrow so vigorously as to maintain or even increase their relative abundance in a community. In other cases, slow-growing species can have their relative abundance reduced by herbivory. Augustine and McNaughton summarized several studies demonstrating that deer pressure can convert stands of conifers such as hemlock (*Tsuga canadensis*) and white pine (*Pinus strobus*) to stands of deciduous species such as beech and paper birch (*Betula papyrifera*). The conversion takes place even though deciduous species experience higher overall tissue loss during summer feeding because the conifers are slow to regrow.

Plants also respond to herbivory with changes in their morphology, becoming more prostrate, for instance, or losing all their twigs and leaves within reach of browsers. These changes can also affect community composition by altering the amount of light that reaches other plants.

Herbivore selectivity and plant tolerance are affected by several factors. Increased herbivore density reduces feeding selectivity. Many ungulate herbivores travel in herds, which means they gain protection from the group but are less able to be selective about what they eat. Herbivore selectivity is also affected by the timing of plant growth. At certain times of year, preferred foods are unavailable. Early in the growing season, before plants have invested in chemical defense, herbivores find a wider range of plants palatable and therefore have less of a selective effect on community composition. The frequency with which herbivores return has a large impact on the potential for regrowth by grazed or browsed plants. How plants respond also depends on the availability of nutrients in the ecosystem.

USE HERBIVORES TO MANAGE PLANT COMMUNITIES

Management of white-tailed deer populations in the eastern United States is an ongoing challenge and relies mostly on controlled hunting. The expansion of coyotes into eastern states may help reduce deer populations. For property owners the most effective means of deer control is exclusion. Where building tall fences is impractical, designers may have to make a preemptive shift in community composition by planting only deer-resistant plants. Remember, however, that feeding choices are always relative. In areas with high populations, or at times when food supplies are low, even less palatable plants may suddenly be eaten.

Herbivorous mammals may also have positive effects on plant community composition. Because of their long history of domestication, ungulates offer a means of efficiently managing larger landscapes. Healing Hooves is a contract grazing company in the state of Washington that uses goats to help clients clear brush, remove invasive species, and manage weeds. One of their clients is the US Fish and Wildlife Service's Leavenworth National Fish Hatchery, located along Icicle Creek on the lower slopes of the eastern Cascades. The Fish and Wildlife service was looking for help managing a community of introduced and native grasses growing in a large, flat area of the site that is used seasonally for a pow wow and other events. Before Healing Hooves' involvement, two invasive plants—diffuse knapweed and Dalmatian toadflax (*Linaria dalmatica*)—had established themselves amid the grasses. Because of the area's proximity to the hatchery and the creek, herbicides could not be used. Instead, the hatchery staff turned to mechanical removal, mowing, and goats.

Goats are considered to be browsers, and they love to eat tough species such as blackberry and poison ivy, but really they are opportunistic generalists and will eat a variety of plants depending on their palatability and the animals' familiarity with them. Because of their smaller body and rumen size compared with cattle and horses, goats need to eat a higher-quality diet and are more selective feeders. Their small mouth and nimble lips allow them to nip preferred plants. They also have a large liver and can process toxins that would be harmful to other ruminants. For all these reasons, in a grassland community such as at the Leavenworth hatchery, goats will eat more broadleaf plants than grasses. Healing Hooves co-owner and shepherd Craig Madsen points out, "For goats, weeds are a resource" (fig. 7.7).

Madsen and his dog, Harvey, influence the impact of the goats on the plant community by controlling their relative density and the timing of their grazing. Madsen's herd consists of 260 does and kids. When on site, Madsen delineates an area of several acres each day using portable electric fencing, and he and Harvey move the goats when they have consumed much of the broadleaf vegetation (mostly invasives) but before they begin heavily eating the grasses. The best time for the goats to consume knapweed and Dalmatian toadflax is between bolting and flowering. Then the plants are highly palatable and there is little danger of spreading mature seeds in the goats' manure. Madsen generally brings his herd to Leavenworth in May and sometimes again later in the season to eat flowers off plants that have regrown from the first grazing.

After 5 years of grazing at the Leavenworth hatchery, the populations of invasives have been diminished and the desirable grasses are responding positively. Dalmatian toadflax especially has been

Figure 7.7 A Healing Hooves' goat preferentially eating diffuse knapweed at the Leavenworth National Fish Hatchery. (Photo by Healing Hooves, LLC.)

reduced, whereas knapweed continues to regenerate from the seedbank. Madsen emphasizes that goats are one tool among many, and not a silver bullet. Eradication of invasive species is tough, in his experience, but grazing can reduce infestations to more manageable levels. Once problem populations have been reduced, Madsen often encourages his clients to use seeding to increase populations of desired species.

Herbivores are part of the ecosystems we design and manage. We must acknowledge their preferences in our selection of plants. We can also use their behavior to shift community composition in ways we desire.

PLANTS HAVE A VARIETY OF CHARACTERISTICS THAT PREVENT THEIR OBLITERATION BY HERBIVORES

With thundering herds and buzzing swarms of herbivores out there, why is the world still covered in plants (fig. 7.8)? Plants capture the energy of the sun, forming the basis of the food chain, and represent an enormous food resource. Why don't herbivores eat more of them, as they do in aquatic systems, where primary consumers claim 50 percent or more of annual primary production? After all, the oceans are blue, not green. In terrestrial systems, however, herbivores consume only 10 to 20 percent of net primary production (Hartley and Jones 1997).

Figure 7.8 Japanese beetles (*Popillia japonica*), an invasive pest in the eastern United States, skeletonize a leaf. (Photo by Bob Kipfer.)

Ecologists have been debating this puzzle for several decades and have developed two main lines of reasoning. One is that herbivore populations are controlled from the bottom up by the poor food quality of plants. The other is that herbivores are controlled from the top down by the organisms that consume them. First we will explore bottom-up control of herbivores, and in the next section we will examine top-down control. Both factor into the continued abundance of green plants.

Part of bottom-up control comes from the fact that plants are a heterogeneous resource, in both space and time. Many insect herbivores are specialized to feed on only certain plant parts of certain plant species. Ungulates cannot reach leaves above a certain height. Less common plants in diverse communities can be less apparent to herbivores. In temperate regions, plant parts such as buds or chemically less well-defended new growth are available only at certain times of the year. This spatial and temporal heterogeneity of plant food causes herbivores to expend more energy searching for food and limits their populations.

Also, for all their biomass, terrestrial plants make poor food. Compared with animal tissues, plant tissues are much higher in carbon. Much of this carbon comes in the form of the tough fibers and lignin that plants need to stay upright and internally circulate food and water while living on land.

Selfishly, plants protect their more nutritious tissues with a variety of defenses. Thorns and hairs present physical defenses. Chemical defenses include the tannins in oak leaves, which bind with proteins, blocking nutrients from being assimilated and interfering with digestive enzymes. Other secondary chemicals (so called because they are not necessary for a plant's primary activities of photosynthesis, respiration, growth, and reproduction) deter animals from feeding in the first place, or are toxic, or interfere with the growth and reproduction of insect herbivores.

It can be costly for plants to maintain chemical defenses. In general, slow-growing plants and plants in nutrient-poor environments have higher levels of chemical defenses, because it is not easy for them to replace lost tissues. Plants will also marshal so-called induced chemical defenses in the days or even minutes after herbivores feed on their tissues. These responses can be remarkably specific and biochemically sophisticated (Schultz 2002). Fascinatingly, when one plant in a population is damaged by herbivores, neighboring plants will also build up their chemical defenses, probably in response to airborne and soilborne chemical signals.

With their high carbon content, seasonal growth cycles, physical defenses, and complex biochemical armaments, land plants are difficult for herbivores to consume.

HELP PLANTS DEFEND THEMSELVES

From the perspective of those who appreciate gardens, it is a good thing the world is green. The challenge in an ecological landscape is to allow the necessary levels of feeding that provide habitat and maintain community structure, without losing important individual plants, threatening the survival of desired populations, or sacrificing the growth needed to achieve the design intent and perform ecosystem services.

When thought of in these terms, consumption of about 10 to 20 percent of annual production seems fair. The real concern is outbreaks that can cause higher levels of damage. The idea of thresholds, as used in integrated pest management, is a useful concept in this regard. A threshold is the level of damage past which further feeding becomes unacceptable. In agricultural crops, the threshold is usually defined in economic terms. At what point does damage begin to reduce the value of the crops by more than it would cost to address the problem? In ornamental plants, thresholds are thought of more in terms of plant appearance and plant health. In an ecological landscape, a threshold might be the point at which damage risks reducing ecological function, eliminating a key functional group (see chap. 5), or directing succession in an unwanted direction (see chap. 8).

The bottom-up side of herbivore control suggests several ideas that can be used to prevent insect outbreaks and keep consumption below threshold levels. Nothing says "feast" to an herbivorous insect like a field of their target species all at its most vulnerable stage. Applying the principles of spatial and temporal heterogeneity can eliminate this opportunity. As they do with pathogens, diverse plantings prevent a single specialized herbivore from doing widespread damage. They can also reduce the apparency of any one species to its coevolved herbivores, as its chemical clues are less obvious. Also, when a plant is less predominant at a site, that location will be less tempting to a searching herbivore than a more densely populated one. Using varied size and age structures will reduce the vulnerability of a population to herbivores that prefer either juvenile or mature tissues (see chap. 2).

We can also control resource availability to help keep the food quality of the plants in our landscape poor. Herbivores track available nitrogen and will preferentially feed on plants with higher nitrogen levels. Fertilizing plants increases the nitrogen content of their tissues and encourages them to put on less chemically defended new growth, which in turn attracts greater levels of herbivory. Creating a healthy soil ecosystem gives plants access to the nutrients they need without artificial pulses of nitrogen (see chap. 6). Irrigation can also promote succulent growth that is attractive to herbivores, especially in comparison to unirrigated surroundings. Using adapted plants that can survive without supplemental watering thus also helps those plants avoid herbivore damage (see chap. 1).

Growers can induce plants to activate their own chemical defenses using a variety of compounds. A simpler approach, however, is to allow plants to experience environmental stresses as they occur and to permit subthreshold levels of feeding. Both of these occurrences will stimulate plants to protect their own tissues with no involvement beyond monitoring on our part.

PREDATORS REGULATE HERBIVORE POPULATIONS

The original observation that we need to explain why the terrestrial world is green was in an article by Nelson Hairston, Frederick Smith, and Lawrence Slobodkin in 1960. The authors argued against the assumption that organisms at all trophic levels are controlled by competition for limited resources (see chap. 3). Hairston and his co-authors noted that in the few situations where herbivore populations have grown large enough to deplete vegetation, this was due to a lack of predators. As an example, they cite outbreaks of scale insects in forests after spraying targeted at caterpillars. The scales were protected by their waxy covering, while the spray killed the caterpillars and also the beetles that normally prey on scales. Hairston, Smith, and Slobodkin also used top-down control to explain why introduced insect herbivores can be so successful: They have left their natural predators behind. Unlike producers, decomposers, and even carnivores, which are all resource limited, Hairston et al. concluded, herbivores are controlled by the predators in the trophic level above them (fig. 7.9). It is important to note that

Figure 7.9 Birds such as this eastern bluebird (*Sialia sialis*) consume spiders as well as insects that feed on plants. (Image by Doug Tallamy.)

Hairston and his co-authors intend predation to be understood in the broadest possible sense, including parasitism. Conceptually, we can also add disease-causing pathogens to the organisms that exert top-down control on herbivore populations.

Ecologists have since found strong examples of top-down control in aquatic ecosystems and in terrestrial ecosystems as well. Researchers from the Smithsonian Tropical Research Institute covered plants in a lowland forest in Panama with mesh exclosures that allowed most insects to come and go but prevented birds and bats from gleaning insects off the plants (Kalka et al. 2008). They then counted the insects present and assessed the damage to the plants' leaves. By putting the exclosures in place during either the day or the night, they distinguished between the effects of birds (active during the day) and bats (active during the night).

They found that both daytime and nighttime exclosures increased the number of insects found on the plants. Exclosures also increased the percentage of total leaf area consumed by herbivores. The effect in both cases was stronger for nighttime exclosures. They concluded that birds, but to a greater degree bats, were reducing insect abundance on plants through predation and thereby reducing herbivory. They note that the effect may be even stronger than their data indicate for several reasons, including that predation can take place away from the immediate vicinity of plants covered by the exclosures and that the exclosures did not prevent top-down control of insect herbivores by insect predators.

Top-down control by predators, along with bottom-up control, places important limits on herbivore populations and helps keep the world full of plants.

INVITE NATURAL ENEMIES TO CONTROL PEST POPULATIONS

Despite the importance of herbivores and their potential usefulness in affecting community structure, in the built landscape most herbivores are regarded as pests. In addition to the various strategies for making plants poor food for herbivores, maintaining populations of predators and parasites is a key aspect of controlling pests in an ecological landscape. Such organisms are often called natural enemies of pests. Natural enemies include vertebrate predators such as hawks that consume rabbits, snakes that prey on field mice, and bats and songbirds that eat both predatory and herbivorous insects, as well as insects such as ladybug larvae that love to munch on aphids, and parasitoid wasps whose larvae consume caterpillars and beetles from the inside out.

Miguel Altieri, whose work at the University of California, Berkeley has been key to the development of agroecology, has studied how vegetational diversity can increase and maintain natural enemy populations, which in turn control insect pests. Altieri and his partners (2005) distinguish between planned biodiversity and associated biodiversity. Planned biodiversity is all the plant species planted on a site. Associated biodiversity is all the soil fauna, insects, and other species that will colonize a site from nearby. Planned biodiversity influences associated biodiversity, which in turn affects how well the originally planted species perform.

In the vineyards that Altieri and his colleagues studied, three planting strategies influenced the abundance of insect natural enemies. One was planting summer cover crops between vineyard rows in Mendocino County (fig. 7.10). Another, at the same vineyard, was the use of a corridor of flowering plants running from an adjacent riparian forest and across the vineyard. The third, at a vineyard in Sonoma County, was the planting of an island of flowering shrubs and herbs in the center of the vineyard. All three of these strategies allow populations of natural enemies to build up and maintain themselves in a site by providing nectar, pollen, and populations of neutral insects on which they can feed. In all three cases, vineyard rows close to summer cover crops, the corridor, and the planted island all had increased abundances of natural enemies and decreased abundances or increased parasitization of grape leafhopper (*Erythroneura elegantula*) and thrips (*Frankliniella occidentalis*). Well-timed mowing of cover crop rows was effective at moving populations of parasitoid wasps from the cover crops to the grapes themselves.

In a landscape setting, diverse plantings with a range of bloom times can help maintain populations of natural enemies. Connections with adjacent natural areas can provide an important means for beneficial organisms to become part of the associated biodiversity of a site (see chap. 9). Planting

Figure 7.10 Cover crops planted between vineyard rows support populations of insect natural enemies that help control grape pests. (Photo by Albie Miles and Houston Wilson, Laboratory of Agroecology, UC Berkeley.)

insectary plants such as members of the aster and carrot families can help support populations of parasitoid wasps. It is also important to avoid the use of broad-spectrum insecticides, which can kill beneficial organisms as well as the target species.

Birds and bats, which as we have seen are important insect predators, can also be encouraged with the provision of cover, alternate food (fruits) during winter for birds, housing, and water. Perches, whether specially designed or naturally occurring, can encourage birds of prey to patrol areas for rodents. Even where they do not consume every last rodent, the presence of predators can influence the behavior of prey species, making them less brazen consumers of plants.

KEYSTONE SPECIES AND ECOSYSTEM ENGINEERS STRUCTURE ECOSYSTEMS

When the tide draws out along the coastline of the Pacific Northwest, it exposes a rich community of seaweed, barnacles, gooseneck barnacles, mussels, rock snails, and starfish lining the rocks and pools. Ecologist Robert Paine (1966) studied this community at Mukkaw Bay, near the very tip of the Olympic Peninsula in Washington State. Paine marked off two areas of the shoreline. One he left alone as a control. The other he kept free of the predatory starfish *Pisaster ochraceus*, commonly known as purple sea star (fig. 7.11). He then established transects across the two areas and from time to time measured the numbers and density of seaweed and the various shellfish. The control community remained as it was before. In the *Pisaster*-free area, however, the community began to change. As competition played out between its sessile residents, the plot became dominated first by one species of barnacle and then by mussels. Without predation by *Pisaster*, the community became less diverse, even though predation by rock snails continued. The difference, Paine suggested, was that the rock snails consumed only a few barnacles each time the tide went down and left the barnacle shells in place, whereas the starfish removed twenty to sixty barnacles at once. In the intertidal zone, where space is a limiting resource, this type of predation is critical in maintaining community diversity.

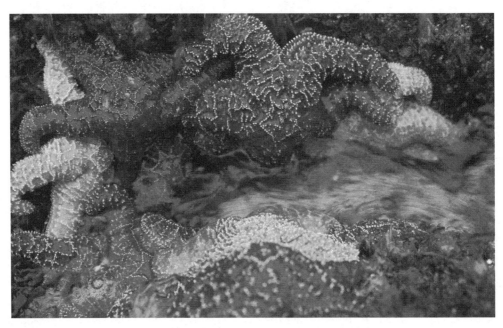

Figure 7.11 The purple sea star in its rocky intertidal habitat. (Courtesy of NOAA.)

Although Paine did not offer the definition in the article in which he described these experiments, ecologists now refer to species such as the purple sea star as keystone species. Like the keystone in an arch, keystone species play a determining role in the structure of their ecosystems, even where their biomass or total abundance is low.

The importance of the physical modification of the community by purple sea star links keystone species to another group of important organisms: ecosystem engineers. Ecosystem engineers modify the physical environment, changing the availability of resources for other organisms and creating habitat (Jones et al. 1994). Autogenic engineers change the environment with their own physical structures. Seagrass, for instance, moderates ocean currents, changing sedimentation rates that determine the food supply for organisms such as clams. Like the eelgrass at Silver Springs (see chap. 4), seagrass itself is a resource of food and living space for organisms, but this is not a case of engineering. Allogenic engineers modify other living or dead organisms or elements of the abiotic environment. Beavers (*Castor canadensis*), to take the classic example, cut down trees and dam streams, changing the entire local environment. Although on a small scale the actions of beavers destroy as much habitat as they create, at a landscape level the creation and abandonment of dams and ponds helps to maintain a patchwork of different habitat types (see chap. 8).

The presence of keystone species and ecosystem engineers is critical in maintaining or creating many ecosystem attributes.

INCLUDE KEYSTONE SPECIES AND ECOSYSTEM ENGINEERS

Every fall, wild salmon return to the rivers and streams of the Pacific Northwest. They dart and leap against the current to find the very gravel beds where they were born. Salmon are recognized as both keystone species and ecosystem engineers. They are keystone species because of their role as a nutrient pump. When salmon return to their spawning grounds, each one carries in its flesh and bones pounds of nutrients accumulated in the Pacific Ocean. As they swim upstream, salmon are pounced upon by grizzly bears (*Ursus arctos horribilis*) and bald eagles (*Haliaeetus leucocephalus*), which consume these nutrients and then excrete them throughout the forest. After spawning, the salmon die. The bodies that are not carried off by scavengers break down in the water and provide an important source of nitrogen and phosphorus in the aquatic ecosystem. Because of their role as a keystone species, decreased salmon runs have a cascading effect through the ecosystems of the Pacific Northwest. During their spawning, salmon also act as ecosystem engineers. To get ready to lay eggs, salmon excavate nests in stream bottoms by vigorously thrashing their bodies and tails. This excavation, when carried out by thousands of spawning salmon, moves sediment downstream and shapes streambeds.

Efforts to restore salmon runs throughout the Northwest, then, are not just a matter of creating habitat for an emblematic species and important food source. They are about restoring a critical component of the broader forest and aquatic ecosystems, one that may be necessary for these ecosystems to function properly.

In Seattle, ambitious work has begun to bring salmon back to even urbanized watersheds. Pipers Creek is a 1.5-mile stream within Carkeek Park in north Seattle that until the 1920s was a spawning ground for steelhead, coho, and chum salmon (*Oncorhyncus mykiss, O. kisutch, O. keta*). Several overlapping efforts have been made to restore these runs. Salmon eggs donated by a local tribe were raised in the watershed and formed the basis of a new salmon population. Meanwhile, as part of Seattle's Urban Creeks Legacy Project, the city performed stream restoration work, placing boulders and logs to prevent scouring of the stream bottom, armor bends, and create pools and riffles (Sovern 1995). Invasive species were removed and replaced with thick plantings of native species along streambanks. In the larger Pipers Creek Watershed, Seattle Public Utilities began implementing its Natural Drainage Systems strategy by installing its first Street Edge Alternative, or SEA Street (Seattle Public Utilities 2012). This block-long SEA Street replaced a ditch and culvert system that dumped stormwater directly into Pipers Creek with vegetated infiltration swales (see chap. 6). These swales reduced stormwater runoff from the block to 1 percent of preproject levels. Other natural drainage projects in the watershed followed. Seattle Public Utilities has also promoted salmon-friendly gardening, which encourages homeowners to capture and infiltrate stormwater on their own properties and reduce their use of fertilizers and pesticides.

Thanks to these efforts, salmon are returning to Pipers Creek, by the hundreds if not yet by the thousands (fig. 7.12). Watching the salmon run has even become an annual event at Carkeek Park (Mapes 2010). Dissolved oxygen levels and temperature within the creek are suitable for salmon. A mysterious new problem has arisen, however, dubbed prespawn mortality. Although other species are largely unaffected, a significant percentage of coho salmon in Pipers Creek and other Seattle streams die before they can spawn, even within hours of reentering the stream. Scientists suspect that contaminants in stormwater are to blame (Pipers Creek Watershed Project 2008).

Figure 7.12   A chum salmon returned to spawn in Pipers Creek in November 2011. (Photo by Christina Wilsdon.)

Accommodating keystone animal species and ecosystem engineers in an urbanized environment is not easy. These species may have demanding requirements, and their engineering activities can be disruptive. However, such species can provide a focal point for larger ecological design efforts and a means of measuring success. Ultimately, we can hope, they may resume their roles as linchpins in a functioning ecosystem, only this time one that is as much built as it is natural.

ANIMALS DISPERSE SEEDS

Ecosystem engineering is not the only way that animals affect the structure of ecosystems. Animal dispersal of plant propagules is another (Herrera 2002). Which plants arrive on and spread across a site is a major driver of the development of a plant community over time (see chap. 8). Seeds that are dispersed away from their parents avoid some of the problems associated with dense stands (see chap. 2) and can spread to vacant favorable sites. Many plants use wind and gravity to disperse their seeds, and others rely on the aid of animals, in a variety of mutualistic and commensal relationships. For instance, trillium seeds come packaged with elaiosomes, fleshy structures rich in lipids and proteins, which encourage ants to bring them back to their anthills. Animal-facilitated dispersal can take place through adhesion of seeds to animal exteriors, as with burrs, collection of seeds for later consumption, as squirrels do, or by consumption of fruits containing seeds. Many different animals disperse plant seeds, including primates, lizards, and bats. However, the most common animal dispersers are birds.

In order to attract animals to ingest and spread their seeds, plants have developed a number of adaptations. Chief among these are fleshy fruits that provide an immediate reward to animal dispersers. Brightly colored fruits attract birds, especially when they occur in masses, and ripe fruits may emit chemical signals, familiar to us as delicious scents. Unlike plant–pollinator mutualisms, there are few specialized relationships in the world of animal dispersal. Most plants attract several dispersers, and most dispersers feed on several different plants. Fleshy fruits are usually the product of trees and shrubs. Therefore, animal dispersal is most common in forest habitats, next most common in shrublands, and least important in primarily herbaceous communities such as grasslands and wetlands.

Fruit is not especially nutrient dense, and indigestible seeds take up valuable digestive space. For these reasons, the digestive tracts of many birds have adapted to rapidly evacuate seeds, in some cases in a matter of minutes after consumption. The consequence of rapid evacuation is a "seed shadow" concentrated close to the parent plant but with a long tail of distribution to more distant locations. This tail is marked by "recruitment foci," spots such as perches where birds are more likely to stop and defecate (fig. 7.13). Studying old fields in New Jersey, Mark McDonnell and Edmund Stiles (1983) found a circular relationship between vegetation structure and seed dispersal. Seeds were dropped most frequently at the forest edge, where birds found both perches and fruits to eat. Where woody vegetation was present in fields, this vegetation served as a recruitment focus, and birds dropped more seeds there than in the open fields, thereby increasing the amount of woody vegetation. Even artificial structures attracted birds and increased the number of seeds dispersed in their area. Some species have a second stage of animal dispersal, when rodents or insects gather seeds initially distributed by birds and move them to a new location. All these patterns can create a clumped distribution of animal-distributed plants.

USE ANIMALS TO PLANT PLANTS

When New York City capped the first enormous mounds of Fresh Kills landfill on Staten Island in the 1990s, the treatment of the site was largely determined by civil engineers. A significant concern was to prevent rainwater from penetrating the landfill mounds, so the engineers covered the mounds with an impermeable barrier, added a layer of poor soil, and sowed grasses on the soil to keep it from erod-

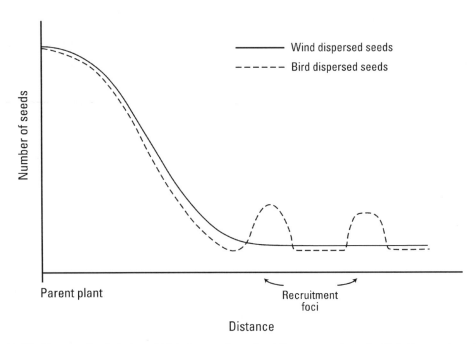

Figure 7.13 Most seeds of wind- and bird-dispersed species fall near parent plants. Bird-dispersed seeds also cluster near recruitment foci such as trees or artificial perches in a field. (From McDonnell, M. J., and E. W. Stiles. Copyright © 1983 Springer. The structural complexity of old field vegetation and the recruitment of bird-dispersed plant species. *Oecologia* 56:109–16. With kind permission of Springer Science+Business Media.)

ing. Given these conditions, succession to woody communities, as would happen on an old field in the Northeast, was very slow and early on was actually prevented by annual mowing. Once research showed that woody plant roots would not penetrate the cap, the question arose: Could something be done to facilitate the growth and spread of woody plants across the site?

Steven Handel, an ecologist from nearby Rutgers University, proposed that dispersal by animals could accelerate the spread of woody plants onto and across the site. To test this idea, he and his collaborators planted clusters of trees and shrubs at various locations on one landfill mound (Mattei et al. 2003). The species they chose, including hackberry (*Celtis occidentalis*), meadow rose (*Rosa nitida*), sumac (*Rhus copallinum*), and beach plum, are all tolerant of stressful conditions and all produce fleshy fruits that are distributed by birds.

Meadow rose tripled the area it covered in 5 years, and sumac spread as well, in both cases largely via vegetative reproduction. Because of the poor soil conditions and competition from perennial grasses, establishment of new seedlings on the site was limited (see chap. 8). However, removing grasses and tilling patches of soil increased establishment from seed. And the seed rain is certainly there. Seed traps at the base of hackberries collected 14,000 seeds from twenty-six different native tree and shrub species in the first season of the experiment. Ninety-five percent of the seeds were bird dispersed. Seed traps in open areas away from the planted clusters collected very few seeds.

Because the research team planted only seven native species, seeds from the other nineteen species found in the traps must have come from offsite. The importance of offsite seed sources was driven home later in the experiment. After a large portion of adjacent woodland was cut down for a construction project, seed deposition on the site fell by more than half. The planting nuclei, it became clear, were serving not primarily as sources of seeds that would spread across the site but as points of attraction for birds that brought in seeds from the nearby community.

To Handel, this is the big lesson learned from the experiments at Fresh Kills: Every site is embedded in a larger regional landscape, and thanks in part to the actions of animal dispersers, that landscape will always intrude on the design and influence its character (see chap. 9). If a project site is surrounded by weedy or invasive plants, many of which are bird dispersed, these species will quickly appear as part of the community and will have to be managed. On the other hand, if a site is surrounded by communities of desirable plants, these plants can be encouraged to spread onto the site by using animal dispersers. Using these animal-dispersed seeds not only is highly cost-effective but, when used in combination with planting, can also quickly create varied size and age structures (see chap. 2) and integrate a planting with the genetics of the surrounding population.

Because woody vegetation attracts birds that disperse the seeds of woody vegetation, the placement of early plantings can determine the spatial pattern of the eventual community. Artificial perches can be moved throughout a site to spread seeds wherever we desire (Handel 1997). Perhaps we could even time this movement to coincide with the ripening of fruit from various species in order to distribute those species to particular locations. In other words, even when we use free natural processes to vegetate a site, there is room for design.

CONCLUSION

Designing landscapes ecologically means integrating animals into them fully. We need to create habitat in more than just a generic way. We need to understand the biology of species we hope to attract and create the environment they need. We need to prioritize plants with which our native fauna have coevolutionary relationships. If we do these things successfully, we can begin to make up for the habitat already lost to development. We will also create built landscapes that are delightfully alive.

Landscapes that are alive include organisms that infect and eat plants. Diverse populations and communities of plants that are appropriate for their environment will stand the best chance of surviving the onslaught of pathogens and pests. We should try not to avoid damage to our plants entirely but to minimize the impact on the overall community, in terms of function, community composition, and successional direction. Enlisting the predators and parasites of herbivores will also help keep their populations in check. Where nuisance herbivores run free, we have little choice but to alter the composition of our plantings toward less palatable species. However, herbivores under proper management can help us fight back invasive species and change community composition in ways we desire.

Keystone species and allogenic ecosystem engineers are important for ecosystems in disproportion to their actual biomass. If we want our designed ecosystems to function fully, we need to find ways to incorporate these species into them. In a truly ecological designed landscape, their natural behaviors should further our management goals. Animal dispersers likewise will bring seeds onto a site whether we want them to or not. With initial plantings and perches, we can guide this process to knit our community into the surrounding vegetation in an intentional way.

Sometimes animals are a directly introduced or managed part of a project. By and large, however, they are part of the associated biodiversity that arrives in response to the biodiversity we planned and planted and to the conditions we created. The better we plan, the more the animals that arrive will be the ones we wanted and play the roles we want and need them to play. They will tell us by their numbers and their engagement how well we have succeeded.

8. When Lightning Strikes: Counting on Disturbance, Planning for Succession

In July 1988 lightning flashed deep within Yellowstone National Park. Grass browned to a crisp by the driest summer on record burst into flame. Needles crackled as the fire climbed nearby lodgepole pines (*Pinus contorta*) and spread from crown to crown. The wind rose, pushing fire and the acrid smell of smoke ahead of it. From a distance, the fire rumbled like a train. Closer, it roared like a jet engine, sucking in air to feed 200-foot towers of flame, spewing forth columns of smoke and embers that landed as far as 2 miles away (Billings Gazette 1995). Fifty fires started in the park that summer. By the time winter's snows put out the last pockets, more than a third of the park had been burned (National Park Service 2006). Debate raged: Was the blaze a natural stand-replacing fire, such as had last occurred in the eighteenth century, or had it been caused by decades of fire suppression? What was unmistakable as soon as the next summer, however, was that the forest was coming back. Wildflowers bloomed in the nutrient-rich ash. Millions of tightly sealed lodgepole pine cones had burst open in the flames, releasing their seeds. In between the charred trunks of their parents, these seeds sprouted into a new forest (fig. 8.1).

Destruction and regrowth are themes as old as nature itself. They are known to ecologists by the names *disturbance* and *succession*, and they provide the framework in which all the processes we have looked at up until now operate. A disturbance is a physical force or event that disrupts the physical or biological structure of an ecological system. Disturbances can be quick and concentrated as a lightning strike or slow and diffuse, like a decade-long drought. They occur at all scales, from a bison's wallow to a massive wildfire. Disturbances can interact, as when after a fire an exposed hillside sloughs off into a stream. Ecologists refer to the set of disturbances that affect a particular area over a long period of time, and their characteristic frequency, scale, intensity, and interactions, as a disturbance regime.

Along with natural disturbances are those of anthropogenic origin (see chap. 10), which have structured many of our most familiar landscapes. Paradoxically, people have also done damage by limiting natural disturbance regimes such as wildfires and floods. Our challenge is to realize that natural

Figure 8.1 Lodgepole pine seedlings in Yellowstone National Park. (Photo by Travis Beck.)

disturbances are regulating and regenerating forces, as well as destructive ones, and to figure out how to make our disturbances regenerative too.

Succession is the change in the plant community on a given site over time. If population dynamics record the year-to-year fluctuations in abundances of different species, succession deals with the long-term trends in these dynamics. As compared with the annual variations in flowering and reproduction that Inghe and Tamm found in their permanent research plots in Sweden and attributed to weather, it is the overall weakening of the hepatica population they studied under the increasing shade of the spruce forest (see chap. 2). Everywhere a patch of ground is disturbed or new land is created, succession occurs. Primary succession occurs in newly formed patches of bare earth, such as those created by volcanoes and receding glaciers. Secondary succession occurs in patches that formerly grew vegetation but have been denuded, by flood or avalanche, for instance. The important distinction is that in primary succession there are almost no plants, seeds, organic matter, or soil, whereas in secondary succession a biological legacy of the previous plant community remains.

It can be heartbreaking to see the natural landscape ravaged, or, as a designer, to watch something you have created be destroyed. It can even be difficult to see it change before your eyes into something you had not imagined. Perhaps for these very understandable reasons, conventional landscaping resists change. Yes, we love the changing seasons and plan exciting effects that will emerge with each one. And we love growth, maturation, and filling in—all that shows our landscape is healthy and living up to its potential. But if something terrible were to happen, our inclination would be to rush to put things back the way they were. And if things were to get "out of control," we would have a crew in there with loppers or herbicides as soon as we could. By and large, a conventional designed landscape is a set piece, built and maintained to realize a particular vision.

An ecologically designed landscape is, necessarily, a successional landscape growing in a disturbance regime. It is prepared for flood or fire, if these are likely events. It grows one thing and then another and then another. It is amenable to alteration and midcourse correction. In fact, it takes advantage of the natural processes of change to assemble and adjust itself. Let us examine ecologists' understanding of these dynamics and consider how we as designers might apply that understanding to create ecological landscapes that count on disturbance and plan for succession.

ECOSYSTEMS ARE FREQUENTLY DISTURBED

In August 1979, Hurricane David struck the eastern Caribbean island of Dominica. Dominica is a rugged, volcanic island. Its high profile catches and cools the trade winds, coaxing from them copious rains that nourish lush forests of tropical hardwoods. In many areas these forests had been left undisturbed by the residents of the island. David showed less restraint, lashing the island with winds averaging 92 kilometers per hour and gusting up to 241 kilometers per hour.

After David passed, Ariel Lugo flew to Dominica from the Institute of Tropical Forestry in Puerto Rico, along with several colleagues, eager to observe how climax forests (see chap. 2) would respond to such an intense hurricane. What they found caused them to rethink some of their basic assumptions (Lugo et al. 1982). By sampling standing and downed trees in plots of undeveloped forest they found that 42 percent of timber trees were damaged. Flat highland areas and windward slopes suffered the worst damage. Regrowth was rapid, however. Just 40 days after the storm, in wet forest areas seedlings and saplings were growing; some had already reached one and a half meters in height. When Lugo returned 1 year later, the forest appeared in good condition. Dominica's impressive forests were not the products of benign equilibrium, it turned out. With an average hurricane frequency of one storm every 15 years, Lugo and his colleagues (1982: 210) concluded, "stable, steady-state ecosystems probably cannot develop in hurricane-prone regions." The probability of any given tree living into late maturity (up to several hundred years old) under such a disturbance regime is slim. The probability of an entire forest doing so is much slimmer. Instead of seeing how climax forests responded to disturbance, Lugo et al. came away feeling that the entire notion of climax forests in hurricane-prone regions was in need of reexamination.

Earlier in the decade, Orie L. Loucks (1970) set out to measure the diversity and productivity of Wisconsin's temperate forests, forests made up of oaks, maples, hickories, and elms. In each of his measurements—seedling diversity, the difference in composition of the seedling and tree layers, and primary production—Loucks found wave forms, with diversity and productivity rising over time and then falling. These wave form patterns, Loucks realized, must have taken place many times before, triggered by random perturbations (disturbances) every 30 to 200 years (fig. 8.2). Loucks (1970: 23) concluded, "The changes that take place are in fact part of a characteristic series of transient phenomena which collectively make up the 'stable system' capable of repeating itself every time a perturbation starts the sequence over."

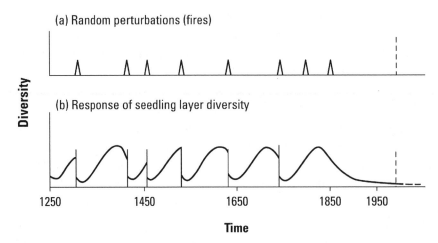

Figure 8.2 Seedling layer diversity rises and then declines in Wisconsin forests, until disturbance restarts the sequence. Repeated disturbances create wave form patterns over time. Suppression of fires since 1850 has led to decreased diversity. (From Loucks, O. L. Copyright ©1970 Oxford University Press. Evolution of diversity, efficiency, and community stability. *American Zoologist* 10:17–25. Reproduced with permission of Oxford University Press.)

Once they began looking, ecologists found signs of disturbance everywhere, and with it a new notion of community dynamics. Instead of a noble climax community, perfectly adapted to its site and persisting there indefinitely, ecologists began to see repeating series of communities, restarted time and time again by disturbance.

BE PREPARED FOR REGIONALLY COMMON DISTURBANCES

Disturbances occur, and our landscapes ought to be ready for them. Hurricanes and wildfires are common natural disturbances whose impacts can be mitigated with sensible landscape design and larger-scale planning (fig. 8.3).

Much of the damage caused by hurricanes stems from falling limbs, flying debris, and the direct force of winds (Abbey 1994). A simple preventive step is to remove dead branches and dead or diseased trees from areas where they might cause a problem. Tall sentinel trees such as cabbage palm (*Sabal palmetto*) and bald cypress placed at the edges of a lot can break up wind flows and act as initial storm buffers (fig. 8.4). Storm walls and wind deflector trees with low centers of gravity and deep root systems, such as live oak (*Quercus virginiana*), can guide winds up and over buildings. These species mentioned can also survive the flooding that accompanies hurricanes. Wind gusts can be slowed with layered plantings, and tightly planted protector plant groves can intercept airborne debris and protect leeward structures. Trees planted in masses will survive high winds better than solitary specimens. Using a variety of native plants in protector groves and plant masses can also provide necessary shelter for wildlife during storms.

Far from the Gulf Coast, state universities, county governments, and local fire departments through-

Figure 8.3 Hurricane Katrina makes landfall, August 29, 2005. (Image courtesy of NOAA.)

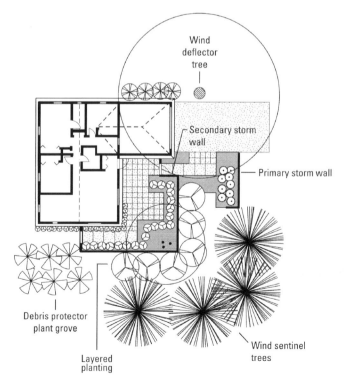

Figure 8.4 Plan for a hurricane-resistant landscape. (Courtesy of Buck Abbey, ASLA, Robert Reich School of Landscape Architecture, Louisiana State University. Original drawing reproduction, LSU CADGIS Lab, Louisiana State University.)

out the American West are issuing guidelines on landscaping in the wildfire zone. As decades of fire suppression give way to "let it burn" policies, fire is returning as a natural element of many environments. The main advice handed out is to reduce fuel (meaning flammable trees, shrubs, and even grasses) in concentric rings of defensible space. The problem with this advice, as Kim Sorvig (2004) found in his analysis of the 2003 Cedar and Wildcat Canyon fires near San Diego, is that it does not guarantee the safety of homes and may actually create the conditions that prompt more intense wildfires. Hot fires driven by strong winds, Sorvig notes, can leap over cleared space, burning one house and then, for no apparent reason, skipping the next. Excessive clearing can increase soil erosion and reduce the leaf litter falling to the soil, leaf litter that otherwise would contribute to the soil's water-holding organic matter. The effective localized drought that results creates the ideal conditions for wildfire.

The damage from Hurricane Katrina in New Orleans showed that preparations by individual property owners can be only so effective when the hurricane resistance of the regional landscape has been degraded. Restoring wetlands and sedimentation cycles in the Mississippi River delta will probably go further to mitigate disturbance than the choice of trees made by citizens. Likewise, when counties allow suburban-style development in fire-prone areas, damage is inevitable even with the best fire-resistant landscapes. Community-wide firebreaks, in the form of parks and constructed wetlands, are probably more effective than smaller clearings around individual homes. At a larger scale, controlled burns that create a mosaic of healthy forests can help prevent catastrophic wildfire (see chap. 9). Planning and management at the neighborhood, county, and regional levels are necessary to create landscapes that are truly prepared for disturbance.

PLANTS HAVE EVOLVED WITH REGIONAL DISTURBANCE REGIMES

Just as plants have adapted to the seasonal stresses and abundances of the climate in which they live (see chap. 1), plants have evolved to live in the conditions imposed by their regional disturbance regime. Some plant species, sometimes called fugitive species (similar to Grimes's ruderal species; see chap. 3), inhabit a niche created by disturbance. One such plant is the pin cherry (*Prunus pensylvanica*), whose life history and ecological role were studied by Peter Marks (1974). Pin cherry is a short-lived tree species that flourishes on disturbed sites in the hardwood forests of the northeastern United States. In the spring its branches are covered with masses of small white flowers with a fuzz of protruding stamens. In summer, these flowers give way to bright red fruit that is prized by birds (fig. 8.5). Before the pin cherries are overtaken by taller and more shade-tolerant maples and beeches, birds distribute large quantities of their seed. Working in New Hampshire's Hubbard Brook experimental forest, Marks found an average of five viable seeds per square foot buried in the soil along one transect. When fire, windthrow, or clearing opens up another gap in the forest, these seeds quickly germinate and fill the area with pin cherry seedlings. Not only is this a viable life history strategy for pin cherry, but, Marks found, it plays an important role in the northern hardwood forest ecosystem. The pin cherries that quickly grow up on disturbed sites reduce runoff and loss of nutrients from the forest ecosystem. Thus they help create stability for the overall ecosystem in a context of disturbance.

Fugitive species such as pin cherry are not the only plants to evolve in response to disturbance. In a 1980 article on the nonequilibrium coexistence of plants, Steward Pickett pointed out that disturbance

Figure 8.5 Pin cherry's fruits are attractive to birds, which spread seeds throughout the northeastern forest. When disturbance occurs, these seeds sprout and quickly fill the disturbed patch.

occurs within the lifetimes of most perennial plants and therefore exerts regular selective pressure on plants. Pickett argued that plant species have specialized for various points along the continuum of disturbance to recovery just as they have along all resource continua (see chap. 3). Some species, such as pin cherry, have evolved to take advantage of the abundance of light and nutrients freed up by disturbance. The cones of lodgepole pines, for instance, will open only after being exposed to a fire. Other plants have evolved to outcompete others in the low-resource environment of a community that has not been disturbed for some time.

A provocative suggestion, made by Robert Mutch in 1970, was that fire-adapted plants such as ponderosa pine (*Pinus ponderosa*) and eucalyptus (*Eucalyptus obliqua*) may actually encourage fires with their flammable litter, in order to clear the area around them of competitors. These plants may have gained an evolutionary advantage by going beyond adaptation to the inevitable and actively facilitating their regional disturbance regime.

INCLUDE PLANTS FROM DIFFERENT POINTS ALONG THE DISTURBANCE–RECOVERY CONTINUUM

In order to be fully prepared for disturbance, designed plant communities should include species evolved for different points along the continuum from disturbance to recovery. Fugitive species, and early successional species generally, have conventionally been regarded as lesser species that are short-lived and weedy. We want to plant the trees that will last for 100 years. In the context of disturbance, however, planting both fugitive and long-lived species can help create a landscape that can persist indefinitely.

As Marks's research showed, fugitive species play an important role in the stability of a landscape. By quickly stabilizing disturbed areas, they reduce erosion and prevent the loss of nutrients. When their propagules are present on site in the way pin cherry seeds were in Marks's research plots, they do all this by themselves, without the need for emergency planting, seeding, or mechanical erosion control. Native fugitive species also play an important role in maintaining community composition. As the first species to grow on a disturbed site, it is they who have to face off against weeds and invasive species.

Because they are adapted to grow quickly in open patches, they have a much better chance of success than slow-growing, long-lived plants. These late successional plants have their role too, of course, as it is they who can command a site in the intervals between disturbances.

In the Northeast, where windthrow is a major disturbance, early successional species include strawberry, raspberry, and blackberry, shrubs such as shadbush (*Amelanchier canadensis*), and trees such as pin cherry and aspen. Long-lived species that grow in undisturbed habitat include maples, beech, and hemlock.

A landscape that is planted to pass through several successional stages will probably accumulate the necessary propagules from early successional species just as a function of its growth and development. On larger sites, a purposely patchy environment can be created and maintained through deliberate disturbance in order to maintain populations of species adapted to each patch (see chap. 9). On smaller sites, fugitive species can be "borrowed" from adjacent properties, although it is important to assess whether these species are desirable before planning on incorporating them into a community.

Communities that incorporate plants from points all along the disturbance continuum are prepared to live in a disturbance regime. Between disturbances they can grow majestically. And when disturbances occur they can bounce back quickly. Should we also include plants that may encourage disturbance? Perhaps not next to the house. In the broader landscape of their native environment, however, these plants can help nature perform its own maintenance.

ECOLOGICAL RESILIENCE

Ecosystems across the globe have developed under various disturbance regimes, and continue to exist and function in spite of the disturbances they face. In 1973 C. S. Holling introduced the term *resilience* to describe this characteristic of natural systems. Resilience is the capacity of a system to absorb disturbance, reorganize if necessary, and retain essentially the same structure and function.

We can envision resilience with the metaphor of a stability landscape (fig. 8.6). A stability landscape is a topographic surface with various undulations and basins. Each basin represents an alternative stable state (see chap. 4). A ball placed into the landscape will roll into one or another basin and remain there, unless a force or a reconfiguration of the stability landscape pushes it out.

Disturbance is a force that can shift a system out of its current basin of attraction. Resilience is the ability of a system to avoid such a shift and depends on several factors (Walker et al. 2004). One is resistance, which we might think of as the depth of a basin, and is a measure of how difficult it is to change a system in the first place. For instance, the trees of a forest will not fall over every time the wind blows but only when the wind reaches a certain strength. Negative feedback loops increase resistance and keep ecosystems in their current stable state. Another factor is latitude, which we can think of as the breadth of a basin, or how much change a system can absorb before becoming something else. If the trees blow down but others regrow, is it still the same forest? At the edge of each basin is a threshold, on the other side of which change from one state to another will take place. Thresholds exist in nonlinear systems, in which a small amount of additional disturbance, if it pushes a system over a threshold, can have a huge effect. A third factor is precariousness, or how close a system is already to a threshold. If deer have eaten all the tree seedlings, maybe the forest will not be able to regrow if the mature trees blow down.

Figure 8.6 A stability landscape with three basins, representing alternative stable states, and unstable areas leading to no basin.

The stability landscape represents another possibility as well, namely that an ecosystem can slip away from all basins of attraction and into a realm of instability where unregulated biotic interactions or unremitting stochastic events keep it in a state of constant flux (Wu and Loucks 1995). Resilient systems are those that are able to experience a disturbance and not shift into this realm or to another stable state. Note, however, that ecosystems can be resilient when faced with a certain type or scale of disturbance but vulnerable to complete destruction from other, larger, or more powerful disturbances.

CREATE RESILIENT LANDSCAPES

How can we design landscapes that are more resilient? If we have succeeded in establishing a functioning ecosystem, how do we keep it going when the inevitable disturbances occur? One answer we know already: More diverse ecosystems better resist disturbance because the performance of important functions is spread over multiple species (see chap. 5). Planting plants from all points along the disturbance continuum is a way of increasing resilience through diversity. Another answer will come later, when we discuss the hierarchical organization of landscapes (see chap. 9).

We can also address the factors of resilience. Healthy and robust ecosystems, with regulating feedback loops, are more resistant to disturbance. Where populations of plants and natural enemies are well established, for example, an insect outbreak is less likely to have a devastating impact. We may be able to move thresholds and increase the latitude of our current stable state by addressing potential issues. Reducing populations of invasive species in the area decreases the basin of attraction that is being overrun. We should also try to reduce the precariousness of the systems we manage. A landscape within the wildfire zone is in a vulnerable position if fuels have built up through years of fire suppression. Fuel removal and controlled burning can ease such a system away from the brink.

Resilient landscapes are also multifunctional and have a high degree of flexibility. Where we maximize for a single function, including a single form of resilience, we risk making our landscapes vulnerable to another disturbance (Walker 2007). Where irrigation is used to ramp up the productivity of agricultural landscapes, for instance, salinization can ruin the entire system. If we have focused our design and management efforts entirely on fire resistance by removing vegetation, we may have made ourselves vulnerable to landslides. A balanced approach will create a more resilient landscape.

PERIODIC DISTURBANCE DIVERSIFIES HABITAT

Disturbances are not just blows to be bounced back from, however. They are integral to how many landscapes function. For instance, stream ecologists have come to appreciate how disturbance contributes to the creation of aquatic habitat diversity. By their very nature, disturbances disrupt established communities and, sometimes, the environment where they live. Disturbances are generally stochastic, meaning they result from processes that include an element of chance. We don't know exactly when or where a fire will break out or how severe it will be. Over time, however, we can get a sense of probabilities. When mapped onto the landscape, a probabilistic disturbance regime creates a matrix of different habitats (see chap. 9).

With this perspective in mind, Lee Benda and colleagues (2003) from the Earth Systems Institute examined the aftereffects of the 1995 Rabbit Creek fire on streams in the Boise River watershed in Idaho. The Rabbit Creek fire was a large stand-replacing fire that swept through the ponderosa pine and Douglas fir forests of Idaho's Sawtooth Mountains. The next summer, intense thunderstorms hit the area. The hydrophobic soil that resulted from the fire could not absorb the water. Sediment and runoff gathered in upstream channels, quickly scouring stream bottoms and tearing off downstream in a wall of water, dirt, rocks, and fallen trees. Where side channels joined larger channels, much of the sediment and wood came spilling to a stop in the form of large alluvial fans. In the short term, these storm events buried existing habitat and killed large numbers of aquatic organisms. In the long term, however, Benda et al. concluded, such events are an intrinsic part of the stream ecosystem and create diverse habitats within the stream environment (fig. 8.7). A new alluvial fan, they found, forms a nick point in the channel gradient. Upstream, where water and sediment are impounded, the channel is flattened for as far as 4 kilometers. Downstream, the gradient increases, and a boulder cascade results. The channel upstream widens, where topography allows, and a braided stream often results. Pools form in the vicinity of alluvial fans. Where streams cut through the aggraded sediment, terraces form. Existing terraces are often renewed by the flash flood that created the alluvial fan. Pools, side channels, and the gravel-bottomed flat areas upstream of alluvial fans are important microhabitats for certain aquatic organisms. Floodplains and terraces are significant habitats in the riparian forest. Although Benda et al. looked only at stream morphology, it is logical that the diversification of habitat resulting from flash flooding supports the biological diversity of the stream ecosystem and the riparian forest.

Figure 8.7 Terraces, flat-bottomed sections, and riffles are evident in this stream, at the base of an avalanche run in Idaho's Caribou National Forest. (Photo by Tony Varilone.)

WORK WITH THE FORCES OF DISTURBANCE

Ecological landscaping involves more than just being prepared for the negative impacts of an inevitable disturbance. It involves creating landscapes that embrace the forces of wind, fire, and flood as part of their natural cycles. That may mean not just letting nature run its destructive course but harnessing its energies to periodically resculpt the land on which we work, creating desired growing environments along the way.

Bruce Blair and his family have implemented such an approach on the banks of the Cannon River in Minnesota. After experiencing a devastating flood in 1998, the Blairs realized that they needed to move beyond conventional engineering and revegetation approaches. The key problem was not just high water levels during flood events but the energy of the floodwaters and the massive quantities of sediment moved. The 1998 flood both dug an enormous hole in the driveway and deposited hundreds of cubic yards of sand elsewhere on the property. To accommodate these flows, the Blairs laid out their entire landscape around the flow of floodwaters. In 2010, waters rose to nearly 1998 levels, but this time they first encountered a double row of hedges. These hedges are laid out parallel to the river, and they direct floodwaters downstream and slow the waters that rise toward the house. The intention is to slow floodwaters enough to allow deposition of the heaviest particles (i.e. sand) in low spots on the property. Evening out low spots this way should reduce turbulence and damaging erosion in future floods. Beyond the hedges, the road that crosses the property parallel to the river functions as a dike. It has also been graded so that water crosses at a planned point and is directed into the flood management zone. In the flood management zone, more hedges are laid out across the path of the flood and parallel to it to further absorb its energy and direct its flow. By this point, floodwaters have lost enough of their energy to begin dropping some of their finer particles. The nutrient-rich silt and clay particles left in the pasture provide natural fertilization. Immediately around the house Blair has designated a no-damage zone, protected by a rock retaining wall and a flood fence. Even the flood fence is permeable on its downstream side, however, and in 2010 it functioned as designed, allowing quiet waters in to keep more destructive waters out (see fig. 8.8).

In a natural context, floods reshape and regenerate riparian and low-lying environments. The natural cycle of flooding on the Cannon River has been altered through deforestation and development. Through careful design, however, the Blairs' property not only survived recent flooding but profited from it as landscape features directed the water's energy and orchestrated the deposition of sediment.

Figure 8.8 Calm waters within the permeable flood fence prevented damage from more forceful flows and debris in the zone adjacent to the Blairs' house during the 2010 flood. (Photo by Bruce B. Blair.)

INTERMEDIATE LEVELS OF DISTURBANCE INCREASE DIVERSITY BY PREVENTING COMPETITIVE EXCLUSION

Disturbance also supports local biodiversity by preventing competitive interactions from reaching their conclusion. Tropical rainforests and coral reefs are famous for their high levels of diversity. The equilibrium explanation of such diversity runs like this: In a stable environment species develop unique niches over time that allow many species to coexist quite closely (see chap. 3). However, as ecologists were coming to realize in the late 1970s, if disturbances are frequent enough to prevent these communities from reaching equilibrium, what explains the great diversity found there? Joseph Connell set out to examine this issue in a classic article that appeared in *Science* in 1978. Citing published studies and experiments of his own, Connell produced evidence that undisturbed areas of tropical forests and coral reefs are actually low in diversity. Along the Western Rift Escarpment in Uganda, for instance, near what is today one of the last refuges of the mountain gorillas, large areas are covered by a climax forest composed almost entirely of ironwood (*Cynometra alexandri*). Ironwood makes up 75 to 90 percent of the canopy, and its seedlings and saplings dominate the understory. These forests occur in areas that destructive storms never reach. In areas of coral reefs off Queensland, Australia that are protected from damaging hurricanes, Connell observed, just a few species of staghorn coral (*Acropora cervicornis*, named for its uncanny resemblance to deer antlers) dominate. In both cases, competitive exclusion has had ample time to operate without disturbance, and one or just a few species have come to dominate (see chap. 3). In areas where tropical rainforests are recovering from disturbance, on the other hand, Connell found, a mixed forest is likely to occur, in which some species are well represented in the canopy and other, more shade-tolerant species are coming up from the understory. On coral reefs disturbed by hurricanes numerous species of coral have colonized disturbed areas, but none has yet choked out all the others. These findings led Connell to support what he called the intermediate disturbance hypothesis as the primary explanation for the high levels of diversity in tropical rainforests and coral reefs. In areas that are disturbed too frequently or too severely, or over too large an area, diversity will have little chance to develop because only the earliest colonists will ever survive. In areas that are disturbed very infrequently or only slightly, or only in small patches, competitive exclusion will lead to low levels of diversity. In areas that are disturbed at intermediate levels of frequency, severity, or area, diversity will be high (fig. 8.9). The nonequilibrium explanation for diversity offered by the intermediate disturbance hypothesis has since come to be widely accepted. The wonderful circle that is created, of course, is that as disturbance promotes local biodiversity, local biodiversity increases the stability of the community in the face of disturbance (see chap. 5). Diversity is part and parcel of life in a changing world.

USE DISTURBANCE AS A MANAGEMENT TOOL

Especially where natural disturbance regimes have been altered, disturbance can make a useful management tool.

The prairies of North America evolved in relationship with several forms of disturbance, including grazing and wallowing by herds of buffalo, soil movement by ground-dwelling animals such as prairie dogs, and fire. Undisturbed, a prairie is likely to lose diversity as short-lived forbs and grasses give way

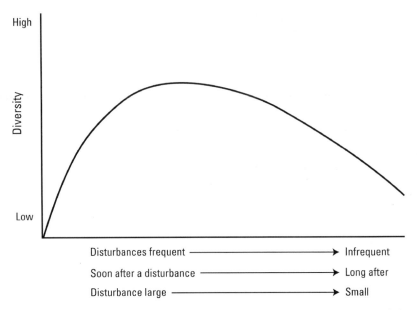

Figure 8.9 Diversity is highest where disturbances are intermediate in frequency, severity, and size. (From Connell, J. H. Copyright ©1978 The American Association for the Advancement of Science. Diversity in tropical rain forests and coral reefs. *Science* 199:1302–10. Reprinted with permission from AAAS.)

to fewer long-lived species. Woody plants may invade and nutrients become tied up in aboveground biomass. Whenever attempting to recreate prairie, either in a prairie garden or a restoration setting, it is best to plan for some similar form of disturbance.

For prairies in developed areas, mowing is often considered the safest form of disturbance to practice. Mowing begins the recycling of organic matter and opens up access to sunlight for new plants. Where practical, however, burning may be the preferred alternative (fig. 8.10). Choosing the timing of a burn has important ramifications for which species recover most rapidly and can be used to adjust the species mix of a managed prairie or prairie garden (Wasowski and Wasowski 2002). Spring burns favor warm season grasses, whereas fall burns benefit cool season grasses and most forbs. Frequency of burns also affects the balance of short- and long-lived perennials, annuals, and woody plants. Combining these variables produces a range of management options. Naturally, safety precautions must be observed whenever a controlled burn is attempted.

On the largest prairie properties, grazing may be a suitable form of disturbance. After observing wild grasslands in Africa, Allan Savory (1988) determined that grasslands do best when they are intensively disturbed by ungulates, then allowed a lengthy period to recover. This is the natural cycle of grasslands subject to seasonal use by migrating herds. It can be mimicked in pasture systems by using fixed or mobile fences to pen herds in small areas for short periods of time. These areas are thoroughly grazed and manured, the soil is turned up by hooves, and then they have a long period for vigorous new growth to emerge and increase in biomass.

On a much smaller scale, and usually not in a prairie setting, the rotational grazing principle can be

Figure 8.10 Land managers set a controlled burn in Kansas. (Photo by Jeff Vanuga, Natural Resources Conservation Service.)

applied by use of a chicken tractor (Lee 1994). In its simplest form, a chicken tractor is a bottomless mobile chicken coop. Wherever it is located the chickens will scratch the soil, weeding and turning it, eat weed seeds and insects, and leave a quantity of their manure already incorporated into the soil. By moving a chicken tractor through a garden or orchard and planting behind it, one creates a patchy environment in which newly disturbed ground and several short-term successional stages are present at all times (see chap. 9). This should help support a diversity not only of plants but also of insects and soil organisms.

When we use disturbance as a management tool, we can seek to emulate natural disturbance regimes in several respects (Hunter 2007). Spatially, we can duplicate the patterns of natural disturbances. Temporally, we can initiate disturbances on a cycle similar to the natural disturbances we are replacing. We can also leave behind legacies of organic matter or seed sources to initiate succession in the ways our reference disturbances would.

DISTURBANCE BY HUMANS HAS LONG INFLUENCED THE STRUCTURE AND COMPOSITION OF PLANT COMMUNITIES

As we seek to emulate natural disturbances, we should recall that in places with long histories of habitation, natural and human disturbances have long interacted. Take, for example, Horse Cove, a diverse and productive stand of forest nestled into the southeastern Blue Ridge escarpment in North Carolina, where Hazel and Paul Delcourt used pollen and charcoal particles captured in layers of peat to examine the relationship between fire and vegetation. Remarkably, Delcourt and Delcourt (1997) found that even in this humid region where lightning-caused fires are rare, fire-dependent trees such as chestnut and oak dominated the forests surrounding the Cove for close to 4,000 years. A clue came in pollen found in the peat core from weedy and cultivated species such as plantain (*Plantago*) and corn. This pollen indicated human activity in the Horse Cove area throughout the time period covered by their peat core. In fact, archaeological remains there date back 8,000 years. By examining the distribution of various charcoal particle sizes in the layers of peat (smaller particles can travel from farther away), Delcourt and Delcourt concluded that Native Americans in the area made selective use of fire, burning dry areas to encourage the growth of useful fire-adapted species, without creating fires of such intensity that they would impinge on wetter areas and north-facing slopes. In effect, Native Americans were using an intermediate disturbance regime to create a patchy landscape with high levels of vegetational diversity.

Since European settlement, humans have continued to affect plant communities in North America through their patterns of land use. David Foster (1992) examined the impact of land use since 1730 on 380 hectares of land in central Massachusetts known as Prospect Hill. From the beginning, Foster noted, physiographic and soil conditions significantly determined land use. Swamps, seepages, steep slopes, and rocky areas were left as woodland. Better-drained land was tilled, and most of the remaining land was used as pasture. Poorly drained pastures were often the first to be abandoned and tilled lands the last. In the early twentieth century, landowners on Prospect Hill planted many abandoned fields with white pine plantations. When a destructive hurricane hit the region in 1938, these plantations were disproportionately affected. Today's vegetation reflects this complex interaction between land conditions and land use and between anthropogenic and natural disturbance (fig. 8.11). Structurally, today's forests on Prospect Hill are young and even-aged, with abrupt discontinuities based on property lines and past land management decisions. Compositionally, land use history plays a role as well. Spruce (*Picea rubens*) and hemlock are largely restricted to undisturbed woodlots. Former pasture areas, on the other hand, are dominated by pine, chestnut sprouts, and early successional forests of birch and red maple (*Acer rubrum*). To understand the structure and composition of today's forests on Prospect Hill, it is necessary to understand their history of disturbance by humans.

DISTURB FOR THE BETTER

Human disturbance is such a ubiquitous feature of the landscape that a sensible rule in site planning should be not to disturb any remaining undisturbed areas (see chap. 10). The complexity arises when we recognize that even areas that appear "natural," such as the wooded areas of Prospect Hill or Horse Cove, reflect a legacy of human disturbance.

Understanding a site's history and reading the signs of disturbance and recovery are important aspects of site analysis. Just as the settlers of Prospect Hill did, we will choose certain lands for certain purposes. We should seek to lay our plans onto the existing landscape in relation not only to site conditions but to what has happened before. Following the footprint of past disturbance may have

Figure 8.11 Second-growth forest and remains of a dam constructed in the 18th century for a tannery on Prospect Hill, Massachusetts. The tannery affected nearby vegetation not only through clearing but through selective harvesting of hemlock, whose bark was used in the tanning process. (Courtesy of Harvard Forest Archives, Harvard Forest, Petersham, MA. Photograph by David R. Foster.)

the least impact. Where recovery is well under way, however, past disturbance alone does not justify redisturbance. There we must step between the lines and seek opportunities to disturb areas whose alteration will least affect the overall landscape. Perhaps we would remove an area of older pine plantation because it is vulnerable to disturbance anyway. Or we could remove a stand of even-aged trees if similar stands are nearby (see chap. 9).

We might also wonder whether all the disturbances we initiate in the landscape could support diversity and ecosystem processes, the way the Native American use of fire at Horse Cove did. Could we clear land for timber in a manner that initiates pulses of growth and maintains the age structure of forest tree populations (see chap. 2)? Could our road cuts serve, landslide like, as habitat patches for native ruderal species and animals that need open ground? Could our suburbs excise damaged lands and act as nuclei for restoration? Could we actually live on the land in a manner that leaves it enhanced? Disturbance not only damages what existed before but also makes way for something new.

SUCCESSION, CLASSICALLY VIEWED

Early ecologists recognized that plant communities respond to disturbance by growing anew through a series of stages. They called the change in plant communities over time *succession*. Their observations and interpretations of this phenomenon laid the groundwork for our current understanding. They also made strong claims that have shaped the debate that followed.

Henry Chandler Cowles's PhD thesis, published in 1899, set the direction of the study of succession in North America for the next 70 years. Cowles studied the ever-changing sand dunes at the southern end of Lake Michigan. Just a streetcar's ride from the University of Chicago, beside the flat blue waters of the lake, these white sand dunes crawl restlessly before the wind. Advancing dunes bury preexisting plant communities before being recolonized and stabilized by new plant life.

What we would today call a plant community, Cowles called a plant society, and he put these societies in order of their historical development. Irregular patches of beachgrass and the occasional cottonwood (*Populus* x *canadensis*) begin the process of dune formation closest to the beach. Behind them is a wandering maze of dunes covered only by the succulent annual bugseed (*Corispermum hyssopifolium*) and occasional cottonwood. Farther from shore, where the wind abates, the wandering dunes may be captured by plants that get started at the base of the lee slopes. Beachgrass appears again, and then a dense shrubby growth of dogwood, willow, and chokecherry (*Prunus virginiana*). Once the slope is captured this way, basswood (*Tilia americana*) grows up. Maple and beech succeed the basswood, establishing a deciduous mesophytic forest. On the windward slopes a different progression occurs, with manzanita and junipers arising first, then giving way to forests of pine or, on protected or southern slopes, oak.

Cowles called this process of vegetation change a genetic succession. He saw it as a process by which the plant life of the region modified the harsh physical environment of the dune to ever more genial environments (except when shifting winds tear into established dunes and destroy the preexisting vegetation) until the conditions were at last right for the normal climax type of the region, a diversified deciduous forest.

The idea of an orderly development of the vegetation of a region into a climax community received more general expression in the work of Frederic Clements, with whose ideas on well-integrated communities we are already familiar (see chap. 2). Clements was aware that the plant communities he observed throughout the American West were not entirely static, and he accounted for the changes he saw through an elaborate description of succession.

Clements (1916) distinguished six successional processes: (1) nudation (disturbance), (2) migration, (3) ecesis (establishment), (4) competition, (5) reaction, and (6) stabilization. Initially, in Clements's framework, early successional plants struggle only against the elements, the harsh environment of a denuded area. Once many plants are able to establish and reproduce, competition for nutrients, water, and light ensues (fig. 8.12). Reaction is the effect that the competitively successful plants have on their habitat. For example, a growing grove of trees reduces wind, casts shade, and drops leaves that molder to form duff and then humus in the soil. Clements contended that the reactions of early pioneer stages create an environment more favorable to late successional species. These species are then able to invade and exert their own reactions on the environment. This process continues until the

Figure 8.12 A plate from Clements (1916). Original caption: "*Ceanothus* consocies surrounded by *Pinus ponderosa* climax, which replaces it as a result of competition for light, Spearfish Cañon, Black Hills, South Dakota."

point of stabilization, when a vegetation type reaches dominance and, through the process of reaction, creates an environment more favorable to itself than to any invaders. This vegetation type is the climax. As Clements described it, the entire sere has brought us from a harsh, denuded environment subject to invasion to a controlled, moderate environment presided over by a vegetation type (almost always trees) that, barring disturbance, will remain dominant as long as the climate remains the same.

Clements jumped to several broad conclusions about succession. First, he claimed that the development of a community through succession is akin to the development of an organism. "As an organism," he wrote, "the formation [plant community] arises, grows, matures, and dies" (Clements 1916: 3). When allowed to proceed naturally, succession will always follow its appointed path. Thus, like an organism, each climax community can faithfully reproduce itself within its range. Second, Clements claimed that succession results from the process of reaction described earlier. In the course of development, each stage creates the conditions that favor the next, until no further development can occur. "Reaction," Clements (1916: 80) wrote, "is thus the keynote to all succession, for it furnishes the explanation of the orderly progression by stages and the increasing stabilization which produces a final climax." Third, Clements proclaimed the existence and necessity of the climax. As a developmental process, succession must be progressive, reaching its highest stage in the climax. The climax is an optimized community that, through the process of succession, flourishes where bare rock once stood.

DESIGN SUCCESSIONAL SERIES

Although our understanding of succession has evolved since the days of Cowles and Clements, the central idea of a changing series of plants is useful to landscape designers.

Nearly all major landscape projects begin with a disturbance, whether as significant as the demolition and reshaping of a former industrial site or as slight as pulling out the unwanted vegetation in an overgrown garden. This disturbance automatically sets in motion a process of succession, whether we choose to acknowledge it or not.

Conventional landscaping practice is to envision a mature landscape—a climax, if you will—and attempt to move directly from disturbance to this climax community, or at least a miniature version of it. The problems with this approach are so common as to go unrecognized: acres of mulch, thousands of weeds, transplant shock, scorching plants waiting for the shade trees under which they would grow so well to mature, impatience with these little sticks that are supposed to be screening that view! Alternatively, we pay outrageous sums for large trees that struggle to reestablish themselves on their new site.

Instead, we should recognize that plant communities evolve in successional stages. We can arrange plants from different points along the disturbance continuum in a temporal series. This allows us to implement not just a single vision but a series of visions that reveal themselves over time. To borrow a successional series from Marks, we might purposefully plant beech between the pin cherry seedlings amid the blackberries that have filled the clearing we made to build our New Hampshire dream house. Each could be arranged in an appealing layout, so that when the beech were small the blackberries would be bountiful, then for many years the pin cherries would be gorgeous in spring, and when the blackberries and the pin cherries were long gone the beech would be orderly and grand. Even better, the interplay of the three could be arranged so that the rising beech saplings would play nicely against the canopy of the pin cherries above the last long shoots of blackberry.

There is not only a design logic to a sequence like this but a horticultural one. As Clements's framework recognizes, the first plants on a disturbed site have to establish in newly open conditions. Early successional plants, such as blackberry and pin cherry, are adapted to these open conditions and can quickly fill a space. However, early successional plants are often short-lived. Their evolutionary strategy is to exploit disturbance, not to stick it out in the long run. For a landscape designer, this gives time for late successional species to establish and grow. Through the process of reaction, well-chosen early successional species can also prepare the ground for other species to grow, accumulating nutrients through nitrogen fixation, building soil organic matter, and moderating the site microclimate.

Planning a successional landscape offers opportunities to design over time and to let natural processes do some of the hard work of establishing a plant community on a disturbed site.

MIGRATION MATTERS

When Mt. St. Helens erupted in 1980, the disaster presented the opportunity of a lifetime to ecologist Roger del Moral: a chance to study primary succession from the very beginning. Del Moral and his colleagues and students quickly set out permanent plots on the devastated slopes of Mt. St. Helens to track the return of plant life (del Moral and Bliss 1993; del Moral and Wood 1993).

Contrary to the classical theories of succession, early invaders were not lichens and lower plants. Instead, stress-tolerant ruderals drawn from the available flora moved in directly. In areas adjacent to intact vegetation, invasion of plants from these communities commenced within 2 years. In more isolated areas, however, even 13 years after the eruption, plant cover was sparse (fig. 8.13). In specially designed seed traps del Moral and his colleagues collected samples of the "seed rain" falling at numerous sites. Not surprisingly, seeds of wind-dispersed species such as western pearly everlasting (*Anaphalis margaritacea*) and fireweed (*Epilobium*) were the most common in their traps. These seeds grew most often in particular microsites, such as on rocky surfaces, or at the edge of rills where they were protected from the sun and able to benefit from some extra moisture. Del Moral and his colleagues applied the term *safe sites* to these microsites.

When more than one plant species has the opportunity to establish in a given safe site, the first to gain a foothold there has an advantage over any subsequent invaders. Just as community composi-

Figure 8.13   Plants regrowing where conditions allow on Studebaker Edge, Mt. St. Helens. (Photo by Roger del Moral.)

tion at the edges of the blast area was affected by the makeup of adjacent vegetation, composition in isolated areas was largely determined by who got there first.

In secondary succession, the effects of what plants are already present are even more important. Several decades before the eruption of Mt. St. Helens, Frank Egler (1954) turned his attention to nothing so dramatic as a volcanic landscape but to common abandoned agricultural land. By the time of an old field's last disturbance (plowing), it is full of the seeds and living roots of numerous plants. When the field is abandoned, these plants begin to grow and come to dominance in turn. The pattern is familiar: first weeds, then grasses, then woody shrubs, and finally trees. What Egler pointed out, however, is that these species did not each arrive on the site after it had been prepared by their predecessors; they were all there from the beginning. This single factor, which he called initial floristic composition, he estimated is responsible for 95 percent of the development of the subsequent vegetation.

Rather than being an orderly sequence of invasions and reactions, succession on Mt. St. Helens and in Egler's old fields has emerged as a historical process, dependent on which plants arrive and establish first.

VEGETATE THROUGH MANAGED MIGRATION

In conventional landscaping, how the plants get to the site goes without saying: We order the plants we want from the nursery and they come in a big truck. This can be seen as an aggressive version of initial floristic composition. It is worth taking a step back, however, and considering the many ways by which plants can arrive on a site and the uses to which they might be put.

Chris Reed and his colleagues at Stoss Landscape Urbanism developed a planting plan that relies largely on successional processes in their plan for Riverside Park in New Bedford, Massachusetts (Reed 2005) (fig. 8.14). Riverside Park is a 27-acre brownfield site along the Acushnet River with a lingering industrial legacy in the form of environmental contamination, brick rubble, and altered landforms. The city of New Bedford had limited and uncertain funds for park development and maintenance. To accommodate these realities, Reed and his colleagues called for larger specimens of trees with wind-dispersed seeds to be planted around the south and west perimeters of the naturalistic park. Not only were the strips of trees located in visible areas, thereby providing a high-value location for investment in larger specimens, but they were also upwind of the rest of the park. As time goes on, these trees would seed themselves throughout the park. The landscape architects also planned to include "seed pods," loose clusters of inexpensive tree whips and other plants whose seeds are dispersed by gravity. These clusters would grow denser through time and expand downslope. The seed trees and the seed pods provided a means for low-cost vegetation of a large area. Furthermore, in the event of a flood, hurricane, or other disturbance, the park would be primed to revegetate itself.

Using wind and gravity as agents of migration does not have to be a random affair, giving rise to an artless landscape. As del Moral found on Mt. St. Helens, plant propagules migrating into a project area have a much higher rate of germination and establishment in safe sites. Chris Reed and his colleagues, in their plan for Riverside Park, called for a dendritic network of landforms that collect and disperse on-site stormwater. They located their seed pods in wet catchment areas, where the planted material is likely to establish with minimal attention and where seeds from the planted material and from the

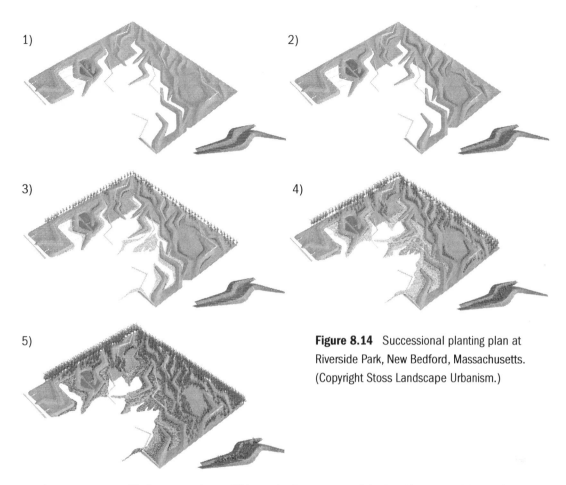

1)

2)

3)

4)

5)

Figure 8.14 Successional planting plan at Riverside Park, New Bedford, Massachusetts. (Copyright Stoss Landscape Urbanism.)

seed trees are more likely to germinate. Ultimately, the pattern of the landforms would be reflected in the distribution of the growing trees and shrubs.

SUCCESSION PROCEEDS BY MULTIPLE MECHANISMS

Frederic Clements made reaction, in which early successional species obligingly prepare the way for late successional species to take their place, the keynote to all succession. In one of the most widely cited articles on succession, Joseph Connell and Ralph Slatyer (1977) argued that the Clementsian model of succession, which they called facilitation, operates in some cases, but less genial models also exist.

Facilitation assumes that late successional species are unable to establish in a newly disturbed area until early successional species prepare the ground for them. Connell and Slatyer cited the giant saguaro cactus, whose seedlings are unlikely to survive except in the shade of nurse plants, as an example of facilitation in action. Often, however, as Egler recognized with initial floristic composition, late successional species establish right alongside early successional ones.

If most of the plants of a community are present from the beginning in many cases, what then accounts for the observed changes in community composition over time? Connell and Slatyer proposed two further models. The first is tolerance. Maybe late successional species are simply better able to tolerate the changing resource environment (e.g., less light in a maturing forest) and therefore come to dominate over time. Or perhaps, once established, some species actually prevent others from growing. Connell and Slatyer called this model inhibition. In the inhibition model, early successional species hold their ground until they die off or are removed by some type of disturbance. Late successional species may then move in. Sugar maple, for instance, has been shown to establish primarily in the gaps opened up by the death of other trees.

Even the Connell and Slatyer models do not represent the full complexity of successional change. Steward Pickett and two colleagues (1987) argued that facilitation, tolerance, and inhibition rarely apply to a full successional sequence and are more properly seen as mechanisms to account for specific transitions within that sequence. They cited the example of grasses, trees, and sumac (*Rhus typhina*) in a Michigan old field. Initially, a dense herbaceous groundcover prevents the establishment of trees. This is a case of inhibition. Where the sumac invades, its shade thins out the grasses and allows for the easier establishment of tree seedlings. The interaction between the sumac and the trees at that point is an example of facilitation. Once the tree seedlings are established, however, the sumac might actually compete with them for resources, and we would be back to inhibition. Rather than argue for one or another broad model, Pickett and his colleagues suggested, we should look more carefully at how numerous factors—differential ability to exploit resources, specific life history characteristics, and populations' interactions with disturbance regimes—drive successional change.

ACCELERATE SUCCESSION INTELLIGENTLY, RETARD IT NATURALLY

We can use our understanding of the mechanisms of succession to guide the development of a constructed ecological landscape.

In cases where we want to speed up the transition to a desired community, an obvious first step is to remove or weaken plants that are inhibiting the community we desire from getting established. If the old agricultural field is not returning to prairie on its own, it may be because it is choked with weeds. In cases where initial floristic composition is a primary determinant of succession, simply removing undesired elements can create a stable plant community. We may also wish to plant late successional species, where conditions are right for them. There is no use planting plants that do best in a well-developed soil into exposed subsoil, even if we have worked soil amendments into the top few inches. However, if the species we have in mind are able to grow in all conditions and outlast other species because of their long lifespan or tolerance of root competition, we might as well get them started at the beginning.

In the ecological landscape, we can go beyond the removal of inhibitors or the planting of tolerant plants to the active use of facilitators. Longer-lived plants that facilitate the growth of other plants are called nurse plants. Nurse plants provide shade and shelter in hot, dry environments. They may enrich the soil underneath them through their leaf litter, or they may even add nitrogen to the soil through relationships with nitrogen-fixing bacteria (see chap. 6). As we have seen, saguaro cacti have difficulty surviving as seedlings except in the shade of nurse plants such as palo verde and mesquite (fig. 8.15). Conventional Sonoran Desert landscaping relies on transplanting single-shoot cacti up to 10 feet tall.

Figure 8.15 Young saguaros grow under a nurse tree in Saguaro National Park, Arizona. (Courtesy of National Park Service.)

An ecological approach would be to scatter seeds into the shade of a clump of young palo verde. For the first 30 years or so, the palo verde will be the principal landscape element in that area. As the saguaro begin to flower and fruit, however, the palo verde can be removed (it may have even begun to naturally senesce), leaving in their place a nice grouping of well-established cacti. If the patience called for by this approach seems excessive, consider that even the 10-foot saguaro shoot may take another 25 years to grow arms and develop the distinctive saguaro look.

In certain circumstances, we might want to use inhibitory effects to retard succession. Millions of dollars are spent annually on pruning, mowing, and spraying to keep trees from obstructing power lines and encroaching on highway right-of-ways. As an alternative, if we selectively remove tree seedlings and can get canopy closure of dense clonal shrubs such as black huckleberry (*Gaylussacia baccata*) or nannyberry (*Viburnum lentago*) in the Northeast, we can create a shrub community that resists invasion by trees through natural inhibitory effects (Niering 2006). The same principle can be used by homeowners trying to preserve a view or solar access to their house.

HOW SUCCESSION UNFOLDS DEPENDS ON MULTIPLE FACTORS

Where Clements saw succession as the predetermined development of a climax community through reaction, contemporary ecologists view succession as a contingent process, dependent on multiple factors, that can lead to multiple possible outcomes.

Pickett, Cadenasso, and Meiners (2009) outlined a framework for succession in which changes in plant community composition and structure are driven by three general causes: differential site availability, differential species availability, and differential species performance. Differential site availability refers to the character of disturbance, whether it opens new substrates, for instance, and also to the available levels of resources. Differential species availability stems from both species whose propagules were in place before disturbance and species that migrate onto a site. Differential species performance covers an entire gamut of familiar processes from plant adaptations to life history strategies, competition, and mutualistic interactions.

Lawrence Walker (1999) used the glacier forelands at Glacier Bay, Alaska as a case study in which the interaction of these factors can be observed. When Captain George Vancouver sighted Glacier Bay in 1794 it was a solid sheet of ice as far as the eye could see. Ever since, the glaciers of Glacier Bay have been retreating farther and farther inland, opening up into two large watery arms with numerous inlets, home to humpback whales (*Megaptera novaeangliae*) and reintroduced sea otters (*Enhydra lutris kenyoni*), and leaving behind bare moraines of tilled soil and rock (fig. 8.16). A generalized successional sequence for this area is cryptogamic crust → the low nitrogen-fixing shrub *Dryas drummondii* → nitrogen-fixing alder (*Alnus viridis*) or cottonwood trees (*Populus trichocarpa*) → spruce (*Picea sitchensis*) or hemlock (*Tsuga heterophylla*). Within this general framework, however, multiple patterns of succession occur.

Walker explained the ways in which different factors affect the successional patterns of Glacier Bay. Resource availability is one factor. The wet and warm conditions at Glacier Bay that allow the predomi-

Figure 8.16 The first shrubs establish themselves on the outwash plain below Brady Glacier in Glacier Bay National Park, Alaska. (Courtesy of National Park Service.)

nance of alder and the rapid growth of spruce forests are unusual among glacial forelands. Differential species availability also influences the pattern of succession. At the mouth of the bay, spruce forests are in close proximity to what was once newly exposed glacial terrain. Here spruce probably colonized at an earlier stage. In more remote inland areas of the East Arm, alder dominates initially. Differential species performance too comes into play. Alder facilitates the growth of spruce seedlings by adding nitrogen and organic matter to the soil. At the same time, alder thickets inhibit seedling growth through light and root competition. The balance of facilitative and inhibitory effects determines the rate of successional change. Ultimately, it is the life histories of the various species involved that seems to determine the overall pattern of succession: Spruce simply live longer than alders or cottonwoods. Because of all these contingencies, any conclusions about succession at Glacier Bay, Walker emphasized, may not apply to other glacial areas.

MANAGE SUCCESSION TO REACH DESIRED OUTCOMES

Because of the interactions of the numerous determining factors, a successional landscape can develop from its initial conditions to one of several alternative stable states. If we view a landscape we create as a self-organizing ecosystem undergoing a successional process (see chap. 4), then the drivers of succession become our points of influence on the process, by which we can help guide our landscape to a desired state. This framework unites many of the individual principles presented earlier.

The way we prepare a site sets the general availability of resources. We might simply burn an existing meadow before overseeding a new community. Or we might engineer an entire soil profile where there was previously only rubble. With the addition of organic matter and priming of the soil community we can create a resource-rich environment, or we can prepare a leaner soil to sustain a more species-rich community.

We can influence the availability of species by directly planting and seeding, of course, including planting and seeding species that will spread either vegetatively or by seed from their initial location. We can allow vegetation whose propagules were already on the site to emerge and select certain species and individuals to remain. We can draw in seeds from offsite using animal dispersers. And we can create safe sites to encourage establishment of new migrants in desired locations.

As species establish on the site we have made ready, the long chain of mechanisms related to differential species performance kicks in. If we have selected adapted species with appropriate life history strategies in an understood competitive hierarchy, then to some degree we can step back and let the ecosystem evolve in relation to the stochastic stresses that arise and the effects those have on the various populations. We can also continue to adjust resource availability, introduce or control consumers, and use intentional disturbances to guide the process.

Successional management also offers a low-cost means of steering existing landscapes to desired endpoints, even landscapes that have been neglected or were never designed to begin with. On former industrial sites, in abandoned agricultural areas, in untended backyards, and in less intensively maintained parkland, spontaneous vegetation springs up. This vegetation is always adapted to site conditions and is an expression of natural successional processes (see chap. 10). In a 2006 article in the *Journal of Landscape Architecture*, Norbert Kühn proposed that spontaneous vegetation can be managed or even enhanced to create design effects. In general, he suggested, we can take one of several approaches: We can maintain the current state of a spontaneous plant community (e.g., through mowing), we can allow succession to proceed naturally, we can intervene in the successional pathway of the existing community (e.g., through limited clearing), or we can introduce new species to the existing community.

The Montgomery County Department of Parks in Maryland plans to apply a number of these techniques in order to manage the successional landscape in the Gateway Area of Little Bennett Regional Park. The Gateway Area consists of 65 acres on the western edge of the 3,600-acre park, bordering Maryland Route 355. Historically, the area was farmed and has been managed as a hay meadow ever since it was acquired by the Department of Parks. The expanse of meadow is interrupted by several drainages whose lower reaches were impractical for farming and remain wooded. A hedgerow has appeared along the fenceline bordering the highway.

Landscape architect Ching-Fang Chen has proposed applying management techniques inspired by Kühn to the existing vegetation of the Gateway Area, in order to reach different endpoints in different portions of the site (fig. 8.17). For the majority of the area, she envisions annual or semiannual

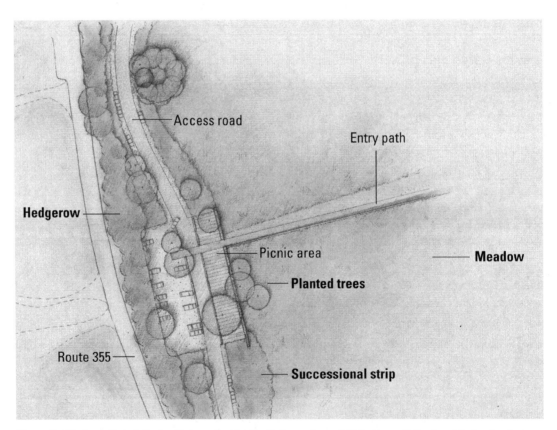

Figure 8.17 A portion of the landscape plan for the Gateway Area at Little Bennett Regional Park, showing areas to be managed on different successional paths. (Courtesy of the Maryland-National Capital Park and Planning Commission.)

mowing of the meadow, to maintain habitat for ground-dwelling birds (see chap. 7) and to preserve the historic cultural landscape. For areas along the existing hedgerow and the proposed access road, her plan is to stop mowing and to allow woody plants to emerge through natural succession (fig. 8.18). The strip will eventually merge with the hedgerow and form a buffer for the meadow and shelter for wildlife. Selective removal, particularly of invasive species, would be practiced to keep succession on the desired track. In areas immediately adjacent to proposed picnic areas and other visitor facilities, planting of native trees would supplement the spontaneous growth of woody plants to more rapidly shade and screen these areas.

Chen's approach takes the existing plant community of the Gateway Area and, through targeted interventions, keeps the largest part of it in its current steady state and moves other parts of it into new alternative steady states. This process depends not on a heavy-handed reworking of the landscape and plant community but on managing the natural successional process and the ongoing invasion of new species. It promises to be not only economical but an intelligent and effective way to enhance the site.

Figure 8.18 An image of the successional strip area that is to be managed for natural growth of woody plants. (Courtesy of the Maryland-National Capital Park and Planning Commission.)

CONCLUSION

In the landscapes we design, as in the natural world, change is the only constant. We should expect periodic physical disruption of everything we create. We can build our landscapes to be resilient to these disturbances and even to harness their energies. Recognizing that disturbance structures and diversifies natural ecosystems, we can use it as a management tool and be intentional, even productive, with our impacts on the land.

We should also design our landscapes for the changes that come from within. Instead of envisioning a fixed creation that we install and maintain, we can plan a series of emerging communities. Or we can make management an ongoing act of design and guide the establishment of plants and the relations between them to reach a desired end state.

No state, no matter how stable, is the end, however. There are always changes to come, surprises to be had, and decisions to be made. If we are successful, the landscapes we design and manage will continue to adapt, becoming new again and again as circumstances require.

9. An Ever-Shifting Mosaic: Landscape Ecology Applied

Landscapes are filled with patterns. Consider figure 9.1, a satellite image of the Mississippi River as it flows along the border of Arkansas and Mississippi south of Memphis, Tennessee. Equally striking are the sinuous course of the river and the grid of farms that surround it. Landscape patterns result from processes—in this case the erosion and deposition of sediments along the river's banks and the clearing of land for agriculture along property lines determined by the Public Land Survey System. Patterns also influence processes. The array of oxbow lakes formed from the river's meanders creates a series of wetlands that guide the movement of waterfowl through the region. The checkerboard of farms isolates small pockets of woods whose microclimates are influenced by their proximity to open fields. Neither of these two dominant landscape elements can be understood without reference to the other. The farmlands along the river are subject to periodic flooding. The river, in turn, is filled with water, sediment, and nutrients that run off the fields. It can be useful to break a landscape into discrete ecosystems with clear boundaries for the purposes of analysis (see chap. 4), but landscape ecology recognizes that ecosystems are in fact open systems. What flows into an ecosystem can be as important in determining the qualities of that ecosystem as what takes place within its boundaries. No single entity can be understood without considering its relationship to what is nearby. Furthermore, the spatial pattern in which those entities are arranged is important to how a landscape works.

Designers are attuned to the importance of context and to the relationship between form and function. We understand how the patterns of a landscape affect the ways it is used. We are accustomed to scaling and shaping spaces for their human occupants, to locating various elements in an efficient relationship to one another, and to creating useful connections between them. By applying the principles of landscape ecology, we can extend this same thinking to the needs of other organisms and to ecological processes in general. Landscape ecology makes clear the challenges we are up against to preserve biodiversity in an increasingly human-dominated environment (see chap. 5).

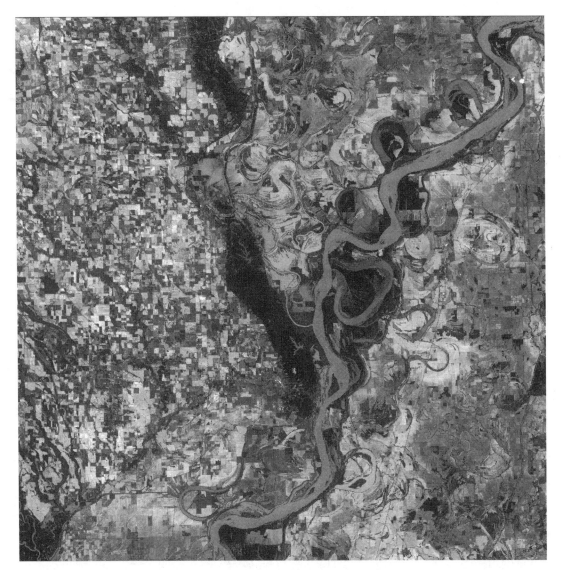

Figure 9.1 The Mississippi River on the border of Arkansas and Mississippi as captured by Landsat 7. (Image courtesy of the US Geological Survey.)

It suggests the best ways to configure preserved, restored, or constructed habitat and how to link such habitats across a landscape. It also offers broader insights into how considerations of spatial structure and context can help us build and manage landscapes to achieve higher overall levels of ecological function.

The term *landscape ecology* was coined by German biogeographer Carl Troll in 1939, but the field did not gain ground in North America until the 1980s. In their seminal book, Richard Forman and Michel Godron offered the following description:

Landscape ecology explores how a heterogeneous combination of ecosystems—such as woods, meadows, marshes, corridors and villages—is structured, functions, and changes. From wilderness to urban landscapes, our focus is on (a) the distribution patterns of landscape elements or ecosystems; (b) the flows of animals, plants, energy, mineral nutrients, and water among these elements; and (c) the ecological changes in the landscape mosaic over time. (Forman and Godron 1986: vii)

Structure, function, and change—these three terms provide a useful framework for exploring landscape ecology and its applications. We will look first at the structure of landscapes as a hierarchy of patches. Then we will examine how various landscape configurations influence ecological functions such as the survival or extinction of local populations and how to design the best patterns to achieve our goals. We will then set these patterns in motion and consider how to create built landscapes for an ever-changing world.

Throughout this chapter we will use the word *landscape* in its ecological sense, to refer to any area composed of multiple patches that differ from one another. To discuss landscapes as an object of design, as we have done throughout this book, we will say "built landscape," "designed landscape," or some other term to indicate that these landscapes are created or constructed. Although landscape ecology originated with the consideration of terrestrial landscapes at a human scale (the "woods, meadows, marshes, corridors and villages" that Forman and Godron mentioned), the concept has since been extended to marine and aquatic systems and, as we shall see, to every scale relevant to the biosphere. Often we will discuss landscapes at the scale of square miles. One of the foundational ideas of landscape ecology was to look beyond the boundaries of individual ecosystems to the processes that animate entire regions. At the same time that ecologists began studying processes at larger scales, technology was advancing that made analysis and application at these levels more feasible.

A geographic information system (GIS) connects databases to maps, allowing great efficiency and flexibility in analyzing conditions across a landscape (Hanna 1999). GIS can help ecologists and designers understand the interaction of multiple elements, including aspect, vegetation, animal migration routes, infrastructure, and property values. Data provided via remote sensing, such as tree canopy heights provided by airborne Light Detection and Ranging (LIDAR, like radar with a laser), is increasingly being integrated in analyses.

Although GIS is a powerful tool for examining landscapes at a large scale, it is just a tool. Planners and designers must still interpret the information the software provides and envision built landscapes that perform the functions we need. An understanding of landscape ecology will help us optimize the patterns we lay down on the land.

LANDSCAPES ARE MADE OF HETEROGENEOUS PATCHES AND ARE ARRANGED IN NESTED HIERARCHIES

Looking again at figure 9.1, we can see many different elements: the river, oxbow lakes, fields, ponds, the large stand of natural vegetation at the center of the photograph, canals, streams, and roads, just to name a few. Landscape ecologists use the word *patch* to describe each of these elements. A patch is simply an area that differs from what surrounds it. The word *patch* encourages one to think of patches as they would appear on a map, in two dimensions, but patches all have a three-dimensional structure. Imagine, for example, the patch defined by the rhizosphere of an oak.

Patches emerge from several sources. One is the unevenness of the physical environment. Hills and valleys, mountain ranges that catch moisture and keep it from other regions, geologic discontinuities in rocks and soils, and the shade cast by a tree all create patches. Another source of patchiness is biological processes. The spread of a colony of suckering aspen, the decomposition of a dead elk (*Cervus canadensis*), and the passage of a pod of blue whales (*Balaenoptera musculus*) through a school of krill all contribute to a patchy environment. An obvious source of patchiness is disturbance (see chap. 8). Gaps in a forest canopy after a windstorm or scorched areas of prairie after a fire are clear patches. Human activity also creates patches, be they clearings for agriculture, new suburban developments, or plantings of windbreaks or gardens. The patches created by disturbance are layered over the patches created by geography and topography. Hurricanes move from the ocean inland. Their winds affect trees on ridgelines more than trees on sheltered slopes. Their floods inundate low-lying areas. People settle first along coastlines and in level areas. The landscape mosaic that emerges from these different factors and their interactions is multilayered and complex.

Patches occur at all scales, from a patch of lichen on a rock to continents in the ocean. A landscape, in an ecological sense, is an area of any size composed of multiple three-dimensional patches that differ from one another. We may examine landscapes at every scale, from rocks to continents, and find different patterns and processes at each.

This is not just a question of magnification but a matter of important functional relationships at and between scales. All smaller patches are nested within larger patches; all large patches are made up of smaller patches. Together these patches form what ecologists call a hierarchy. A hierarchy describes an organized complex system that can be broken down into discrete functional components operating at different rates and scales (O'Neill et al. 1986). Hierarchies have both a horizontal and a vertical structure. Horizontally, functional components, like patches, are differentiated by rates of interaction. The soils, plants, and animals in a patch of forest interact with each other more than with the equivalent elements in a neighboring field. Vertically, a hierarchy consists of different levels, each governed by processes at a characteristic temporal frequency and spatial scale. Smaller, faster processes characterize lower levels. Larger, slower processes define higher hierarchical levels. Individual elements with strong interactions at one level of a hierarchy form a component that can be viewed as an individual element at the next highest level (fig. 9.2). In a nested hierarchy, lower levels come together to make up higher levels. At the same time, higher levels set conditions that constrain lower levels.

Dean Urban, Robert O'Neill, and Herman Shugart Jr. (1987) developed as an example a hierarchy for a deciduous forest in the eastern United States. When a large tree dies, a gap-sized patch will emerge in which new trees will actively compete with (interact with) each other for the same light resources. A mosaic of gaps at various stages of succession, which share seeds between them, and all of which are governed by similar environmental conditions, form a stand. A watershed is made up of many such stands, all of which share similar hydrology and interact more than with stands in other watersheds. Together, all the watersheds that make up a mountain range form another larger patch,

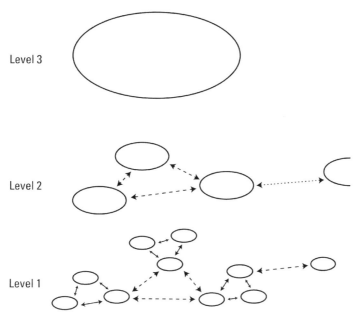

Figure 9.2 In this schematic diagram of a nested hierarchy, ovals represent individual elements and arrows their interactions. An arrow's solidity indicates the strength of the interaction it represents. Elements that interact strongly at one level can be viewed as a single element at the next highest level. (From Urban, D. L., R. V. O'Neill, and H. H. Shugart Jr. Copyright ©1987, American Institute of Biological Sciences. Landscape ecology. *BioScience* 37(2):119–27. With permission of American Institute of Biological Sciences.)

defined by weather patterns and species movement. Many such broad patches compose a regional forest province, governed by climate and long-term patterns of dispersal.

Depending on the level at which you examine a hierarchy, different patterns will emerge. If an ecologist is interested in the feeding patterns of a population of tent caterpillars in the eastern deciduous forest, she might look at the stand level and see individual trees that are affected or not. If another ecologist wants to explore how wildfire structures the same forest, he might look at the watershed level and see a mosaic of stands burned at different times in the past. To analyze any question of interest from a landscape ecological view, we have to identify the relevant scale and the different elements at that scale. We should also look at the hierarchical level below, to understand the interacting elements that make up the components we are interested in, and at the level above, to understand the constraints that affect the elements at our level of interest.

CREATE PATCHES THAT NEST NEATLY WITHIN THE EXISTING HIERARCHY

Landscape architects work at a variety of scales, from small residential yards to urban planning schemes for large metropolitan areas. At every scale, it can be useful to view the project site horizontally as a landscape, in the ecological sense, consisting of multiple interacting patches that are governed by characteristic processes, and vertically as a level in a nested hierarchy.

Imagine that we have been asked to advise the owners of the small farm near Lyme, New Hampshire shown in figure 9.3. They are interested in reducing their livestock operation and increasing the value of timber on their property. What is the appropriate level at which to view this property? This area is part of the eastern deciduous forest, in Urban, O'Neill, and Shugart's hierarchy, but it is not the forest as a whole, or even an entire watershed. We can most usefully see it at the level of a stand. At this level a pattern emerges consisting of patches such as fields, which we can relate to gaps, and tree cover of different ages and types. Shrubby growth occupies a recently abandoned field in the lower right, and midsized trees compose a patch of intermediate age behind the barns. A pine-dominated patch grows on the slope of the hill behind the farm.

Looking horizontally, we should understand how each patch interacts with adjacent patches. The bands of trees that divide the fields act as windbreaks and shade the pasture there. The fields in turn expose the woods that border them to sunlight and wind. Trees along the stream buffer the water from sediment and nutrients that might come off the fields.

Looking vertically, we should consider how these patches relate to the next smallest and largest hierarchical levels. At a smaller level, within the wooded patches, trees compete for light and nutrients, and in the fields trees attempt to establish to take advantage of the nutrients there and are knocked

Figure 9.3 A patchy landscape near Lyme, New Hampshire. (Photo by Travis Beck.)

back by grazing and mowing. At the next highest level, the watershed, constraints emerge. In the background of the photograph, a large expanse of forest runs up the slope of the distant mountain. Forest is the dominant element in the surrounding landscape and must influence all the processes on the farm. Wildlife is ever present and may come to feed at the edges of the fields. Seeds are constantly being dispersed from the forest and will sprout wherever they are allowed.

Any interventions we make in this landscape will create new patches that, to be most successful, should function well with adjacent patches and integrate into the existing nested hierarchy. The narrow field on the upper right, just below the pine-covered hill, is surrounded by trees on all sides and will revegetate rapidly if the owners cease to graze or mow it. A young stand of trees there would also blend easily into the processes of the adjacent forest and further protect water quality in the stream. At the same time that they allowed succession to proceed in the one field, the owners could also thin the trees growing in the younger patch behind the barn, to create an early yield and allow the remaining trees to grow larger. In doing so they would effectively eliminate one field-sized gap with straight edges and create many smaller irregular gaps, more like those produced by windthrow.

This modest proposal works with the landscape as a series of patches at a relevant scale. It takes advantage of the spatial relationships and interactions between patches. The actions it proposes would create new patches (a regenerating field and a series of tree-sized gaps) that fit structurally and functionally within the nested hierarchy present on the site.

PATCH SHAPE INFLUENCES ECOLOGICAL FUNCTION

The structure of a landscape mosaic and the patches that compose it affect ecological processes. Let us begin our study of landscape function by looking at patch shape. Landscape designers have some freedom to determine the shape of patches in the built environment. At times we are constrained by property lines, or existing features, but at other times we get to draw the lines.

Patch shape, as described by Richard Forman (1995), results from a balance of internal and external forces. Internal forces include the growth and expansion (or, conversely, death and contraction) of vegetation, succession, and accompanying alterations in microclimate. External forces include the movement of water and wind, disturbances, and the effect of processes taking place in adjacent patches. A strong unidirectional flow, such as that caused by a river or an ancient glacier, will produce elongated patches. Where there is spatial or temporal heterogeneity, convoluted patches with multiple lobes or peninsulas form.

The shape of a patch is important for its ecological function. Compact, rounded patches will have less edge and a greater interior area, which, as we will see, increases their ability to maintain microclimatic conditions different from the surrounding environment and to host certain species. In contrast, an elongated patch can be almost all edge. A patch with several lobes will have greater internal genetic differentiation, as the groups of organisms living in different lobes can almost form separate populations. The shape of a convoluted patch also makes it less vulnerable to the spread of pests or disturbances such as fire. Colonization of an adjacent patch by vegetation will proceed most rapidly in the cove between two lobes. Animal movement, on the other hand, is likely to be funneled through lobes, when a patch extends into less inviting adjacent areas. Long lobes can also serve as a "drift fence" and draw animals passing through adjacent patches into the interior of a preferred patch. Wherever a patch has a convoluted edge and multiple lobes, it increases its interactions with adjacent patches, which will increase exchanges of materials and organisms and can make a patch more subject to invasion by exotic species. The orientation of a patch is also significant. For instance, migratory birds are more likely to make use of a suitable patch that is set perpendicular to their direction of travel.

SHAPE PATCHES FOR ECOLOGICAL FUNCTION

Designed patches will be easiest to maintain when they conform with the natural processes that determine patch shape. Following topography and microclimate will immediately produce rational patch shapes. Elongating designed patches along the flow of water will keep us from being surprised when they spread in that direction on their own. Except where they stem from topographical rarities such as kettle ponds, compact, lobeless shapes with smooth perimeters will take effort to keep in that shape. Growth and disturbance are likely to soon create irregular margins.

The shape of a patch is also relevant to what ecological functions we intend it to accomplish. If we want to preserve or create an interior core for habitat or microclimate, then we need to maximize the central area of our patch. If instead we want interaction with surrounding patches, to build genetic diversity, spread the risk of disturbance, encourage animal movement, or promote vegetative spread from a nucleus, then a convoluted shape is more desirable. We might orient a patch at different angles depending on our goals as well. We might want to intercept or channel animals moving in certain directions. We might also want to redirect the movement of wind or water.

Forman (1995) promoted a "spaceship" shape (fig. 9.4) as having the best balance of all features, especially in the context of biological conservation. He acknowledged that determining the optimum shape for a group of patches is a more complicated question, however. This is where a designer's art truly comes into play, balancing several sets of needs with what is possible on site to configure multiple interlocking patches.

EDGE EFFECTS

People love edges. We are drawn to shorelines. We sit happily on a porch and look out onto the street. In our primeval brain we feel safer at the edge. Viscerally we sense the richness of adjoining ecosystems. This is one reason why edges are a prominent feature of designed landscapes. Another is that we truly have divided the landscape. We have carved fields from forests, built roads across expanses, and marked property lines with fences, walls, and planted screens. All of these activities create edges. Backyard woods, urbanized stream corridors, and most planted beds are effectively all edge, more subject to outside influences than to any internal dynamics. Edges can be one of the more difficult areas of a constructed landscape to maintain. Lawn grass is always getting into the planting beds. Brambles and weedy shrubs pop up incessantly along woody margins. To minimize these common problems, and to make the most of edges everywhere, it is critical that we understand how they function.

An edge is formed wherever two contrasting landscape patches come together, at whatever scale. Where the taiga transitions into the tundra, an edge exists. Where the waters of a lake come to shore, an edge is formed. Perhaps the most intensively studied category of edges is that between forests and

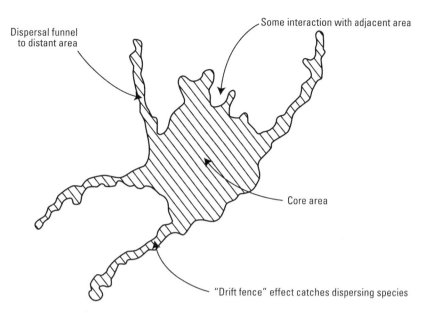

Dispersal funnel
to distant area

Some interaction with adjacent area

Core area

"Drift fence" effect catches dispersing species

Figure 9.4 A spaceship-shaped patch combines the benefits of a consolidated core with the advantages of long lobes that facilitate exchanges with the surrounding landscape. (From *Landscape Ecology Principles in Landscape Architecture and Land-Use Planning* by Wenche E. Dramstad, James D. Olson, and Richard T. T. Forman. Copyright ©1996 President and Fellows of Harvard College. Reproduced by permission of Island Press, Washington, DC.)

fields. In some ways, an edge forms a patch of its own. Edges can be straight or tortuous. They can be continuous or perforated. They can be sharp or transition gradually (fig. 9.5).

Edge effects are changes in ecological function that occur as we transition between two adjacent patches. Recall Sophia Gehlhausen's studies of Trelease and Brownfield Woods in Illinois (see chap. 1). Moving from forest edge to interior, Gehlhausen found that soil moisture and relative humidity climbed. These changes occurred because the vegetation of the edge dampened the intensity of sunlight and wind penetrating the forest. Mary Cadenasso and colleagues (2003) found other examples of an edge mediating ecological flows in their study of a forest–field boundary in the Hudson Valley of New York. Using transects across the edge, they determined that seed numbers of field species declined as one moved from field to forest. Herbivory by voles (*Microtus pennsylvanicus*) was greatest in the field and by deer greatest in the forest. The deposition of nitrogen from rain and the atmosphere was greatest at the edge itself. When the scientists removed all vegetation along the edge below half the canopy height, these flows changed. Field seeds penetrated farther into the forest. Vole damage decreased at the edge, and deer damage increased. Nitrogen deposition peaked 25 meters into the forest interior. These findings demonstrate that the vegetation at the boundary controlled flows across the edge. The structure of the edge therefore also affected dynamics within the forest itself, influencing nutrient deposition, immigration of species from the adjacent patch, and herbivore pressure.

Edges affect the abundance and diversity of animals. Edges can host species from both adjacent

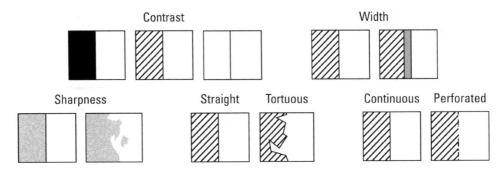

Figure 9.5   Characteristics of edges. (Adapted from Strayer, D. L., M. E. Power, W. F. Fagan, S. T. A. Pickett, and J. Belknap. Copyright ©2003, University of California Press Journals. A classification of ecological boundaries. *BioScience* 53(8):723–29. With permission of University of California Press Journals.)

patches, as well as edge specialist species, and therefore have greater species richness. Animals, such as deer, that take advantage of the resources of both patches will also increase in abundance along edges. These were the first edge effects noted, and wildlife managers promoted the creation of edges. As ecologists' focus shifted to the conservation of nongame species, however, they began to notice negative edge effects. Species that depend on interior patch habitat are negatively affected by edges. Edges also serve as entry points for invasive plants and animals. Leslie Ries and Thomas Sisk (2004) proposed that positive, negative, and neutral edge effects on animal populations can be explained by the distribution of resources, as they relate to the species in question. Positive effects will be found where resources are concentrated at an edge or where two adjacent patches have complementary re-sources. Negative effects will be seen when one patch has higher-quality resources than the adjacent patch and these resources are not complementary.

DESIGN EDGES

Because edges are critical components of natural and designed landscapes, and because how they are structured influences so many ecological functions, we need to be attentive to the forms we give them. Rather than just butt up two dissimilar landscape patches, we need to design edges in their own right. Luckily, edges are one of the most readily altered features of a built landscape. We may not have perfect freedom to determine how large, or even what type, a patch will be, but we can address its edge. Any time we alter patch shape, we automatically reconfigure its edge. The form we give our edges will determine how they function.

Successful edge plantings respond to the shifts in microclimates across boundaries. Where trees border open areas, it is a mistake to assume that shade- and moisture-loving species will march all the way up to one side of a line and sun-loving, more drought-tolerant species to the other. We need to plan the transition, using shrubs, vines, and adapted herbaceous plants that can take part-sun condi-tions. Lawn grasses will peter out naturally along a shaded edge. Where we want lawn to meet other sun-loving plantings we might place an intervening path, as an alternative to edging, or transition to grass species that can be allowed to grow up and flower amid the other plants.

Edges control flows of all sorts within a landscape, and their structure modulates those flows. How we design an edge depends on what we want it to do. If we want to protect interior forest from sun, wind, excessive nutrients, and invasive species, Cadenasso's study suggests that constructing an abrupt edge and allowing it to seal with vegetative growth may be most appropriate. This will give a cooler, secluded feel to the forest interior. On the other hand, if we want animals to move across an edge, for viewing at a nature center, say, or perhaps to guide them to other habitat nearby, then we might create a more convoluted or perforated edge. How we orient an edge will also affect how energy, materials, and organisms will move across it. Cutting into an intact patch on the windward or sunward side increases the effective edge width for those two flows.

Edges clearly affect the habitat value of a landscape. If we are looking to increase overall diversity and give a place a sense of life, creating and lengthening an edge is a good thing. Complicating the line of an edge and adding to its structural diversity with plants of different heights creates a variety of habitats and increases its species richness. If we are trying to defend or develop habitat for particular rare organisms, however, we probably want to reduce the edge of their favored habitat. We can do this by altering the shape of their higher resource patch to reduce its edge to interior ratio or by making adjoining patches less different.

Creating ecological function in a patchy landscape requires designing edges.

FRAGMENTS EXPERIENCE ECOLOGICAL DISTORTION

Land clearing, agricultural expansion, and suburban development have all left, embedded in their matrix, fragments of native ecosystems, parcels of land that whether for reasons of topography, law, economics, or owner's whim are not wiped out. When a forest, grassland, or chaparral is broken up this way, the amount of edge and the influence of edge effects increase tremendously, changing the entire system. Ecologists have studied the functioning of these fragments. Can some of their findings apply to the small, edge-dominated landscape patches built by humans as well as to the fragments of natural ecosystems that persist in the mosaic of our built environment?

In the late 1970s, Thomas Lovejoy, then head of the World Wildlife Fund's conservation program, convinced landowners near Manaus, Brazil, in the heart of the Amazon rainforest, to set aside parcels of precise dimensions within the properties they were slashing and burning to prepare land for cattle ranching. Eleven parcels were created, ranging from 1 to 100 hectares in size (fig. 9.6). Field teams surveyed life in these parcels both before and after the surrounding areas were cleared. More than 30 years later, the Biological Dynamics of Forest Fragments Project (BDFFP) continues, though not the surrounding cattle ranches, which, because of low productivity, have been largely abandoned. Ironically, as second-growth forest moved in, the researchers have had to clear 100-meter strips around the edges of their plots several times in order to maintain the integrity of those plots as fragments.

Summarizing 32 years of research, William F. Laurance and a host of colleagues (2011) wrote that the ecology of the forest fragments is far different from the ecology of equivalent areas in the midst of intact rainforest. The species richness of many groups of organisms decreased with decreasing fragment size, and the smallest fragments lost species most quickly. Some plant species have lost their animal pollinators or dispersers and hang on as ecological ghosts, unable to reproduce or spread.

Figure 9.6 A 10-hectare and a 1-hectare forest fragment studied in the Biological Dynamics of Forest Fragments Project shortly after clearing of the surrounding landscape. (Photo by Richard O. Bierregaard.)

Edge effects dominate the ecology of the fragments, especially at the corners where two edges join. The penetration of wind and sunlight into the fragments changes their microclimates substantially, making them hotter and drier and leading to the decline of plant and animal species adapted to the humid forest interior. Compared with intact forest, the fragments are hyperdynamic. Populations fluctuate markedly, tree species disappear and appear rapidly, and disturbances such as droughts and windstorms can alter the entire composition of the community. The plant communities in the fragments come to be defined by the microclimatic stresses, the disturbance events, and the decline of species whose mutualists have disappeared. The fragments experience a kind of ecological distortion, with disrupted food webs and unstable transitional states not seen in the intact rainforest. These effects alter ecosystem function as a whole, changing streamflows, altering nutrient cycling, and reducing carbon storage.

As the surrounding landscape has changed from pasture to second-growth forest, some birds and other animals have recolonized the fragments. Early successional species in the old pastures also increase in abundance within the fragments. These effects show that the changing community composition of the fragments is greatly affected by what lives in neighboring patches.

MANAGE FRAGMENTS TO OFFSET DISTORTING EFFECTS

The findings of the BDFFP make it clear that we will be hard pressed to replicate the diversity and functioning of extensive native ecosystems in small remnant, restored, or constructed patches. Fragments of all types have lower species richness, altered microclimates, and reduced ecological function. For these reasons, Wenche Dramstad, James Olson, and Richard Forman (1996: 22) argued for the importance of preserving large patches of natural vegetation:

Figure 9.7 The Thain Family Forest at the New York Botanical Garden is a fragment of a once extensive natural ecosystem, now embedded in the urban fabric of the Bronx. (© 2012 Google and © 2012 TerraMetrics. Data SIO, NOAA, US Navy, NGA, GEBCO.)

Large patches of natural vegetation are the only structures in a landscape that protect aquifers and interconnected stream networks, sustain viable populations of most interior species, provide core habitat and escape cover for most large-home-range vertebrates, and permit near-natural disturbance regimes.

They noted that small patches can host uncommon species and facilitate species movement across an inhospitable landscape. Scale being relative, we can also add that what we humans perceive as small patches may be large to smaller species, including insects and microbes. Small natural, restored, or ecologically designed patches can still provide a measure of ecosystem services too, especially when compared with the simplified built landscape that often surrounds them (see chap. 4). Later we will discuss how linkages can overcome some of the problems of fragmentation to knit together small and large patches into a functioning network, but for now let us consider the dynamics within the patches themselves.

The 50-acre Thain Family Forest at the New York Botanical Garden is the largest remnant of the deciduous forest that once covered New York City. Though protected and managed by the Botanical Garden since 1895, it has experienced the combined effects of fragmentation and urbanization of the surrounding area (fig. 9.7). These effects include local extinction of plant populations, growth of invasive plants, elevated levels of heavy metals in the soil from air pollution, and microclimatic changes caused by the urban heat island. As the findings of the BDFFP would predict, the Forest plant community is influenced by what grows nearby. Common invasives such as Amur honeysuckle (*Lonicera maackii*) and Japanese knotweed have established themselves amid the old-growth oaks, along with Amur corktree (*Phellodendron amurense*), a less well-known invasive that probably entered the Forest from an adjacent collection. In order to maintain the integrity of the Forest community, the Botanical Garden staff has begun removal and control of these invasive species, along with vigorous replanting of natives. Like Laurance's Amazonian plots, urban forest fragments are not intact natural ecosystems in miniature but altered pieces of a larger landscape. If we want to offset the ecological consequences of this condition, active management is needed.

Patches of designed landscape should also be expected to experience a certain ecological distortion. The communities and food webs we construct will not perfectly duplicate those found in nature and may be unstable. We will have to contend with hyperdynamism, in which disturbance and various stresses alter the community in nonlinear ways. Left alone, a patch and its neighbors will become more similar over time. We should be attentive and assess when to intervene to keep the evolving community on the desired track. The smaller the patch and the more different from its surroundings we try to make it, the more active our management of it will have to be.

ISLAND BIOGEOGRAPHY

The study of fragments of native ecosystems embedded in the landscape mosaic, and debate over how best to size, locate, and shape preserved and restored patches of habitat, have their roots in the theory of island biogeography.

In the 1960s, Robert MacArthur (whose study of resource partitioning in warblers we discussed earlier) and E. O. Wilson (1963, 1967) offered a new explanation for the numbers of animal and plant species found on various islands. They began with two observations: Larger islands contain more species than smaller islands, and islands closer to the mainland have more species than islands farther away. We have already seen that the number of species found increases with the area sampled (see chap. 2). In part this is because larger areas are more likely to contain different habitats, which can host different species. However, MacArthur and Wilson suggested another reason, based on population dynamics.

Populations are subject to several factors that can make them vulnerable to extinction: demographic fluctuations, environmental variability, disturbances, and genetic troubles such as inbreeding depression (Shaffer 1981). When these factors combine, a local population can get sucked into an extinction vortex and disappear. To guard against this possibility, populations need to achieve a minimum viable population size. A common measure of minimum viable population is the number of individuals necessary to have a 95 percent chance of avoiding extinction over a 100-year time period. Although this number varies by species, it is often estimated to be in the hundreds or thousands.

MacArthur and Wilson proposed an equilibrium model of species richness. On larger islands, species are able to develop larger populations, which are less likely to go extinct than the smaller populations on smaller islands. On closer islands, immigrating species will more easily fill the vacancies left by species that go locally extinct than they can on less accessible, farther islands. The number of species on an island, the authors suggested, is determined by the point at which the rate of local extinctions equals the rate of arrival of new species (fig. 9.8a). The rate of extinction drives the relationship between species richness and island size. The rate of immigration drives the relationship between species richness and distance from the mainland (fig. 9.8b).

The theory of island biogeography offered a comprehensive explanation for why the largest number of species is found on larger, closer islands and fewer species on smaller, more remote islands. It also suggested that the species composition of islands is far from static. Because of the ever-present risk of extinction and the rain of potential new immigrants, an island community will experience regular turnover. Some species may arrive, establish populations, and go extinct numerous times. Despite this dynamism, the number of species present remains roughly the same.

Wilson and then graduate student Daniel Simberloff were able to confirm this theory in an experiment in the Florida Keys (Simberloff and Wilson 1969; Wilson and Simberloff 1969). They selected six very small islands consisting of one or a few red mangroves (*Rhizophora mangle*) between 2 and just over 500 meters away from a source island. They exhaustively surveyed the existing land arthropod

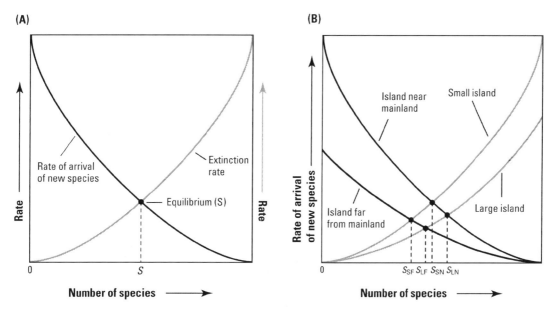

Figure 9.8 MacArthur and Wilson's theory of island biogeography. **(A)** The number of species on an island (S) is determined by the point at which the rate of arrival of new species equals the rate of extinction. **(B)** On islands nearer (subscript N) to the mainland, the rate of arrival of new species is higher, leading to higher species richness. On smaller islands (subscript S), the rate of extinction is higher, leading to lower species richness. Thus larger islands (subscript L) closer to the mainland have higher species richness than smaller islands farther (subscript F) from the mainland. (From Sadava, D., D. M. Hillis, C. Heller, and M. R. Berenbaum. Copyright ©2011, Sinauer Associates. *Life: The Science of Biology*, 9th edition. Reproduced with permission of Sinauer Associates.)

communities on these islets, digging in the mud and climbing to the very tips of the trees, and found the expected relationship: The closer islets contained more species than the ones farther away. Then, working with a pest control company, they tented and fumigated each of the islets to kill off the entire existing arthropod community. For the next year they regularly surveyed arthropod life as it returned to each of the islets. Powerful fliers, such as wasps and moths, arrived first. Weak fliers and nonfliers followed, some coming in on birds and nesting material. Some species persisted once they arrived, but others went extinct, some of which recolonized the islands again. The rates of immigration and extinction were highly variable but quite high, between 0.05 and 0.50 species per day, or about 1 percent of the pretreatment number of species. At the end of the year, the number of species found on each of the islets was nearly identical to the number that had existed before, although the actual species present differed from the pretreatment communities. The quick return to pretreatment species richness and then oscillation around that level provided powerful evidence of MacArthur and Wilson's equilibrium theory.

CONSIDER PATCHES AS ISLANDS

Not all islands rise from the sea. Fragments cut from the cloth of once extensive natural ecosystems can become functional islands, as can designed landscapes built in the midst of the urban fabric, or acres of lawn. Island biogeography theory highlights some of the constraints these landscape patches operate under and the dynamic processes that take place there.

Island biogeography theory adds another dimension to our understanding of species–area relationships. We know that a landscape patch can accommodate more species when there is more space to physically fit them and multiple habitats are included (see chap. 2). To this we must now add that populations will persist in a patch only if it is large enough for them to maintain a minimum viable population. If we protect a small remnant wetland to provide habitat for the dozen or so turtles that live there, it will probably be only a matter of years before those turtles get sucked into an extinction vortex and disappear. If we hope to maintain a population of wildflowers in the corporate landscape we have designed, we need to be sure there are enough of them, over a large enough area, that they can withstand the vicissitudes of weather, disturbance, and variable reproductive success. Let us add two caveats. One, minimum viable population and area needed vary by species. The preserved wetland that is too small for turtles may support a population of thousands of minnows indefinitely. Two, for plant populations in the designed landscape, our standards for viability may be less strict. It may be adequate for a population to have an 80 percent chance of surviving for 10 years, for example, in which case the size of the population and the area it needs will be substantially smaller.

The degree of isolation of a patch is important as well. We might lose the turtles from our wetland but gain them back quickly through immigration if there are other populations nearby. If a designed landscape is close to source populations of desirable plants, weeds, or animals of all sorts, we can expect those organisms to attempt to colonize it. If we are far from these species, they may never appear on their own. Laurance and others' work on Amazonian forest fragments reminds us that the exact makeup of the surroundings is important. Not all adjacent patches on land are as inhospitable as the ocean. The relative isolation of terrestrial landscape patches can vary depending on what surrounds them.

Island biogeography theory also suggests that community turnover is inevitable. If we assemble an initial community tightly, it will resist invasion as long as its component populations persist. As populations drop out, however, new species may take their place. In fragments of natural ecosystems and isolated designed landscapes the communities will always be in flux, hovering around a level of species richness based on, among other factors, the intersection of patch size and degree of isolation.

ORGANISMS INHABIT THE LANDSCAPE IN METAPOPULATIONS

Island biogeography theory has proved suggestive for imagining how plants and animals survive in a landscape of fragmented, sometimes transitory patches. Species can disappear from an island or patch and reappear later because they are connected to other populations. Ecologists call such an interacting set of populations a metapopulation.

Susan Harrison, Dennis Murphy, and Paul Ehrlich (the same Paul Ehrlich who suggested coevolution in butterflies and plants [see chap. 7]) illustrated metapopulation dynamics in a study of the bay checkerspot butterfly (*Euphydryas editha bayensis*). The bay in this case is the San Francisco Bay, where the butterflies live on grasslands that grow on outcrops of serpentine rock. Harrison, Murphy, and Ehrlich (1988) followed a discrete metapopulation of bay checkerspot butterflies occurring near Morgan Hill, southeast of San Jose. On Morgan Hill itself, an area of approximately 2,000 hectares supports a population of hundreds of thousands of checkerspot butterflies. Within about 20 kilometers of Morgan Hill the researchers identified fifty-nine other potential habitat patches ranging in size from 0.1 to 250 hectares in size. These are the metaphorical islands to the Morgan Hill mainland. The researchers surveyed these patches in 1987 and found breeding populations on seven of them (fig. 9.9). Distance from Morgan Hill was the most important factor in explaining which patches were inhabited. All of the patches inhabited in 1987 were within 4.4 kilometers of the Morgan Hill patch. Habitat quality was also important. The orientation and steepness of slopes within the patches (which interacts with weather to determine how long the butterflies host plants grow before senescing) and the abundance of host plants clearly influenced the presence or absence of butterflies. The inhabited patches were those that were both close enough to the source population and of high enough quality.

However, 1987 is just one moment in time. Between 1975 and 1977 the region had experienced a severe drought that probably wiped out all the populations of bay checkerspot butterfly on the smaller patches in the area studied. The Morgan Hill population had been able to persist and had served as a source for the recolonization of the surrounding patches. Harrison and her colleagues suggested that the metapopulation was still regaining its equilibrium.

In addition to the mainland-island model observed at Morgan Hill, metapopulations can have other dynamics (Hanski 1998). A source area can feed several sinks, less suitable habitat areas where populations will never persist. Or there can be no single source population, and the metapopulation persists by establishing and losing a fluctuating number of individual populations over a network of habitat patches. Or a population with high dispersal ability can exist in patches, without developing the separation of local populations characteristic of a metapopulation. The metapopulation concept emphasizes the dynamic nature of biogeography (see chap. 1). Plants and animals are not distributed evenly based on environmental tolerances. Less suitable habitat may host species year after year as a

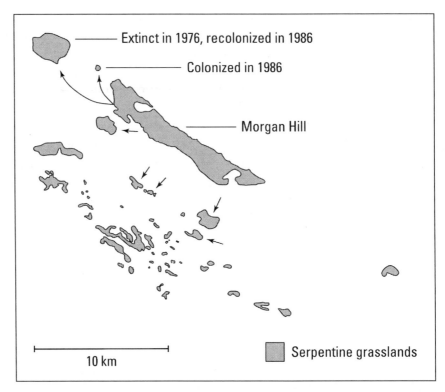

Figure 9.9 A metapopulation of bay checkerspot butterflies inhabits some but not all patches of serpentine grassland on and around Morgan Hill. The large Morgan Hill patch serves as a source for colonization of other patches. Which patches besides Morgan Hill are inhabited fluctuates over time. (From Harrison, S., D. D. Murphy, and P. R. Ehrlich. Copyright ©1988, The University of Chicago. Distribution of the bay checkerspot butterfly, *Euphydryas editha bayensis*: Evidence for a metapopulation model. *American Naturalist* 132(3):360–82. With permission from the University of Chicago Press.)

sink. Patches of suitable habitat may be temporarily vacant but part of the network of a shifting meta-population. Or they may never be inhabited at all, because of their isolation.

Since Harrison conducted her study, the importance of the Morgan Hill metapopulation has only grown. The bay checkerspot butterfly was listed as a threatened species in 1987. A decade later, scientists observed the extinction of the second largest metapopulation of the butterfly on Stanford's Jasper Ridge Biological Preserve (McGarrahan 1997). And in 2002 the last individual of the Edgewood County Park population farther north on the San Francisco Peninsula was seen. Restoration plans for Jasper Ridge have been discussed using checkerspot butterflies from the Morgan Hill metapopulation (now usually identified as Kirby Canyon or Coyote Ridge), and in 2011 caterpillars from there were released at Edgewood as phase one of a 5-year reintroduction (Friends of Edgewood Natural Preserve 2011). Thus one discrete metapopulation is now serving as the source population for the entire subspecies.

MANAGE METAPOPULATIONS

As we discussed earlier, when we design and plant a landscape, we are dealing with populations of plants (see chap. 2). The animals that come to inhabit these landscapes likewise form populations. Now we take the further step of conceiving of these populations as part of metapopulations. Some metapopulations (such as those of animals for which we have created habitat) we hope to increase. Others (such as those of insect pests and invasive species) we hope to decrease. Even when we simply hope to maintain a population on our site that is not part of a regional metapopulation, we have to understand that many of its competitors, consumers, and mutualists are linked to larger metapopulations. The weeds that crop up no matter how many times we pull them, the pests that appear, and the pollinators we desire are all moving through a dynamic network of habitat patches in the immediate neighborhood and beyond.

In order to contribute to the maintenance or growth of a metapopulation, habitat fragments and newly restored or created habitat patches need to meet several criteria. First, the habitat patch needs to offer habitat of sufficiently high quality. Because site conditions interact with weather and disturbance events, habitat quality can vary from year to year. Thinking in terms of metapopulation survival, then, it is valuable to have a range of available habitats, some of which are of high quality under any given set of conditions. Second, the patch must be close enough to other inhabited patches to exchange immigrants. If we introduce a new, or reintroduce an extirpated, species, then our patch will serve as a source, and to succeed it should be close to other high-quality habitats. Third, the habitat patch must be large enough to support an independent population for at least several years. Habitat that is created immediately adjacent to existing patches or within the range of a group of mobile animals can effectively increase the size of an existing patch and population without being large itself. We should be careful, though, not to create a sink, or ecological trap, where our target organisms set up shop but fail to reproduce. Arthur Shapiro (2006), a longtime butterfly researcher at the University of California at Davis, noted the following in his recommendations for butterfly gardens for the northern California foothills:

> Few butterfly species can maintain an ongoing population within the confines of a residential lot— even a big one. If you get breeding, it will be as part of a larger "metapopulation" whose borders are constantly changing. . . . The principal function of a butterfly garden is to intercept individual butterflies as they move through an area and detain them where they can be observed and enjoyed. Occasionally, one can actually boost numbers by planting nectar sources or larval hosts, but only if these are otherwise in short supply. More often, one is just moving individuals around from one place to another.

Broader efforts beyond the creation of small habitat patches are usually needed to augment metapopulations.

The same holds true if we seek to decrease a metapopulation, such as an invasive plant species that is displacing butterfly larval host plants. We can decrease habitat quality by reducing nutrient inputs that favor invasive species, for instance. We can increase the isolation of a population by revegetating other nearby patches. And we can seek to reduce patch size by restoring disturbed areas that are most subject to invasion. Here source–sink dynamics can be more troubling, because even as we remove invasive plants, our site may be constantly reinfested by immigrants from a source population.

Metapopulation dynamics can be difficult to work with because they involve things that happen at sites and scales beyond our immediate control. They offer the truest means of understanding many of the changes in local communities we do observe, however. They also emphasize the importance of tying the work we do at any one site into the context of the larger landscape.

LANDSCAPE CONNECTIVITY SUPPORTS BIODIVERSITY

Plants and animals are able to move fairly easily through extensive naturally vegetated landscapes, subject only to natural barriers such as rivers and mountain ranges. In the fragmented human-dominated landscape, however, populations can be cut off from one another in isolated habitat islands. As we have seen, isolation of populations increases their risk of extinction. Also, wide-ranging animals such as top carnivores cannot support themselves in smaller patches, and they often put themselves at risk when they travel between patches. The long-term persistence of wide-ranging species and of metapopulations of many other species depends on their ability to move through the landscape. Isolated communities are also subject to being radically altered by disturbance, without being able to regenerate from adjacent undisturbed areas, and are vulnerable to changes in environmental conditions.

In the mid-1980s, coinciding with the rise of landscape ecology, conservation biologists began to recognize that efforts to preserve biodiversity by protecting individual areas were incomplete. This view was articulated strongly by two scientists from the University of Florida, Reed Noss and Larry Harris (1986: 303), who wrote, "We cannot consider our parks and preserves as closed, self-supporting systems, but rather as parts interacting within still larger systems." They proposed instead that conservation strategy be focused on nodes of diversity connected by corridors into a regional network.

In Noss and Harris's terminology, nodes include not only biologically significant areas, such as an undrained swamp, but also entities that move over time, such as a heron rookery. Ideally, they argued, nodes should be preserved wherever they may shift. Identifying nodes recognizes that not all patches within a landscape are equally significant in terms of biodiversity and allows us to prioritize our conservation efforts.

Corridors are linear features such as ridgelines, streamcourses, animal trail systems, power lines, and roads that connect landscape patches and allow organisms to move between them. In order to be effective, corridors have to account for the perceptions and behavior of individual species. What looks like a corridor to a kestrel might not to a frog. A corridor going in one direction can also serve as a barrier to movement in the opposite direction. For instance, a road may facilitate the spread of roadside weeds along its length but disrupt the passage of animals across its width. The wider a corridor, the more effective it usually is at facilitating species movement. Corridors are most often thought of in terms of animal movement, but they can also provide avenues for the movement of plants in response to environmental change (see chap. 10).

Networks are formed where corridors connect multiple nodes through alternate pathways. These alternate pathways provide insurance in the case of disruption of any one corridor. Noss and Harris proposed that networks should allow metapopulations of multiple species to persist across a regional landscape. The most difficult species to maintain, such as large carnivores, provide the ultimate test of the success of a network.

To illustrate these points, Noss and Harris described a proposed network for north Florida and south Georgia. This network would encompass nodes such as the Okefenokee Swamp, surrounded by buffer zones and connected by corridors such as the Suwannee River. Such an interconnected network, they claimed, could both support the reintroduction of endangered species such as the Florida panther (*Puma concolor coryi*) and allow the perpetuation of large-scale ecological patterns and processes (fig. 9.10).

Figure 9.10 One of the few remaining Florida panthers, a species whose recovery depends on landscape connectivity over large areas. (Photo by Rodney Cammauf, National Park Service.)

STRIVE FOR CONNECTIVITY

Noss and Harris's vision of an interconnected landscape has been carried forward in the form of the Florida Ecological Greenways Network (FEGN). The FEGN grew out of the work of nonprofits and the state to envision and implement a statewide system of linked conservation lands based on extensive public input and the best available science (Conservation Fund 2004). The goals of the network were to

- Conserve critical elements of native ecosystems and landscapes
- Restore and maintain connectivity between native ecological systems and processes
- Facilitate the ability of ecosystems and landscapes to function as dynamic systems
- Maintain the evolutionary potential of the components of the ecosystems to adapt to future environmental changes

A team at the University of Florida used GIS to design the network (Hoctor et al. 2000). They identified hubs, similar to Noss and Harris's nodes, which included ecologically significant areas such as biodiversity hotspots (see chap. 5), roadless areas, and rare plant communities greater than 2,000 hectares in size. Then they analyzed the areas between hubs to identify the most effective linkages. Once optimal paths were determined, the researchers widened them by including adjacent natural and low-intensity use areas. Combining the hubs and the linkages created the network. The proposed network included 57.5 percent of the state's area, more than half of which was already protected. The researchers updated the network in 2004, refining the ecological information on which the analysis was based and eliminating areas that had been converted to more intensive land use. The FEGN now serves as a basis for land acquisition by the State of Florida and private conservation groups.

A critical section of the FEGN would connect the Ocala National Forest in central Florida to the Osceola National Forest in northern Florida, and ultimately to the Okefenokee National Wildlife Refuge in southeast Georgia, protecting several watersheds and providing habitat connections for populations of Florida black bear (*Ursus americanus floridanus*) (fig. 9.11). This section, known as the O2O Greenway, has met with both success and challenges.

At the northern end of the O2O Greenway, a variety of public acquisitions and private conservation agreements have successfully protected a large portion of the Pinhook Swamp, an area of swamp and pine flatwoods that had been previously logged but otherwise undisturbed. In the center, however, important links are still missing to connect the existing conservation lands within the US Army's Camp Blanding to the Raiford Wildlife Management Area and on to the Osceola National Forest.

Statewide networks such as the FEGN protect biodiversity and ecological processes at the regional scale. However, the idea of connectivity applies at smaller scales too. Reed Noss (1991) describes how fencerows can connect isolated woodlots, supporting metapopulations of white-footed mice (*Peromyscus leucopus*) and facilitating movement by birds and other animals. At whatever scale we work, we should strive to create linkages and networks that promote landscape functioning. Connectivity offers the means to knit together remnant natural ecosystems, restored areas, and constructed landscapes into an ecological whole whose sum is greater than its parts.

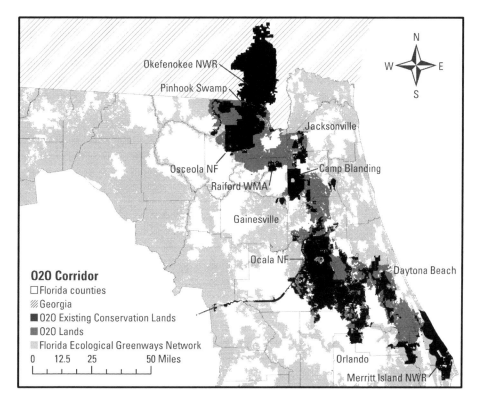

Figure 9.11 The Ocala to Osceola (O2O) corridor within the Florida Ecological Greenways Network, showing both proposed and already protected lands. (Courtesy of Tom Hoctor, PhD, Center for Landscape Conservation Planning, University of Florida.)

HIERARCHICAL PATCH DYNAMICS DESCRIBE LANDSCAPE CHANGE

Connectivity is critical because landscapes are always in flux. As disturbances arrive, as succession proceeds, and as shifts in climate and landforms occur, the mosaic of patches that make up a landscape change. All of these changes are described as patch dynamics (Pickett et al. 1999).

The idea of patch dynamics was first introduced by Alex Watt in his presidential address to the British Ecological Society in 1947. Watt described as one example the supposed phases of growth and drowning of hummocks in a peat bog, which he referred to as the regeneration complex. First sphagnum moss invades an open pool of water and forms a hummock. Heather (*Calluna vulgaris*) and other plants then grow atop the hummock. Eventually the rise of surrounding hummocks forces water over the existing plants, drowning them and creating a new open pool of water. If each patch (open water, sphagnum hummock, heather) is constantly turning into the next, how does the community remain recognizable? Watt proposed that in a constant environment the community enters a phasic equilibrium, where the proportions occupied by each phase are fixed, even as the individual patches rotate.

Notice that Watt juxtaposed two spatial and temporal scales. At the scale of the hummock, change happens quickly. At the scale of the entire bog, stability is maintained over a long period of time. This is one of the hallmarks of hierarchy theory. At the lower levels of a hierarchy, change is small and rapid. At the higher levels, change is large and infrequent (Urban et al. 1987). Infrequent changes, such as hurricanes, can overwhelm the stabilizing mechanisms of lower levels of hierarchy by wiping out entire stands of trees, for instance. Instability at small scales can translate into stability at a higher level, however. For example, a series of small fires over many years can leave a forest less vulnerable to a catastrophic burn than a long period without disturbance would. The patches that make up a forest may go through successional stages in turn, but as long as the proportion of patches at each successional stage remains even, the forest as a whole is relatively stable. Bormann and Likens (1979) referred to this as a shifting mosaic. Now, ecologists are more likely to say that such a system has achieved metastability.

Hierarchical patch dynamics offers a framework that explicitly deals with heterogeneity and the processes that renew it. It recognizes the vulnerability of ecological systems to unmanageable devastation, as well as the adaptability of those systems. It explains both the moments of equilibrium that occur and the changes that are ever taking place. As Jianguo Wu and Orie Loucks (1995: 459) put it in their review of the concept, "Harmony is embedded in the patterns of fluctuation, and ecological persistence is 'order within disorder.'"

MAKE THE RIGHT CHANGES

Already we know that our landscapes change and that we must plan for and manage that change (see chap. 8). Hierarchical patch dynamics provides a broader perspective. The whole landscape mosaic is changing. The changes occurring in the patches we manage both affect and are affected by these larger changes.

Let us think again of the New Hampshire farm pictured in figure 9.3. The valley floor and even some of the slopes beyond were probably substantially more open 100 years ago, having been cleared for agriculture. The wooded patches we see today are second growth, each at a different successional stage, depending on when the fields they overtook were let go. Continued disturbance keeps the remaining fields open.

We might advise the owners of this property to create a sort of phasic equilibrium in their woods, by cutting small areas at a time, so that all successional stages are represented on their property. This is easiest to imagine as a regular rotation, but it could also be done following natural models, removing patches of irregular size and shape at irregular frequency, including cutting over of more recently cleared patches and preservation of some undisturbed areas. A series of such clearings at a smaller scale would work to create metastability at the scale of the farm, offering regular harvests over time and decreasing the possibility of catastrophic loss.

Viewed at a higher level, this farm is but a single stand-sized patch in the watershed. It might not be necessary to represent all phases of growth on the farm itself, because some of them are already present in the area. The owners can "borrow" patches from nearby, in the same sense that designers "borrow" views. As long as the forest remains intact on the mountain slopes, the farm owners do not need to have mature forest on their property to produce seed for revegetation or provide other ecological services. As long as other properties in the valley include open and recently abandoned fields, early successional species will remain available. The owners of this property could manage all their lands at an intermediate stage of succession by eliminating their livestock entirely and regularly removing all trees above a certain diameter. This would keep their woods at a productive spot on the growth curve and could actually increase the metastability of the larger landscape. Of course, if the surrounding forest is cut down or all the other farms in the valley start managing their land as intermediate successional woodlots, then the equation changes, and our responsive owners would want to allow their woodland to mature or clear patches to preserve early successional species.

It can be difficult to manage land in reaction to the changes that take place in the surrounding landscape, but we have to in any case. Changes at a larger scale will still drive whatever happens on this farm. If a major ice storm or fire arrives, the entire property could be knocked back to the start of succession. If a shifting climate alters the species composition of the forest, the plant community on this property will be altered too (see chap. 10). Or if economic trends change and the land became more valuable again in crops, it could seem pressing to clear it all once again.

Every change that occurs in the larger landscape affects the situation on the site for which we are responsible. Every change we make contributes to the overall hierarchical patch dynamics.

CONCLUSION

The landscapes we design are also landscapes in the ecological sense, mosaics of heterogeneous patches at any chosen scale. Good landscape design is always about creating forms that support intended functions, about the relationships of different elements, and about the context in which they are situated. Landscape ecology brings these same concerns to the study of ecosystem processes and the maintenance of biodiversity.

Forman and Godron (1986) emphasized three focuses of landscape ecology: structure, function, and change. We have learned how to analyze landscapes as interacting patches in a nested hierarchy and how to fit our designs into that structure. We have looked at how to shape patches and design their edges to improve their function and how to connect them together to promote landscape-level processes and the survival of metapopulations. And we have discussed how to step into the ever-evolving array of patches and make changes that increase overall stability. In order for the landscapes we design to function ecologically, they have to be integrated with their surroundings as part of a dynamic hierarchical arrangement of patches.

The challenge that underlies all this is the fragmentation of the natural landscape at human hands. We will not see again the extensive, unmolested biomes that once covered this continent. However, we can offer this surrogate: an interconnected network of large preserves, forest fragments, riparian corridors, restored grasslands, working landscapes, constructed wetlands, and well-designed parks and yards. Landscapes have always consisted of patches. We can enhance the ecological performance of the landscape at large if we are far more intentional with the patches we create.

10. No Time Like the Present: Creating Landscapes for an Era of Global Change

For millennia humans have interacted with the physical environment and other living organisms to shape ecosystems and landscapes. As our population has skyrocketed, our development of land accelerated, our consumption of energy, fresh water, and other resources risen, and our production of toxic chemicals, synthetic fixation of nitrogen, and release of carbon dioxide to the atmosphere surged, we have become more and more entangled in the workings of the biogeochemical system that is the planet Earth. As we have seen, this system is not necessarily the self-regulating Gaia that James Lovelock (2000) envisioned. Instead, it is best understood as a complex adaptive system characterized by nonlinearity (see chap. 4). Thanks to our prodigious efforts as a species, we are now entering an era of global change in which interacting stresses can lead to cascading, unpredictable effects (Steffen et al. 2004). Natural ecosystems may be thrown into chaos or flip to alternative stable states. We may witness unusually severe disturbances and see the biogeographical map of the planet redrawn within our lifetimes. Centuries-old landscapes will be stressed. Time-tested agricultural methods may cease to work.

Maintaining the ecological functioning of the planet and maintaining our quality of life are two sides of the same coin. As we always have, we will continue to rely on ecosystem services to provide the food we eat, the water we drink, and the air we breathe. In the twenty-first century, these services will have to come from an interwoven landscape of natural, restored, managed, and constructed patches. We must simultaneously strengthen this vital network, minimize the pressures on it as best we can, and prepare for it to adapt as changes unfold.

HUMAN ACTIVITY HAS DAMAGED NATURAL ECOSYSTEMS AND LANDSCAPES

By many measures, humanity has transformed the face of the planet. An influential article in *Science* in 1997 by a group of illustrious ecologists first pulled together data from a variety of sources to quantify these changes (Vitousek et al. 1997). The authors estimated that between one third and one half of the land surface of the planet had been significantly altered by human activity, including urban and industrial areas, row crop agriculture, and pastureland (fig. 10.1). They cited this land transformation as the primary driving force behind the global loss of biodiversity (see chap. 5). In addition to its immediate effects, land transformation contributes to carbon dioxide emissions and produces pollution and erosion that disrupt river and ocean ecosystems. By destroying or degrading natural ecosystems and landscapes, we humans have impeded the ability of the planet to provide the ecosystem services we depend on, including the provision of clean water, renewal of soil, and buffering against catastrophic storms (see chap. 4).

Eric Sanderson and a group of colleagues (2002) produced a similar analysis in graphic form. They mapped the "human footprint," using geographic information system (GIS) data for four proxies: population density, land transformation, road and river transportation networks, and penetration of electrical infrastructure. Because they included broader measures of human impact (e.g., buffer areas along roads not just the roads themselves), their estimates are higher. They estimated that 83 percent of the earth's land surface is directly affected by human beings. This impact ranges along a continuum from areas of the boreal forest and the Amazon, for instance, that score zero on their scale to major

Figure 10.1   Phoenix, Arizona and adjacent agricultural lands encroach on the desert landscape, 2009. (Image courtesy of NASA's Earth Observatory.)

metropolitan areas such as Beijing and São Paulo at the upper end. Sixty percent of the planet, they find, falls in between these extremes, in areas of "moderate but variable human influence."

The extent of human influence over the biosphere makes us responsible for its continued functioning. The ecologists writing in *Science* wrap up their article with the statement, "There is no clearer illustration of the extent of human dominance of the Earth than the fact that maintaining the diversity of 'wild' species and the functioning of 'wild' ecosystems will require increasing human involvement" (Vitousek et al. 1997: 499). Sanderson et al. (2002: 902) put it more simply: "The global extent of the human footprint suggests that humans are stewards of nature, whether we like it or not."

PRESERVE THE REMAINING NATURAL ECOSYSTEMS AND LANDSCAPES

What does it entail, in the twenty-first century, to be a steward of nature? Certainly, when so much of the surface of the planet has been affected by human activity, it entails conserving the natural ecosystems and landscapes that remain. It is easy to envision what this means in remote regions such as the Amazon or Alaska, but how about in already populated areas? How can the practice of landscape planning and landscape design support conservation in the context of development? The Avon Hills in Stearns County, Minnesota provide an instructive example.

The Avon Hills are approximately 80 square miles of rolling hills and kettle lakes at the western edge of the northern deciduous hardwood forest. Held in many places by the descendants of original homesteaders, the Avon Hills landscape retains large areas of forest and hosts several rare plant and animal species, including populations of American ginseng (*Panax quinquefolius*) and Cerulean warbler (*Setophaga cerulea*). The Avon Hills have been recognized for the important native plant communities they contain by the Minnesota Department of Natural Resources (1999) and are designated by the Nature Conservancy (2000) as an ecologically significant area.

Still, the area faces development pressure. Stearns County is the seventh most populous county in Minnesota and anticipates an approximately 33 percent increase in population by 2030 (Stearns County 2008). The nearby city of St. Cloud has grown over the past several decades, and St. Joseph's Township, the Avon Hills township closest to St. Cloud, has seen the spread of small hobby farms and unplanned subdivisions.

Recognizing these threats, Saint John's Abbey and University partnered with the Nature Conservancy in 2003 to bring in Applied Ecological Services (AES) and together lead a community planning process for the four townships that include the core of the Avon Hills. The process began with local tours to show community members the differences between high-quality and low-quality natural areas (e.g., intact wetlands versus wetlands that receive polluted runoff). AES developed base maps of the resources and land use in coordination with a small group of invited local leaders. Then, in a series of workshops, the public was asked to envision the Avon Hills in 2050 and mark their ideas on maps. The conservation vision that emerged from this process identified areas of the four townships to be preserved for recreational purposes, working forest and agriculture, rural character, and important upland and lowland conservation areas (fig. 10.2). Further workshops solidified community consensus and led a citizens' committee to recommend including stronger conservation elements in the county's new comprehensive plan. These recommendations were heard, and the 2008 Stearns County Comprehensive Plan called for

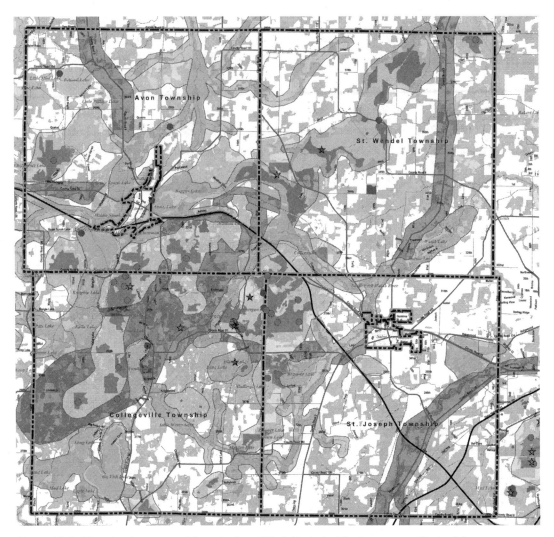

Figure 10.2 The map that emerged from the Avon Hills Initiative's visioning process. Much of the area indicated for conservation here is now governed by the Avon Hills Natural Resource Conservation Design Overlay District. (Courtesy of Applied Ecological Services, Inc.)

any planning process for the Avon Hills to consider natural resources first. The plan emphasized the protection of open space through parkland acquisition, conservation easements on private land, and limited residential development using conservation design. Conservation design is an approach to development in which new construction is adapted to natural features and large portions of a site are left as open space (Arendt 1996). Stearns County's land use and zoning ordinance now requires that development in the township-identified natural resources conservation design overlay district must permanently set aside at least 80 percent of the land for natural resource protection, possibly the strongest level of protection in the country (Stearns County 2010).

Thanks to community efforts, the regionally important ecosystems of the Avon Hills are being protected even in the context of continued population growth and land development. An ecological landscape design, whether for an entire region or a single site, should recognize and preserve intact natural ecosystems. However, this is just one element of our larger stewardship responsibilities. Another key piece is to try to repair the damage that has already been done.

RESTORATION ECOLOGY

Along with the recognition that ecosystems have been damaged by human activity has come a field of ecology dedicated to understanding how to reverse that damage. Restoration ecology is simply the science dealing with the restoration of ecological systems.

Restoration ecology occupies a mediating position between the basic theoretical science of ecology and the practical pursuit of ecological restoration (fig. 10.3). It has the potential to improve restoration efforts by bringing to them clear scientific understanding of the ecological mechanisms at play. Restoration ecology can also improve ecological theory by testing concepts such as assembly rules,

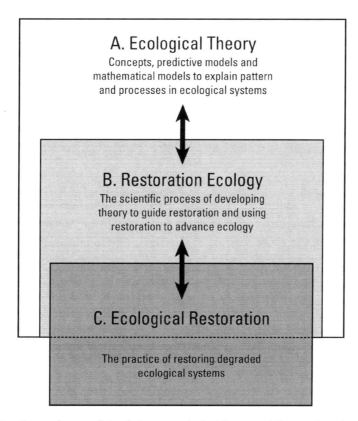

Figure 10.3 Restoration ecology mediates between ecological theory and the practice of ecological restoration. (From *Foundations of Restoration Ecology*, edited by Donald A. Falk et al. Copyright ©2006 Island Press. Reproduced by permission of Island Press, Washington, DC.)

succession, and plant–herbivore interactions in on-the-ground experiments. Where restoration fails, it may be because ecological theory was not applied properly, or it may be because the ecological theory applied was unable to predict the response of natural systems. Working as a bridge between the theoretical and the practical, restoration ecology has the potential to improve our understanding in both areas (Palmer et al. 2006).

This is an urgent endeavor but one that can be approached positively. Taking the long view of the current global biodiversity crisis (see chap. 5), restoration ecologist Truman Young (2000) predicted that by 2050 we will have lost most of the species and habitats we are going to lose and that the critical issue will be helping those that survived the crisis to recover. Viewed in this light, he suggested, "the long-term future of conservation biology is restoration ecology" (Young 2000: 77). Young also pointed out that even as human impact has become so extensive, we are witnessing a trend toward land abandonment. While cities are growing, many rural areas in both the developed and the developing world are being depopulated. As this happens, marginal agricultural areas fall out of production. Many of these areas are degraded but have the potential to be restored.

In addition to recreating habitat, restoring ecosystems can rehabilitate the many ecosystem services that natural areas provide, from controlling floodwaters to serving as a genetic bank. Although it is no substitute for the preservation of intact natural ecosystems and landscapes, restoration ecology can guide the process of reversing the direct damage that humans have already done.

RESTORE DAMAGED ECOSYSTEMS

The practical counterpart of restoration ecology is ecological restoration, which is defined by the Society for Ecological Restoration as the process of assisting the recovery of an ecosystem that has been degraded, damaged, or destroyed (Society for Ecological Restoration International Science & Policy Working Group 2004).

One example of damage and restoration is the ongoing story of road removal in Idaho's Clearwater National Forest. Hundreds of thousands of miles of mostly dirt roads have been built on public lands in the United States. According to Adam Switalski, science program director with Wildlands CPR, a non-profit group committed to reviving wild places by restoring unneeded roads, this makes the US Forest Service the largest road-managing agency in the world. As Sanderson's map of the human footprint suggests, these roads have numerous impacts on the forests they penetrate. They fragment animal habitat, provide access for poachers, become sites for the establishment of invasive species, disrupt the natural hydrology, and chronically contribute sediment to streams in their watershed.

The roads in the Clearwater National Forest were built largely in the 1940s and 1950s to support "jammer" logging, in which felled logs were hauled by cable directly onto trucks. Roads were put in every 200 vertical yards on the steep mountain slopes, leading to densities of up to 30 miles of road per square mile, which, Switalski relates, is greater than the road density in New York City. These roads were built by cutting into the slope, piling the material as fill on the downside of the cut, and compacting the resulting flat bed. Where roads crossed streams, logs were laid side by side, or later metal pipes were used, to create culverts. Especially where culverts have clogged, water can build up on the uphill side of roads and then trigger an entire section of road to slide. Because the roads are stacked up the slopes, a landslide at one can set off a cascade of road failures. In the Clearwater National Forest the impacts of roads were brought home during the winter of 1995–1996, when heavy rainfall on top of snowpack triggered more than 900 landslides, more than half of which were associated with roads. Although landslides are a natural land-forming process in this area, the amount of sediment released that winter buried several streams and choked many others.

The next summer the Forest Service, in cooperation with the local Nez Perce tribe, who have rights to the co-management of the forest, began removing some of the roads. Fifteen years later, this work continues, and a proven road removal procedure has been developed, essentially reversing the road construction process. Any shallow-rooted trees that have grown up in the center of the road are cut down and stockpiled to the side. A large excavator drives to the end of the road to be removed and begins by scraping up the fill that was placed on the downhill side of the road. The machine operator places this fill back on the cut side of the slope that it came from. Underneath the fill lies the original duff and topsoil that was buried 60 or 70 years ago and all the seeds that it contains. The operator spreads several buckets of this duff and topsoil across the restored area and then places a couple of the stockpiled downed trees across the slope. The operator then backs the excavator up and starts the procedure again. At stream crossings the operator removes all the fill material to expose the original stream channel, which again is evident because of its layer of buried topsoil. In erosion-prone spots, slopes are backed down to 2:1, and supplemental seeding and mulching is sometimes used.

Initially the restored roadbeds can erode more sediment than they did before, but soon grasses, horsetail (*Equisetum arvense*), clover, and dandelions cover the exposed soil. Then fruiting shrubs such as thimbleberry (*Rubus parviflorus*), elderberry (*Sambucus cerulea*), and serviceberry (*Amelanchier alnifolia*) begin to grow. On the first slopes to be restored, conifers have begun to reclaim the old road-way. Salmon have begun to appear in reaches of streams that were formerly blocked by culverts, and camera traps record use of the restored roads by deer, moose (*Alces alces*), lynx (*Lynx canadensis*), and bears (fig. 10.4).

Along with protection of remaining wild ecosystems, restoration of areas where human impacts can be reversed is an important aspect of our emerging twenty-first-century relationship with the land. But what about areas where the degree of human impact makes restoration to a "wild" state impossible?

URBAN AREAS CAN BE UNDERSTOOD AS ECOSYSTEMS

One of the primary changes in land use that is transforming the face of the planet is ever-increasing urbanization. In 2008 the world passed a milestone in human development. For the first time ever, more people now live in cities than in rural areas. The United Nations (2008) estimates that between 2007 and 2050 the world's population will grow by 2.5 billion and the population of cities by 3.1 billion, meaning that urban areas will absorb all of this astounding growth in population and continue to draw people from rural areas. Most of that growth will occur in the less developed world. In the United States, more than 80 percent of the population already lives in metropolitan areas.

As urbanization has increased, a new field of urban ecology has emerged. One of the signs of the arrival of this field was the designation of two US cities—Phoenix and Baltimore—as Long Term Ecosystem Research (LTER) sites, putting them in the same company as Hubbard Brook (see chap. 4) and

Figure 10.4   Deer photographed with a camera trap on a restored section of road in the Clearwater National Forest. (Photo courtesy of Wildlands CPR.)

the Konza Prairie (see chap. 2). The focus of the urban LTERs is not on remnant natural communities and vegetated areas, what can be thought of as ecology *in* cities, but on the performance of overall metropolitan areas—the ecology *of* cities.

A key conceptual leap is that in the urban LTERs human structures and social processes are explicitly incorporated into the research program. If we think back to Bormann and Likens's model of a watershed ecosystem at Hubbard Brook, it included the atmosphere, soil and rock minerals, available nutrients in the soil, and organic matter, both living and dead. To these components, scientists at the Baltimore Ecosystem Study have added buildings and built infrastructure, the human population, and various linked human institutions (Pickett et al. 2004). All of these components interact to determine nitrogen fluxes in the Baltimore area, which, given nitrogen pollution of Chesapeake Bay, is an issue of tremendous concern (see chap. 6).

Among the findings of the Baltimore Ecosystem Study is that urban riparian areas do not function as nitrogen sinks, removing nitrates through denitrification in wet soils (Pickett et al. 2008). Because much of the water that enters urban streams does so as surface flow over hard surfaces or in pipes, rather than as groundwater, it bypasses the riparian buffer zone. Furthermore, the flashy flows of streams incise deep channels, drying adjacent riparian areas and leading to lower rates of denitrification. Cities such as Baltimore are not uniform environments. Like natural landscapes, they are heterogeneous, with multiple patches that change through time (see chap. 9). The patchiness of the urban environment influences ecosystem processes. Somewhat counterintuitively, nitrate levels in Baltimore's Gwynns Falls watershed are lower in urban than in suburban reaches of the stream. The use of septic systems rather than sanitary sewer in the suburbs is a leading contributor. Fertilization of expansive lawns is likely to be another. Thus human-driven patterns and processes interact with biophysical elements in a spatially heterogeneous manner to determine the characteristics and behavior of the urban ecosystem.

Ecologists who study urban ecosystems argue that their research offers scientific means to improve the quality of life (by both social and environmental measures) in cities. They even suggest that as urbanization increases and the environmental problems associated with cities become more widespread, urban ecology will be central to creating a sustainable future (Grimm et al. 2008).

IMPROVE THE FUNCTIONING OF URBAN ECOSYSTEMS

Looking at cities as ecosystems offers a sophisticated approach to dealing with various environmental and social issues, such as nitrogen pollution. This is the approach taken by urban-interface, a design consultancy that has been working alongside the Baltimore Ecosystem Study team to apply their findings and develop practical solutions (McGrath et al. 2007).

The first premise of the designers' approach is that, in order to be effective, they have to understand and work with the heterogeneity of urban ecosystem. To that end, they chose model neighborhoods to represent a range of conditions. Two of these provide a study in social and ecological contrasts. Springfield Farm Court, in the Baisman Run watershed, has only recently been converted from agricultural land to upscale residences on large lots. Sewage is treated with septic systems. Wide streets and long driveways concentrate stormwater and direct it immediately into local streams. Closer to Baltimore Harbor, the inner-city community of Harlem Park in Watershed 263 is a neighborhood of row homes, residential squares, and vacant lots. Here streams are completely buried. The sanitary sewer system prevents regular discharge of pollutants to the watershed, but storms collect whatever litter and spills have accumulated on the neighborhood's various hard surfaces and take them directly to the Patapsco River and from there into the bay.

The designers' second premise is that social and ecological factors interact in the urban ecosystem (fig. 10.5). No doubt the residents of Springfield Farm Court chose their neighborhood in part for its feel of genteel country living. Being far from city infrastructure and having a long driveway across a large lawn help create this feel and, unfortunately, contribute to nitrate pollution. Design solutions will have to work with the homeowners' expressed landscape preference. Luckily, the large lots allow ample opportunities for individual homeowners or immediate neighbors to make effective improvements. Rain gardens, with front yard and back yard variations, can filter water from roofs and driveways. Subtle detention basins in lawn can capture stormwater in the low spots between neighboring properties.

The residents of Harlem Park probably have fewer choices about where to live and fewer resources to tackle stormwater improvements at the individual level. Nonprofit groups such as Parks and People have stepped in, however, coordinating and funding local stormwater improvement projects at the com-

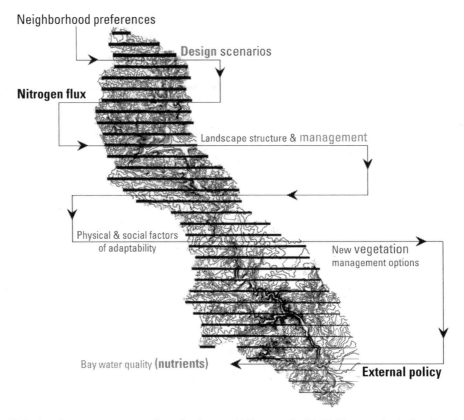

Neighborhood preferences

Design scenarios

Nitrogen flux

Landscape structure & management

Physical & social factors
of adaptability

New vegetation
management options

Bay water quality **(nutrients)**

External policy

Figure 10.5   In urban ecosystems such as the Gwynns Falls watershed in Baltimore, physical and social factors interact and can be influenced by landscape design to affect ecological outcomes. (Courtesy of urban-interface, llc.)

munity level. Solutions such as replacing asphalt in local schoolyards with green spaces that infiltrate runoff, cleaning alleys, and greening vacant lots help reduce the amount of polluting nitrogen that reaches the bay. They also improve recreational opportunities in the neighborhood, create green-collar jobs, and serve as community development programs.

In a heterogeneous urban ecosystem, broadscale best management practices for stormwater management and mitigating nitrogen pollution are less useful than design solutions that are tailored to the specifics of the physical and social environment. Because people are part of the ecosystem, our learning and the design changes we implement can alter the patch dynamics of the system and improve ecological function.

ATMOSPHERIC POLLUTION AFFECTS ECOSYSTEMS

The impact of humans on the biosphere is not confined to bulldozers' blades. Atmospheric pollution is changing the chemistry and ecology of aquatic and terrestrial ecosystems (fig. 10.6).

Photos of dying forests and sterile lakes have made acid rain one of the best-known examples of

Figure 10.6   Humans' pollution of the atmosphere is a potent force for ecological change. (Courtesy of US Fish and Wildlife Service.)

such damaging pollution. Burning fossil fuels, especially coal, releases large quantities of sulfur dioxide (SO_2) and nitrogen oxides (NO_x). In the atmosphere, these gases react with water vapor to form an acidic solution that, when it falls to the earth, reduces the pH of lakes, streams, and soils. Acidic waters can directly harm fish and also mobilize toxic aluminum. Where the buffering capacity of soils is exceeded, acid rain can leach out nutrients and, again, mobilize aluminum. In regions such as New York's Adirondack Mountains that are downwind of industrial areas in the Midwest, acid rain has decimated fish populations and weakened stands of red spruce (*Picea rubens*). Emissions of sulfur dioxide and nitrogen oxides have peaked in the United States thanks to increased regulation and more efficient technology, but acid rain continues (US Environmental Protection Agency 2011).

Nitrogen oxides carried on the wind are not only a precursor to acid rain, but also, along with ammonia (NH_3) from agricultural sources, unintended fertilizer for large swaths of land. In California, a recent study found that 55,000 square kilometers of the state were exposed to atmospheric deposition of more than 5 kilograms per hectare per year, with a high of 21 kilograms per hectare per year in central Los Angeles (Weiss 2006).

Atmospheric nitrogen deposition, like overuse of agricultural fertilizers, can pollute streams and bodies of water. It also reduces the biodiversity of native plant communities by favoring more aggressive plants (see chap. 2). In southern California's coastal sage scrub and on serpentine grasslands in the San Francisco Bay area, home to the checkerspot butterfly (see chap. 9), nitrogen deposition favors the growth of invasive annual grasses and has contributed to the decline of endemic species.

Oxides of nitrogen and sulfur are not the only gases that human activity is releasing into the atmosphere. Carbon dioxide (CO_2) from fossil fuel combustion and land transformation has accumulated in the atmosphere since the beginning of the industrial revolution and now stands at record levels. Jack Morgan and colleagues exposed sections of shortgrass prairie in northeastern Colorado to elevated levels of carbon dioxide for a period of 5 years in order to assess plant community response (Morgan et al. 2004, 2007). With higher CO_2 concentrations, plants need to open their stomata for less time in order to absorb the CO_2 they need for photosynthesis and growth. This means they also lose less water. On the shortgrass prairie, this has the effect of reducing the competitive advantage of warm-season grasses. Morgan found that with elevated CO_2 the cool-season needle and thread grass (*Hesperostipa comata*) increased its productivity and abundance in the community. Fringed sage (*Artemesia frigida*), a woody subshrub, also increased forty-fold in biomass and twenty-fold in cover under elevated CO_2. Morgan and his co-authors conclude that although the diversity of the community did not change with the increase in carbon dioxide, overall species composition did. The resulting community in some ways more closely resembled a mixed-grass prairie but with more woody plants and lower forage value for cattle and wildlife.

Effects such as these from atmospheric pollution create growing conditions different from those to which preexisting plant communities are adapted and challenge our ability to restore native ecosystems.

ANTICIPATE THE EFFECTS OF ATMOSPHERIC POLLUTION

Acid rain, nitrogen deposition, and higher levels of carbon dioxide complicate the restoration, design, and management of plant communities in affected areas. This is especially the case in urban areas, where all three problems are magnified.

We should at a minimum be aware of how these pollutants may contribute to management problems. Reduced pH from acid rain and the accompanying metal toxicity may affect plant health. Increased productivity from nitrogen deposition and elevated CO_2 will probably reduce community diversity. They may also encourage the growth of invasive plants.

There are horticultural management approaches that can alleviate the affects of atmospheric pollution. In areas affected by acid rain, continued pH monitoring of soils and liming may be needed. Nitrogen deposition should be taken into account when planning the fertility program of a site. High-carbon mulches such as sawdust could be used to immobilize excess nitrogen in planting beds. Aggressive grasses promoted by higher nitrogen or carbon dioxide levels can be managed with timed grazing (see chap. 7) or fire (see chap. 8). Grazing can also potentially reduce nitrogen levels at a site by converting plant biomass to meat, which is then exported and consumed.

Because of the large scale of these problems and the fact that pollutants often have effects far from their source, policies and regulations will continue to be the most effective response. Until these pollution problems can be resolved through legislation and agreement, however, we may have to accept as fact their impacts on the landscape. Their assessment, even if only anecdotally, should be part of site analysis. Is a site near a highway, downwind of a fossil fuel–burning power plant or an animal feedlot, or in an urban watershed? If so, the plant communities we try to create there will have to respond to these conditions. We may not be able to restore diverse native communities. We may have to allow the community to adjust to the conditions and expect more rampant growth of certain species and faster or altered succession. We may even be led to embrace novel communities suited to these conditions.

LAND TRANSFORMATION HAS DISRUPTED TERRESTRIAL CARBON SINKS

It is a well-established fact that atmospheric carbon dioxide has hit record levels. The Intergovernmental Panel on Climate Change noted that the atmospheric concentration of CO_2 of 379 parts per million in 2005 far exceeds levels captured in ice cores covering the last 650,000 years (Solomon et el. 2007). Elevated CO_2 threatens to have disruptive effects on the global climate and the ecosystems on which we depend. After the burning of fossil fuels, the largest contributor to the increase in CO_2 levels is land transformation (Le Quéré et al. 2009). As forests are cleared for farm fields or pasture, the carbon stored in the trees is released into the atmosphere. As agricultural lands are worked over time, soil organic carbon levels generally decrease, and that carbon too finds its way into the atmosphere. When agricultural lands are stripped of their topsoil to allow new construction on the edges of metropolitan areas, the carbon stored in that soil is again subject to rapid decay. So not only does the development of new lands for agriculture and cities directly disrupt native ecosystems, but it also indirectly contributes to climate change across the planet.

By calculating annual changes in land use and the carbon flux associated with each, Richard Houghton (1999, 2008) came up with what are widely regarded as the most definitive estimates available of carbon release due to land transformation (fig. 10.7). Houghton estimated that between 1850 and 1990 the area of cultivated lands worldwide more than quadrupled, from 320 million hectares to 1.36 billion hectares. Most of that increase occurred since 1950 and took place in the tropics. On top of this, another 180 million hectares of forest were cleared for pasture. Over the period 1850–2000, Houghton calculated a total net flux to the atmosphere of 148.6 billion metric tons due to land transformation. Worldwide in the first 5 years of the twenty-first century, the net annual flux of carbon dioxide from terrestrial areas to the atmosphere averaged 1.47 billion metric tons. Tropical deforestation drove the global figures. In North America, however, where forests cleared for agriculture in the eastern half of the country largely regrew during the period studied, Houghton calculated that annual fluxes of carbon dioxide actually entered negative territory. This demonstrates the potential of terrestrial ecosystems to serve not only as sources of atmospheric carbon but as carbon sinks.

Only about 45 percent of the carbon released from burning fossil fuels and clearing and farming land each year remains in the atmosphere. The rest is reabsorbed by the ocean and by terrestrial ecosystems. Continuous sampling over forest canopies shows daily fluxes in carbon dioxide levels, similar to the oxygen measurements taken by Odum in the waters of Silver Springs (see chap. 4). At a broader scale of space and time, during summer in the northern hemisphere scientists have actually measured the drawdown in atmospheric carbon dioxide as photosynthesis kicks in. Summarizing the findings of ground-level and atmospheric measurements as well as global models, John Grace (2004) concluded that temperate, boreal, and tropical regions all serve as carbon sinks, through both mature and de-

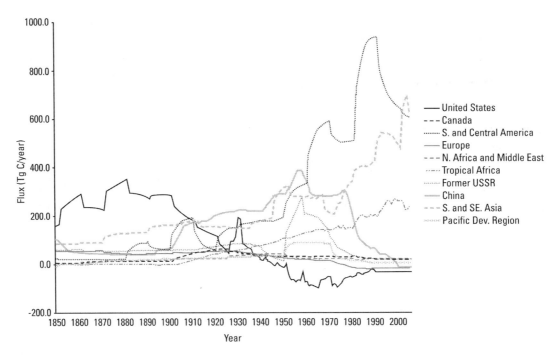

Figure 10.7   Annual net carbon flux to the atmosphere from land transformation for different regions between 1850 and 2005. Note the dramatic increase in emissions from South and Central America and South and Southeast Asia and the fact that the United States, Europe, and China have all crossed into negative territory, meaning that their landscapes serve as carbon sinks. (Adapted from Houghton 2008.)

veloping ecosystems. Grace goes on to point out that new carbon sinks can be created, as with tree planting programs. Development of carbon sinks could offset 1 billion metric tons or more of carbon emissions a year.

SEQUESTER CARBON IN THE BUILT ENVIRONMENT

Preserving intact natural areas will help minimize ongoing contributions to atmospheric carbon dioxide from land transformation. It is also worth exploring how the constructed landscapes we are creating can function as carbon sinks. When we hear of carbon sequestration, it is most often in the form of pumping power plant emissions deep underground. Land use practices too can create carbon sinks, and efforts are being made at reforestation, afforestation, and no-till farming. In urban areas, tree planting and green roofs have also been promoted for their ability to capture carbon.

Landscape architect Denise Hoffman Brandt went beyond the obvious remedies in a project called City Sink. City Sink proposes a number of interventions, in both the design and planning of the constructed environment and in policies that help to shape it, that can create sinks for carbon in New York City and, by extension, other metropolitan areas. Hoffman Brandt imagines City Sink as a "meta-park of dispersed landscape infrastructure" (Buckminster Fuller Institute 2012). As multiple strategies are used in numerous locations, the overall system becomes more resilient. The aim is not to replace the natural ecosystems lost to development but to create high-functioning analogs to them. Although many of the constructed features could seem like conventional city greening efforts, their intent is more sophisticated and specific: to use the multiple interactions of ecological systems to capture and store carbon in plants and in soil.

One of the strategies Hoffman Brandt proposes is highway bio-sound barriers. Cars and trucks driving along highways emit CO_2, and the concrete used in conventional barriers also contributes to carbon dioxide emissions. What if instead these barriers absorbed CO_2 from passing vehicles? Hoffman Brandt first suggests a system to convert existing sound barriers into living walls. Steel mesh drapes, folded to retain vertical soil pockets, could be fastened to the sides of existing barrier walls. The folding increases surface area and creates a variety of microclimates, including recesses that are protected from wind. Hoffman Brandt envisions seeding these drapes with tough perennials, grasses, and vines.

New sound barriers could be built as vertical living systems surrounding a soil–gravel core (fig. 10.8). Hoffman Brant has designed a modular frame of intersecting rebar (or perhaps bamboo) that could be set between steel posts in four different orientations, again forming a varied surface and allowing for flexible installation while creating a continuous run of the sound-attenuating core. The frame encourages several types of planting. The outside edges of the soil core could be planted with plugs as a living wall. Another section could serve as a trellis for vines. And a third offers the possibility of serving as a frame to guide topiary-style pruning of shrubs planted within.

In both the drape retrofit and the new bio-sound barrier systems, solar panels can be integrated to provide energy to run irrigation pumps that circulate stormwater captured from the highways through internal drip tubing in the bio-sound barriers.

Although a single installation of bio-sound barrier would not create much carbon storage capacity, a network of installations could have a significant effect. A quick estimate by Hoffman Brandt shows that installing bio-sound barriers along 56 miles of highway in New York's five boroughs would create 127.8 acres of planted area.

There are many practical details to be worked out in a novel system such as this. Hoffman Brandt is working now on setting up a pilot project to test and refine the bio-sound barriers in practice. However, this creative concept suggests the potential for capturing carbon in urban ecosystems in ways that might not have been previously envisioned.

CLIMATE CHANGE WILL ALTER BIOGEOGRAPHY

Plants are adapted to certain ranges of temperature and available moisture. This is among the factors that drive the distribution of plants, and of the communities and biomes they compose, across the earth's surface (see chap. 1). Increased temperatures and changing weather patterns associated with rising levels of greenhouse gases in the atmosphere will necessarily affect the biogeography of plants and of the animals, including humans, that depend on them. Scientists at Caltech recently used modeling software to predict that, under an intermediate climate change scenario identified by the Intergovernmental Panel on Climate Change, 49 percent of the earth's land surface will experience a change in plant communities and 37 percent a change in biome (Bergengren et al. 2011).

Figure 10.8 New highway bio-sound barrier.
Modular frames set between steel posts
attenuate sound with a continuous gravel–soil
core and provide opportunities for planting of
perennials, vines, and shrubs. The bio-sound
barrier is designed to be less carbon-intensive
in its production and to sequester carbon
dioxide emissions from highway in vegetation,
internal soil medium, and surrounding soil. (From
Denise Hoffman Brandt, *City Sink: Carbon Cycle
Planning for Future Cities*, Oscar Riera Ojeda
Publishers 2012.)

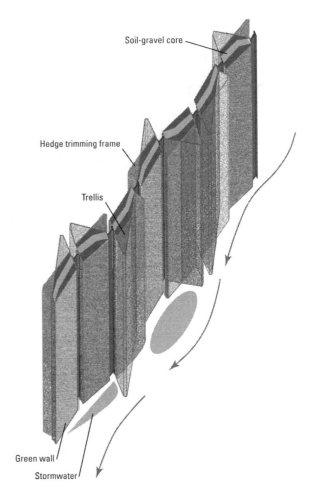

Soil-gravel core

Hedge trimming frame

Trellis

Green wall

Stormwater

Scientists with the US Forest Service have concluded that the forests in the eastern United States
will be among the communities affected (Iverson et al. 2008). Early evidence indicates that some of
those changes are already taking place. Louis Iverson and his colleagues have spent a decade and a
half modeling suitable habitat for 134 tree species under a range of scenarios. Using the predicted
high and low atmospheric carbon ranges presented by the Intergovernmental Panel on Climate Change,
three climate models, information from more than 100,000 forest inventory and analysis plots, and
thirty-eight predictor variables, they have estimated the potential suitable habitat for all the tree species in the year 2100.

Using a combination of importance values and area of habitat, they determined that sixty-six species would experience increases in potential habitat, fifty-four decreases, and fourteen no change. Not
surprisingly, habitat for most species would move northward, and much farther north in the hotter scenarios. Trees of the spruce–fir forest would lose almost all their habitat within the borders of the United
States, whereas southern species of oak and pine would increase their potential habitat (fig. 10.9).

The Forest Service scientists pointed out a couple of limitations to their findings. One is that the

Figure 10.9 Comparison of **(A)** current (from Forest Inventory and Analysis plots) and **(B)** projected (under average of three models in low atmospheric carbon scenario) habitat for loblolly pine (*Pinus taeda*). (From Prasad et al. 2007.)

climate models do not account for land use changes that may take place or for changes in disturbance regimes that may accompany climate change. The other is that their findings indicated only potential habitat. In order for species with increasing potential habitat to actually increase their ranges, they will have to successfully migrate to the newly suitable areas. Because of lag times, fragmentation of remaining forests, and barriers to dispersal such as large bands of cities or agricultural land, natural colonization is likely to be a slow and fitful process. Iverson and his colleagues estimated that for four species studied, only 15 percent of the new potential habitat available (that closest to the current range limits) had a 2 percent or greater chance of being colonized within 100 years.

Margaret Davis, who used pollen trapped in cores of lake sediment to track the expanding ranges of eastern trees after the last ice age (see chap. 1), has suggested that along with migration, adaptation is an important response to climate change (Davis and Shaw 2001). We know that plant species consist of populations with adaptations to different areas. Rates of evolution are affected by gene flow and the intensity of selective pressure. At the leading edge of a species' northward migration, populations are likely to undergo rapid evolution, as pollen from preadapted southern populations mixes in and plants better adapted to the newly available habitats have greater reproductive success. Like the Forest Service researchers, however, she and her co-author expressed concern that fragmentation of the landscape makes the necessary gene flow difficult. They also suggested that the rates of climate change predicted may create greater differences between the genetic resources of populations and the new environmental realities they face than adaptation can surmount. They concluded that extirpation of populations at the southern end of species' ranges, and even extinction of species, is a possibility.

ASSIST THE MIGRATION OF PLANTS

In addition to reducing carbon emissions from land transformation and to sequestering carbon in order to minimize climate change, we will have to adapt to the changes already unfolding. If the models created by scientists at Caltech and the US Forest Service are right, the twenty-first century will be a time of severe ecological disruption. The plant communities we are accustomed to seeing will shift before our eyes as species migrate, adapt, and go locally extinct. We may feel compelled to minimize this disruption.

Where interconnected regional networks of habitat are in place, plants may be able to migrate successfully on their own (see chap. 9). Given the rapid rate of climate change predicted and the barriers that lie in the path of migrating species, however, human involvement may be necessary in order for many tree species to extend their ranges to keep pace with changing conditions.

The first question we face when contemplating assisted migration is, "What are its goals?" Are we seeking to preserve ecosystem function? To maintain economically important species? To conserve species that risk extinction? Each of these goals suggests a somewhat different course of action.

The next question is, "How do we decide when to act?" There is a danger of disrupting existing communities and trophic relationships, some of which may be in the process of reestablishing their own equilibria. Unaided migration will lead to changes in community composition, so changing community composition itself is not a trigger for action. In many ways, changing community composition is a sign that natural processes are working. Lack of regeneration of existing species on a site is one possible sign that intervention is needed, although there could be explanations for such a phenomenon other than climate change. Increases in invasive species are another sign, suggesting that niches are available that no current member of the community is filling, although, again, other explanations for this phenomenon are possible. For species at risk of extinction, minimum viable populations can be determined and action taken when actual populations fall below a threshold.

Then we come to the question, "How can we best help plants migrate?" Davis's research suggests that selecting source populations is an important aspect of the problem. We should look for populations that are likely to be already adapted to the conditions of a site that is being targeted for introduction of new migrants. Populations at the northern edge of species' current ranges may be at the front of a wave that is still cresting from the retreat of the last glaciers and could be well suited for continued dispersal. It may help to introduce diverse genetic material to an introduction site, to facilitate rapid evolution.

It is probably especially important to assist migration where barriers such as large urban conglomerations or swaths of agricultural land stand in the way. Helping species leap these barriers may be a useful place to target limited resources. It would be inefficient, if not downright impossible, to plant continuous waves of northward migration. It would be more effective to establish outlying populations to simulate successful random long-distance dispersal. These populations would form the ragged edge of a wave and could coalesce with a naturally advancing core to fill out newly available habitat. Species that have formed important mutualistic relationships may have to be moved as pairs or multiples (see chap. 7). Or we may hope, in the case of plant–animal mutualisms, that if we keep the plants moving, the animals will keep up.

If taken seriously, assisted migration would be an act of attempted ecological management on an enormous scale. To be done effectively, it would entail coordination between multiple public and private entities. It would require the best scientific information available but would probably have to be done in the realm of uncertainty. The enormous scale of global climate change may call for such measures, however.

WITH GLOBAL CHANGE, NOVEL PLANT COMMUNITIES WILL EMERGE

As Margaret Davis's work with pollen cores revealed, the forest communities of eastern North America that we are familiar with today are relatively recent associations, based on the individual dispersal of various taxa (see chap. 1). Subsequent research has further illustrated this point. Thompson Webb (1987) used pollen samples from radiocarbon-dated cores of lake sediment to track the ranges of several families and genera in the eastern United States over the last 18,000 years, that is, since the approximate beginning of the retreat of the Laurentide ice sheet. During this time, he noted, "the changes were large enough to result in the appearance and disappearance of major biomes and ecotones" (Webb 1987: 177). Most unfamiliar to us among these vanished biomes was the extensive spruce parkland that 18,000 years ago covered the current range of the eastern deciduous forest. In this parkland, broadly spaced spruce trees grew amid sedges and cold-tolerant sage, providing excellent habitat for wandering mastodons (*Mammut americanum*). Note that all these species (except the mastodon) are still present but occur in different community combinations: spruce along with pines, fir, birch, and alder in the boreal forest; sedges in the prairies; cold-tolerant sages in the tundra. Webb (1987: 184) reminded us that on the time scales he studied, plant communities "are ephemeral features, and plant taxa are capable of growing in a variety of locations and associations."

The sorts of changes documented by Webb have only accelerated. Richard Hobbs, Eric Higgs, and James Harris (2009: 599) claimed,

The rapid pace of current change, coupled with the breakdown of biogeographic barriers through the global human transport of species, sets the current era apart from previous times in terms of the increasing rate of appearance of novel environments, species combinations and altered ecosystem function.

Climate change is only one of the driving forces that can give rise to new plant communities. Invasive species, land use change, atmospheric pollution, and changing disturbance regimes are others, all of which we are currently facing.

Hobbs, Higgs, and Harris distinguished between historic ecosystems, hybrid ecosystems (which retain some of the characteristics or functions of the original ecosystem), and novel ecosystems (in which the species composition or ecosystem function have been entirely altered). They argued that the traditional restoration goal of re-creating historic ecosystems may not be possible in all cases and propose accepting a range of management options. They claimed that at some point in the development of a hybrid ecosystem a threshold is crossed, where the best outcome becomes acceptance of certain changes and restoration of only some aspects of historic ecosystem structure or function. In cases of the most significant alteration to both biotic and abiotic factors, they suggested, restoration may be practically impossible, and the focus should be on management of the new resulting ecosystem.

ALLOW AND TAKE PART IN THE CREATION OF NOVEL COMMUNITIES

In the twenty-first century that Hobbs, Higgs, and Harris described, novel plant communities will play an increasingly significant role. Where ecological restoration typically tries to recreate communities observed in less disturbed reference ecosystems, we may, in some cases going forward, have to accept the development of communities without references.

Peter Del Tredici, senior research scientist at the Arnold Arboretum of Harvard University, argues that the spontaneous vegetation that appears in neglected urban areas gives us a foretaste of what these novel communities might look like. Like the cities that house them, they are melting pots. Of the 222 species described in Del Tredici's *Wild Urban Plants of the Northeast* (2010), 32.5 percent are from the Americas, 47.5 percent from Europe and Central Asia, 7.5 percent are native to both Europe and North America, 12 percent from Eastern Asia, and just one (Bermuda grass) from Africa. Many are pre-adapted to the stressful conditions of urban living, being drought resistant, tolerant of a wide range of soils, and able to recover quickly from disturbance. Some, such as purslane (*Portulaca oleracea*), have been associated with human settlements for so long that their natural origins have been obscured.

Del Tredici argues that spontaneous urban vegetation performs a number of ecosystem services, including temperature reduction, erosion control, soil building, and carbon sequestration (see chap. 4). However, he has admitted that "unfortunately, the aesthetics of ecologically functional, spontaneous urban landscapes often leave something to be desired" (Del Tredici 2010: 20). This does not have to be the case, however. As a first sketch of an intentionally designed novel plant community, he has proposed the "cosmopolitan urban meadow," which contains grasses such as tall fescue (*Festuca arundinacea*) and purple lovegrass (*Eragrostis spectabilis*), legumes such as white clover (*Trifolium repens*), and flowering perennials such as yarrow and chicory (*Cichorium intybus*).

The Europeans are further along in their development of these ideas. Since the mid-1990s, James Hitchmough and Nigel Dunnett at the University of Sheffield in England have been developing novel herbaceous plant communities for use in urban parks and on green roofs (Hitchmough 2004, 2008). Their naturalistic plantings use a broad palette of native and nonnative plants, screened for invasiveness, tested for horticultural compatibility, and tuned for aesthetic display (fig. 10.10). They create intentionally diverse plantings in stacked layers, to better support invertebrate biodiversity and exclude weeds. These plantings are more clearly cultural creations than Del Tredici's spontaneous vegetation. However, both approaches offer a view of how we might allow and take part in the creation of novel plant communities as significant components of the landscapes of the twenty-first century.

PANARCHY EXPLAINS THE PERSISTENCE OF NATURAL ECOSYSTEMS

The environmental changes we can expect in this century are upon us already. Their largest effects may not come gradually, however. We understand that ecosystems can exist in one of several alternative stable states and that resilient ecosystems can absorb a degree of disturbance, reorganize if necessary, and continue to function. However, even these ecosystems may undergo episodic abrupt shifts between states. If disruptive change is not an uncommon experience for natural ecosystems, how have they survived?

Refining his original inquiry into resilience (see chap. 8), C. S. Holling proposed a Möbius-strip like figure to explain the cycle of such events (fig. 10.11). On the front side of the loop, the r phase

Figure 10.10 In this planting at London's Olympic Park, designed by James Hitchmough, Nigel Dunnett, and LDA/Hargreaves, North American prairie plants maximize summer display while mostly British native plants (including purple loosestrife) process runoff at the base of the slope. (Photo by James Hitchmough.)

involves rapid exploitation of newly available resources, followed by the K phase of steady growth and development of connections. You might think of this as the classic description of succession after a disturbance. At some point during the process of growth, another disturbance triggers the omega phase of creative destruction, breaking the established connections and releasing the accumulated resources, beginning the back loop of the cycle. The alpha phase of reorganization quickly follows. During this phase unpredictability is at its highest. Resources can be lost, accidents can happen that set the course of future events, and flips to alternative stable states can occur. Together the front and back loops represent the interplay between predictability and unpredictability, between accumulation of resources and the introduction of opportunity. We can think of the full loop as an adaptive cycle that an ecosystem, as a complex adaptive system, undergoes repeatedly through time (see chap. 4).

Remember, however, that what we view as an ecosystem at a particular scale is part of a hierarchy of larger and smaller systems (see chap. 9). Holling and Lance Gunderson named a nested set of adaptive cycles a panarchy, like a hierarchy, but with a nod to the Greek god of nature, Pan (Gunder-

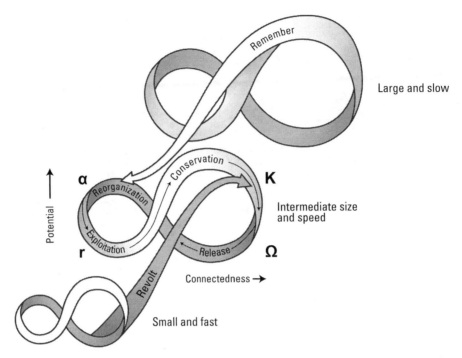

Figure 10.11 A figure depicting a panarchy, a nested set of adaptive cycles. (From *Panarchy*, edited by Lance H. Gunderson and C. S. Holling. Copyright ©2002 Island Press. Reproduced by permission of Island Press, Washington, DC.)

son and Holling 2002). In a panarchy it is the interactions between the larger, slower cycles and the smaller, faster cycles that cause episodic change. When change spreads from a smaller, faster level to the next larger or slower level, Holling and co-authors called that change "revolt." Revolt can occur most easily when the next larger level is at the end of its own K phase and is at its least resilient. A small ground fire, for instance, can spread into the crowns of senescing trees and cause a major wildfire. "Remember" is when processes at a larger, slower level of a panarchy frame the reorganization that occurs in the next smaller or faster level. For instance, the seedbank will promote recovery to a similar community after a wildfire. As in a single adaptive cycle, conservatism enforced by large, slow cycles is balanced by novelty in the form of experimentation and evolution in small, fast cycles. Holling and his co-authors intended panarchy to describe the behavior not just of ecosystems but of human societies and economy. Panarchy therefore is of special interest in this time of urban ecosystems and human responsibility for the welfare of the planet.

Holling and his co-authors' emphasis on accident, opportunity, and adaptation, along with conservation of resources, distinguish panarchy from simple multiple stable-state models and begin to provide the answer to the original question: Why are natural ecosystems still here? Not all stable states are simultaneously available. Some may not yet be possible, and some may no longer be attainable. Not so long ago, remember, the northeastern forests were buried under glacial ice. As the climate changes, they will face entirely new conditions. The stability landscape that we diagrammed with multiple basins that a ball might roll into is a shifting landscape. In order to persist, all living systems need to be able to not only preserve the gains they have made but also evolve.

USE NESTED ADAPTIVE CYCLES TO SURVIVE UNPREDICTABLE CHANGES

As the last several sections have identified, we and the landscapes we create face an uncertain future. Land transformation has dramatically degraded the earth's natural ecosystems and created new human-made ecosystems whose properties are just being realized. Atmospheric pollution is creating unusual growing conditions. Climate change could disrupt established patterns of season and weather with unpredictable results. Meanwhile, resource pressure and concern about the fate of chemicals in the environment are changing many previously standard landscape maintenance practices. Throw economic uncertainty into the mix, and it becomes clear that the landscapes we create today will have to be uncannily tough to survive.

Resilience, as explained by Gunderson and Holling, requires both persistence and change, the ability to go through adaptive cycles without losing everything in the transition. To understand these qualities, landscape architect Joan Woodward (2005a, 2005b, 2008) studied "feral" landscapes in the Los Angeles area. These are landscapes that, for a variety of reasons, had been "released from care" after establishment. Some withered, some became overgrown, and some retained their design framework or even increased their ecological function. Woodward's studies were particularly focused on disruptions to maintenance, but some of the lessons she identified can apply to our broader concerns about unpredictability. Her findings, along with Gunderson and Holling's proposals, suggest strategies to help landscapes both persist and adaptively change.

Several factors enable landscapes to persist in the face of changing conditions. Woodward emphasized the importance of "good bones." The design and microclimatic effects of grading or well-built hardscape can be very persistent and will continue to influence a landscape through its future incarnations. We can go further to intentionally create topography with memory. For instance, low spots will continue to collect water and nutrients for decades or centuries to come. Vegetation will return to these spots, even after disturbance. Designing landscapes whose physical form, soils, and vegetation can retain nutrients during the creative destruction phase of an adaptive cycle is important for long-term persistence. In order to do this, landscapes have to harmonize with the prevailing forces of wind, water, and human use. Imagine how things will perform without leaf-blowing, irrigation, and "Stay off the grass" signs. Sturdy plants—usually trees—placed well in relation to other elements and to their mature size can also form the bones of a persistent landscape. These plants should be established well, with careful soil preparation, watering, and care in this time of relatively abundant resources and well-understood conditions, to set us up for the future. We should also use resilient plants, those that are able to survive discontinuities in care or altered circumstances. Woodward encouraged study of abandoned landscapes to identify such plants and suggested that they are not necessarily drought-tolerant natives. Each of these strategies can help a landscape "remember" its earlier form after disruption.

Retaining strong elements of earlier forms is not enough; landscapes also need to change with changing conditions. They should include flexible elements that can maintain some function even in new circumstances. Tough rootstocks for grafted plants, for instance, can sprout and take over if the scions fail. Ephemeral elements such as decorative plantings can be allowed to come and go. In order to change, landscapes should be in communication with their surrounding context, distributing and accepting migrant propagules. To mitigate against catastrophic reorganizations, periodic intermediate disturbance (e.g., gap opening or withholding irrigation or pest control) can sort the weak from the strong and open opportunities for small-scale reorganization by the community itself and learning by land managers (see chap. 8). Humans have the ability to add foresight to the equation, to anticipate changing conditions and get ahead of them. Above all, however, we need to take an experimental approach to managing our landscapes and lend our efforts to support, rather than resist, their evolution.

CONCLUSION

We who work with the land will be at the forefront of dealing with many aspects of global change. We should remember that, whatever happens, the principles of ecology will still apply. For every foreseeable challenge, there is an ecological course we can take.

We must preserve the remaining natural ecosystems and landscapes, even in the face of development pressure. Human needs and desires can be accommodated, and even better met, through planning that prioritizes conservation. Vast areas of terrestrial and aquatic ecosystems have been degraded but not destroyed. Our well-being, and the well-being of many other species, depends on us restoring these ecosystems to higher-functioning states. Developed areas, even the densest cities, are ecological systems too, in which biophysical forces interact with social and economic trends. Recognizing this fact, we can work to improve the performance of these systems for both nature and people.

Atmospheric pollution extends human impact beyond the areas immediately affected by development. We must be aware of and prepared to deal with this phenomenon. Rising carbon dioxide concentrations in the atmosphere are already beginning to affect the growing conditions plants and other organisms face. Landscape designers can play a role in dealing with increased atmospheric CO_2 by planning communities that rely less on fossil fuels and by increasing the ability of our landscapes to serve as carbon sinks. As the climate changes, plants will move, as they always have. We may need to facilitate that movement by providing corridors for natural dispersal and, potentially, through proactive planting. In this process, novel communities will emerge, probably including species that we currently battle as invasives. We will have to accommodate these changes in some cases and focus on maintaining ecosystem function rather than hewing to preconceived notions of what a community should look like.

Uncertainty about the impacts of climate change is just one of the uncertainties we face in this century. From this point forward, we need to design landscapes that can handle possible stresses and shocks and adapt and persist. Our greatest chance of success is to learn from the evolving natural systems that have survived on this planet through far greater upheavals. We can build in and maintain negative feedback loops that help ecosystems remain stable (see chap. 4). We can preserve biodiversity and incorporate it into our designed landscapes in order to take advantage of differential responses to various stresses (see chap. 5). We can be prepared for likely disturbances and prime our landscapes to respond vigorously (see chap. 8). We can work to increase the resilience of the ecosystems for which we are responsible by reducing their precariousness and managing for multifunctionality. We can nest the patches we create within a larger landscape that can incorporate smaller-scale disturbances and that is connected so that important nodes of biological activity can move as needed (see chap. 9). We can create landscapes that both remember their essential forms and are flexible enough to evolve into something new. These landscapes may look somewhat different than we are accustomed to, but they will be the landscapes that perform in challenging times.

With will and through negligence, with powerful tools and often the best of intentions, we have shaped the environment we live in today. We have equal capability to reshape it for the better. This is not an easy task, but we bring to it a greater understanding than ever before. And if we act with intelligence and humility, we can count on a resilient and dynamic natural world as our partner.

Bibliography

Abbey, D. G. 1994. *Hurricane Resistant Landscapes: Preparing the Landscape to Resist Hurricane Storms.* Louisiana State University. Available at http://www.greenlaws.lsu.edu/hurricanecover.htm.

Agricultural Research Service. 2000. Phytoremediation: Using plants to clean up soils. *Agricultural Research* 48(6):4–9.

Agrios, G. N. 1997. *Plant Pathology*, 4th ed. New York: Academic Press.

Al-Mufti, M. M., C. L. Sydes, S. B. Furness, J. P. Grime, and S. R. Band. 1977. A quantitative analysis of shoot phenology and dominance in herbaceous vegetation. *Journal of Ecology* 65:759–91.

Altieri, M. A., L. Ponti, and C. I. Nicolls. 2005. Manipulating vineyard biodiversity for improved insect pest management: Case studies from northern California. *International Journal of Biodiversity Science and Management* 1:1–13.

American Chestnut Foundation. 2012. *Restoring the American Chestnut Tree.* Available at http://www.acf.org/pdfs/help/restoration_crop_sm.pdf.

American Horticultural Society. 2012. *The AHS Plant Heat Zone Map.* Available at http://www.ahs.org/publications/heat_zone_map.htm.

Anderson, C. 2007. Landscape grounded in northwest natural history. *Landscape Architecture Magazine*, August, p. 107.

Arendt, R. 1996. *Conservation Design for Subdivisions: A Practical Guide to Creating Open Space Networks.* Washington, DC: Island Press.

Augustine, D. J., and S. J. McNaughton. 1998. Ungulate effects on the functional species composition of plant communities: Herbivore selectivity and plant tolerance. *Journal of Wildlife Management* 62(4):1165–83.

Benda, L., D. Miller, P. Bigelow, and K. Andras. 2003. Effects of post-wildfire erosion on channel environments, Boise River, Idaho. *Forest Ecology and Management* 178:105–19.

Bergengren, J. C., D. E. Waliser, and Y. L. Yung. 2011. Ecological sensitivity: A biospheric view of climate change. *Climatic Change* 107:433–57. doi:10.1007/s10584-011-0065-1.

Billings Gazette. 1995. Yellowstone on fire! *Billings Gazette.*

Billings Gazette. 2011. Prairie bioblitz finds 480 species. *Billings Gazette*, July 7.

Blair, B. 2004. Going with the flow. *Permaculture Activist* 54:19–21.

Bohlen, P. J., S. Scheu, C. M. Hale, M. A. McLean, S. Migge, P. M. Groffman, and D. Parkinson. 2004. Non-native invasive earthworms as agents of change in northern temperate forests. *Frontiers in Ecology and the Environment* 2(8):427–35.

Bormann, F. H., and G. E. Likens. 1967. Nutrient cycling. *Science* 155(3761):424–29.

Bormann, F. H., and G. E. Likens. 1979. *Pattern and Process in a Forested Ecosystem*. New York: Springer Verlag.

Braun-Blanquet, J. 1932. *Plant Sociology: The Study of Plant Communities*. Translated by G. D. Fuller and H. S. Conrad. New York: Hafner, 1972.

Buckminster Fuller Institute. 2012. *City Sink*. Accessed July 21, 2012, http://challenge.bfi.org/application_ summary/1158.

Burghardt, K. T., D. W. Tallamy, C. Philips, and K. J. Shropshire. 2010. Non-native plants reduce abundance, richness, and host specialization in lepidopteran communities. *Ecosphere* 1(5):art11. doi:10.1890/ES10-00032.1.

Burghardt, K. T., D. W. Tallamy, and W. G. Shriver. 2008. Impact of native plants on bird and butterfly diversity in suburban landscapes. *Conservation Biology* 23(1):219–24.

Cadenasso, M. L., S. T. A. Pickett, K. C. Weathers, and C. G. Jones. 2003. A framework for a theory of ecological boundaries. *BioScience* 53(8):750–58.

Cadotte, M. W., K. Carscadden, and N. Mirotchnick. 2011. Beyond species: Functional diversity and the maintenance of ecological processes and services. *Journal of Applied Ecology* 48:1079–87.

City of Tucson. 2009. *Development Standard No. 10-03.0 Commercial Rainwater Harvesting*. Available at http://www.tucsonaz.gov/ocsd/docs/CMS1_035089.pdf.

Clausen, J., D. Keck, and W. Hiesey. 1948. *Experimental Studies on the Nature of Species III. Environmental Responses of Climatic Races of Achillea*. Publication 581. Washington, DC: Carnegie Institute of Washington.

Clements, F. E. 1916. *Plant Succession: An Analysis of the Development of Vegetation*. Publication 242. Washington, DC: Carnegie Institution of Washington.

Clements, F. 1936. Nature and structure of the climax. *Journal of Ecology* 24:252–84.

Collins, S. L., and S. M. Glenn. 1990. A hierarchical analysis of species' abundance patterns in grassland vegetation. *American Naturalist* 135:633–48.

Connell, J. H. 1978. Diversity in tropical rain forests and coral reefs. *Science* 199:1302–10.

Connell, J. H., and R. O. Slatyer. 1977. Mechanisms of succession in natural communities and their role in community stability and organization. *American Naturalist* 111:1119–44.

Conservation Fund. 2004. *Florida's Ecological Network*. Green Infrastructure: Linking Lands for Nature and People, Case Study Series. Accessed March 24, 2012, http://www.greeninfrastructure.net/sites/greeninfrastructure.net/ files/2-Florida Case Study 2012.08.04.pdf.

Costanza, R., R. d'Arge, R. de Groot, S. Farber, M. Grasso, B. Hannon, K. Limburg, et al. 1997. The value of the world's ecosystem services and natural capital. *Nature* 387:253–60.

Cowles, H. C. 1899. The ecological relations of the vegetation on the sand dunes of Lake Michigan. *Botanical Gazette* 27:5–117, 167–202, 281–308, 361–91.

Cox, J. 1993. *Plant Marriages: What Plants Look Good Together: How to Choose the Perfect Plant Combinations for Your Garden*. New York: HarperCollins.

Craul, P. J. 1992. *Urban Soil in Landscape Design*. New York: Wiley.

Craul, P. J. 1999. *Urban Soils: Applications and Practices*. New York: Wiley.

Crawley, M. J., and J. E. Harral. 2001. Scale dependence in plant biodiversity. *Science* 291:864–68.

Crawley, M. J., A. E. Johnston, J. Silvertown, M. Dodd, C. de Mazancourt, M. S. Heard, D. F. Henman, and G. R. Richards. 2005. Determinants of species richness in the Park Grass Experiment. *American Naturalist* 165:179–92.

Curtis, J. T. 1959. *The Vegetation of Wisconsin: An Ordination of Plant Communities*. Madison: University of Wisconsin Press.

Darke, R. 2002. *The American Woodland: Capturing the Spirit of the Deciduous Forest*. Portland, OR: Timber Press.

Darwin, C. 1859. *The Origin of Species*. New York: Random House.

Darwin, C. 1881. *The Formation of Vegetable Mould through the Actions of Worms with Observations on Their Habits*. London: John Murray.

Davey Resource Group. 2009. *Tree Inventory Analysis Report: Ann Arbor, Michigan*. City of Ann Arbor. Available at http://www.a2gov.org/government/publicservices/fieldoperations/forestry/Documents/Urban Forestry Management Plan/Tree Inventory Analysis Report.pdf.

Davis, M. B. 1981. Quaternary history and the stability of forest communities. In *Forest Succession: Concepts and Applications*, edited by D. C. West, H. H. Shugart, and D. B. Botkin. New York: Springer Verlag.

Davis, M. B., and R. G. Shaw. 2001. Range shifts and adaptive responses to Quaternary climate change. *Science* 292(5517):673–79.

Delcourt, H. R., and P. A. Delcourt. 1997. Pre-Columbian Native American use of fire on southern Appalachian landscapes. *Conservation Biology* 11:1010–14.

del Moral, R., and L. C. Bliss. 1993. Mechanisms of primary succession: Insights resulting from the eruption of Mount St. Helens. In *Advances in Ecological Research*, edited by M. Begon and A. H. Fitter, 1–66. New York: Academic Press.

del Moral, R., and D. M. Wood. 1993. Early primary succession on a barren volcanic plain at Mount St. Helens, Washington. *American Journal of Botany* 80(9):981–91.

Del Tredici, P. 2010. *Wild Urban Plants of the Northeast: A Field Guide*. Ithaca, NY: Cornell University Press.

De Luis, M., J. Raventós, T. Wiegand, and J. C. González-Hidalgo. 2008. Temporal and spatial differentiation in seedling emergence may promote species coexistence in Mediterranean fire-prone ecosystems. *Ecography* 31:620–29.

Diamond, J. M. 1975. Assembly of species communities. In *Ecology and Evolution of Communities*, edited by M. L. Cody and J. M. Diamond, 342–444. Cambridge, MA: Belknap Press.

Diboll, N. 1997. Designing seed mixes. In *The Tallgrass Restoration Handbook*, edited by S. Packard and C. F. Mutel, 135–50. Washington, DC: Island Press.

Dirzo, R., and P. H. Raven. 2003. Global state of biodiversity and loss. *Annual Review of Environment and Resources* 28:137–67.

Dramstad, W. E., J. D. Olson, and R. T. T. Forman. 1996. *Landscape Ecology Principles in Landscape Architecture and Land-Use Planning*. Washington, DC: Island Press.

Dunnett, N. P., and A. J. Willis. 2000. Dynamics of *Chamerion angustifolium* in grassland vegetation over a thirty-nine year period. *Plant Ecology* 148(1):43–50.

Egler, F. E. 1954. Vegetation science concepts I. Initial floristic composition, a factor in old-field vegetation development. *Vegetatio* 4:412–17.

Ehrlich, P. R., and P. H. Raven. 1964. Butterflies and plants: A study in coevolution. *Evolution* 18:586–608.

Ellenberg, H. 1953. Physiologisches und ökologisches Verhalten derselben Pflanzenarten. *Bericht der Deutschene Botantischen Gesellschaft* 65:351–61.

Ellstrand, N. C., and M. L. Roose. 1987. Patterns of genotypic diversity in clonal plant species. *American Journal of Botany* 74:123–31.

Environment Maryland Research and Policy Center. 2011. *Urban Fertilizers and the Chesapeake Bay: An Opportunity for Major Pollution Reduction*. Available at http://www.environmentmaryland.org/center/reports.

Falk, D. A., M. A. Palmer, and J. B. Zedler, eds. 2006. *Foundations of Restoration Ecology*. Washington, DC: Island Press.

Falk, D. A., C. M. Richards, A. M. Montalvo, and E. E. Knapp. 2006. Population and ecological genetics in restoration ecology. In *Foundations of Restoration Ecology*, edited by D. A. Falk, M. A. Palmer, and J. B. Zedler, 14–41. Washington, DC: Island Press.

Fischer, T. 2009. *Perennial Companions: 100 Dazzling Plant Combinations for Every Season*. Portland, OR: Timber Press.

Flynn, D. F. B., N. Mirotchnick, M. Jain, M. I. Palmer, and S. Naeem. 2011. Functional and phylogenetic diversity as predictors of biodiversity: Ecosystem-function relationships. *Ecology* 92(8):1573–81.

Forbes, S. A. 1887. The lake as a microcosm. *Bulletin of the Peoria Scientific Association* 77–87. Reprinted in *Bulletin of the Illinois State Natural History Survey* 15(1925):537–50.

Forman, R. T. T. 1995. *Land Mosaics: The Ecology of Landscapes and Regions*. New York: Cambridge University Press.

Forman, R. T. T., and M. Godron. 1986. *Landscape Ecology*. New York: Wiley.

Foster, D. R. 1992. Land use history (1730–1990) and vegetation dynamics in central New England, USA. *Journal of Ecology* 80:753–71.

Francis, M., and A. Reimann. 1999. *The California Landscape Garden: Ecology, Culture, and Design*. Berkeley: University of California Press.

Friends of Edgewood Natural Preserve. 2011. *Welcome Home, Checkerspot!* Accessed December 4, 2011, http://www.friendsofedgewood.org/butterfly/chapter1.htm.

Gause, G. F. 1934. *The Struggle for Existence*. Baltimore, MD: Williams and Wilkins.

Gehlhausen, S. M., M. W. Schwartz, and C. K. Augspurger. 2000. Vegetation and microclimatic edge effects in two mixed-mesophytic forest fragments. *Plant Ecology* 147:21–35.

Generoso, L. 2002. Calculate your landscape's water needs: On-line tool provides customized schedule. *San Diego Earth Times*, August. Accessed April 21, 2012, http://www.sdearthtimes.com/et0802/et0802s4.html.

Gleason, H. 1926. The individualistic concept of the plant association. *Bulletin of the Torrey Botanical Club* 53:7–26.

Goodenough, A. E. 2010. Are the ecological impacts of alien species misrepresented? A review of the "native good, alien bad" philosophy. *Community Ecology* 11(1):13–21.

Grace, J. 2004. Understanding and managing the global carbon cycle. *Journal of Ecology* 92:189–202.

Greig-Smith, P. 1979. Pattern in vegetation. *Journal of Ecology* 67:755–79.

Grime, J. P. 1977. Evidence for the existence of three primary strategies in plants and its relevance to ecological and evolutionary theory. *American Naturalist* 111(982):1169–94.

Grime, J. P. 2001. *Plant Strategies, Vegetation Processes and Ecosystem Properties*, 2nd ed. New York: Wiley.

Grimm, N. B., S. H. Faeth, N. E. Golubiewski, C. L. Redman, J. Wu, X. Bai, and J. M. Briggs. 2008. Global change and the ecology of cities. *Science* 319:756–60.

Grubb, P. J. 1977. The maintenance of species-richness in plant communities: The importance of the regeneration niche. *Biological Reviews* 52:107–45.

Guarino, L., V. Ramanatha Rao, and R. Reid, eds. 1995. *Collecting Plant Genetic Diversity: Technical Guidelines*. Wallingford, UK: CAB International.

Gunderson, L. H., and C. S. Holling, eds. 2002. *Panarchy: Understanding Transformations in Human and Natural Systems*. Washington, DC: Island Press.

Gurda, J. 2012. *The Menomonee Valley: A Historical Overview*. Accessed March 4, 2012, http://www.renewthevalley.org/media/mediafile_attachments/04/4-gurdavalleyhistory.pdf.

Gurevitch, J., L. L. Morrow, A. Wallace, and J. S. Walsh. 1992. A meta-analysis of competition in field experiments. *American Naturalist* 140:539–72.

Hairston, N. G., F. E. Smith, and L. B. Slobodkin. 1960. Community structure, population control, and competition. *American Naturalist* 94:421–25.

Handel, S. N. 1997. The role of plant-animal mutualisms in the design and restoration of natural communities. In *Restoration Ecology and Sustainable Development*, edited by K. M. Urbanska, N. R. Webb, and P. J. Edwards, 111–32. New York: Cambridge University Press.

Hanna, K. C. 1999. *GIS for Landscape Architects*. Redlands, CA: ESRI Press.

Hansen, R., and F. Stahl. 1993. *Perennials and Their Garden Habitats*, translated by R. Ward. New York: Cambridge University Press.

Hanski, I. 1998. Metapopulation dynamics. *Nature* 396:41–49.

Harker, D. F., G. Libby, K. Harker, S. Evans, and M. Evans. 1999. *Landscape Restoration Handbook*, 2nd ed. New York: CRC Press.

Harlan, H. V., and M. L. Martini. 1938. The effect of natural selection in a mixture of barley varieties. *Journal of Agricultural Research* 57:189–99.

Harper, J. L. 1977. *Population Biology of Plants*. New York: Academic Press.

Harrison, S., D. D. Murphy, and P. R. Ehrlich. 1988. Distribution of the bay checkerspot butterfly, *Euphydryas editha bayensis*: Evidence for a metapopulation model. *American Naturalist* 132(3):360–82.

Hart, R. 1996. *Forest Gardening: Cultivating an Edible Landscape*. White River Junction, VT: Chelsea Green Publishing.

Hartley, S. E., and C. G. Jones. 1997. Plant chemistry and herbivory, or why the world is green. In *Plant Ecology*, 2nd ed., edited by M. J. Crawley, 284–324. Malden, MA: Blackwell.

Herrera, C. M. 2002. Seed dispersal by vertebrates. In *Plant–Animal Interactions: An Evolutionary Approach*, edited by C. M. Herrera and O. Pellmyr, 185–208. Malden, MA: Blackwell.

Hillebrand, H., D. M. Bennett, and M. W. Cadotte. 2008. Consequences of dominance: A review of evenness effects on local and regional ecosystem properties. *Ecology* 89(6):1510–20.

Hitchens, M. J. 1997. The structure of plant populations. In *Plant Ecology*, 2nd ed., edited by M. J. Crawley, 325–58. Malden, MA: Blackwell.

Hitchmough, J. 2004. Naturalistic herbaceous vegetation for urban landscapes. In *The Dynamic Landscape*, edited by N. Dunnett and J. Hitchmough, 130–83. London: Taylor and Francis.

Hitchmough, J. 2008. New approaches to ecologically based, designed urban plant communities in Britain: Do these have any relevance in the United States? *Cities and the Environment* 1(2):1–15.

Hobbs, R. J. 2000. Land-use change and invasions. In *Invasive Species in a Changing World*, H. A. Mooney and R. J. Hobbs, 55–64. Washington, DC: Island Press.

Hobbs, R. J., E. Higgs, and J. A. Harris. 2009. Novel ecosystems: Implications for conservation and restoration. *Trends in Ecology and Evolution* 24(11):599–605.

Hoctor, T. S., M. H. Carr, and P. D. Zwick. 2000. Identifying a linked reserve system using a regional landscape approach: The Florida Ecological Network. *Conservation Biology* 14(4):984–1000.

Hole, F. D. 1981. Effects of animals on soils. *Geoderma* 25:75–112.

Holling, C. S. 1973. Resilience and stability of ecological systems. *Annual Review of Ecology and Systematics* 4:1–23.

Hooper, D. U., F. S. Chapin III, J. J. Ewel, A. Hector, P. Inchausti, S. Lavorel, J. H. Lawton, et al. 2005. Effects of biodiversity on ecosystem functioning: A consensus of current knowledge. *Ecological Monographs* 75(1):3–35.

Houghton, R. A. 1999. The annual net flux of carbon to the atmosphere from changes in land use 1850–1990. *Tellus* 51B:298–313.

Houghton, R. A. 2008. Carbon flux to the atmosphere from land-use changes: 1850–2005. In *TRENDS: A Compendium of Data on Global Change*. Oak Ridge, TN: Carbon Dioxide Information Analysis Center, Oak Ridge National Laboratory, US Department of Energy.

Howard, A. H. 1943. *An Agricultural Testament*. Oxford, UK: Oxford University Press.

Hubbell, S. P. 2001. *The Unified Neutral Theory of Biodiversity and Biogeography*. Princeton, NJ: Princeton University Press.

Hubbell, S. P. 2010. Neutral theory and the theory of island biogeography. In *The Theory of Island Biogeography Revisited*, edited by J. B. Losos and R. E. Ricklefs, 264–92. Princeton, NJ: Princeton University Press.

Humboldt, A. 1805. Essay on the geography of plants. In *Foundations of Biogeography*, trans. F. Kern and P. Janvier, edited by M. V. Lomolino, D. F. Sax, and J. H. Brown, 49–57. Chicago: University of Chicago Press, 2004.

Humboldt, A., and A. Bonpland. 1818–1825. *Personal Narrative of Travels to the Equinoctial Regions of America during the Years 1799–1804*, Vol. II, trans. H. M. Williams. London: Longman, Hurst, Rees, Orme, and Brown. Reprinted 1966, AMS Press, New York.

Hunter, M. L. Jr. 2007. Core principles for using natural disturbance regimes to inform landscape management. In *Managing and Designing Landscapes for Conservation: Moving from Perspectives to Principles*, edited by D. B. Lindemayer and R. J. Hobbs, 408–22. Malden, MA: Blackwell.

Hutchinson, G. E. 1957. Concluding remarks. *Cold Spring Harbor Symposia on Quantitative Biology* 22:415–27.

Inghe, O., and C. O. Tamm. 1985. Survival and flowering of perennial herbs. IV. The behavior of *Hepatica nobilis* and *Sanicula europaea* on permanent plots during 1943–1981. *Oikos* 45:400–420.

Iverson, L. R., A. M. Prasad, S. Matthews, and M. Peters. 2008. Estimating potential habitat for 134 eastern US tree species under six climate scenarios. *Forest Ecology and Management* 254:390–406.

Jacke, D., and E. Toensmeier. 2005. *Edible Forest Gardens: Ecological Vision and Theory for Temperate Permaculture*. White River Junction, VT: Chelsea Green.

Jenny, H. 1941. *Factors of Soil Formation: A System of Quantitative Pedology*. New York: McGraw-Hill.

Jobin, B., and G. Falardeau. 2010. Habitat associations of grasshopper sparrows in southern Québec. *Northeastern Naturalist* 17(1):135–46.

Jones, C. G., J. H. Lawton, and M. Shachak. 1994. Organisms as ecosystem engineers. *Oikos* 69(3):373–86.

Jönsson, K. I., E. Rabbow, R. O. Schill, M. Harms-Ringdahl, and P. Rettberg. 2008. Tardigrades survive exposure to space in low earth orbit. *Current Biology* 18:R729–31.

Kalka, M. B., A. R. Smith, and E. K. V. Kalko. 2008. Bats limit arthropods and herbivory in a tropical forest. *Science* 320(5872):71.

Kearney, R. F. 2003. *Partners in Flight Bird Conservation Plan, the Mid Atlantic Piedmont (Physiographic Area 10)*. Accessed February 18, 2012, http://www.blm.gov/wildlife/plan/pl_10_10.pdf.

Keddy, P. 2001. *Competition*, 2nd ed. Norwell, MA: Kluwer Academic Publishers.

Keddy, P. 2005. Putting the plants back into plant ecology: Six pragmatic models for understanding and conserving plant diversity. *Annals of Botany* 96:177–89.

Keddy, P. A., and B. Shipley. 1989. Competitive hierarchies in herbaceous plant communities. *Oikos* 54:234–41.

Kershaw, K. A., and J. H. H. Looney. 1985. The causal factors of pattern. In *Quantitative and Dynamic Plant Ecology*, 3rd ed., 138–55. Baltimore, MD: Edward Arnold Publishers.

Kühn, N. 2006. Intentions for the unintentional: Spontaneous vegetation as the basis for innovative planting design in urban areas. *Journal of Landscape Architecture* 1:46–53.

Lancaster, B. 2008. Rainwater Harvesting for Drylands and Beyond, Vol. 2: *Water-Harvesting Earthworks*. Tucson, AZ: Rainsource Press.

Lancaster, B. 2012. *Rainwater Harvesting for Drylands and Beyond*, Vol. 1, 2nd ed. Tucson, AZ: Rainsource Press.

Laurance, W. F., J. L. C. Camargo, R. C. C. Luizão, S. G. Laurance, S. L. Pimm, E. M. Bruna, P. C. Stouffer, et al. 2011. The fate of Amazonian forest fragments: A 32-year investigation. *Biological Conservation* 144:56–67.

Lee, A. W. 1994. *Chicken Tractor: The Gardener's Guide to Happy Hens and Healthy Soil*. Shelburne, VT: Good Earth Publications.

Le Quéré, C., M. R. Raupach, J. G. Canadell, G. Marland, et al. 2009. Trends in the sources and sinks of carbon dioxide. *Nature Geoscience*. doi:10.1038/NGEO689.

Levin, S. A. 1998. Ecosystems and the biosphere as complex adaptive systems. *Ecosystems* 1:431–36.

Levin, S. A. 1999. *Fragile Dominion: Complexity and the Commons*. Cambridge, MA: Perseus.

Li, H. L. 1952. Floristic relationships between eastern Asia and eastern North America. *Transactions of the American Philosophical Society* 42:371–429.

Likens, G. E., F. H. Bormann, N. M. Johnson, D. W. Fisher, and R. S. Pierce. 1970. Effects of forest cutting and herbicide treatment on nutrient budgets in the Hubbard Brook watershed ecosystem. *Ecological Monographs* 40:23–47.

Lindeman, R. L. 1942. The trophic-dynamic aspect of ecology. *Ecology* 23:399–417.

Lord, T. 2002. *The Encyclopedia of Planting Combinations*. Toronto, ON: Firefly Books.

Loreau, M. 2010. Linking biodiversity and ecosystems: Towards a unifying ecological theory. *Philosophical Transactions of the Royal Society: Biological Sciences* 365:49–60.

Loucks, O. L. 1970. Evolution of diversity, efficiency, and community stability. *American Zoologist* 10:17–25.

Lovelock, J. E. 2000. *Gaia: A New Look at Life on Earth*. Oxford, UK: Oxford University Press.

Lowenfels, J., and W. Lewis. 2010. *Teaming with Microbes*. Portland, OR: Timber Press.

Lugo, A. E., M. Applefield, D. J. Pool, and R. B. McDonald. 1982. The impact of Hurricane David on the forests of Dominica. *Canadian Journal of Forest Research* 13:201–11.

MacArthur, R. H. 1958. Population ecology of some warblers in northeastern coniferous forests. *Ecology* 39:599–619.

MacArthur, R. H., and E. O. Wilson. 1963. An equilibrium theory of insular zoography. *Evolution* 17(4):373–87.

MacArthur, R. H., and E. O. Wilson. 1967. *The Theory of Island Biogeography*. Princeton, NJ: Princeton University Press.

Mapes, L. V. 2010. Chum-salmon survivors welcomed at Piper's Creek. *Seattle Times*, November 13.

Marks, P. L. 1974. The role of pin cherry (*Prunus pensylvanica* L.) in the maintenance of stability in northern hardwood ecosystems. *Ecological Monographs* 44:73–88.

Mattei, J. H., S. N. Handel, and G. R. Robinson. 2003. Lessons learned in restoring an urban forest on a closed landfill (New York). *Ecological Restoration* 21(1):62–63.

May, R. M. 2000. The dimensions of life on earth. In *Nature and Human Society: The Quest for a Sustainable World*, edited by P. H. Raven and T. Williams, 30–45. Washington, DC: National Academies Press.

McDonnell, M. J., and E. W. Stiles. 1983. The structural complexity of old field vegetation and the recruitment of bird-dispersed plant species. *Oecologia* 56:109–16.

McGarrahan, E. 1997. Much-studied butterfly winks out on Stanford preserve. *Science* 275:479–80.

McGrath, B., V. Marshall, M. L. Cadenasso, J. M. Grove, S. T. A. Pickett, R. Plunz, and J. Towers. 2007 *Designing Patch Dynamics*. New York: Columbia University Press.

McHarg, I. L. 1969. *Design with Nature*. Garden City, NY: Published for the American Museum of Natural History by the Natural History Press. 1992. *Design with Nature: 25th Anniversary Edition*. New York: Wiley.

Michon, G., J. Bompard, P. Hecketsweiler, and C. Ducatillion. 1983. Tropical forest architectural analysis as applied to agroforests in the humid tropics: The example of traditional village-agroforests in West Java. *Agroforestry Systems* 1:117–29.

Millennium Ecosystem Assessment. 2005. *Ecosystems and Human Well-Being: Synthesis*. Washington, DC: Island Press.

Miller, S. C. 2003. *Central Park: An American Masterpiece*. New York: Harry N. Abrams.

Minnesota Department of Natural Resources. 1999. *Minnesota County Biological Survey Map Series No. 19. Stearns County, Minnesota*. Accessed March 31, 2012, http://files.dnr.state.mn.us/eco/mcbs/maps/stearns.pdf.

Mitsch, W. J., X. Wu, R. W. Nairn, P. E. Weihe, N. Wang, R. Deal, and C. E. Boucher. 1998. Creating and restoring wetlands: A whole-ecosystem experiment in self design. *BioScience* 48:1019–31.

Mohler, C. L., P. L. Marks, and D. G. Sprugel. 1978. Stand structure and allometry of trees during self-thinning of pure stands. *Journal of Ecology* 66:599–614.

Morgan, J. A., D. G. Milchunas, D. R. LeCain, M. West, and A. R. Mosier. 2007. Carbon dioxide enrichment alters plant community structure and accelerates shrub growth in the shortgrass steppe. *Proceedings of the National Academy of Sciences* 104(37):14724–29.

Morgan, J. A., A. R. Mosier, D. G. Milchunas, D. R. LeCain, J. A. Nelson, and W. J. Parton. 2004. CO_2 enhances productivity, alters species composition, and reduces digestibility of shortgrass steppe vegetation. *Ecological Applications* 14:208–19.

Morrone, J. J. 2009. *Evolutionary Biogeography*. New York: Columbia University Press.

Mutch, R. W. 1970. Wildland fires and ecosystems: A hypothesis. *Ecology* 51:1046–51.

Myers, N., R. A. Mittermeier, C. G. Mittermeier, G. A. B. da Fonseca, and J. Kent. 2000. Biodiversity hotspots for conservation priorities. *Nature* 403:853–58.

Naeem, S., D. E. Bunker, A. Hector, M. Loreau, and C. Perrings, eds. 2009. *Biodiversity, Ecosystem Functioning, and Human Wellbeing: An Ecological and Economic Perspective*. New York: Oxford University Press.

Nardi, J. B. 2007. *Life in the Soil: A Guide for Naturalists and Gardeners*. Chicago: University of Chicago Press.

National Park Service. 2006. *Wildland Fire in Yellowstone*. Accessed January 19, 2007, http://www.nps.gov/yell/naturescience/wildlandfire/

National Wildlife Federation. 2012. *Create a Certified Wildlife Habitat*. Accessed February 18, 2012, http://www.nwf.org/Get-Outside/Outdoor-Activities/Garden-for-Wildlife/Create-a-Habitat.aspx.

Nature Conservancy. 2000. *The Prairie–Forest Border Ecoregion: A Conservation Plan*. Accessed May 21, 2011, http://east.tnc.org/east file/46/PrairieForestBorder_FINALREPORT_wExhibits.pdf.

Niering, W. A. 2006. *Working with Succession: An Ecological Approach in Preserving Biodiversity*. Available at http://www.environment.fhwa.dot.gov/ecosystems/vegmgmt_rdsduse12.asp.

Noss, R. F. 1991. Landscape connectivity: Different functions at different scales. In *Landscape Linkages and Biodiversity*, edited by W. E. Hudson. Washington, DC: Island Press.

Noss, R. F., and L. D. Harris. 1986. Nodes, networks, and MUMs: Preserving diversity at all scales. *Environmental Management* 10(3):299–309.

Nowak, D. J., and P. R. O'Connor. 2001. *Syracuse Urban Forest Master Plan: Guiding the City's Forest Resource into the 21st Century*. Newtown Square, PA: USDA Forest Service.

Odum, H. T. 1957. Trophic structure and productivity of Silver Springs, Florida. *Ecological Monographs* 27:55–112.

O'Neill, R. V., D. L. DeAngelis, J. B. Waide, and T. F. H. Allen. 1986. *A Hierarchical Concept of Ecosystems*. Princeton, NJ: Princeton University Press.

Ouroussoff, N. 2009, June 10. On high, a fresh outlook. *New York Times*.

Owen, J. 2010. *Wildlife of a Garden: A Thirty-Year Study*. London: Royal Horticultural Society.

Pacala, S. W. 1997. Dynamics of plant communities. In *Plant Ecology*, edited by M. J. Crawley, 532–55. Malden, MA: Blackwell.

Packard, S., and C. F. Mutel, eds. 1997. *The Tallgrass Restoration Handbook*. Washington, DC: Island Press.

Paine, R. T. 1966. Food web complexity and species diversity. *American Naturalist* 100:65–75.

Palmer, M. A., D. A. Falk, and J. B. Zedler. 2006. Ecological theory and restoration ecology. In *Foundations of Restoration Ecology*, edited by D. A. Falk, M. A. Palmer, and J. B. Zedler, 1–10. Washington, DC: Island Press.

Pickett, S. T. A. 1980. Non-equilibrium coexistence of plants. *Bulletin of the Torrey Botanical Club* 107:238–48.

Pickett, S. T. A., M. L. Cadenasso, and J. M. Grove. 2004. Resilient cities: meaning, models, and metaphor for integrating the ecological, socio-economic, and planning realms. *Landscape and Urban Planning* 69:369–84.

Pickett, S. T. A., M. L. Cadenasso, J. M. Grove, P. M. Groffman, L. E. Band, C. G. Boone, W. R. Burch Jr., et al. 2008. Beyond urban legends: An emerging framework of urban ecology, as illustrated by the Baltimore Ecosystem Study. *BioScience* 58(2):139–50.

Pickett, S. T. A., M. L. Cadenasso, and S. J. Meiners. 2009. Ever since Clements: From succession to vegetation dynamics and understanding to intervention. *Applied Vegetation Science* 12:9–21.

Pickett, S. T. A., S. L. Collins, and J. J. Armesto. 1987. Models, mechanisms and pathways of succession. *Botanical Review* 53:335–71.

Pickett, S. T. A., J. Wu, and M. L. Cadenasso. 1999. Patch dynamics and the ecology of disturbed ground: A framework for synthesis. In *Ecosystems of Disturbed Ground*, edited by L. R. Walker, 707–22. Amsterdam, the Netherlands: Elsevier.

Pimentel, D., R. Zorniga, and D. Morrison. 2005. Update on the environmental and economic costs associated with alien-invasive species in the United States. *Ecological Economics* 52(3):273–88.

Pipers Creek Watershed Project. 2008. *Pipers Creek Watershed Annual Status Report 2008.* Accessed February 20, 2012, http://www.seattle.gov/parks/Environment/pipers_annual_rpt2008.pdf.

Prasad, A. M., L. R. Iverson, S. Matthews, and M. Peters. 2007. A Climate Change Atlas for 134 Forest Tree Species of the Eastern United States [database], Northern Research Station, USDA Forest Service, Delaware, Ohio. Available at http://www.nrs.fs.fed.us/atlas/tree.

Quammen, D. 1998. Planet of weeds: Tallying the losses of earth's animals and plants. *Harper's Magazine*, October, pp. 57–69.

Quigley, M. F. 2003. Reducing weeds in ornamental groundcovers under shade trees through mixed species installations. *HortTechnology* 13(1):85–89.

Quigley, M. F. 2010. Potemkin gardens: Biodiversity in small designed landscapes. In *Urban Ecology: Patterns, Processes, and Applications*, edited by J. Niemelä, 85–92. Oxford, UK: Oxford University Press.

Raventós, J., T. Wiegand, and M. De Luis. 2010. Evidence for the spatial segregation hypothesis: A test with nine-year survivorship data in a Mediterranean shrubland. *Ecology* 91:2110–20.

Rawinski, T. J. 2008. *Impacts of White-Tailed Deer Overabundance in Forest Ecosystems: An Overview.* US Forest Service. Accessed February 19, 2012, http://na.fs.fed.us/fhp/special_interests/white_tailed_deer.pdf.

Reed, C. 2005. Performance practices. *306090 Architecture Journal* 9:82–91.

Reichard, S. H., and C. W. Hamilton. 1997. Predicting invasions of woody plants introduced into North America. *Conservation Biology* 11(1):193–203.

Ries, L., and T. D. Sisk. 2004. A predictive model of edge effects. *Ecology* 85(11):2917–26.

Risser, P. G., J. R. Karr, and R. T. T. Forman. 1983. *Landscape Ecology: Directions and Approaches.* Illinois Natural History Survey, Special Publication no. 2. Champaign: Illinois Natural History Survey.

Rothamsted Research. 2006. *Guide to the Classical and Other Long-Term Experiments, Datasets and Sample Archive.* Rothamsted Research. Available at http://www.rothamsted.bbsrc.ac.uk/Research/Centres/Content.php?Section=Resources&Page=LongTermExperiments.

Sanderson, E. W., J. Malanding, M. A. Levy, K. H. Redford, A. V. Wannebo, and G. Woolmer. 2002. The human footprint and the last of the wild. *BioScience* 52(10):891–904.

Savory, A. 1988. *Holistic Resource Management.* Washington, DC: Island Press.

Scheffer, M., S. H. Hosper, M.-L. Meijer, B. Moss, and E. Jeppesen. 1993. Alternative equilibria in shallow lakes. *Trends in Ecology and Evolution* 8(8):275–79.

Schroon Lake Watershed Management Planning Committee. 2010. *Schroon Lake Watershed Management Plan*, draft. Available at http://www.warrenswcd.org/reports/schroon.pdf.

Schultz, J. C. 2002. How plants fight dirty. *Nature* 416:267.

Seattle Public Utilities. 2012. *Seattle's Natural Drainage Systems: A Low-Impact Approach to Stormwater Management.* Seattle, WA: City of Seattle. Accessed February 20, 2012, http://www.seattle.gov/util/groups/public/@spu/@usm/documents/webcontent/spu02_019984.pdf.

Shaffer, M. L. 1981. Minimum population sizes for species conservation. *BioScience* 31(2):131–34.

Shapiro, A. M. 2006. *Butterfly Gardening in the Northern California Foothills*. Accessed March 18, 2012, http://butterfly.ucdavis.edu/doc/garden/foothills.

Silvertown, J. 2004. Plant coexistence and the niche. *Trends in Ecology and Evolution* 19:605–11.

Silvertown, J. 2005. *Demons in Eden: The Paradox of Plant Diversity*. Chicago: University of Chicago Press.

Silvertown, J., and D. Charlesworth. 2001. *Introduction to Plant Population Biology*, 4th ed. Oxford, UK: Blackwell.

Simberloff, D. S., and E. O. Wilson. 1969. Experimental zoography of islands: The colonization of empty islands. *Ecology* 50(2):278–96.

Simmons, M., M. Bertelsen, S. Windhager, and H. Zafian. 2011. The performance of native and non-native turfgrass monocultures and native turfgrass polycultures: An ecological approach to sustainable lawns. *Ecological Engineering* 37(8):1095–1103.

Society for Ecological Restoration International Science & Policy Working Group. 2004. *The SER International Primer on Ecological Restoration*. Tucson: Society for Ecological Restoration International.

Solomon, S., D. Qin, M. Manning, Z. Chen, M. Marquis, K. B. Averyt, M. Tignor, and H. L. Miller, eds. 2007. *Contribution of Working Group I to the Fourth Assessment Report of the Intergovernmental Panel on Climate Change, 2007*. Cambridge, UK: Cambridge University Press.

Sorvig, K. 2004, March. Crying "fire!" in a crowded landscape: Do firewise initiatives ward off—or help spark—catastrophic wildfires? *Landscape Architecture*, p. 26.

Sovern, D. 1995. Pipers Creek: Salmon habitat restoration in the Pacific Northwest. *Watershed Protection Techniques* 1(4):179–81.

Stalter, R. 2004. The flora on the High Line, New York City, New York. *Journal of the Torrey Botanical Society* 131(4):387–93.

Stankey, G. H., R. N. Clark, and B. T. Bormann. 2005. *Adaptive Management of Natural Resources: Theory, Concepts, and Management Institutions*. General Technical Report PNW-GTR-654. Portland, OR: US Department of Agriculture, Forest Service, Pacific Northwest Research Station.

Stearns County. 2008. *2030 Stearns County Comprehensive Plan*. Accessed March 31, 2012, http://www.co.stearns.mn.us/Government/CountyDevelopment/StearnsCountyComprehensivePlan.

Stearns County. 2010. *Land Use and Zoning Ordinance #439*. Accessed March 26, 2012, http://www.co.stearns.mn.us/Portals/0/docs/Document Library/ordinances/ord439.pdf.

Steffen, W., A. Sanderson, P. D. Tyson, J. Jäger, P. A. Matson, B. Moore III, F. Oldfield, et al. 2004. *Global Change and the Earth System: A Planet under Pressure*. New York: Springer Verlag.

Sternfield, J. 2001. *Walking the High Line*. Göttingen, Germany: Steidl.

Strayer, D. L., M. E. Power, W. F. Fagan, S. T. A. Pickett, and J. Belknap. 2003. A classification of ecological boundaries. *BioScience* 53(8):723–29.

Sumner, M. E., editor in chief. 2000. *Handbook of Soil Science*. Boca Raton, FL: CRC Press.

Sustainable Sites Initiative. 2009a. *The Case for Sustainable Landscapes*. Available at http://www.sustainablesites.org/report.

Sustainable Sites Initiative. 2009b. *The Sustainable Sites Initiative: Guidelines and Performance Benchmarks 2009*. Available at http://www.sustainablesites.org/report.

Tallamy, D. 2007. *Bringing Nature Home*. Portland, OR: Timber Press.

Tansley, A. G. 1935. The use and abuse of vegetational concepts and terms. *Ecology* 16:284–307.

Thompson, J. N. 2009. The coevolving web of life. *American Naturalist* 173:125–40.

Tilman, D. 1982. *Resource Competition and Community Structure*. Princeton, NJ: Princeton University Press.

Tilman, D. 1997. Mechanisms of plant competition. In *Plant ecology*, 2nd ed., edited by M. J. Crawley, 239–61. Malden, MA: Blackwell.

Tilman, D., P. B. Reich, and J. M. H. Knops. 2006. Biodiversity and ecosystem stability in a decade-long grassland experiment. *Nature* 441:629–32.

Tilman, D., D. Wedin, and J. Knops. 1996. Productivity and sustainability influenced by biodiversity in grassland ecosystems. *Nature* 379:718–20.

Todd, N. J., and J. Todd. 1993. *From Eco-Cities to Living Machines: Principles of Ecological Design*. Berkeley, CA: North Atlantic Books.

Troll, C. 1939. Luftbildplan und okologische Bodenforschung. *Zeitschrift der Gesellschaft für Erkund, Berlin, Germany*, pp. 241–98.

Turesson, G. 1922. The species and the variety as ecological units. *Hereditas* 3:100–13.

United Nations Department of Economic and Social Affairs, Population Division. 2008. *World Urbanization Prospects, the 2007 Revision, Highlights*. New York: United Nations.

Urban, D. L., R. V. O'Neill, and H. H. Shugart Jr. 1987. Landscape ecology. *BioScience* 37(2):119–27.

US Department of Agriculture. 1999. *Soil Taxonomy: A Basic System of Soil Classification for Making and Interpreting Soil Surveys*, 2nd ed. Washington, DC: US Government Printing Office.

US Department of Agriculture. 2011. *Invasive and Noxious Weeds*. Accessed October 9, 2011, http://plants.usda.gov/java/noxiousDriver#federal.

US Department of Agriculture. 2012. *Plant Hardiness Zone Map*. Available at http://planthardiness.ars.usda.gov.

US Environmental Protection Agency. 2011. *Acid Rain*. Accessed March 31, 2012, http://www.epa.gov/acidrain/.

Vitousek, P. M., H. A. Mooney, J. Lubchenco, and J. M. Melillo. 1997. Human domination of Earth's ecosystems. *Science* 277(5325):494–99.

Walker, B. 2007. Disturbance, resilience, and recovery: A resilience perspective on landscape dynamics. In *Managing and Designing Landscapes for Conservation: Moving from Perspectives to Principles*, edited by D. B. Lindemayer and R. J. Hobbs, 395–407. Malden, MA: Blackwell.

Walker, B., C. S. Holling, S. R. Carpenter, and A. Kinzig. 2004. Resilience, adaptability, and transformability in social-ecological systems. *Ecology and Society* 9(2):5. Available at http://www.ecologyandsociety.org/vol9/iss2/art5.

Walker, L. R. 1999. Patterns and processes in primary succession. In *Ecosystems of Disturbed Ground*, edited by L. R. Walker, 585–610. Amsterdam, the Netherlands: Elsevier.

Walker, T. S., H. P. Bais, E. Grotewold, and J. M. Vivanco. 2003. Root exudation and rhizosphere biology. *Plant Physiology* 132:44–51.

Wang, B., and Y.-L. Qiu. 2006. Phylogenetic distribution and evolution of mycorrhizas in land plants. *Mycorrhiza* 16:299–363.

Warming, E. 1895. *Plantesamfund*. Copenhagen.

Wasowski, S., and A. Wasowski. 2002. *Gardening with Prairie Plants*. Minneapolis: University of Minnesota Press.

Watt, A. S. 1947. Pattern and process in the plant community. *Journal of Ecology* 35:1–22.

Webb, T. 1987. The appearance and disappearance of major vegetational assemblages: Long-term vegetational dynamics in eastern North America. *Vegetatio* 69:177–87.

Weinstein, G. 1999. *Xeriscape Handbook: A How-To Guide to Natural, Resource-Wise Gardening*. Golden, CO: Fulcrum.

Weiss, S. B. 2006. *Impacts of Nitrogen Deposition on California Ecosystems and Biodiversity*. Sacramento: California Energy Commission.

Wen, J. 1999. Evolution of eastern Asian and eastern North American disjunct distributions in flowering plants. *Annual Review of Ecology and Systematics* 30:421–55.

Whittaker, R. 1956. Vegetation of the Great Smoky Mountains. *Ecological Monographs* 26:2–80.

Whittaker, R. H. 1972. Evolution and measurement of species diversity. *Taxon* 21(2/3):213–51.

Wilson, E. O. 2010. *The Diversity of Life*. Cambridge, MA: The Belknap Press of Harvard University Press (Orig. pub. 1992).

Wilson, E. O., and D. S. Simberloff. 1969. Experimental zoography of islands: Defaunation and monitoring techniques. *Ecology* 50(2):267–78.

Wilson, J. B., T. C. E. Wells, I. C. Trueman, G. Jones, M. D. Atkinson, M. J. Crawley, M. E. Dodd, and J. Silvertown. 1996. Are there assembly rules for plant species abundance? An investigation in relation to soil resources and successional trends. *Journal of Ecology* 84:527–38.

Woodward, J. 2005a. Letting Los Angeles go: Lessons from feral landscapes. *Landscape Review* 9(2):59–69.

Woodward, J. H. 2005b, December. Lessons from a feral landscape: What's become of a Tommy Church garden since it was released from intended irrigation and other care? *Landscape Architecture*, pp. 52–59.

Woodward, J. H. 2008. Envisioning resilience in volatile Los Angeles landscapes. *Landscape Journal* 27(1-08):97–113.

Wu, J., and O. L. Loucks. 1995. From balance of nature to hierarchical patch dynamics: A paradigm shift in ecology. *The Quarterly Review of Biology* 70(4):439–66.

Xerces Society. 2011. *Attracting Native Pollinators: Protecting North America's Bees and Butterflies*. North Adams, MA: Storey Publishing.

Yoda, K., T. Kira, H. Ogawa, and K. Hozumi. 1963. Self-thinning in overcrowded pure stands under cultivated and natural conditions. *Journal of Biology, Osaka City University* 14:107–29.

Young, T. 2000. Restoration ecology and conservation biology. *Biological Conservation* 92:73–83.

Zavaleta, E. S., J. R. Pasari, K. B. Hulvey, and G. D. Tilman. 2010. Sustaining multiple ecosystem functions in grassland communities requires higher biodiversity. *Proceedings of the National Academy of Sciences* 107(4):1443–46.

Zerbe, S., U. Maurer, S. Schmitz, and H. Sukopp. 2003. Biodiversity in Berlin and its potential for nature conservation. *Landscape and Urban Planning* 62(3):139–48.

Index

diversity: biological (*see* biodiversity); genetic, 36-40,
    42, 162, 216; of habitats (*see* heterogeneity,
    environmental). *See also* disturbance, diversity and;
    species richness
dominance. 82, 83-85, 197, 200. *See also* hierarchy,
    competitive
dominance switching, 47, 122
drainage: of soils, 129-30, landscape, 150. *See also*
    stormwater, green infrastructure
Dramstad, Wenche, 217, 220
Dunnett, Nigel, 47, 254-55

earthworms, 125, 127, 145
ecological restoration, 239-40, 254
ecosystem: as complex adaptive system, 91-92;
    concept, 89-90; designing, 90-91; function, 101-
    2, (*see also* biodiversity, ecosystem function and);
    hybrid, 253; novel (*see* community, plant, novel);
    services, 5, 103-6, 150, 154, 159, 221; stability of,
    47, 97-101, 121-23, 184, 186-88, 254-59; urban,
    241-44
ecosystem engineer, 114, 171-74, 177
ecotype, 23-26, 31, 36, 108-9
edge, 20-21, 215-19; effects, 217-18, 219-20
Egler, Frank, 200-201
Ehrlich, Paul, 158, 225-26
El Monte Sagrado, 96-97
Ellenberg, Heinz, 80-82
endemism, 109, 112, 123, 246
energy flow, 94-96, 127, 141
equilibrium, 66-67, 97-99, 181, 191, 222-24, 225,
    231-32. *See also* nonequilibrium
erosion 101, 130, 142, 179, 184, 188-90
eutrophication 99-100, 140
exotic plants, 27-28, 31, 74, 107, 111-15, 123, 163,
    216, 254. *See also* invasive species
extinction, 46, 68, 107, 110-11, 211, 221, 222-24,
    226, 228, 251-52

feedback loop, negative, 97, 99-100, 186-87, 258
FEGN. *See* Florida Ecological Greenways Network
fertilization: atmospheric pollution as, 245;
    environmental problems with, 140, 174, 243, 245;
    plant growth and, 57, 65-66, 80, 117, 123, 127,
    134; species richness and, 57; without fertilizer
    123, 127, 142, 144, 146-47, 152, 190
fir, balsam, 10, 40-41, 45
fire: as management tool, 35, 192-93, 194, 246; as
    natural disturbance, 179, 182, 184, 188, 191, 212,
    213, 256; landscaping for, 181, 183-84, 188; plant

adaptation to, 184-85; suppression, 111, 179, 182,
    183, 184, 188; promoted by invasive species, 111,
    113; decreasing vulnerability to 184, 215, 232; use
    by Native Americans, 194
Fischer, Tom, 65
flood, 91, 103, 138, 142, 150, 179, 180, 182, 188-90,
    200, 209, 212, 240
Florida Ecological Greenways Network, 230-31
food web, 94-95, 101, 126, 142, 220, 222
Forbes, Stephen, 90, 94
forest garden, 53-54
Forman, Richard, 133, 210-11, 215-17, 220, 233
Foster, David, 194-95
fragmentation, 111, 156, 228, 233, 240, 251; effects
    of, 219-22, 224-25
Franklin, Colin, 91-92
Fresh Kills Landfill, 24, 175-77
Freshkills Park, 24
fugitive species, 184-86
fungi, 94, 107, 111, 125, 126, 127, 142, 143, 160-61

Gaia, 235
gap, 72, 76-77, 163, 184, 202, 212, 214-15, 258
Gause, Georgii F., 66-67
Gause's Law. *See* competitive exclusion
geographic information system, 211, 230, 236
GIS. *See* geographic information system
glaciation, 29-30, 252, 253
glacier, 29, 135, 136, 180, 204, 215
Glacier Bay, 204-5
Gleason, Henry, 51-52, 90
global change, 1, 27, 235, 253, 258
goats, 164-66
Godron, Michel, 133, 210-11, 233
grading, 23, 127, 131, 138, 150, 257
grazing, 145, 147, 155, 163-66, 191-92, 215, 246
Great Smoky Mountains, 51-52
green infrastructure, 148-51, 173-74
green roof, 89, 248, 254
green world hypothesis, 166-69
Greenbelt Native Plant Center, 24-25
Grime, J. Philip, 58, 78-80, 83, 184
groundcover, 14, 46, 68, 74, 202
Grubb, Peter, 75-76
guild, 73-75
Gunderson, Lance, 255-57

habitat: creating and managing, 13, 50, 91, 105-6, 146,
    154-59, 167, 177, 195, 207, 210, 216, 219, 222,
    227, 229-30: definition, 155; diversity within an